CLASSICS AND CELTIC LITERARY MODERNISM

Celtic modernism had a complex history with classical reception. In this book, Gregory Baker examines the work of W. B. Yeats, James Joyce, David Jones and Hugh MacDiarmid to show how new forms of modernist literary expression emerged as the evolution of classical education, the insurgent power of cultural nationalisms and the desire for transformative modes of artistic invention converged across Ireland, Scotland and Wales. Writers on the "Celtic fringe" sometimes confronted, and sometimes consciously advanced, crudely ideological manipulations of the inherited past. Yet, even as they did so, their eccentric ways of using the classics and its residual cultural authority animated new decentered idioms of English – literary vernaculars so inflected by polyglot intrusion that they expanded the range of Anglophone literature and left in their wake compelling stories for a new age.

GREGORY BAKER is Assistant Professor of English and Director of Irish Studies at the Catholic University of America in Washington, DC.

CLASSICS AFTER ANTIQUITY

Editors:

Alastair Blanshard
University of Queensland

Shane Butler
Johns Hopkins University

Emily Greenwood
Yale University

Classics after Antiquity presents innovative contributions in the field of Classical Reception Studies. Each volume explores the methods and motives of those who, coming after and going after antiquity, have entered into a contest with and for the legacies of the ancient world. The series aims to unsettle, to provoke debate, and to stimulate a re-evaluation of assumptions about the relationship between Greek and Roman classical pasts and modern histories.

Other titles in the series

Brecht and Tragedy: Radicalism, Traditionalism, Eristics
MARTIN REVERMANN
ISBN: 978-1-108-48968-3

The Nero-Antichrist: Founding and Fashioning a Paradigm
SHUSHMA MALIK
ISBN: 978-1-108-49149-5

Dionysus after Nietzsche: The Birth of Tragedy *in Twentieth-Century Literature and Thought*
ADAM LECZNAR
ISBN: 978-1-108-48256-1

Feeling and Classical Philology: Knowing Antiquity in German Scholarship, 1770–1920
CONSTANZE GÜTHENKE
ISBN: 978-1-107-10423-5

The Vernacular Aristotle: Translation as Reception in Medieval and Renaissance Italy
EUGENIO REFINI
ISBN: 978-1-108-48181-6

Afterlives of the Roman Poets: Biofiction and the Reception of Latin Poetry
NORA GOLDSCHMIDT
ISBN: 978-1-107-18025-3

The Perpetual Immigrant and the Limits of Athenian Democracy
DEMETRA KASIMIS
ISBN: 978-1-107-05243-7

Borges' Classics: Global Encounters with the Graeco-Roman Past
LAURA JANSEN
ISBN: 978-1-108-41840-9

Modernism and Homer: The Odysseys of H. D., James Joyce, Osip Mandelstam, and Ezra Pound
LEAH CULLIGAN FLACK
ISBN: 978-1-107-10803-5

Classical Victorians: Scholars, Scoundrels and Generals in Pursuit of Antiquity
EDMUND RICHARDSON
ISBN: 978-1-107-02677-3

CLASSICS AND CELTIC LITERARY MODERNISM

Yeats, Joyce, MacDiarmid and Jones

GREGORY BAKER

The Catholic University of America

CAMBRIDGE
UNIVERSITY PRESS

CAMBRIDGE
UNIVERSITY PRESS

University Printing House, Cambridge CB2 8BS, United Kingdom

One Liberty Plaza, 20th Floor, New York, NY 10006, USA

477 Williamstown Road, Port Melbourne, VIC 3207, Australia

314–321, 3rd Floor, Plot 3, Splendor Forum, Jasola District Centre, New Delhi – 110025, India

103 Penang Road, #05–06/07, Visioncrest Commercial, Singapore 238467

Cambridge University Press is part of the University of Cambridge.

It furthers the University's mission by disseminating knowledge in the pursuit of education, learning, and research at the highest international levels of excellence.

www.cambridge.org
Information on this title: www.cambridge.org/9781108844864
DOI: 10.1017/9781108953825

First published 2022

A catalogue record for this publication is available from the British Library.

Library of Congress Cataloging-in-Publication Data
NAMES: Baker, Gregory, 1980– author.
TITLE: Classics and Celtic literary modernism : Yeats, Joyce, MacDiarmid and Jones / Gregory Baker.
OTHER TITLES: Classics after antiquity.
DESCRIPTION: New York : Cambridge University Press, 2022. | Series: Classics after antiquity | Includes bibliographical references and index.
IDENTIFIERS: LCCN 2021035031 (print) | LCCN 2021035032 (ebook) | ISBN 9781108844864 (hardback) | ISBN 9781108953825 (ebook)
SUBJECTS: LCSH: English literature – Classical influences. | Yeats, W. B. (William Butler), 1865–1939 – Criticism and interpretation. | Joyce, James, 1882–1941 – Criticism and interpretation. | MacDiarmid, Hugh, 1892–1978 – Criticism and interpretation. | Jones, David, 1895–1974 – Criticism and interpretation.
CLASSIFICATION: LCC PR471 .B35 2022 (print) | LCC PR471 (ebook) | DDC 820.9/00912–dc23
LC record available at https://lccn.loc.gov/2021035031
LC ebook record available at https://lccn.loc.gov/2021035032

ISBN 978-1-108-84486-4 Hardback

For Ciara

Pour qu'un héritage soit réellement grand,
il faut que la main du défunt ne se voie pas.

For an inheritance to be truly great,
the hand of the dead should not be visible.

René Char (1907–88), *Feuillets d'Hypnos*

Contents

Preface

The state is concentric, man is eccentric.

James Joyce (1882–1941)[1]

In a previous volume of this series, the editors of *Classics after Antiquity* noted suggestively how tempting and easy it is to conceive of literary modernism as a "fixed point" in history, one whose diverse engagements with classical learning we may consolidate by "culling" its past selectively with academic shorthand.[2] One need only to think of Wilfred Owen's "old Lie," James Joyce's reputed "mythical method," Virginia Woolf's salient discussion on "Not Knowing Greek," or Ezra Pound's "Died some pro patria, non dulce non et decor" to find a "clutch of well-known and well-worn quotations" by which we sometimes dilute, or package, the heterogeneity of modernist classical receptions for broader scholarly discussion and classroom-ready understanding.[3] This kind of error is in no way endemic to reception studies in classics, or to the study of modernist writings at large: it remains a threat to scholarship of many types, for when contextualizing or theorizing the tendencies of any artwork(s) or period, the temptation to employ categories or other abstract principles as a blunt instrument has a strong concentric pull – perhaps even more so when dealing with works notorious for their lexical difficulty, thematic ambiguity and avant-garde distortions of received stylistic convention. We might choose to ignore certain historical details and seize on others; we might develop certain theoretical complexities while the nuance of other aspects may be recentered or lost; we may smooth out the distinctive formal ambiguities of a particular text, object or period of study where its characteristics, to say nothing of its genesis, could in fact be much rougher, much less tidy. In this way the densely

---

[1] Borach (1954) 326.
[2] Blanshard, Butler and Greenwood (2015) ix.
[3] Blanshard, Butler, and Greenwood (2015) ix.

packed eccentricities of particular creative moments in history are made to seem less volatile, less ambiguous and perhaps more comparable to phenomena we can recognize more easily. Reception studies in the classics has long sought to counter this tendency, plunging scholars deep into the thicket of style and history while making them aware of the very historicity of interpretative activity itself. All encounters with classical literature, with the complex circulation of its knowledge and meaning, are always mediated afterwards – in a labyrinth of ways – and it is these serpentine movements of transmission that create stories whose call and response may be worth retelling. Yet no matter how dispassionately we may conceptualize the nexus of past encounters, our understanding is always framed within our own moment, caught in parallel pathways of interpretation and transmission. Thus, as we narrate stories of reception, we do so always for our own place, in our own time, and often with intentions towards, and representations of, the 'classical' known only in part. "Understanding in which 'the dead trace of meaning' is 'transformed back into living experience,'" writes Charles Martindale in *Redeeming the Text* (1993), "is always made *within history*; indeed our own historicity is a necessary concomitant of understanding of this kind."[4] As the evolutionary force of "previous readings by previous communities" takes hold, present interpretative work is drawn into that "chain of receptions" that has made possible our knowledge and retellings of literature and its past.[5]

There is no doubt that a book devoted to classics and its place in the work of Yeats, Joyce, Jones and MacDiarmid could not exist without a vast chain of receptions. Many previous readings have helped set the dimensions and defining characteristics of Anglo-American literary modernism, while often also assigning Yeats and Joyce among its most prominent figures. On the whole, this book does not dispute that assignment, nor does it discount the fact that many of the earliest scholarly accounts – especially of Yeats and of Joyce – were attuned to something of the significance that Celtic modernists attached to the Greek and the Roman. Yet from the beginning, I would argue, the compulsion to periodize, to canonize – to cut a cleaner picture of modernism in unambiguous lines – has been a powerful force, one that has often overwhelmed more detailed and local consideration of specific writers' eccentric engagements with classical learning. Yeats and Joyce in particular,

---

[4] Martindale (1993) 7.
[5] Martindale (1993) 5, 7.

from an early stage in their scholarly reception, were sometimes cast as the latest inheritors of a so-called classical tradition in 'Western' literature, an insistence whose crude theorization diminished how conflicted, how subtly enmeshed their own receptions were in their time and place. Following the upheaval of the First World War and the collapse of the world economy nearly a decade later, the notion of an enduring 'classical tradition' in European literature took on new importance in Anglophone societies. Over the course of the previous fifty years, classical education had seen its role shift dramatically. Once critical in marking rank – in settling deeper questions of civic enfranchisement – among the governing and the governed, the value of classical knowledge gradually came under profound scrutiny across the British Empire, and to some its value seemed largely discredited. Nonetheless, as the Pax Americana began to emerge, the Anglo-American academy reinvigorated the study of classical antiquity and recast its importance in universities and in English-speaking societies at large. Influential scholars from the 1920s through the 1950s – figures such as Gilbert Murray, Douglas Bush, Gilbert Highet, R. R. Bolgar among others – salvaged something of its institutional and cultural prominence by stressing the existence of a classical tradition. The formative and benevolent impact of this tradition, they argued, could be traced in the development of all major European civilizations and their literatures – and perhaps nowhere was it more apparent than in English literature whose study at Anglo-American universities was fast becoming a widely available means to acquire a liberal education. Though classical works were then predominantly read in English translation, the literatures of Greece and Rome were still regarded as spiritual ideals, forms from which the postwar world would have to learn if it were to contribute something lasting to the progress of Anglophone civilization. This stress on the invigorating power of an enduring 'classical tradition' injected some life, in new contexts, into some of the older, Victorian claims that knowledge of Greek and Latin had previously maintained on social prestige, cultural fluency and political enfranchisement. Thus its study became, for a time, a critical organizing principle in the expansion of liberal education and in the social cohesion of democratic 'Western' civilization, newly reborn amid the Cold War.

Under these auspices, many of modernism's more prominent receptions of Greek and Roman antiquity were first studied and curricularized for broad institutional consumption, and some figures of 'high modernism' were seen as contemporary exemplars of a more or less unbroken line of descent from classical antiquity, one whose apparent 'purity' or cultural stability ran back behind the ravages of world war, genocide and economic devastation. The apparent longevity of this tradition was thus cast in terms of broad civic consolation – the classics existed as a model of 'wisdom literature' that could still provide examples of aesthetic unity and social order for a generation tempered by war and beset with the desire to recover. Nonetheless, this 'traditional' way of presenting the heterogenous stories of classics and its modernist receptions tells much more about the importance of antiquity in the immediate postwar period than it does about exceptional encounters with the *Nachleben* of Greek and Latin a generation earlier, not least because many of the period's most innovative interventions with classics were born, not in efforts to conform with 'timeless tradition' but with skepticism, envy and sometimes outright antagonism against customary ways of institutionalizing and transmitting classical knowledge. The last thirty years of study in modernism and classical reception have helped demonstrate the dynamism of these struggles, even as the very definition of modernism(s) has come under renewed scrutiny and new forms of revision. Reimagining the critical paradigms that first prized modernism's mainly European and American expressions, studies of the period have been engaged in what the editors of *The Oxford Handbook of Modernisms* (2010) have called "an ongoing process of redefinition that takes its cue from analyses of a modernity that is increasingly seen in globalizing and thus transnational terms."[6] The shift, moreover, towards new historicist approaches and to genetic criticism of prominent literary texts has further discouraged pursuits of "grand unified accounts" of modernism at large and instead opened up and expanded its scholarly fields empirically and theoretically.[7] This expansion has been predicated largely on the view that modernity itself represents a geographically diverse phenomenon across the globe, one whose intermittent temporal paths in specific places can be better analyzed with forms of "local historicism."[8] It is with this in mind that this book brings together some of the disparate stories that have helped determine the specific histories of classical reception within the evolution of so-called Celtic literary modernism. What follows is thus not a unified account of a movement per se but an attempt rather to

---

[6] Brooker et al. (2010) 3.
[7] Hacking (1989–1990) 345. See also Brooker et al. (2010) 3.
[8] Brooker et al. (2010) 4, and Hacking (1989–1990) 345.

document the eccentric character, and stylistic consequences, of five particular encounters with the traces of classical antiquity. Broadly speaking, these encounters took place at a moment when classics' diminished cultural authority had become entangled across the British Isles with a variety of insurgent ideologies centered on Celtic revival and proto-postcolonial resistance. As that happened, receptions of the ancient world became contested sites among an emerging literary avant-garde, palimpsests on which a variety of popular nationalist receptions of antiquity were enmeshed with and radically overwritten by imaginative – often linguistically hybrid – reworkings of the Greek and the Roman. These receptions – fired by skepticism, satirical mimicry, outright mistranslation and creative adaptation – made the 'classical' a disputed "third space" within Celtic modernism, one where national self-determination and experimental poetics could be, as Homi Bhahba has written, "appropriated, translated, rehistoricized and read anew."[9]

The scholarly approach adopted in this book joins interest in the hermeneutics of modernist reception with what has recently been called narrative historicism. This critical method emerged as a way to examine works of twentieth-century literature, and the specific contexts of their genesis and reception, in part with the 2014 publication of Kevin Birmingham's *The Most Dangerous Book: The Battle for James Joyce's Ulysses*. While Birmingham's book is not concerned with the *Nachleben* of classical literatures, his approach is evidence of a broader desire to see the active voice of narrative history, of storytelling, reinvigorated in literary criticism. On being awarded the 2016 Truman Capote prize for the book, Birmingham insisted that the telltale sign of so-called narrative historicism was the embedding of "arguments in a story" instead of "embedding stories in an argument."[10] In seeking "patterns in the boggling immensity of the past," narrative historicism

> asserts relevance, identifies influence and qualifies importance. It draws out nuances of personality, of moments in time, of settings and disputes and gestures. Criticism is not distant. Literary history accumulates from a litany of intimacies, from the small, day-to-day experiences of men and women of letters. Recreating those experiences is as crucial as forming arguments about them. In fact, it doubles as an argument about them.

---

[9] Bhabha (2004) 55.
[10] Birmingham (2017).

Narrative details serve critical purposes. The size and style of James Joyce's notebooks are important.[11]

Although *Classics and Celtic Literary Modernism* does not tell the story of a single work in twentieth-century literature, its approach to documenting key moments in the history of modernist classical receptions works in something of the way Birmingham describes. The analysis of pivotal, creative encounters with classical learning (and the institutions that guarded the diffusion of that knowledge) can not only generate fresh exegetical accounts of modernist literature but also deepen our understanding of modernisms at large, reenacting the complex ways in which classical allusions, adaptations and translations of the 'past' were mediated to and then renovated by widely regarded writers. Thus the narrative details of this book – its "litany of intimacies" – serve critical purposes: the stories of each chapter are designed to show how classics' different institutional and ideological receptions remained transformative in the early twentieth century. Despite evolving prestige, classics and its receptions shaped not just the nationalist ideologies of Celtic revival and renaissance but the unusual, hybrid literary responses of Anglo-Celtic writers as well. The emphasis this book places on narrative history is not to sideline wider discussion of theoretical implications but to suggest rather that sound reflection can best be made when key contextual differences are drawn out from the receptions under examination. The prominent Irish, Anglo-Welsh and Scottish writers selected for this study were chosen because the thick historical contexts that molded their forms of reception (and transformed their reputations) are parallel, if not altogether shared. However, even when similarities of place, style or ideology can be noted, it is equally important to remain skeptical of patterns observed, to retain, as Peter Burke has suggested, "a variety of concepts" – a variety of stories even – when investigating 'classical' encounters with cultural nationalisms.[12] This seems especially salient at present as more critical forms of reception studies have taken hold recently amid the rise of new kinds of populism and nationalism. The classics and reception have again been implicated in ideologies and movements that have sometimes cast themselves as 'rightful' inheritors of the so-called classical tradition or legacy of 'Western' civilization. In this moment, to remain rigorous about describing and judging differences of context and situa-

---

[11] Birmingham (2017).
[12] Burke (2009) 66.

tion in specific cultural encounters is essential, I believe, to gaining perspective on how receptions of antiquity continue to foment nationalist fervor and crude political animus – even while offering, in some cases, fertile ground on which eccentric modes of collusion with, or profound resistance against, these receptions can stand. As this study demonstrates, the aesthetic of Celtic literary modernism did not emerge from or produce an ossified 'classical tradition' of predetermined significance. Instead it catalyzed a variety of insurgent ideologies, literary idioms and experimental expressions across languages – forces that left, in their wake, compelling stories for a new age.

Acknowledgments

I am indebted to many who have helped me bring this book to life. Along the way my research has been generously supported by involvement with the Modernist Studies Association, the American Comparative Literature Association, the American Conference for Irish Studies and the Association of Literary Scholars, Critics and Writers; with Brown University, the Graduate School of Arts and Sciences and the departments of Classics, Comparative Literature and English; and with the Catholic University of America, especially the English department. Thanks are due also to the staff of the Rockefeller Library at Brown University, as well as the staff at the National Library of Wales, Aberystwyth; the National Library of Scotland, Edinburgh; the National Library of Ireland, Dublin; the British Library; and the Burns Library of Boston College. Without their help many essential pieces of scholarly interest would have passed unnoticed.

I am grateful to the trustees of the David Jones Estate for allowing me to publish excerpts from the correspondence of David Jones. Éditions Gallimard have also generously permitted me use of René Char's poetry for the epigraph of this book. I thank also the publishers at Bloomsbury Academic who granted me permission to reprint the parts of Chapter 3 that originally appeared in *The Classics in Modernist Translation* (2019).

All intellectual endeavors, I believe, are enmeshed in a complex web of influence, criticism and creativity. Over the last years I feel fortunate to have been caught, productively, in such a nexus – in conversations with scholars whose work and encouragement have helped me deepen my own research. In particular, I thank Fran Brearton, Gregory Castle, Thomas Dilworth, Leah Culligan Flack, Eamon Grennan, Miranda Hickman, Lynn Kozak, Florence Impens, Peter Liebregts, the late Margery Palmer McCulloch, Fearghal McGarry, Salvatore Pappalardo, Kathy Staudt, Nathan Suhr-Sytsma, Isabelle Torrance, Phil Walsh and Daniel G. Williams. At the Catholic University of America, I have enjoyed generous support from colleagues and friends both past and present. Their work and dedication have my profound admiration. I count among these Ernie Suarez, Chris Wheatley, Rebecca Rainof Mas, Taryn Okuma, Megan Murton, Lev Weitz, Daniel Gibbons, Tobias Gregory, Jennifer O'Riordan, Jenny Paxton, Lilla Kopár, Claudia Bornholdt, Kevin Rulo, Joe Sendry, Patrick Tuite, Michael Mack and Glen Johnson.

I am especially grateful for the editorial assistance and advice provided by all involved with the *Classics after Antiquity* series at Cambridge University Press. Michael Sharp, Alistair Blanshard, Shane Butler and Emily Greenwood have my deepest gratitude for shepherding this book through the processes of peer review and publication. The anonymous reviewers of my initial manuscript suggested many substantive ways of improving this book. Their critiques have been indispensable in making my work better. I extend my thanks also to Linsey Hague, Nicola Maclean, Emily Grace and to Pam Scholefield for their dedicated and efficient work in turning my manuscript into a proper book.

I undertook this project as doctoral work under the guidance of Ken Haynes. Throughout the revision of my dissertation, Ken has remained an important source of support, criticism and friendship. I am profoundly in his debt. The broad conceptual framework of this book, however, did not begin in my thesis alone but was fostered also in the teaching and mentoring I received at the University of Chicago and Brown University. I would particularly like to thank the late Mutlu Konuk Blasing, David Konstan, Arnold Weinstein, Shadi Bartsch, Peter White, David Wray, the late Nicholas Rudall and the late David Bevington.

Finally, I would never have had strength enough to devote largely solitary hours to research and writing without my family and close friends. Michael, Anne-Marie, Cian and Sapna Brogan have all been tireless supporters of me for many years. I have known few people in life so generous, so invested in seeing others thrive and live well. My mother, Evelyn, has been a deep source of hope and faith since the beginning. Her devotion amid life's joy, her resilience amid its pain, inspire me each day. The memory of both my father, Howard, and my brother, Matt, is, I feel, stitched in ways into this book – as through a glass darkly. Both left this world too soon, yet the warmth, the depth of love they bestowed on me, and on others whom I cherish, remains. Both are sorely missed. Some of the friends I treasure most have offered me encouragement and support during the many stages of writing and revising my work. I thank Sam Coren, Greg, Jen and Madeleine DePardo, David and Gail Stokes, Nora Peterson and, especially, Travis Andersen and Jeff Peckham.

I dedicate this book to Ciara. She has been there with me through the dark moments, and in the bright, too. Without her I would know far less about all the happiness and love that can course through a life led together. That abounds across ours – in Aoife, Emma and Eoin. This book could be for no other.

Abbreviations

Eliot *LTSE1* (2009) – Eliot, T. S. *The Letters of T. S. Eliot, Vol. 1: 1898–1922*, rev. ed. Ed. Valerie Eliot and Hugh Haughton. London: Faber and Faber, 2009.

Eliot *LTSE2* (2009) – Eliot, T. S. *The Letters of T. S. Eliot, Vol. 2: 1923–1925*. Ed. Valerie Eliot and Hugh Haughton. London: Faber and Faber, 2009.

Jones *DG* (1980) – Jones, David. *Dai Greatcoat, A Self-Portrait of David Jones in His Letters*. Ed. René Hague. London: Faber and Faber, 1980.

Jones *IN* (1984) – Jones, David. *Inner Necessities: The Letters of David Jones to Desmond Chute*. Ed. Thomas Dilworth. Toronto: Anson Cartwright Editions, 1984.

Joyce *CWJJ* (1989) – Joyce, James. *The Critical Writings of James Joyce*. Ed. Ellsworth Mason and Richard Ellmann. Ithaca, NY: Cornell University Press, 1989.

Joyce *Dubliners* (1993) – Joyce, James. *Dubliners*. Ed. Hans Walter Gabler, with Walter Hettche. New York: Garland Publishing, 1993.

Joyce *LJJ* (1957) – Joyce, James. *Letters of James Joyce*. Ed. Stuart Gilbert. New York: Viking Press, 1957.

Joyce *LJJ2* (1966) – Joyce, James. *Letters of James Joyce, Volumes 2 and 3*, Vol. 2. Ed. Richard Ellmann. New York: Viking Press, 1966.

Joyce *LJJ3* (1966) – Joyce, James. *Letters of James Joyce, Volumes 2 and 3*, Vol. 3. Ed. Richard Ellmann. New York: Viking Press, 1966.

Joyce *Portrait* (1993) – Joyce, James. *A Portrait of the Artist As a Young Man*. Ed. Hans Walter Gabler, with Walter Hettche. New York and London: Garland Publishing, 1993.

Joyce *SLJJ* (1975) – Joyce, James. *Selected Letters of James Joyce*. Ed. Richard Ellmann. New York: Viking Press, 1975.

Joyce *Ulysses* (1986) – Joyce, James. *Ulysses*. Ed. Hans Walter Gabler. New York: Random House, 1986.

MacDiarmid *CP1* (1993) – MacDiarmid, Hugh. *Complete Poems*, Vol. 1. Ed. Michael Grieve and W. R. Aitken. Manchester: Carcanet Press, 1993.

MacDiarmid *CP2* (1994) – MacDiarmid, Hugh. *Complete Poems*, Vol. 2. Ed. Michael Grieve and W. R. Aitken. Manchester: Carcanet Press, 1994.

MacDiarmid *CSS* (1995) – MacDiarmid, Hugh. *Contemporary Scottish Studies*. Ed. Alan Riach. Manchester: Carcanet Press, 1995.

MacDiarmid *LHM* (1984) – MacDiarmid, Hugh. *The Letters of Hugh MacDiarmid*. Ed. Alan Bold. Athens: University of Georgia Press, 1984.

MacDiarmid *LP* (1994) – MacDiarmid, Hugh. *Lucky Poet*. Ed. Alan Riach. Manchester: Carcanet Press, 1994.

MacDiarmid *NSLHM* (2001) – MacDiarmid, Hugh. *New Selected Letters of Hugh MacDiarmid*. Ed. Dorian Grieve, O. D. Edwards and Alan Riach. Manchester: Carcanet Press, 2001.

MacDiarmid *RT1* (1996) – MacDiarmid, Hugh. *The Raucle Tongue: Hitherto Uncollected Prose*, Vol. 1. Ed. Angus Calder, Glen Murray and Alan Riach. Manchester: Carcanet Press, 1996.

MacDiarmid *RT2* (1997) – MacDiarmid, Hugh. *The Raucle Tongue: Hitherto Uncollected Prose*, Vol. 2. Ed. Angus Calder, Glen Murray and Alan Riach. Manchester: Carcanet Press, 1997.

MacDiarmid *RT3* (1998) – MacDiarmid, Hugh. *The Raucle Tongue: Hitherto Uncollected Prose*, Vol. 3. Ed. Angus Calder, Glen Murray and Alan Riach. Manchester: Carcanet Press, 1998.

MacDiarmid *SEHM* (1970) – MacDiarmid, Hugh. *Selected Essays of Hugh MacDiarmid*. Ed. Duncan Glen. Berkeley: University of California Press, 1970.

MacDiarmid *SP* (1992) – MacDiarmid, Hugh. *Selected Prose*. Ed. Alan Riach. Manchester: Carcanet Press, 1992.

Woolf *EVW2* (1987) – Woolf, Virginia. *The Essays of Virginia Woolf, Vol. 2: 1912–1918*. Ed. Andrew McNellie. London: Hogarth Press, 1987.

Woolf *EVW4* (1994) – Woolf, Virginia. *The Essays of Virginia Woolf, Vol. 4: 1925–1928*. Ed. Andrew McNellie. London: Hogarth Press, 1994.

Yeats *CL1* (1986) – Yeats, W. B. *The Collected Letters of W. B. Yeats, Vol. 1: 1865–1895*. Ed. John Kelly and Eric Domville. Oxford: Clarendon Press, 1986.

Yeats *CL2* (1997) – Yeats, W. B. *The Collected Letters of W. B. Yeats, Vol. 2: 1896–1900*. Ed. Warwick Gould, John Kelly and Deirdre Toomey. Oxford: Clarendon Press, 1997.

Yeats *CL3* (1994) – Yeats, W. B. *The Collected Letters of W. B. Yeats, Vol. 3: 1901–1904*. Ed. John Kelly and Ronald Schuchard. Oxford: Oxford University Press, 1994.

Yeats *CL4* (2005) – Yeats, W. B. *The Collected Letters of W. B. Yeats, Vol. 4: 1905–1907*. Ed. John Kelly and Ronald Schuchard. Oxford: Oxford University Press, 2005.

Yeats *CL5* (2018) – Yeats, W. B. *The Collected Letters of W. B. Yeats, Vol. 5: 1908–1910*. Ed. John Kelly and Ronald Schuchard. Oxford: Oxford University Press, 2018.

Yeats *CLWBY* – Yeats, W. B. *The Collected Letters of W. B. Yeats*. Intelex Past Masters Database. www.nlx.com/collections/130.

Yeats *CW3* (1999) – Yeats, W. B. *The Collected Works of W. B. Yeats, Vol. 3: Autobiographies*. Ed. William H. O'Donnell and Douglas N. Archibald. New York: Scribner Press, 1999.

Yeats *CW4* (2007) – Yeats, W. B. *The Collected Works of W. B. Yeats, Vol. 4: Early Essays*. Ed. Richard J. Finneran and George Bornstein. New York: Scribner Press, 2007.

Yeats *CW5* (1994) – Yeats, W. B. *The Collected Works of W. B. Yeats, Vol. 5: Later Essays*. Ed. William H. O'Donnell. New York: Charles Scribner and Sons, 1994.

Yeats *CW6* (1989) – Yeats, W. B. *The Collected Works of W. B. Yeats, Vol. 6: Prefaces and Introductions*. Ed. William H. O'Donnell. New York: Macmillan, 1989.

Yeats *CW8* (2003) – Yeats, W. B. *The Collected Works of W. B. Yeats, Vol. 8: The Irish Dramatic Movement*. Ed. Mary Fitzgerald and Richard J. Finneran. New York: Scribner Press, 2003.

Yeats *CW9* (2004) – Yeats, W. B. *The Collected Works of W. B. Yeats, Vol. 9: Early Articles and Reviews*. Ed. John P. Frayne and Madeleine Marchaterre. New York: Scribner Press, 2004.

Yeats *CW10* (2000) – Yeats, W. B. *The Collected Works of W. B. Yeats. Vol. 10: Later Articles and Reviews*. Ed. Colton Johnson. New York: Scribner Press, 2000.

Yeats *LWBY* (1955) – Yeats, W. B. *The Letters of W. B. Yeats*. Ed. Allan Wade. New York: Macmillan, 1955.

Yeats *Mem* (1972) – Yeats, W. B. *Memoirs*. Ed. Denis Donoghue. New York: Macmillan, 1972.

Yeats *UP1* (1970) – Yeats, W. B. *Uncollected Prose by W. B. Yeats, Vol. 1: First Reviews and Articles, 1886–1896*. Ed. John P. Frayne. New York: Columbia University Press, 1970.

Yeats *UP2* (1976) – Yeats, W. B. *Uncollected Prose by W. B. Yeats, Vol. 2:*
Reviews, Articles and Other Miscellaneous Prose, 1897–1939. Ed. John
P. Frayne and Colton Johnson. New York: Columbia University
Press, 1976.

Yeats *VE* (1987) – Yeats, W. B. *The Variorum Edition of the Poems of W. B.*
Yeats. Ed. Peter Allt and Russell K. Alspach. New York: Macmillan,
1987.

Introduction
"At Once the Bow and the Mark": Classics and Celtic Revival

"On the morning when I heard of his death a heavy storm was blowing and I doubt not when he died that it had well begun."[1] So wrote W. B. Yeats (1865–1939) in March 1909, four days after the death of his friend and protégé, the 37-year-old playwright John Millington Synge (1871–1909). For Yeats, the death of Synge marked an important turning point in his life and, broadly, in the development of modernist expression across the literatures of Ireland and Britain. A heavy storm was indeed blowing; and in the weeks that followed Synge's death, Yeats, though awash in grief, slowly began to envision his reinvention as a poet, elaborating a new theory of artistic genius anchored in reflection over Synge's art and life. A "drifting, silent man, full of hidden passion," he wrote, Synge had long been marked by "physical weakness," but that weakness had done little to diminish his imagination.[2] On the contrary, as his body grew weak in the last months of life, Synge's imagination became "fiery and brooding," undimmed by disease and decay.[3] Even as death approached, Yeats argued, Synge could not be stopped from embodying in literature all his "hidden dreams."[4] Deprivation and impending death had been vital to the final flourishing of Synge's art. "[L]ow vitality," Yeats explained,

> helped him to be observant and contemplative … What blindness did for Homer, lameness for Hephaestus, asceticism for any saint you will, bad health did for him by making him ask no more of life than that it should keep him living, and above all perhaps by concentrating his imagination.[5]

Illness had driven Synge "to reject from life and thought all that would distract" him from struggling with "despair or a sense of loss produced in

---

[1] Yeats *Mem* (1972) 200. The phrase in the introductory title is taken from MacDiarmid (1967–1968) 15.
[2] Yeats *Mem* (1972) 203.
[3] Yeats *Mem* (1972) 203.
[4] Yeats *Mem* (1972) 204.
[5] Yeats, "J. M. Synge & the Ireland of His Time" (1909) in Yeats *CW4* (2007) 232–33.

us by the external world."[6] In that struggle Synge had discovered "creative joy," a phenomenon Yeats defined as "an acceptance of what life brings, because we have understood the beauty of what it brings, or a hatred of death for what it takes away."[7] Far from drowning Synge's voice, deprivation emerged as a creative force, its pressure provoking "through some sympathy perhaps with all other men, an energy so noble, so powerful, that we laugh aloud and mock, in the terror or the sweetness of our exaltation, at death and oblivion."[8] Synge's death, as Roy Foster has noted, drove Yeats into a "long process of self-examination," one in which a preoccupation with loss would lead him to scrutinize not only his friend's life but the very grounds of the "intellectual movement" that he, Lady Augusta Gregory (1852–1932) and Synge had tried to foster through the Irish Literary Revival.[9] Shaken by the idea that they had, perhaps, not 'understood the clock', that the Revival had faltered in the face of public pressure and propaganda, Yeats nonetheless began to wonder whether he too, amid his grief, might discover a renewed sense of "creative joy."[10] Drawn to memories of childhood, Yeats began composing "reveries about the past," ruminating, in part, over the ways in which his early education had left him unprepared for the aims of the Revival.[11] Central among these reflections was the lasting fascination Yeats expressed for the ancient worlds of Greece and Rome, worlds that had – though he bemoaned his

---

[6] Yeats *Mem* (1972) 203; Yeats, "Theatre of Beauty – December 1913." Yeats Papers, MS 30052, National Library of Ireland, Dublin (NLI).

[7] Yeats *CW4* (2007) 233.

[8] Yeats *CW4* (2007) 233.

[9] Foster (1997) 526; Yeats, "*Samhain*: 1901," in Yeats *CW8* (2003) 5. The years following Synge's death proved to be a time of discouragement, as Yeats watched the Abbey Theatre, then under the stewardship of Lennox Robinson (1886–1958), gradually make new accommodations with popular taste, accommodations that he thought derivative of bourgeois expectations for the theatre. That served Robinson's work well but, as David Krause notes, Robinson's "benign light comedy" possessed none of the depth that Synge, Yeats and Gregory had prized, having "no rogue heroes, no sharp ironies, no dark shadows." Yeats lamented what had become of the Abbey, admitting to Lady Gregory in 1919 that, "not understanding the clock, [we] set out to bring again the Theatre of Shakespeare or rather perhaps of Sophocles ... We thought we could bring the old folk-life to Dublin, patriotic feeling to aid us, and with the folk-life all the life of the heart ... but the modern world is more powerful than any propaganda or even than any special circumstance." Krause (1982) 195; Yeats, "A People's Theater, A Letter to Lady Gregory" (1919) in Yeats *CW8* (2003) 129, 130. On this period at the Abbey Theatre, see C. Murray (1997) 113–37.

[10] Yeats *CW8* (2003) 129; Yeats *CW4* (2007) 233. In a similar manner, Yeats noted losses of great imaginative significance in the life of Dante Alighieri, namely "the death of Beatrice which gave him a vision of heavenly love, and his banishment which gave him a vision of divine justice." Caught in the "contest between dream and reality," Dante required recompense for such loss; he sought in poetry what life did not provide, namely "some compensation, something that would complete his vision of the world." Yeats Papers, MS 30052, NLI.

[11] Yeats, Letter to Susan Mary "Lily" Yeats (July 28, 1914) in Yeats *CW3* (1999) 16.

lack of fluency in both Latin and Greek – stirred his imagination and guided his desire to "build up a national tradition, a national literature" in Ireland, an Anglo-Irish 'classical' literature "none the less Irish in spirit from being English in language."[12]

Although Yeats played a critical role in the Irish Revival – and though he felt, after some years, that his own lack of a classical education had left him unprepared for its onerous demands – scholars ignored, for some time, the prominent place classical reception occupied in the spread of Celtic revivals – not only in Ireland but in Scotland and Wales as well.[13] While the "Graeco-Roman classical tradition" was broadly regarded as pivotal to the development of history and culture across the Celtic countries, the critical assessment of classics and the Irish Revival from W. B. Stanford's *Ireland and the Classical Tradition* (1976) was characteristic for some time.[14] Stanford had insisted that "classical quotations and appeals to classical precedents" became scarce as the "Gaelic revival reached its full strength," leading many to believe that Greek and Roman receptions had little part in fomenting distinctively Celtic forms of literary dissidence and dissatisfaction with English rule.[15] Because formal study of Greek and Latin at university was central to the socialization and education of Britain's governing elite, the classics were thought to be no friend, no "natural ally" to Anglophobic movements bent on resurrecting Celtic literature, let alone compelling political movements, untethered from the 'main line' of English dominance.[16] Accordingly, the institutional presence of classics in Ireland, in Scotland and in Wales was often seen as inimical to movements of Celtic revival or, at the very least, as something whose allegiance and affiliation could best be described as benignly 'unionist'.

However, as Fiona Macintosh first observed in *Dying Acts* (1994), the classics were not, in fact, an "alien adversary" to movements of Celtic revival but instead a contested site wherein a wide range of literary and ideological manipulations of antiquity were employed – not only by those eager to hold fast to the security of union but by a variety of cultural nationalists keen to confront a growing 'anglicization' across the British

---

[12] Yeats, "To the Editor of *United Ireland*, 17 December 1892," in Yeats *CL1* (1986) 338. See Chapter 1, pp. 53–55; Chapter 2, pp. 105–08; Chapter 4, pp. 163–65.
[13] Yeats *CW3* (1999) 108.
[14] Stanford (1976) viii.
[15] Stanford (1976) 219.
[16] Macintosh (1994) 3. On this untethering, see O'Connor (2006) xi–xviii. See also Impens (2018) 6–7 on Stanford.

Empire.[17] Thus, often in the rhetoric of late nineteenth- and early twentieth-century Celtic revival, the classics – with its enduring devotion to dead Mediterranean languages – became allied to what Nicholas Allen has called a "fluid resistance to the solid presence of empire."[18] Joined to efforts to revive dead and dying tongues from the Celtic world, classical *exempla* and precedents were cited widely in attempts to challenge English rule and to envision a world beyond the United Kingdom, a world where new forms of 'vernacular classics' could aid the social and linguistic purification of the Celtic nations.[19] Since the publication of Macintosh's work, significant scholarship in the diverse fields of Celtic studies, translation studies, classical reception and comparative literature – work by Macintosh and Allen but also by Declan Kiberd, Michael Cronin, Len Platt, Robert Crawford, Ceri Davies, Laura O'Connor, Lorna Hardwick, Richard Martin, J. Michael Walton, Marianne McDonald, Leah Flack, Tony Crowley, Gregory Castle, Matthew Hart and Margery Palmer McCulloch, among others – has widened our understanding of how receptions of the ancient world, both classical and Celtic, became pivotal forces in the "nationalist imaginary."[20] Employed in efforts towards purportedly national renewal, the classics were not merely a "useful guide" for defending against further English incursion but a catalyst

---

[17] Macintosh (1994) 3. See also the discussion in McDonald (1995) 183–203. For a broad overview of literary devolution in this period and the place of 'Anglocentricity', see Robert Crawford's extensive account of "British Literature" and "Modernism as Provincialism" in Crawford (2000) 45–110, 216–70, Declan Kiberd's examination of revivalist rewritings of William Shakespeare in Kiberd (1996) 268–85, as well as Ceri Davies' discussion of the Welsh university system in Davies (1995) 115–55.

[18] Allen (2010) 18.

[19] Numerous examples of this practice exist. For example, when announcing the third Oireachtas festival of 1899, *An Claidheamh Soluis*, the bilingual journal of the Gaelic League, insisted that "after community of blood and community of language, community of festivals was the strongest bond that held the various independent Greek republics together as one Greece. What the Pythean, the Olympic, the Nemean and Isthmian games were to the Greeks, the assembles of Tara, Emania, Carman, and Tailtenn, were to the men of Ireland." "The Oireachtas," *An Claidheamh Soluis* I.2 (March 25, 1899) 24. For other accounts analyzing reception and the development of various modern nationalisms and imperialisms, see Stephens and Vasunia (2010), Bradley (2010), Stead and Hall (2015), Goff (2005) as well as Hardwick and Gillespie (2007).

[20] Allen (2010) 18. See Kiberd (1996) 131–88; Cronin (1996) 1–7, 131–66; Platt (1998) 99–127; Crawford (2011) 131–46; Davies (1995); O'Connor (2006); Hardwick (2000) 79–95; Martin (2007) 75–91; Walton (2002) 3–36; McDonald (2002) 37–86; Flack (2015); Crowley (2005) 128–63; Hart (2010) 3–25, 51–78, and McCulloch (2009). On primitivism and the Irish Revival, see Castle (2001) 1–39. For a discussion of earlier 'revivals' and the contexts of earlier eighteenth- and nineteenth-century classical receptions in Ireland, see especially Vance (1990) 1–164, Cronin (1996) as well as O'Higgins (2017). On Scottish reception, see Davie (1961) and Crawford (1998) 225–46. On the role of 'minor' literatures in literary modernism, see McCrea (2015) 1–46. For a broad examination of so-called Hellenizing impulses in modern Irish literature, see Arkins (2005).

for reinventing the collective "social fabric and cultural unconscious" of the British Isles.[21] Nevertheless, though greater attention has been given to the links between classics and Celtic revival, considerably less has been written about the eccentric associations that Irish, Anglo-Welsh and Scottish practitioners of literary modernism had with institutions of classical learning and with movements of national revival.[22] In considering the work of Yeats, James Joyce (1882–1941), David Jones (1895–1974) and Hugh MacDiarmid (1892–1978), this book documents part of this history. It traces a comparative genealogy that shows how modernism's so-called Celtic fringe was roused to life as the evolution of classical education, the insurgent power of cultural nationalisms and the desire for new, transformative modes of literary invention converged.[23] Writers on the 'fringe' sometimes confronted, and sometimes consciously advanced, ideological manipulations of the 'inherited' past. As they did so, however, their modes of receiving the classics also helped animate freshly decentered idioms of English, literary vernaculars "so twisted and posed" that they expanded the "stock of available reality" across Anglophone literature.[24]

Throughout the first of his memoirs, *Reveries over Childhood and Youth* (1914; 1916), Yeats detailed his preoccupation with pain and deprivation, principally by examining his early life. "Indeed I remember little of childhood but its pain," he declared, and nowhere was that felt more acutely than in "the ordinary system of education."[25] As a young boy, he confessed, he had been thoroughly "unfitted" to formal instruction:

> though I would often work well for weeks together, I had to give the whole evening to one lesson if I was to know it. My thoughts were a great excitement, but when I tried to do anything with them, it was like trying to pack a balloon into a shed in a high wind. I was always near the bottom of my class, and always making excuses that but added to my timidity.[26]

[21] Macintosh (1994) 3; O'Connor (2006) xvii.

[22] There have also been surveys detailing the evolving engagements that Yeats and Joyce maintained, individually, with the literatures and civilizations of classical antiquity. Included among these are Arkins (1990); Liebregts (1993) as well as Schork (1997, 1998). More recent is Flack (2020). See also Arkins (1999) as well as Arkins (2009) 239–49.

[23] The phrase "Celtic fringe" is here borrowed from Jones (2016) [10]. Jones elaborated on the phrase further in a 1962 letter to Aneirin Talfan Davies (1909–80). See Jones (1980) 86–88. See also Simon Gikandi's use of the term in Gikandi (1996) 29, as well as O'Connor's extensive discussion of the Pale/Fringe distinction in O'Connor (2006) xiv–xvii.

[24] Blackmur (1935) 108.

[25] Yeats *CW3* (1999) 45, 99.

[26] Yeats *CW3* (1999) 64–65.

As the firstborn son of the barrister John Butler Yeats (1839–1922), expectation loomed over Yeats: it was thought he would excel, continuing the family's history of success at university. "My father had wanted me to go to Trinity College," he recalled, "and, when I would not, had said, 'My father and grandfather and great-grandfather have been there.' I did not tell him that neither my classics nor my mathematics were good enough for any examination."[27] Yeats was a poor student of Greek and Latin, evidently unable to manage even the memorization necessary to pass Latin.[28] "I was expected to learn with the help of a crib a hundred and fifty lines [of Virgil]," he remembered,

> The other boys were able to learn the translation off, and to remember what words of Latin and English corresponded with one another, but I, who, it may be, had tried to find out what happened in the parts we had not read, made ridiculous mistakes.[29]

Though he labored at times to correct his errors, his trouble with Latin and Greek persisted. No vision, no passion induced by ignorance seemed to grow in him; he was left then, he wrote, with only a "timidity born of excuse and evasion," one that gnawed at him even as his reputation began to flourish.[30] Yet Yeats would find solace in the example of John Keats (1795–1821), who, he suggested, had composed much of his work in struggle with a lack of education. Born the "ill trained son of a livery stable keeper," Keats was "ignorant," Yeats contended, "separated from all the finest life of his time."[31] Nevertheless, despite that lack of inherited wealth, he still managed to cultivate what Yeats called "a passion of luxury," a passion that manifested itself in his verse as "Greece and the gods of greece [sic]."[32] Keats had no formal training in Greek, and despite his fervor for the language, he failed to teach it to himself. He once hoped, he told Joshua Reynolds, to "feast upon Old Homer as we have upon Shakespeare," but his progress with the language was slow.[33] So, by

---

[27] Yeats *CW3* (1999) 90. John Butler Yeats firmly believed his son could pursue classics at Trinity: "When he entered the VI form its master, who is now a classical fellow in TCD [George Wilkins, the Headmaster's brother], told me that he could be as good in classics as in science if it were not that, having read Huxley, he despised them. When the other boys of the form entered Trinity he on his own responsibility decided to remain outside, and he entered the art school, where he studied for two years." John Yeats, "Memoirs," 8, as in Foster (1997) 35.

[28] On Yeats' knowledge of Greek and Latin, see Arkins (1990) 1–23 and Liebregts (1993) 7–21. See Chapter 1, p. 55n35; Chapter 3, pp. 131–32, especially n60.

[29] Yeats *CW3* (1999) 75.

[30] Yeats *CW3* (1999) 76.

[31] Yeats Papers, MS 30052, NLI.

[32] Yeats Papers, MS 30052, NLI.

[33] John Keats, "To J. H. Reynolds" (April 27, 1818) in Keats (1958) 1:274.

the autumn of 1819, Keats gave up on Greek, insisting that he would make himself "complete in latin, and there my learning must stop. I do not think of venturing upon Greek."[34] Because of this, Yeats envisioned Keats "always as a boy with his face pressed to the window of a sweet shop."[35] "Kept from Greece by his ignorance, kept from luxury by his unlucky birth," he had been "denied all expression in his surrounding life";[36] and yet, because the poet lacked what Simon Goldhill has called the "position of cultural assurance" that knowing Greek might grant, Keats was driven to spend his days "reading the classics in translation," and from these "frantic strivings after Greece and luxury," he drew inspiration.[37] Keats had desired, Yeats believed, some vision of beauty commensurate to what he himself lacked in wealth, education and training.[38] Therefore it was not from intimate knowledge but rather from ignorance of Greek – from a partial knowledge or understanding of the language – that Keats forged his singular vision of the Hellenic world. He could not translate its letter, but his verse was said to breathe an English marked with Greek, marked with "the very spirit of antiquity, – eternal beauty and eternal repose."[39]

Keats' achievements notwithstanding, Yeats still could not shake the feeling that "the system of education from which [he] had suffered" had prepared him inadequately for the future.[40] His father, he complained, could have spared him, teaching him nothing but the classics himself;[41] but John Yeats was "an angry and impatient teacher," and when he "often interfered" in the poet's education, he did so "always with disaster, to

---

[34] Keats, "To George and Georgiana Keats" (September 17, 18, 20, 21, 24, 25, 27, 1819) in Keats (1958) 2:212.

[35] Yeats Papers, MS 30052, NLI.

[36] Yeats Papers, MS 30052, NLI.

[37] Goldhill (2002) 189; Yeats Papers, MS 30052, NLI.

[38] Yeats may have developed an abiding interest in privation, in part, from his reading of Friedrich Nietzsche (1844–1900). Nietzsche's discussion of art and suffering in *Menschliches, Allzumenschliches: Ein Buch für freie Geister* (1878) suggested that an artist's genius was often possessed by a "moving and ludicrous pathos," generated by the "lack of others" to enjoy his work. Needing *Compensation für diese Entbehrung*, the artist's "sufferings are felt to be exaggerated because the sound of his lamentations is louder, his mouth more persuasive; and *sometimes* his sufferings really are great, but only because his ambition and envy are so great." See Nietzsche (1878) 142. See also Nietzsche (1986) 83. On Yeats' knowledge of Nietzsche, see Heller (1988) 127–40, as well as Oppel (1987) and Liebregts (1993) 116–26.

[39] Smith (1857) 57.

[40] Yeats *CW3* (1999) 98.

[41] Though Yeats regarded his father as a capable, amateur classicist, John Yeats' own account of his experience at Trinity College, Dublin, was one of alienation. He found his fellow students to be "noisy and monotonous, without ideas or any curiosity about ideas, and without any sense of mystery, everything sacrificed to mental efficiency." The college was "intellectually a sort of little Prussia." John Yeats, "Memoirs, 1," in Murphy (1978) 33.

teach me my Latin lesson."[42] If he had perhaps been a better teacher, he might have

> taught me nothing but Greek and Latin, and I would now be a properly educated man, and would not have to look in useless longing at books that have been, through the poor mechanism of translation, the builders of my soul, nor face authority with the timidity born of excuse and evasion. Evasion and excuse were in the event as wise as the house-building instinct of the beaver.[43]

Though Yeats would never gain fluency, he continued to associate knowledge of Greek and Latin with intellectual achievement, social prestige and political confidence.[44] The lack of a classical education did provoke timidity in him; but, as Yeats aged, he began to draw strength from a desire to overcome that timidity, to incite a vision deeper than excuse and schoolboy evasion. Just as Keats' ignorance of Greek resulted in an English laced with passion for antiquity, the partial knowledge of classics Yeats did possess provoked both sharp thematic engagements with classical subjects and a broader transformation of style across his poetry and drama.

Though Yeats felt that his failure to acquire fluency in Latin and Greek had a detrimental effect on his intellectual life, his experience of youth was not unusual for the time. At the end of the nineteenth century, knowledge of Greek and Latin still remained central to the "organization of expert knowledge by university scholars and the civil service" in both British and Irish civic institutions, but the preeminent position classics occupied in liberal education was by then beginning to erode, due in large part to the successful rise of professionalism within the academy and the "increasingly pluralized nature of the curricular field."[45] To trace the institutional history of classics in the British Isles from the late nineteenth century through the early twentieth is to trace, as Christopher Stray notes, "just how marginalized" a once dominant subject could become, a subject "which once lay at the heart of English high culture."[46] As the

---

[42] Yeats *CW3* (1999) 53, 75.

[43] Yeats *CW3* (1999) 76.

[44] R. R. Bolgar's remark in 1954 that the "classical student of Edwardian times" felt that in studying Greek and Latin "he, if any man, possessed the magic key which would unlock the kingdoms of this world" aptly describes Yeats' belief in the power of classical learning – a power he did not possess. Bolgar (1954) 1.

[45] Haynes (2019a) xiii; Stray (1998) 259.

[46] Stray (1998) 1. See also the discussion in Richardson (2013). Richardson notes that the "narrative of antiquity in Victorian Britain" was predominantly one of "cultures triumphant, of a classically

"relaxed amateur scholarship of Anglican gentlemen" gradually "gave way to the specialized, methodic activity of a community of professional scholars," classics became a contested field of knowledge, one whose preeminence in university education was soon to be supplanted by a variety of competing academic interests, perhaps most powerfully by the study of English.[47] The rise of English was swift, so much so that, by 1921, Henry Newbolt (1862–1938), the principal author of a government report on *The Teaching of English in England* (often cited as the Newbolt Report), declared:

> it is now, and will probably be for as long a time as we can foresee, impossible to make use of the Classics as a fundamental part of a national system of education. They are a great watershed of humanistic culture, but one to which the general mass of any modern nation can, at present, have no direct access ... The time is past for holding, as the Renaissance teachers held, that the Classics alone can furnish a liberal education. We do not believe that those who have not studied the Classics or any foreign literature must necessarily fail to win from their native English a full measure of culture and humane training.[48]

With classics' importance diminished, the social and political utility of Greek and Latin also came under scrutiny. Where once a "knowledge of the Classics conferred a certain social distinction," that "glamour," with its "traditional association with high place," began to fade: English became "not less valuable than the Classics and decidedly more suited to the necessities of a general or national education."[49] One might "have expected an élitist subject centered on the learning of dead languages to have been discarded after the industrial revolution, the emergence of parliamentary democracy, and the triumph of the vernacular."[50] Yet the value of studying Greek and Latin in the prewar period managed to maintain – however tenuously – something of the promise of

---

educated British elite, commanding all corners of the world." Yet, in spite of that, the period was also marked by an unstable "insecure relationship with the ancient world." "The past rarely satisfied the present's whims – and triumphant Victorian classicism was never assured: its grandeur could disintegrate in a heartbeat; its disciples were lost in longing, not fulfillment." Richardson (2013) 4.

[47] Stray (1998) 2. On the history of classics at Trinity College and other prominent Irish universities, see Stanford (1976) 45–72; Dillon (1991) 239–54; Stubbs (1892) 113–24, and Ross (2013) 22–33.

[48] Newbolt Report (1921) 13, 18.

[49] Newbolt Report (1921) 39, 15. On the 'invention' of English literature in the academy, see Court (1992) 119–61; Palmer (1965) as well as Eagleton (1996) 15–46, and Crawford (2000) 1–44. See Conclusion, pp. 239–50. On the diminishment of classics' institutional presence in the United Kingdom and Ireland after 1960, see Harrison (2009) 1–16.

[50] Stray (1998) 1.

"entitlement to full civic participation."[51] Though its credibility would diminish, the grip Greek and Latin maintained over the public imagination proved tenacious, not only in England but across the British Isles. In this context, as the institutional structures governing the transmission of classical knowledge shifted slowly, new burgeoning forms of cultural nationalism and language purism in Ireland, in Scotland and in Wales emerged. These movements – calling for devolution, new national literatures and the preservation of Gaelic and Brythonic languages – would soon set their sights on the dominant institutions of English society and struggle to ally their cause with what remained of classics' claims to social prestige, political authority and intrinsic literary value. In this way, though classics was soon surpassed by English as the preeminent subject of liberal arts education, what was left of its "cultural glory from the era of Victorian Hellenism" was deployed – often in *ressentiment* – as a blunt, ideological weapon in the 'Celtic nations'.[52] Scholars, critics, controversialists and poets – figures such as Douglas Hyde (1860–1949), Saunders Lewis (1893–1985) and Hugh MacDiarmid – argued for the preservation or resuscitation of the Celtic on 'classical' grounds: the Irish, the Welsh and the Scottish could confront the "Anglocentric voice" of the British Isles because each bore what MacDiarmid called "an alternative value of prime consequence when set against the Greek and Roman literatures which are all that most of us mean when we speak of 'the Classics'."[53]

As classics became pervasive in the rhetoric of revival, interest in its creative potential likewise grew among the 'Celtic' avant-garde, and new experimental forms of expression began to rise in response to the ideological pressures of cultural nationalism. Poets and artists at times promoted, and at times interrogated, the visions of classical antiquity advanced by these pressures, using their work to contest the meaning of the ancient world for contemporary 'Celtic' societies. Yet it is worth noting that comparatively few of the writers considered critical to Celtic literary modernism possessed a fluent knowledge of classical languages. This was a bitter reality about which Yeats wrote in *Reveries over Childhood and Youth*. A similar sense of deprivation also dogged James Joyce who, despite a high degree of competence with Latin and other modern European languages, lamented in midlife (just months before the

---

[51] Haynes (2019b) 3.
[52] Stray (1998) 2.
[53] Crawford (2000) 11. MacDiarmid, "English Ascendancy in British Literature," *The Criterion* 10.41 (July 1931) 593–613, in MacDiarmid *SP* (1992) 63.

publication of *Ulysses* [1922]) that "I don't even know Greek though I am spoken of as erudite. My father wanted me to take Greek as third language, my mother German and my friends Irish. Result, I took Italian."[54] David Jones, the poet, painter and engraver, likewise complained of a "terrible ignorance one is trying to make up all the time" that kept him from mastering "even one language besides English."[55] "If I'd gone to school," he exclaimed, "at least they'd have taught me Greek and Latin."[56] Hugh MacDiarmid too, though he lived life as a brash autodidact, received little formal instruction in classics: "alas I can speak no Greek," he complained, "And am now too old to learn / And nil leiyeas ogam air."[57] For each writer, however, the largely untutored exposure to antiquity they did have pushed them towards the "fertile chaos" of bold literary experimentation.[58] Like Keats, the loss of immediate access to antiquity in no way kept classics from becoming midwife to literary invention. On the contrary, it was the tension between knowledge and ignorance, between the apparent loss of classics and the cultural significance still attached to its traceable presence, that proved powerful.

---

[54] Joyce, "Letter to Harriet Shaw Weaver, 24 June 1921," in Joyce *LJJ* (1957) 167. Joyce first chose to study Italian instead of Greek when he enrolled at Belvedere College around the age of eleven. The classical Greek he did acquire later was, as Ron Bush notes, "self-taught and mixed up also with his self-taught study of modern Greek." His instruction in Latin was more consistent and effective, beginning at Clongowes Wood College, and continuing through his studies at University College, Dublin. The results of Joyce's formal examinations were often better in Latin than in English. See Bush (2019) 349, as well as Bradley (1982) 112, 115, 129, 138–39; Ellmann (1982) 46–47 and Sullivan (1957) 80–81, 94–95, 98, 159–61, 236–37. On classical education at University College, Dublin, in Joyce's time, see Fathers of the Society of Jesus, comp. (1930) 194–203.

[55] David Jones, as in Roberts (1964) 7.

[56] Roberts (1964) 7. On Jones' education, Dilworth (2017) 23–34; on his approach with Latin, see Miles (1990) 45–46. Jones' Greek was poor. In 1952 when thanking his friend Rev. Desmond Chute for sending an engraved Greek inscription, he told him: "I can't read Greek but someone staying in this house translated it for me and I like the sound of it and what it says very much." David Jones, Letter to Rev. Desmond Chute (December 29, 1952) in Jones *IN* (1984) 25. For further discussion, see Chapter 4, pp. 182–84.

[57] MacDiarmid *CP2* (1994) 797. The Irish Gaelic of this quotation may be translated in English as, "There is no cure for it." MacDiarmid encountered a slight variation of this quotation in the letters of Stephen MacKenna (1872–1934), the linguist and translator of Plotinus' *Enneads*. In a 1926 letter to a friend, MacKenna had complained of his lingering knowledge of Irish: "God knows why I don't let the Irish die in me but I don't, can't: I always have – for one thing – the idea, which would make Bergin snort, of one day quite suddenly and gan fhios dom fhéin blossoming out into a Irish Essayist. Anyhow this bee has built his nest in my bonnet and nil leiyeas agam air. No fool like an old Gael." "gan fhios dom fhéin" is glossed as "unbeknownst to myself." See MacKenna (1936) 229–30, as well as Grieve (2011) 33–34. When MacDiarmid moved to Edinburgh to train as a teacher at Broughton Junior Student Center in 1908, he did receive some training in languages and the classics, but he was never fluent in Latin or Greek. See Kerrigan (1988). See Chapter 5, pp. 225–27.

[58] Carne-Ross (1979) 11.

Untethered from more conventional modes of reception, Yeats, Joyce, Jones and MacDiarmid therefore redeployed classical receptions variously with "unexpected freshness," eccentrically overwriting competing visions of the classical past in the contemporary moment.[59] Their work would challenge not only institutionalized receptions articulated in common educational establishments but those advanced by ideologues of Celtic nationalism 'at home' as well. Because – to paraphrase Declan Kiberd – the very notion of classics, or a 'classical tradition', was then rapidly evolving, the Greek and the Roman could no longer be presented as a "museum of nostalgias" commanding obeisance from contemporary artists.[60] Instead, among the avant-garde, the classical past appeared as a "reopened future" where the loss and discrediting of its so-called tradition had unleashed new and unstable creative forces.[61] With classical knowledge more dis-embedded from institutions that had long dominated its transmission, the range of reception became more multivocal, and the shapes of Celtic modernism reflect that diversity. With hybrid idioms notable for their appropriation, polyglot collage, retranslations and outright mistranslations of antiquity, Yeats, Joyce, Jones and MacDiarmid variously contested ideological reconfigurations of classics in their own time, giving voice to work no one "yet had ears to hear."[62]

Despite the growing 'recession' in classical education – for Yeats, Joyce, Jones and MacDiarmid – a fluent knowledge of classics still carried prestige, civic entitlement and compelling claims to a sense of cultural continuity and social stability. That reputation, however, was met variously: sometimes with admiration, sometimes with fear, skepticism or resistance. As a young poet in Dublin, Yeats felt that the classics might threaten the advent of a national literature in Ireland, for, since the Renaissance, imitation of Greece and Rome had often been implicated in the reputed loss of 'native' capacities for literary achievement. Many countries in Europe, he thought, had seen their own art and literature emerge stillborn in the presence of antiquity. The desire to study, to mimic classical form was too compelling, too powerful, he claimed, so much that when "learning turned [human minds] to Greece and Rome,"

---

[59] Arendt (2006) 94.
[60] Kiberd (1996) 292. See Conclusion, pp. 248–56.
[61] Kiberd (1996) 292. Arendt (2006) 94.
[62] Arendt (2006) 94.

the sanctity has dwindled from their own hills and valleys, which the legends and beliefs of fifty centuries had filled so full of it that a man could hardly plough his fields or follow his sheep upon the hillside without remembering some august story, or walking softly lest he had divine companions.[63]

Instead of cultivating what Johann Gottfried Herder (1744–1803) had called, a century before, the *Gedankenvorrat eines Volks* or *Schatzkammer*, the "treasure-chest" of the nation, foreign stories and forms were imported from Greece and Rome.[64] For this reason, classics was both feared and envied among those intent on reviving Celtic language and literature in the British Isles. Neoclassical imitation might thwart the flowering of indigenous genius, and no vernacular forged with foreign forms, whether classical or otherwise, could serve the literary aspirations of a new and emerging nation. A national literature had to be a native growth.[65] Yet it was without caution or wariness of classical examples that the Irish revolutionary Pádraic Pearse (1879–1916) once claimed for the modern 'Gael' great forerunners in antiquity, "the Greeks – the pioneers of intellectual progress in Europe."[66] "What the Greek was to the ancient world," Pearse declared, "the Gael will be to the modern; and in no point will the parallel prove more true than in the fervent and noble love of learning which distinguishes both races. The Gael, like the Greek, loves learning, and he loves it solely for its own sake."[67] In a similar spirit, Douglas Hyde, the first president of the Gaelic League, claimed a Hellenic bloodline for Ireland, insisting in 1892 that the Irish were a living remnant of the civilization that "established itself in Greece," a civilization then "making its last stand for independence in this island of Ireland."[68] Likewise, George William Russell, known as Æ (1867–1935), held the emulation of Greek literature aloft, seeing the classics as a model for "building up an overwhelming ideal" of Irish nationality.[69] "Since the

---

[63] Yeats, "The Literary Movement in Ireland" (December 1899) in Yeats *CW9* (2004) 468.

[64] Herder (1985) 552–56. See also Herder (1993) 260. On Herder and the broad influence of German Romanticism in Ireland, see McCormack (1985) 219–28.

[65] See Stanford (1976) 219–20. See pp. 3–5 of this Introduction.

[66] Pearse, "The Intellectual Future of the Gael," in Pearse (1898) 49.

[67] Pearse (1898) 56. Later, as plans for armed resistance against British rule began to develop, Pearse became bolder, asserting Irish superiority over ancient Greek, as in a December 1912 speech when he claimed "for Irish literature, at its best, these excellences: a clearer than Greek vision, a more generous than Greek humanity, a deeper than Greek spirituality. And I claim that Irish literature has never lost those excellences." Pádraic H. Pearse, "Some Aspects of Irish Literature," in Pearse (1924) 133.

[68] Hyde, "The Necessity for De-Anglicising Ireland" (November 25, 1892) in Hyde (1986) 155.

[69] Æ (1899) 81.

Greek civilization," he explained, "no European nation has had an intellectual literature which was genuinely national."[70] A chance for just such a genuinely national literary culture remained alive in Ireland, however, a chance to expose the country "in clear and beautiful light, to create the Ireland in the heart"; this, he argued, was the "province of a national literature."[71] For Æ, for Hyde, for Pearse and for others sympathetic to Revival, an oppression far worse than neoclassical imitation then loomed over Ireland: Anglicization and the annihilation of all that still remained 'authentically' Gaelic. So, it was thought that if the abiding authority afforded the classics in contemporary society could be harnessed, if professional scholars and amateur classicists could be convinced to support the language movement, then Ireland's Literary Revival would gain a powerful ally.[72] To paraphrase the words of Joyce's Buck Mulligan, if classicists "could only work together" with advocates for revival, then their receptions of antiquity "might do something for the island. Hellenise it."[73]

It was with that desire for cooperation that the Cork-born priest William Francis Barry (1849–1930) urged his contemporaries in 1902 to "snatch from the grave" the "musing, sparkling, tender soul of a nation."[74] Revivalists, though, could not rely on the "dangerous fancy that original minds need no discipline and have had no ancestors."[75] In their struggle they had to look to Greek antiquity, for no national genius had been "created on demand."[76] "[C]ircumstances favourable to genius" could be prepared through educational reform and new creative endeavor, but no revival, no Irish literary culture would spring to "new life" without widespread commitment to the study of classical antiquity.[77] "[A]t the first hour of every revival in literature, in philosophy, in art, in civil polity, how can we fail to perceive," he asked,

> the Greeks, our everlasting schoolmasters, and Athens, the University of mankind? Under the magic of that great ancient literature, more than one nation during the last four hundred years has awakened to a knowledge of itself and what it could do ... However we explain it, the flower and fruit

---

[70] Æ (1899) 81.
[71] Æ (1899) 83.
[72] On the various factions within the Gaelic Revival and the 'Irish' Renaissance, see O'Leary (1994) 281–354.
[73] Joyce Ulysses (1986) 6 (1.157–58).
[74] Barry (1902) 322.
[75] Barry (1902) 324.
[76] Barry (1902) 323.
[77] Barry (1902) 323, 335.

season of our noblest productions in letters, has followed always upon the study of the classics, but especially of the Greeks.[78]

For Barry, the development of Ireland's national genius was predicated on the desire to imitate a "Hellenic model," for he argued, "no European literature of the highest order" had emerged "except in dependence, near or remote, on the classics."[79] "[S]tudents, critics, translators, commentators" were called therefore to advance a "new birth of Greek studies" in Ireland, not simply further "school-exercises or competitive cramming" with the language.[80] "Our ambition is to come into living contact with a people so marvellously endowed," to see this "confused existence of ours as a whole" shaped on a Greek "pattern of beauty" by "[d]iscipline, choice, effort," all the so-called "stages of worthy mental training."[81] When "the creative sap rises," Barry declared,

> and the tree of life puts forth blossom or decks its branches with immortal fruit. Greek literature is studied, and will be studied yet more, in our schools, our universities. And it is surely desirable that, whether as a creative or a critical influence, it should be brought to bear on a movement that is fired with the ambition of equalling it in pure artistic value if not in renown. I wish to see Hellenic scholars bestow an Irish Homer, an Irish Herodotus, on our aspiring youth.[82]

Yet despite the insistence that from "Greek we shall get no harm if our eyes are fixed unswervingly on its golden days," classicists and revivalists remained wary of making common cause.[83] Barry's "much-discussed" recommendations were warmly received by the Gaelic League, but they were welcomed only with the understanding that "Gaels" could not "neglect any deep native forces for foreign ones," that Ireland's "literary or other outcomes would, of course, be Irish and not quasi-Greek."[84] *An Claidheamh Soluis* (The Sword of Light), the Gaelic League weekly, wondered too whether Barry had presented too rosy a view of the Gael and the Greek, writing that

> … we have a great deal of hard, rough, humble home-work to do before we are in the fine mood and temper in which Dr. Barry imagines us to be

[78] Barry (1902) 324.
[79] Barry (1902) 324–325.
[80] Barry (1902) 335, 325, 329.
[81] Barry (1902) 329. See Chapter 1, pp. 55–61.
[82] Barry (1902) 335.
[83] Barry (1902) 334.
[84] "London Notes," *An Claidheamh Soluis* 4.23 (August 16, 1902) 393.

already. There is very little in an Irish village or forlorn town of to-day to
set one dreaming of Attica. Picture Plato in a Midland carriage on the way
to Galway![85]

Some sympathetic to the Revival feared that deepening any alliance with
classics would further commit Ireland to "a plagiarism that imitates but
knows not how to strike out on a path untrodden."[86] At the same time
many across prominent Irish institutions of higher learning – professors,
scholars and students alike – thought the push to resuscitate Irish Gaelic,
could possibly diminish the quality of the established curriculum of
liberal education.

Given the contested position which classics occupied within the
language movement, it is no surprise that controversy surrounding classics' relation to Celtic language spilled out into public debates – in 1899
and again in 1901–02 – when in those years a Royal Commission was
appointed to inquire into "the present condition" of educational practices
in Ireland, and "to report as to what reforms, if any, are desirable in order
to render that education adequate to the needs of the Irish People."[87] In
1899 the Commission focused its attention largely on secondary education while in 1901 and 1902 the matter of the university curriculum was
broadly examined. Prominent teachers, headmasters and academics were
called to give testimony before the Commission in a series of extensive
interviews. Notable among those that appeared in 1899 were Trinity
College faculty, Louis Purser (1854–1932), professor of Latin, Robert
Yelverton Tyrrell (1844–1914), professor of Greek, John Pentland Mahaffy
(1839–1919), professor of Greek history, and Robert Atkinson (1839–
1908), professor of comparative philology and the 1884 Todd Professor of
Celtic Languages, as well as Douglas Hyde of the Gaelic League.[88] In
spring 1902 Hyde was once again interviewed along with many others,
including the Rev. Dr. George Salmon (1819–1904), provost of Trinity
College, and Edward Gwynn (1868–1941), Todd Lecturer in the Royal

---

[85] "London Notes," *An Claidheamh Soluis* 4.23 (August 16, 1902) 393. For a comprehensive account
of the weekly *An Claidheamh Soluis* and its importance within the Gaelic language movement, see
Uí Chollatáin (2004).

[86] Barry (1902) 334.

[87] Royal Commission on University Education in Ireland (1901) 2.

[88] In addition to being a prominent academic and controversialist, Mahaffy is also well known as the
teacher of Oscar Wilde (1854–1900) who once called him the "one to whom I owe so much
personally ... my first and my best teacher ... the scholar who showed me how to love Greek
things." Oscar Wilde, "To J. P. Mahaffy" (April ?, 1893) in Wilde (2000) 562. In April 1877 Wilde
accompanied Mahaffy on a trip to Corfu, Mycenae and Athens. On Mahaffy's character and
scholarly achievements, see Stanford and McDowell (1971) as well as Dillon (1991) 244–46.

Irish Academy and a fellow of Trinity. Before both commissions, Hyde championed the cause of Irish and the interests of the language movement, arguing that requiring instruction in Irish was essential to the future health of the country. In his view Ireland needed to dispense with the current "cosmopolitan" curricular scheme and embrace a "national factor in Irish education."[89] Without that, he argued, schools could not sufficiently serve the "Irish needs and Irish well-being" of their students.[90]

> We desire to see the whole scheme of Irish cosmopolitan education exactly reversed. If this country is to be saved, it is Irish needs which should, in our opinion, be the aim of Irish education in the future ... We believe it to be the steady neglect of the national factor in Irish education which is largely responsible for driving such multitudes of Irishmen into professions, the end of which is emigration. We have steadily refused to make the country interesting to them, and the consequence is, that they are glad to leave it.[91]

Lack of instruction in Irish, he explained, had stunted a common sense of national pride among all social classes in Ireland. As constituted, the present system of education had helped instead to "thoroughly divorce the upper classes from the lower. The lower are still largely penetrated with traditional love of country and national feelings and instincts," but those of greater means were products of "un-Irish teaching" and "divorced from the life and genius of their own country, brought up *non vitae sed scholae.*"[92] For that reason, "all who can afford it, with few exceptions, are sending their sons out of the country altogether to be educated."[93] Such was "the export standard" of Irish schooling.[94] To keep the country from becoming "a sandbank thrown up in some strange sea, inhabited by a race of mongrels," broad reform was needed – one which made instruction in Irish a clear priority.[95] For without its revival, no sense of "national consciousness, and pride of country, and love of country" could be forged for the coming generation.[96] Practically

---

[89] Douglas Hyde, "Thirty-Fourth Day, Tuesday, 10th June 1902," in "Third Report of the Commissioners on University Education (Ireland)." *Reports From Commissioners, Inspectors, and Others: 1902.* 32 (1902) 313 (hereafter *Sessional Papers*). See also *Irish in University Education. Gaelic League Pamphlet,* no. 29 [1902?]. On the diminished position of Irish in the national schools of Ireland, see Wolf (2014) 53–59; Doyle (2015) 118–20 as well as Coolahan (1981) 3–51, 223–26.

[90] *Sessional Papers* 32 (1902) 313.

[91] *Sessional Papers* 32 (1902) 313.

[92] *Sessional Papers* 32 (1902) 314, 313.

[93] *Sessional Papers* 32 (1902) 314.

[94] *Sessional Papers* 32 (1902) 313.

[95] *Sessional Papers* 32 (1902) 314.

[96] *Sessional Papers* 32 (1902) 313.

speaking, Hyde felt, this meant that Irish should maintain equal if not greater standing than Greek and Latin in both intermediate and university curricula. Irish was, he insisted, a classical language in its own right, an ancient tongue possessing "the oldest vernacular literature of any in Europe except Greece, to which she bears, in many respects, the closest comparison. And this literature is not like the great continental literatures, a mere reflex of the Roman, but is wholly indigenous and autochthonous."[97] Irish, "though at present a lost language," was "not a foreign language" to those born in Ireland.[98] Unlike Greek or Latin, it could be reacquired "with vigour and quickness," having once been

> the language, if not of the father, then of the grandfather, and if not of the grandfather, then, certainly, of the great-grandfather, of almost every boy examined before the Intermediate Board at the present day. The very cast of their features, the expression of their faces, their laryngeal peculiarities, their accent in speaking – all this is largely the product of the Irish language spoken for hundreds or thousands of years by all who went before them. The very English which they speak swarms with Irish idioms.[99]

While "a long and tedious training" was needed "to make a Celt or a Teuton read himself into the spirit of classical literature, and into the spirit of the Greeks and Romans," Irish demanded less "pain and loss of time."[100] Though the contemporary student had "lost the Irish language altogether," he might still "imbibe," Hyde suggested, "the benefits of classical study from Irish literature in a way he could not do from any other, because every fibre of his being will pulsate and thrill, responsive to some chord in the Irish language."[101] The "comparative value" of Irish was therefore even "more important than Greek" because the "Irishman

[97] *Sessional Papers* 32 (1902) 314.
[98] *The Irish Language and Irish Intermediate Education. III. Dr. Hyde's Evidence. Gaelic League Pamphlet*, no. 13 [1901?] 6.
[99] *Gaelic League Pamphlet*, no. 13 [1901?] 6. In a 1912 pamphlet, *What Is the Use of Reviving Irish?*, Dermot Chenevix Trench (1881–1909) – Joyce's model for Haines in *Ulysses* – developed the racialist account of Irish biology and language further, insisting that the anatomical structure of the "Irish brain" and "Irish larynx" were organically connected and best-suited to the speaking of Irish Gaelic. Fearing a "mingling of races" and "the forcible extermination of a racial genius through the pressure of political and economic circumstances," Trench provocatively asked whether his countrymen still wished "'to live in an Ireland which reflects your racial type? If so, you will support the language which expresses the Irish nature and which will keep the nation true to itself in all that it sets its hand to accomplish.'" Trench (1912) 27, 29, 32. On Trench and his contributions in debates over Irish, see Crowley (2005) 146–50.
[100] *Gaelic League Pamphlet*, no. 13 [1901?] 6.
[101] *Gaelic League Pamphlet*, no. 13 [1901?] 6.

responds more readily to it."[102] Although the current structure of education had conspired to spread English further, a broad receptivity to Irish remained palpable, and the country's most classical resource, if properly supported, Hyde thought, could reemerge as a catalyst of national reinvention.[103]

That Irish Gaelic was a 'classical' language, that it therefore possessed an "equal educational value – or very nearly so" with Greek – did not win widespread approval among Dublin's academics.[104] Hyde's foremost critics emerged at Trinity College in Robert Atkinson and J. P. Mahaffy, who regarded rising Irish enthusiasm as "not only useless, but a mischievous obstacle to civilisation."[105] When called before the Commission on Intermediate Education in January 1899, Mahaffy tried to settle the matter boldly: little to no educational value could be gained from the study of Irish.[106] The language might be, he quipped, "sometimes useful to a man fishing for salmon or shooting grouse in the West," but as an object of formal study, Irish was not classics.[107] All the newfound fervor for this "out-of-the-way and troublesome language" was, Mahaffy complained, simply a consequence of a pervasive sentimentalism, one that would see

> every miserable remnant of barbarism, every vanquished and half-extinct language which has lost its literary worth, and has become a hindrance to the commercial and political progress of the world ... coddled and pampered as if it were the most precious product of the human mind.[108]

Irish was no precious product, and as Mahaffy saw it, no baseless comparisons could make it so. "Let me not be told that all this applies equally to the study of the dead classical languages."[109] To discourage Irish was "to brave unpopularity" in Dublin where public pronouncements of its value were becoming more frequent and more extravagant.[110] "One Prelate," Mahaffy observed, had gone "so far as to say that of all the

---

[102] *Gaelic League Pamphlet*, no. 13 [1901?] 19, 20.
[103] The linguist Richard Henebry (1863–1916) put it succinctly when he said that "Old Irish must become the study of our boys in school just as Latin and Greek. It must be used as the key to our great wealth." Henebry (1903) 857.
[104] *Gaelic League Pamphlet*, no. 13 [1901?] 20.
[105] Mahaffy (1896) 783. When asked before the Commission of 1899 if "Celtic" were "a subject that should be entered on at all," Mahaffy called its study "a mischievous waste of time." Intermediate Education (Ireland) Commission (1899) 33.
[106] See Diarmid Coffey's account of Mahaffy's appearance before the 1899 Commission in Coffey (1938) 66–78. See also Stanford and McDowell (1971) 104–26, and Mathews (2003) 35–45.
[107] Intermediate Education (Ireland) Commission (1899) 33.
[108] Mahaffy (1882) 465; Mahaffy (1896) 784.
[109] Mahaffy (1896) 786.
[110] Mahaffy (1899) 216.

languages he knew (even including Greek) none was so powerful and expressive as his mother tongue. But for his exalted position, we might have ventured to ask him how many languages he really *knew*, how far Greek could be fairly included."[111] At the third *Oireachtas* festival in June 1899, it was Michael Logue (1840–1924), archbishop of Armagh, who had praised Irish in this way, claiming that

> for public speaking, and for poetry, there is not – not even excepting the Greek – any language on this planet of ours, as the American says, than [*sic*] can surpass the Irish, as it was known by our ancestors, for power and expression. I know some little things about a number of languages. I have a superficial knowledge of French, Italian, Latin, and Greek. I even learned Hebrew in my young days, though I don't remember even a letter now. I assure you it is my firm conviction that the man who can speak Irish, classical Irish, and at the same time simple Irish that can be understood by the people, will produce a greater effect than Demosthenes would have produced upon his countrymen in the very zenith of his power.[112]

That a bishop would go so far, Mahaffy thought, with such "absurd laudations" demonstrated how deeply the "Celtic craze" had taken hold, a craze that "the cool and sceptical few" were called to resist.[113] Otherwise, he argued,

> The few thousands who were till recently ashamed of [Irish] as a mark of ignorance are now likely to dream that they have a nobler heritage than the millions in Ireland who know not a word of it and who have never even heard it spoken, and so we may possibly (though not probably) have a serious recrudescence of Irish speaking, which will have even worse effects than the maintenance and cultivation of Welsh in Wales.[114]

---

[111] Mahaffy (1899) 216.

[112] Logue, cited in Barrett (1899) 12. Logue often made this claim when defending Irish against the charges of Mahaffy and Atkinson. See, for example, "Cardinal Logue at Kilkenny," *An Claidheamh Soluis* 1.5 (April 15, 1899) 75.

[113] Mahaffy (1899) 216, 214. By the turn of the twentieth century, the Catholic Church in Ireland had largely come to view the revival of Irish Gaelic favorably. A number of priests and bishops, most notably William Walsh (1841–1921), archbishop of Dublin, as well as Cardinal Logue were known supporters of the Gaelic League as well as of Home Rule. Nonetheless, when the National University was founded in 1908, the Catholic hierarchy found itself feuding with the Gaelic League over its opposition to making Irish compulsory for enrollment at the university. On the Catholic Church and advocacy for Irish, see Crowley (2000) 175–78 as well as Mathews (2003) 26–28 and Mannix (2012) 29–48.

[114] Mahaffy (1899) 213–14. Mahaffy refers to the view that the Welsh language was "a decided impediment to the mental improvement of the people," a "nuisance and an obstacle, both to the administration of the law, and to the cause of religion." As outlined in the 1848 *Reports of the Commissioners of Inquiry into the State of Education in Wales*, Welsh was thought to have "no liter-

For Robert Atkinson, Irish was to be rejected on grounds both technical and moral. The language was still not "in a settled state," and for that reason alone, it could not be effectively employed in teaching students.[115] Though the amount of material published in Irish during the Revival had begun a movement to standardize the language, the presence of many dialects still suggested "a decline from what was perceived as the perfections of classical languages like Latin."[116] Better to use "Greek or Latin, or French," Atkinson claimed, for there "you have a perfectly definite spelling, definite declensions, definite forms, a definite syntax, and so on."[117] Irish, by contrast, possessed too many linguistic variations: its *patois* were too "numerous" and "no standard of speech absolutely accepted by everybody" existed as yet.[118] Thus it was "impossible for the child to get real educational training out of [Irish]," for the language possessed "extremely little literature" of instructional value.[119] "If a boy learns his French, or learns his Latin," he observed,

> he has the whole world before him in choice of what to read. But I have been surprised in seeing even now, after so many years during which the beauties of Irish literature have been talked of, how little has been done that really could be usefully or properly brought before children.[120]

Moreover, those old Irish stories that did exist were likely to pollute the innocence of youth, for "it would be difficult," Atkinson declared, "to find a book in which there was not some passage so silly or so indecent as to give you a shock from which you would never recover during the rest of your life."[121] When pressed to explain, Atkinson contrasted the "crude realism" of Irish folktales with the bawdy comedies of Aristophanes, insisting that, unlike the Greek poet, Gaelic folklore had no "elevating ideal."[122] The saltiness of Aristophanes – what Plutarch described as the θυμελικὸν καὶ βάναυσον (the vulgarity and ribaldry) of his comedies (*Moralia* 853b) – could, however, stir "positive pleasure" in students,

---

ature of any real value and utility," and its deficiencies had left in Wales the "impress" of an "imperfect civilization." Committee of Council on Education (1848) 319, 406, 401, 519. See also G. A. Williams (1985) 197–213, as well as Brooks (2003) 134.

[115] *The Irish Language and Irish Intermediate Education, IV. Dr. Atkinson's Evidence. Gaelic League Pamphlet*, no. 14 [1901?] 2.

[116] Doyle (2015) 224, and Ó Conchubhair (2009) 194–96.

[117] *Gaelic League Pamphlet*, no. 14 [1901?] 3.

[118] *Gaelic League Pamphlet*, no. 14 [1901?] 2.

[119] *Gaelic League Pamphlet*, no. 14 [1901?] 6.

[120] *Gaelic League Pamphlet*, no. 14 [1901?] 6.

[121] *Gaelic League Pamphlet*, no. 14 [1901?] 14.

[122] *Gaelic League Pamphlet*, no. 14 [1901?] 14.

a *ktema es aei* – a perpetual treasure; but if I read these Irish books, I see nothing ideal in them, and my astonishment is that through the whole range of Irish literature that I have read (and I have read an enormous range of it), the smallness of the element of idealism is most noticeable; and children, my lord, I contend, cannot live without ideals, and should not be brought up without them.[123]

Against this charge, Douglas Hyde took up the matter of obscenity and classics and, citing his friend, the philologist Alfred Trübner Nutt (1856–1910), asked "what language" would the "unfortunate Irish child" then be "allowed to study? Greek? Why you can buy all Aristophanes for 3s., and the erotic poems of the Anthology for 1s. 6d. Latin? Martial and Juvenal can be had unexpurgated for a few shillings."[124] Atkinson persisted, however: Irish was, by contrast with classics, excessively crude. The "filth" found in recent editions of both *Tóraíocht Dhiarmada agus Gráinne: The Pursuit of Diarmuid and Gráinne* (1857) and *The Lay of Oisin in the Land of the Young* (1859) were "nearer to the sod ... lower than low."[125] Even Douglas Hyde's own work with folklore appeared "so low," he thought, that one could not regard his Irish as "good enough for a *patois*. I should call it an *imbroglio*, *mélange*, an *omnium gatherum*."[126] The language could not be accepted until "some man of commanding intelligence" – presumably someone other than Hyde – had emerged to standardize it "in such beautiful form that everybody has accepted it and assented to it, and followed it as a model."[127]

Hyde, for his part, was astounded by the "utterly reckless way" in which Atkinson and Mahaffy had thrown "plenty of dirt in the hope that

[123] *Gaelic League Pamphlet*, no. 14 [1901?] 7. Atkinson's remarks built on those he made in his edition of the Middle Irish text, *The Yellow Book of Lecan* (1896). Enraging both Lady Augusta Gregory and Douglas Hyde, Atkinson asserted there that the "mass of material preserved" in *The Yellow Book* was "out of all proportion to its value as 'literature.'" It contained "so many repetitions of certain tales" that one could say this "series of disconnected collectanea" was largely "mere metrical sawdust and technical scaffolding, so many pages taken up with genealogical fact and speculation, such an amount of problematical scriptural history taken usually from any source but the Bible itself, that the whole mass, when sifted, furnishes in reality but a very small quantity of what may be called imaginative literature." Atkinson (1896) 4, 3.

[124] *The Irish Language and Irish Intermediate Education, VI. Dr. Hyde's Reply to Dr. Atkinson, Gaelic League Pamphlet*, no. 16 [1901?] 17.

[125] *Gaelic League Pamphlet*, no. 14 [1901?] 14, 6. See O'Grady (1857) as well as O'Looney (1859) 227–80. See also Chapter 1, pp. 69–70 for a discussion of O'Looney's translation.

[126] *Gaelic League Pamphlet*, no. 14 [1901?] 13. Atkinson had long opposed Hyde's attempts to make Irish more prominent in scholarly circles around Dublin. In March 1896, when Hyde had sought an appointment as Professor of Irish at Trinity College, Atkinson was reported to have persuaded the provost, George Salmon, that he was unsuitable, largely because he spoke "baboon Irish." Dunleavy and Dunleavy (1991) 200–1.

[127] *Gaelic League Pamphlet*, no. 14 [1901?] 21.

some may stick."[128] Most galling was the accusation Atkinson leveled against folklore itself, namely that all such stories were "at the bottom abominable."[129] The professor, Hyde claimed, possessed no objectivity, nothing of the "deliberate opinion" one would expect from a scholar whose professional expertise was ancient languages.[130] The "wild combativeness and exaggeration" with which he had greeted even the suggestion that Irish folklore might prove valuable was evidence of political bias and personal antagonism.[131] Irish was no more unsettled, Hyde claimed (citing Heinrich Zimmer [1851–1910], professor of Sanskrit and comparative linguistics at the University of Greifswald) than the "language of the Greek epics, of the Homeric poems."[132] Even the celebrated "literary language" of Homer had borne "the imprint of Ionic dialects, quite shot through with the peculiarities of the Aeolic dialect; and as far as forms go, old forms and new forms ... confusedly mingled together."[133] "Where is the 'absolute standard of correctness'?" he exclaimed,

> What would Atkinson, from his schoolmaster standpoint, call the epic literature of the Greeks? "Not good enough for a patois"; "an imbroglio, mélange, an omnium gatherum"? From his point of view that would be the proper answer, and yet – as everyone sees – an absurdity![134]

The matter was simple: Atkinson feared that Irish, a tongue "which he does not understand," could generate a greater sense of national pride, and its teaching might thereby be tantamount to supporting Home Rule.[135] Thus Atkinson had rushed out "with the words 'filth' and 'indecency' upon his lips. Is this political or is it racial," Hyde exclaimed, "or is it both combined? Oh! politics, politics, how much you have to answer for in Irish life!"[136] Hyde, for his part, insisted that efforts to reinvigorate Irish had little to do with Home Rule and more to do with resuscitating "the principle of nationality, rightly understood."[137] That principle, if

---

[128] Hyde (1899) 3.
[129] *Gaelic League Pamphlet*, no. 14 [1901?] 15. See also Douglas Hyde, *The Irish Language and Irish Intermediate Education, VI. Dr. Hyde's Reply to Dr. Atkinson. Gaelic League Pamphlet*, no. 16 [1901?] 13; and Hyde (1899) 3.
[130] Hyde (1899) 3.
[131] Hyde (1899) 3.
[132] "Letter to Dr. Douglas Hyde from Dr. H. Zimmer, Professor of Sanscrit and Celtic Languages, University of Greifswald" (April 4, 1899), printed in *Gaelic League Pamphlet*, no. 16 [1901?] 33.
[133] *Gaelic League Pamphlet*, no. 16 [1901?] 33.
[134] *Gaelic League Pamphlet*, no. 16 [1901?] 33.
[135] Hyde (1899) 3.
[136] Hyde (1899) 3.
[137] *Gaelic League Pamphlet*, no. 13 [1901?] 5.

revived, could bring about a renewed "reverence for antiquity," he insisted, a patriotism that could exist "altogether apart from politics."[138]

Yet where Hyde insisted there was no political provocation, Mahaffy saw ideological resentment and a radical disrespect for the imperial progress of English, for as P. J. Mathews observes, even though "Hyde insisted that the League was strictly non-political, the language controversy" placed advancement of Gaelic revival "in direct collision with the forces promoting English interests in Ireland."[139] To Mahaffy, the "self-developed enthusiasts" of the Gaelic League ("whose trade is to shout") hoped only to gain notoriety by ensnaring the prestige of classics and challenging the scholarly authority of Trinity.[140] "If the present controversy," he told *The Daily Express*,

> should lead to the education of a large number of persons in the classical language, with all its grammatical and philological niceties, no one would be better pleased than myself. But to be worth learning a language must possess a decent literature, or must at least be practically useful. Modern Irish has no literature worthy the name, and the folly of wasting the time of children who will have to work for their living on a language that is for all practical purposes dead is ridiculously obvious.[141]

Though it seemed obvious to Mahaffy that study of the language was a waste, he knew also that there was no hope "of mending, or even of moderating" the thinking of the Gaelic League, an organization too eager to "attribute sordid motives to their opponents in addition to charging them with lack of patriotism and with ignorance."[142] Hyde did believe that Mahaffy and Atkinson lacked patriotism, but as he saw it, the broad influence of Trinity College in Ireland was a more troublesome problem.[143] Though the school's authority was "ever growing smaller and smaller, relatively to the whole mass of educated public opinion in Ireland," Trinity

---

[138] *Gaelic League Pamphlet*, no. 13 [1901?] 5.
[139] Mathews (2003) 44.
[140] Mahaffy (1899) 216.
[141] "Dr. Hyde and the Irish Language – Interview with Dr. Mahaffy," *The Daily Express* (February 16, 1899) 5.
[142] Mahaffy (1899) 216.
[143] The language controversies of 1899 and 1901–02 were nested in the debates over the university education of Irish Catholics – specifically over the establishment of a Catholic college in Dublin "equal in endowment and prestige to Trinity." Led by the Catholic hierarchy, the campaign for such a college was strengthened by a "deepening hostility towards Trinity College" born from the perception that Trinity's scholarly ethos and curriculum were too thoroughly Anglicized, Protestant and thus seemingly antithetical to the emerging reality of a nationalist and Catholic Ireland. Pašeta (1998–99) 16, 18. On the history of Trinity in this era, see Luce (1992) 117–34.

still remained the standard-bearer of Irish academia at the time.[144] Hyde was eager therefore to insist that

> it is not from Trinity College or its pupils, but wholly outside of them, that all the vigorous movements of the intellectual life of the Ireland of to-day have arisen. The soil of its making has been regularly and persistently sterilized by what a Yankee journalist might call "The Great De-nationalizing Anti-Irish Company Unlimited, warrented [*sic*] one of the most perfect devitalisers in the world."[145]

By obstructing the revival of Irish, by not supporting efforts to expand instruction, Trinity had passed up another opportunity to influence Irish intellectual life. The college had set itself up as the "undying opponent of all things Irish," he complained, a place where scholars conspired "to bury the oldest vernacular literature in Europe under a load of obloquy," to "give people the idea that it was a leprous and unclean thing."[146] Despite those efforts, however, the Irish language and the Gaelic League emerged from the dispute in a stronger position, aided by the negative attention that Mahaffy's "patrician disdain" generated.[147] The Commission had ignored the warnings of Trinity scholars and allowed for the instruction of Irish "as an ordinary school language provided it did not hinder the teaching of other subjects."[148]

Fear, however, that the introduction of Irish would diminish what the Oxford classicist Alfred Denis Godley (1856–1925) later called the "old undisputed prerogative of a classical education" still persisted.[149] To cede a place to Irish would be, in the words of Mahaffy, a "retrograde step, a return to the dark ages – nay, even to the famous Tower of Babel in Hebrew legend"; its presence would generate further "provincial isolation" in Ireland by depressing student interest in learning the worldly tongues of Greek and Latin.[150] Douglas Hyde, however, insisted that there was no contest, no competition between the Celtic and the classical. On the contrary, he argued, the teaching of Irish would only encourage further study of antiquity, for to "gain a right outlook upon the art and culture of the world," he explained,

---

[144] *A University Scandal. Gaelic League Pamphlet*, no. 7 [1900?] 2.
[145] *A University Scandal. Gaelic League Pamphlet*, no. 7 [1900?] 2.
[146] *Gaelic League Pamphlet*, no. 7 [1900?] 8; Hyde (1899) 3.
[147] Crowley (2005) 144.
[148] Crowley (2005) 143–44.
[149] Godley (1914) 81.
[150] Mahaffy (1899) 221, 222.

our minds must first be instinct with the spirit of appreciation for some art or some culture. The bulk of Irish minds (as the Gaelic League has, I think, conclusively proved) can only be emotionalised through their own ancestral culture; but once emotionalised in this way, they are open to many further impressions from without. A student who starts by learning Irish may end by learning Greek.[151]

By stressing Irish from a young age, students would possess greater confidence and greater "reverence for antiquity" and would thus, he thought, be likely to pursue learning Greek and Latin, no longer "ashamed of their names, ashamed of their past, of their national games, and of their national songs."[152] Despite Hyde's pleading, Ireland's elite, academic classes – as Yeats himself observed – had little interest in supporting the language movement or the broader aims of a culturally Celtic revival. Trinity College had for too long helped cultivate, he noted, a distinctive "atmosphere of cynicism" in educated Dublin, one that set all its interests "against all Irish enthusiasms in the first instance, and then, by perhaps slow degrees, against all the great intellectual passions. An academic class is always a little dead and deadening; and our political rancours may long have made our academic class even quicker in denial than its association with undeveloped minds."[153] For Yeats, Mahaffy's and Atkinson's recalcitrance was but the latest instance of educated Irishmen opposing "without ideas" and "without charm" the larger work of civilization and imagination.[154] They had not so much as attacked "the often narrow enthusiasm of nationalism with the great intellectual passions of the world," he observed, but instead taken the "easier way, that brings the death of imagination and at last the death of character."[155] "Trinity College, Dublin, makes excellent scholars," Yeats declared, "but it does not make men with any real love for ideal things or with any fine taste in the arts. One does not meet really cultivated Trinity College men as one meets really cultivated Oxford and Cambridge men."[156] Mahaffy, for his part, grumbled that the contemporary 'literary class' of Irish writers and critics were themselves a cautionary tale – evidence enough, he thought, to resist extending the privileges of higher education any further: the

---

[151] *Irish in University Education. Gaelic League Pamphlet*, no. 29 [1902?] 15.
[152] *Gaelic League Pamphlet*, no. 13 [1901?] 5, 4.
[153] Yeats, "The Academic Class and the Agrarian Revolution," *The Daily Express* (March 11, 1899) jn Yeats *UP2* (1976) 151, 150. See also Yeats, "To George Russell (Æ), [6 March 1899]," in Yeats *CL2* (1997) 370–72.
[154] Yeats *UP2* (1976) 151.
[155] Yeats *UP2* (1976) 151.
[156] Yeats *UP2* (1976) 151.

existence of James Joyce alone with his "flair for latrine levity" was, he reputedly claimed, a "living argument in defence of my contention that it was a mistake to establish a separate university for the aborigines of this island – for the corner boys who spit into the Liffey."[157]

Although Trinity seemed out of step to Hyde and to Yeats, the doubts expressed by its faculty were not unusual. As Stanford observed, those who shared the skepticism of Mahaffy were convinced "that the *cursus honorum* of a rich empire offered wider scope for talents than that of a small independent island, no matter how illustrious. This conflict of principle among men who cherished the classical tradition but derived different ideals from it was always bound to occur."[158] The language controversy, far from being a technical or literary debate over the "merits or demerits of the Irish language," became enmeshed in a broad cultural struggle to define not only the contours of Irish liberal education but the very shape of the country's national character as well.[159] Where Trinity College academics defended an aggressive, cosmopolitan vision of Irish education – a vision that regarded "imperialism, not only in politics, but in language" as ultimately advantageous to Ireland, advancing its position within the empire and the wider international community – a growing nationalist insurgency saw the education promoted by Trinity as antithetical to the "principle of nationality, rightly understood."[160] No "revival upon cosmopolitan lines" could ever come about in the country: Irish education had instead to "be intellectually nationalised" for "home consumption."[161] As Mathews suggests, in some ways the "row over the Irish language marks the last flourish of a moribund colonial intelligentsia and, at the same time, the coming of age of a new generation of nationalist intellectuals."[162] At the heart of this ongoing struggle, attempts to redefine access, modes and perception of classical learning, to link its prestige and rigor with the formal study of Irish, proved a crucial point of dispute.[163] For Mahaffy and Atkinson, the classics remained indisputably essential to university education, an area of study whose significance could not be displaced by fashionable forms of political advocacy or mere antiquarian interests: for them, classical learning provided the unique

---

[157] As quoted in Griffin (1938) 23, 24.
[158] Stanford (1976) 220.
[159] Mathews (2003) 44. See Doyle (2015) 183–85.
[160] Mahaffy (1899) 222; *Sessional Papers* 32 (1902) 312.
[161] *Sessional Papers* 32 (1902) 312.
[162] Mathews (2003) 64.
[163] On the evolution of Irish education and popular reading habits during the Literary Revival, see Murphy (2017).

means by which individuals could "recover ... the joys and beauties of life."[164] "This was the aspect of human happiness," Mahaffy wrote,

> which is most perfectly represented, so far as the world has yet run, by the Greeks, and hence the careful and minute study of their life must always appeal to those who desire the aesthetic reformation of modern society. Once and again the Greeks have exercised this vast and beneficent influence; is it vain to hope that even still it is not exhausted, but potent to cure the ills of man?[165]

Stressing the careful "minute study of their life," Mahaffy prized dispassion in approaching the classics; he saw, moreover, in the entrenched institutions governing Irish classical education, not simply Unionist values to be preserved but a broader web of civilized connection between noble societies, a connection that put those educated in the classics in touch with the progressive achievements of all significant imperial civilizations, not only the Greek and the Roman but the British as well.[166] Though his was a compelling vision to some in Dublin, it was not persuasive among those sympathetic to the cause of Celtic revival; and as the prestige of Greek and Latin learning slowly eroded in university, the desire to see its forms of reception redeployed for immediate political and literary ends proved irresistible. Douglas Hyde and the Gaelic League attempted to seize the moment, knowing that a "national factor" might be best introduced into the curriculum by setting Irish on equal footing with Greek and Latin.[167]

Practically speaking, the fear that the revival of Irish might lead to further "provincial isolation" and a lessening of interest in classics was unfounded.[168] Though the position of classics continued to decline, no clear evidence specifically links growth in the study of Irish to a decline in Greek and Latin. Nevertheless, twenty years later, when the British prime minister, David Lloyd George (1863–1945), appointed a committee to report on the status of classical studies in Britain and Ireland, the committee did not steer away from that "topic which has excited much controversy – the Gaelic Revival and the study of Irish in schools and Universities."[169] Noting that knowledge of Irish had been mandated in

---

[164] Mahaffy (1909) 29.
[165] Mahaffy (1909) 29–30.
[166] Mahaffy (1909) 30.
[167] *Sessional Papers* 32 (1902) 313.
[168] Mahaffy (1899) 222.
[169] Committee to Inquire into the Position of Classics in the Educational System of the United Kingdom (1921) 232.

1909 for matriculation at the National University of Ireland (NUI) and that its teaching was then "practically universal in Catholic schools," the report (known as the Crewe Report) suggested that it could "be readily understood how" mandating Irish "has handicapped the study of Greek, and in girls' schools even that of Latin."[170] The growth of Irish notwithstanding, there was little doubt "the pendulum" was "swinging strongly against classical studies" across Irish universities "though Trinity College inherits a classical tradition as strong as that of Oxford or Cambridge."[171] Compulsory Greek had been abolished for enrollment at Trinity after 1903, and the "effect of this change" was reported as "startling."[172] The study of Greek had dramatically receded, the number of undergraduate students being examined falling from fifty-two in 1902 to four in 1920. Latin, too, was no longer obligatory for entrance, though all students were still required to pass responsions, or 'Little-go', in the language. Elsewhere, the committee reported, in the "modern Universities" where there was "naturally less tradition of classical study," the Catholic Church had "strongly operated to preserve classical studies" for the training of clergy.[173] "Greek studies, and therefore Classics," were becoming, the report noted, "specialised as a branch of clerical study, a process which" would, however, as the committee alleged, "inevitably cause injury to humanistic studies as a whole."[174] Nevertheless, at the National University, students of Greek were reputedly "not diminishing in quality or quantity."[175] This was helped in some part by the efforts of Rev. Henry Martyn Browne, SJ (1853–1941), professor of Greek and prior to his appointment at the National University, the founder of the Classical

---

[170] Committee to Inquire into the Position of Classics in the Educational System of the United Kingdom (1921) 232. Pressured by the Gaelic League, the NUI university senate narrowly passed a resolution in 1909 to require Irish for matriculation. As Aidan Doyle has noted, the establishment of an Irish-language requirement at NUI split support for the Gaelic League among Catholic clergy. "The university battle was fought out between Catholic priests. Roughly speaking, the older generation of priests and bishops, and many teaching orders like the Jesuits which ran fee-paying schools, were opposed to Irish, or at best lukewarm about it. Younger priests, and the Christian Brothers' teaching order which catered for the children of the lower middle classes, favoured Irish." Doyle (2015) 183–85.

[171] Committee to Inquire into the Position of Classics in the Educational System of the United Kingdom (1921) 233.

[172] Committee to Inquire into the Position of Classics in the Educational System of the United Kingdom (1921) 233.

[173] Committee to Inquire into the Position of Classics in the Educational System of the United Kingdom (1921) 234, 232.

[174] Committee to Inquire into the Position of Classics in the Educational System of the United Kingdom (1921) 234.

[175] Committee to Inquire into the Position of Classics in the Educational System of the United Kingdom (1921) 234.

Association of Ireland (as well as a successor to Gerard Manley Hopkins [1844–89] at University College, Dublin).[176] Though well aware of classics' diminishing presence within the university curriculum, Browne had grown accustomed to hearing "colleagues of other faculties, in law, in philosophy, in modern languages, in English literature, in Irish studies" pay tribute to "the immense debt which they owe to Classical history and literature."[177] "[T]hey have frequently to borrow from Classics the most vital truths which they have to communicate," he insisted, and thus eyed "with concern any tendency to depress Greek and Roman studies in our common University."[178] With that in mind, Browne sought to have classics "adapt itself, at whatever cost, to modern methods and ideas," for though classical education often claimed, "according to the highest and most representative authority, to be an essentially democratic method of mental training … suited for all classes of the nation," Browne felt that it still "depended largely on class interests" suffused with the "spirit of narrow and even exclusive conservatism."[179] If its study were to survive, and perhaps claim something of a "wider horizon than that of belated tradition," it had to be brought "into line with all that is best in modern education, and all that is sane and progressive in modern life."[180] "Modern life has many complexities," he declared,

> in politics, social intercourse, education, art, literature, religion – to mention a few not unimportant things. What we maintain is that in none of the problems, none of the interests of life, can men afford to lose sight of the storehouse bequeathed to them by the ancients. Not in philosophy and history alone, not in language and literature alone, not in art and religion alone – but in the complexus of everything which differentiates man from the brute creation, the voice of antiquity must be heard, and by antiquity we mean chiefly our own mental and moral forbears, the Greeks and Romans.[181]

To place "the healthful development of Classical teaching on modern, efficient, and democratic lines," Browne encouraged an expansive view of the field, one that did not give "exaggerated prominence to linguistic study" but included other disciplines such as archaeology, music,

---

[176]　Stanford (1976) 65–66.
[177]　Browne (1917) 144.
[178]　Browne (1917) 144.
[179]　Browne (1917) 154, 172, 145.
[180]　Browne (1917) 157, 144.
[181]　Browne (1917) 149–50.

numismatics and art history as well as language and literature.[182] For each "person who learns to read and write Latin and Greek fluently," he argued, "one hundred could be fairly well versed in Greek and Roman literature by means of good translations, and one thousand could be familiarized with many salient facts about ancient life, and even interested in some of the great monuments which have come down to us."[183]

Although Browne's efforts to "revivify the Classical learning in the twentieth century," to "democratize Classical study" in the "educational struggle for existence," had some success in Dublin – most especially through the establishment of the Classical Museum at University College in 1910 – the decline of classical education continued in Ireland as elsewhere on the British Isles.[184] Neither Yeats nor Joyce, it seems, could fairly be said to have been the beneficiaries of a "great Revival of Classical Learning" in Ireland (though Henry Browne did, in fact, instruct Joyce in Latin at University College, Dublin).[185] On the contrary, although both writers received some formal training in classical languages as students at school, their creative engagements with antiquity were developed not from fluency but rather from the half-read or "wounded" stance of being what Joyce once called a "shy guest at the feast of the world's culture."[186] Joyce wrote this woundedness into the *Bildung* of Stephen Dedalus, who in *A Portrait of the Artist As a Young Man* (1916) despondently reflects over the "pages of his timeworn Horace," thinking himself "so poor a Latinist."[187] Nevertheless the pages of Dedalus' edition still "never felt cold to the touch." Just as Stephen was attracted to the "dusky flyleaf" and "dusky verses" of a Roman poet whose "fragrant" writings appeared still "as though they had lain all those years in myrtle and lavender and vervain," Joyce himself was transfixed by the ancient promise and powerful allure of classics.[188] In a similar manner, though Yeats experienced the presence of classics in "useless longing ... through

[182] Browne (1917) 184, 156.
[183] Browne (1917) 183.
[184] Browne (1917) 1, 3. Still the prime minister's committee believed there was "good ground for believing that [classics] will not be allowed to disappear," even though "the study of Classics in the country is somewhat depressed." Committee to Inquire into the Position of Classics in the Educational System of the United Kingdom (1921) 234. On the founding of the Classical Museum, see Haywood (2003).
[185] Browne (1917) 1. Sullivan (1957) 158–63. See also Fathers of the Society of Jesus, comp. (1930) 194–203.
[186] Joyce *Portrait* (1993) 206.
[187] Joyce *Portrait* (1993) 206.
[188] Joyce *Portrait* (1993) 206.

the poor mechanism of translation," the magnetism of classical antiquity prevailed over him as over other writers of the Literary Revival.[189] Yet while advocates of Revival were attracted to the prestige associated with classical learning, many deliberately eschewed the well-known mythologies of ancient Greece and Rome in their work, believing these had become "worn out and unmanageable" having "ceased to be a living tradition."[190] Instead, the "resolute purpose" of Revival was, as Yeats explained in 1895, to bring Ireland's "literary tradition to perfection" by utilizing the "unexhausted and inexhaustible mythology" of Gaelic folklore.[191] In so doing revivalists felt they could "accentuate" in their work "what is at once Celtic and excellent in their nature, that they may be at last tongues of fire uttering the evangel of the Celtic peoples."[192] Preference was given therefore to stories and adaptations involving Celtic figures such as Niamh, Oisin, and Cúchuliann over classical heroes and heroines, whether Odysseus, Aeneas, Helen or Achilles. Yet this devotion was predicated on the notion that knowledge of Gaelic legends could provide a unique path to understanding, as the philologists Alfred Nutt and Kuno Meyer (1858–1919) put it, "the beliefs out of which the beliefs of the Greeks and the other European races arose."[193] Thus, in returning Irish literature to Celtic sources, writers saw themselves as legitimizing a new 'vernacular classics' for Ireland, linking 'Anglo-Irish' work genealogically with the sources of classical civilization. For Yeats, however, returning straightway to Irish legend was a complicated matter. With little knowledge of Irish, his earliest efforts to nationalize an Irish classics would be mediated not by direct translation from Gaelic texts but through the complex prism of re-stylizing and revising his English, sometimes through retranslation (or double translation) or through the absorption of recent English receptions of classics. Yeats' belief that Ireland could, in fact, have "a national literature which would be written to a very great extent in English" was thought by some advocates of Gaelic revival to be a thoroughly "heretical idea ... that a country with a distinct history, distinct traditions, and distinct ideals can possess a national literature in another language ... let them not vex our ears by calling their writings Irish and national."[194] Nevertheless, as discussed

---

[189] Yeats CW3 (1999) 76. See pp. 7–8 in this Introduction.
[190] Yeats, "The Message of the Folk-lorist" (August 1893) in Yeats CW9 (2004) 210.
[191] Yeats, "Irish National Literature, III" (September 1895) in Yeats CW9 (2004) 287, 281.
[192] Yeats CW9 (2004) 287.
[193] Yeats, "Celtic Beliefs about the Soul" (September 1898) cited in Yeats CW9 (2004) 416.
[194] Yeats, as quoted in "Notes," An Claidheamh Soluis 1.13 (June 10, 1899) 200. For this reason, it was sometimes said that the "so-called Irish Literary movement" championed by Yeats was "a

throughout Chapter 1, Yeats pushed ahead, hoping to forge an 'Irish Homer' in a distinctively 'hibernized' form of un-English. However, while he ostensibly set out to blend Irish and English into a new hybrid idiom, an idiom that could persuasively translate a nationalized vision of the Irish past, his early attempts to elevate an 'Irish Homer' moved by the way of misdirection. Recent efforts by English-born poets, efforts that 'dislocated' conventional idioms of English with anglicized imitations of ancient Greek, had long attracted his interest, and their influence would prove critical. In this way Romantic and Victorian receptions of classical antiquity exerted more pressure on Yeats' earliest distillation of a 'Celtic' style than any substantive fusion with Irish.

The tense, politicized space occupied by classics within the Literary Revival fomented further artistic engagements as well, some of which can be counted among the most prominent works of Irish modernism. These often became, stylistically speaking, more experimental and at the same time increasingly skeptical of attempts to nationalize an 'Irish classics' for broad public consumption. Chapters 2 and 3 of this book detail, at length, two divergent forms of resistance to this work of recentering the classics across the *oeuvre* of Yeats and Joyce – in, respectively, their encounters with Sophocles and with Homer. Yeats – frustrated with the management of the Abbey Theatre and incendiary forms of nationalist agitation – became wary of his early idealism. As he did so, Yeats also began to draw on allusions to ancient Greek literature with greater frequency, employing images of classical antiquity, often with the intention of interrogating the very failures he associated with the Revival's once "heroic dream."[195] "Ah, that Time could touch a form," he lamented in 1910, "That could show what Homer's age / Bred to be a hero's wage."[196] Despite his own effort, time, he felt, had not touched Irish literature in Homeric fashion. Even though a powerful vision of Homer's Helen still appeared before him, her "nobleness made simple as a fire," her "beauty like a tightened bow" was then "not natural in an age like this, / Being high and solitary and most stern."[197] No such vision could instantiate what he once sought for Ireland: the striving for a classical ideal had only roiled Irish society with division and class warfare among

---

hindrance and not a help to a genuine revival." "Notes," *An Claidheamh Soluis* 1.13 (June 10, 1899) 200.

[195] Yeats, "A Woman Homer Sung," in Yeats *VE* (1987) 255.

[196] Yeats, "Peace," in Yeats *VE* (1987) 258.

[197] Yeats, "No Second Troy," in Yeats *VE* (1987) 256, 257. See Chapter 2, pp. 88–91, Chapter 3, pp. 135–38, and the Conclusion, pp. 248–50.

"ignorant men."[198] "Why," he exclaimed, "what could she have done, being what she is? / Was there another Troy for her to burn?"[199] In this context of growing distrust Yeats turned his attention to Sophocles – to retranslating his Victorian shape even as he himself was intent on transforming his own poetic mask with "prose directness" and "hard light."[200]

Though Joyce's critique of revivalism did not draw out, by contrast, the same bitterness, he remained fascinated by the Revival's penchant to variously misalign the 'ancients' (Homer, perhaps, above all) to suit present circumstances. Through his own deliberate mistranslations of classical parallels in both *A Portrait of the Artist As a Young Man* (1916) and *Ulysses*, he too misaligned the ancient and the modern to satirize nationalist appropriations of Greek antiquity. A notable feature of Joyce's mistranslations, however, is the different approach he took to Latin and Greek. Latin, still heavy with an ecclesial odor of atonement and purgation – its discipline Joyce knew well from his time at Clongowes Wood College and Belvedere College – was not easily turned to greater expressions of artistic freedom and eccentricity.[201] In *Portrait*'s first chapter Father Arnall's drilling of Latin declensions provides the setting for false accusation and the pandying of Stephen Dedalus, the "[l]azy, little schemer" who is "not writing like the others."[202] As Leah Flack notes, the study of Latin in this episode

> becomes an occasion for the enactment of discipline, control, and punishment as a corrective force against sexual transgression. Knowledge of Latin grammar theoretically offers the means for students to demonstrate submission and obedience to the authority of the priest/Latin teacher and the strictly policed heteronormative code he enforces.[203]

Yet, although Latin promised conformity and punishment, ancient Greek was altogether more enigmatic for Joyce – a force he would associate with Dedalus' particular sense of freedom and destiny. On hearing its distant call, hearing his own name playfully retranslated, or mistranslated in Greek, Stephen Dedalus perceives not just the schoolboy ridicule of his

---

[198] Yeats *VE* (1987) 256.
[199] Yeats *VE* (1987) 257.
[200] Pound (1914) 66, 67.
[201] The view that learning classical languages at school was socially coded to reenforce institutional conformity, and thereby curb outbursts of individual expression, was not a new phenomenon in Joyce's novel but a trope that recurred across Victorian fiction, especially in the work of Charles Dickens and George Eliot. On this point, see Haynes (2013) 421–30.
[202] Joyce *Portrait* (1993) 70.
[203] Flack (2020) 40.

classmates but his own "strange name" in a new light, "Stephanos Dedalos! Bous Stephanoumenos! Bous Stephaneforos!"[204] And it is in the eccentric uttering of this name – in its far-reaching idiosyncratic Greek – that Stephen begins to envision a life beyond the "heaps of dead language" in Dublin, beyond the nets of "nationality, language, religion" that bore the strong mark of the city's most dominant tongues: English, Irish and Latin.[205] The appearance of distorted Greek thus becomes in *Portrait* a "prophecy" whose inscrutable "wild spirit" pushes Dedalus further towards rejecting the "cerements" of the present – "the fear that he had walked in night and day, the incertitude that had ringed him round, the shame that had abased him within and without" – and so to rise "from the grave of boyhood" to "the call of life to his soul."[206] That that call comes not in Latin, not in Irish nor in English, but in Greek, is significant. It was

> not the dull gross voice of the world of duties and despair, not the inhuman voice that called him to the pale service of the altar. An instant of wild flight had delivered him ... Yes! Yes! Yes! He would create proudly out of the freedom and power of his soul, as the great artificer whose name he bore, a living thing, new and soaring and beautiful, impalpable, imperishable.[207]

Though Joyce 'grecified' the unveiling of Dedalus' 'authentic' self, he still remained wary of the melodrama with which he had packaged the "Hellenic ring" of Stephen's name.[208] To represent the presence of ancient Greek as though it were, or could be, an unmolested site of imaginative freedom, of individual ambition in Dublin, was, he knew, terribly naive, menaced as receptions of ancient Greece were by various competing, contemporary claims on its authority and prestige. Thus, in the opening moments of *Ulysses*, Joyce openly subverted the romance he had attached to Stephen's 'Greek' name, further distorting his emerging vision of Homeric reception. Ruminating again over Stephen's "absurd name," Joyce overwrote its epiphanic character with the mocking jibes of Malachi 'Buck' Mulligan:

> – The mockery of it! he said gaily. Your absurd name, an ancient Greek!
> ... Buck Mulligan's gay voice went on.

[204] Joyce *Portrait* (1993) 195, 194.
[205] Joyce *Portrait* (1993) 205, 230.
[206] Joyce *Portrait* (1993) 195, 196, 195.
[207] Joyce *Portrait* (1993) 195–96.
[208] Joyce *Ulysses* (1986) 4 (1.42).

– My name is absurd too: Malachi Mulligan, two dactyls. But it has a
Hellenic ring, hasn't it? Tripping and sunny like the buck himself. We
must go to Athens. Will you come if I can get the aunt to fork out twenty
quid?[209]

The 'authentic' call of destiny that Dedalus had once heard in Greek is
rendered farcical by Mulligan, who joins the false assurance of its classical
correspondence to the Hellenized absurdity of his own "Malachi
Mulligan, two dactyls," a name whose trivial metrical equivalence with
the dominant quantitative unit of Homeric verse possesses no claim on
romance or artistic authenticity. Instead, Mulligan's pseudo-Hellenic
name betrays a habit of forcibly borrowing allusions from Greek antiquity
for clearly self-serving ends. Skeptical that claims to a Hellenic or classical
value were little more than this, Joyce came to see in Greek not an
untrammeled pathway to self-discovery, or national self-invention, but
the specter of error, delusion and misinterpretation. Throughout *Ulysses*
he therefore continually 'mistranslated' the Hellenic correspondences at
work in the novel, juxtaposing stylized forgeries of 'authentic originals' in
a comic palimpsest. Both the book's characters and its various styles are
empowered and yet conditioned by the misaligned parallels Joyce drew
from the literatures of Greece and Rome.

In the world beyond Ireland, those striving to find alternative forms of
'classical' value in Celtic language and civilization drew critical inspiration
from the example set by Yeats and other advocates of Ireland's Literary
Revival. Further modes of revival and renaissance in both Scotland and
Wales used the Irish experience to make claims on Lallans, Highland
Gaelic and Welsh as potential means for national self-determination as well
as literary experimentation. However, at the beginning of the twentieth
century, support in Scotland for the revival of Gaelic languages was not so
broad as it had been in Ireland. For that reason, the institutional structures
associated with classical learning were never so dramatically challenged by
movements for Celtic revival there. According to the "necessarily imperfect
sketch" drawn from the Crewe Report, the study of classics occupied a less
prominent position in Scotland, Latin and Greek having "never enjoyed
anything that can be called a privileged position in Scotland, except,
perhaps, for a short time in the nineteenth century."[210] That lack of privilege meant that "no great classical tradition such as exists in England" had

---

[209] Joyce *Ulysses* (1986) 3–4 (1.34, 40–43).
[210] Committee to Inquire into the Position of Classics in the Educational System of the United
Kingdom (1921) 208.

yet been forged, and by 1892 Scottish universities had already begun to liberalize requirements in classics, making Greek and Latin "alternatives for graduation in Arts, instead of both being compulsory."[211] Thus Scotland's most gifted students in classics, those able to "reach the Scholarship standard of Oxford and Cambridge," were compelled to attend English universities rather than enroll in weaker programs closer to home.[212] The transfer of these students had lamentably served to "accentuate class distinctions" in Scotland, a "great misfortune," the committee warned, for "if classical education were to become associated with a particular social class," it "would surely violate the best Scottish tradition."[213] As the committee saw it, the learning of Latin and Greek possessed a "great and almost irreplaceable value" precisely because of its power to advance the spread of English across Scottish society: classical studies remained a critical "means of promoting the proper use of the English language both in speech and writing by all classes of the community."[214]

Though links in Scotland between nationalist agitation and classical learning appeared less palpable than in Ireland, advocates of Scottish Gaelic were both moved by the disputes that had embroiled Trinity College, Dublin, and inspired by the Gaelic League's spirited defense of Irish as 'classical'. Not long after the public controversy between Atkinson, Mahaffy and Hyde unfolded, members of the advocacy group *An Comunn Gàidhealach* (first established in 1891) began to restructure their promotion of Scottish Gaelic, modeling their "movement, like that of the Gaelic League, on a less academic and more popular basis."[215] However, as the longtime supporter of Scottish Home Rule Ruaraidh Erskine of Marr (1869–1960) observed, the "difficulty in Scotland" lay in persuading "people that this is a serious movement," for there was then "little or no vitality in her language movement, and even less conduct."[216] Compared with the agitation for Gaelic in Ireland, there was "far too

---

[211] The effect of this liberalization was reputedly "disastrous": once there stood "a large number of pass men who, without being Greek scholars, had a competent knowledge of Greek. Students of this type now tend to take subjects which they believe to be easier." This resulted in lessening the "general influence of Greek culture in University education." Committee to Inquire into the Position of Classics in the Educational System of the United Kingdom (1921) 208, 219, 220.

[212] Committee to Inquire into the Position of Classics in the Educational System of the United Kingdom (1921) 219.

[213] Committee to Inquire into the Position of Classics in the Educational System of the United Kingdom (1921) 219, 222.

[214] Committee to Inquire into the Position of Classics in the Educational System of the United Kingdom (1921) 11–12.

[215] "Notes," *An Claidheamh Soluis* 1.31 (October 14, 1899) 488.

[216] Erskine (1904a) 202, 204.

prevalent a disposition," he noted, "to regard the language movement as something that may be played with – as a hobby suitable for dull winter evenings, or as an excuse for 'social gatherings' at which tea and gossip (for the most part in English) may be indulged in."[217] However, on seeing the recent controversy unfold in Dublin, watching as the "rank and file" Irish became "thoroughly persuaded" that their "agitation is a *political one*," Erskine believed that Scotland could take its "thought from the Irish" and find the motivation necessary to "shake off the sloth and indifference of nigh a couple of centuries, and give our kinsmen across the Moyle measure for measure."[218] Intent on drawing "the Gaels of Scotland and Ireland" together to "advance objects and aspirations held in common," Erskine proposed the creation of a "great Gaelic-speaking Confederacy of Nations": the "Gaels of Scotland and the Gaels of Ireland" were on the cusp, he argued,

> of re-establishing the Gaelic tradition, of rejoining and carrying on the long-disconnected threads of our common story, of making the Gaelic cause the cause of Alba at large (as once it was), of replanting our flag upon the ruins of the Lowland policy, of marching shoulder to shoulder in serried and irresistible array towards the realisation of our great national ambition.[219]

Echoing the case Douglas Hyde had made before the Commissions of 1899 and 1902, Erskine insisted on the "compulsory teaching of Gaelic" in all Scottish schools, for only by resuscitating and renewing "the old Scots tongue as the national language of the whole of Scotland," he argued, could "the old artificial barrier between 'Highlands' and 'Lowlands'" be erased.[220] As Erskine saw it, the fragmented state of Scotland's Celtic languages – the separation between Lallans and Highland Gaelic – remained a central obstacle to greater Scottish political unity. The vernacular spoken across the Lowlands had long since given up any claim to a Gaelic essence, and as such, Lallans had become a site of pervasive English incursion into Scottish culture, its reputedly literary tradition being overrun with the "national measures of the Saxon power."[221] "Of old," Lowlanders

[217] Erskine (1904a) 202.
[218] Erskine (1904a) 202, 205, 206.
[219] Erskine (1906) 11, 25.
[220] Erskine (1908) 238.
[221] Erskine (1906) 20.

spoke the Gaelic Language; now their pride is in the purity of their English – particularly in a certain northeasterly town! In olden days, they fought *against* the Gall and the Sassenach to preserve their *own* independence. In modern days they fought *for* the Sassenach to put down nationalities struggling for *their* independence.[222]

Despite Erskine's belief that Scottish Gaelic was the country's rightful national language, his views were not widely embraced or accepted. His defense of the language was, in addition, not helped by his desire to align a Scottish Gaelic revival with the reconversion of Scotland from Protestantism to Roman Catholicism.[223] "Nearly every great evil, religious, political, social and commercial, which Alba labours under," he once claimed,

> owes its existence, or its continuance, to Protestantism … Protestantism robbed Scotland of her independence. Protestantism introduced the English influence which is hostile to our language, manners and customs … Scratch a Scots Protestant and you will find him little better than an Englishman; scratch an Englishman and you will soon find that with him Protestant ascendancy and Englishism mean the same thing – namely, Anglo-Saxon ascendancy.[224]

Although Erskine's joining of the Gaelic revival to "religious propaganda" was not broadly supported by those inclined to advance the cause of Scottish independence, many nationalists nonetheless saw the separation, the fragmentary condition of languages in Scotland, as a serious threat to any developing sense of nationhood and the establishment of an independent literature in Scotland.[225] As Hugh MacDiarmid reiterated two decades later, Scotland's "sense of continuity and tradition" could be rediscovered by overcoming that separation of its languages, "by 'connecting up' again with our lost Gaelic culture. This is the background to which we must return," he declared, "if we are ever to establish a Scottish classical culture."[226] For MacDiarmid, however, Scotland's

---

[222] C. M. P. (1908) 380.

[223] Erskine placed at the front of the first issue of *Guth Na Bliadhna* an essay on "The Church and the Highlands," in which he reported that the "present position of the Church in Scotland … should inspire a Catholic with hope," while adding that "Protestantism and all that it implies, in a civil as well as in a religious way, has been but an unprofitable and melancholy experiment." Erskine (1904b) 1, 4.

[224] Erskine (1905b) 303–304.

[225] Erskine (1905a) 105.

[226] Hugh MacDiarmid, "Scottish Gaelic Policy," *The Pictish Review* 1.2 (December 1927) in MacDiarmid *SP* (1992) 50.

diversity of language offered promise and peril, for to articulate the genius of the nation – its indisputably classical character he thought – one had to embrace the essential "diversity-in-unity" of Scotland's languages, both Lallans and Scottish Gaelic.[227] Repulsed by the "false conception of Scottish Gaelic character," namely the "popular belief" that "the Highlander, a dreamer and a poet, a mystic and a romantic" was to be "contrasted with the shrewd, keen, pushing, practical Lowlander," MacDiarmid saw his vision confirmed by the historian Anna A. W. Ramsay whose work *Challenge to the Highlander* (1933) had exposed the "strange unreality" of this critical distinction.[228]

> Nothing could be more remote from the facts of everyday life, as it appeared in the pages of history. The Highlander had never produced any great poetry or any great art to speak of; and far from being given to dreams, he seemed to be entirely concerned with the more practical aspects of life; money and the ownership of land appeared to be his dominant passions. It has been pointed out, and with perfect truth, that almost every Highland feud took its rise originally from a quarrel about the possession of land. The Highlander excelled in practical work: he made a good colonist, pioneer, soldier, scientist, engineer. But for poetry, romance, idealism – one must go to the Lowlands.[229]

Thus it would be by synthetic experiment, by fusing together Highland Gaelic and Scots Vernacular, that Hugh MacDiarmid would attempt to recast this distinction and forge "a new classicism."[230] As he wrote in 1923, the coming of a renaissance in Scottish writing demanded more invention and experimentation, not nostalgia-driven forms of revival and preservation:

> Our interest, therefore, should centre not so much in what has been done in the Doric as in what has not but may be done in it. No literature can rest on its laurels.

> We lack the courage to be where we are,
> We love too much to travel on old roads,
> To triumph on old fields; we love too much
> To consecrate the magic of dead things.[231]

---

[227] C. M. Grieve, "Introducing 'Hugh M'Diarmid'," *The Scottish Chapbook* (August 1922) in MacDiarmid *SP* (1992) 10.
[228] MacDiarmid (1968) 306; Ramsay (1933) vii.
[229] Ramsay (1933) vii–viii.
[230] MacDiarmid *SP* (1992) 74, 80.
[231] MacDiarmid, "A Theory of Scots Letters," *The Scottish Chapbook* 1.7–9 (February–April 1923) in MacDiarmid *SP* (1992) 20.

Although the "false Highland-Lowland distinction" had often obstructed efforts to compel a greater sense of national unity, the crisis it presented enmeshed northern nationalism in the 'problem' of Scotland's many languages, drawing the history of Scottish classical receptions together with MacDiarmid's admiration for the European avant-garde.[232] Yet, by the early 1930s, as MacDiarmid became increasingly irritated with the lack of fervor he saw among more politically fashionable forms of Scottish nationalism, he began to turn from his heteroglossic 'synthetic Scots'. Estranged from his country's 'popular mind', he redirected his desire for a 'new classicism' to more ambitious heights, insisting on a polyglossic vision of poetry as world language.[233] However, in so doing, MacDiarmid slowly bled his distinctive sense of Scottish classicism of its more substantive links with the literatures of Greece and Rome. Attracted by the "anthologizing of cultures and cultural fragments" prevalent among his modernist contemporaries, MacDiarmid made his idiom progressively more multilingual throughout the 1930s, seeking to articulate "the ever-expanding / And accelerating consciousness Březina has sung so nobly, / *Sdrucciola* – swift and utterly unEnglish / Songs like the transition from the *ùrlar* to the *crunluath*."[234] As he did so, his vision of reception evolved too, foregrounding a highly eccentric form of synthetic English, a communist 'global classics'. Though MacDiarmid, self-preening and brash, often felt his new work was a vision of the 'world literature' to come, its critical fate proved far less persuasive. His work became ideologically idiosyncratic and lexically hermetic, his new "Doric" being for many an idiom without border or tribe – perhaps even "no dialect in particular."[235]

Although it was believed that a revival of Irish Gaelic in Ireland might crowd out the study of classics – a notion that even the Prime Minister's Committee on Classics reenforced in 1921 – the matter of "Celtic, in relation to Classical, Studies" as it existed in Wales was handled in an altogether different fashion.[236] In Wales, the committee suggested, the involvement of classics in the development of modern Welsh literature

---

[232] MacDiarmid *SP* (1992) 51. On the Doric, see Chapter 5, p. 211n104.

[233] On learnedness, classics, and the modernist aesthetic, see Wray (2019) 419–43.

[234] Crawford (2000) 259. MacDiarmid, "The Kind of Poetry I Want," in MacDiarmid *CP2* (1994) 1007. The italicized words in Scottish Gaelic are words for time signatures in pipe music.

[235] MacDiarmid under the pseudonym, J. G. Outterstone Buglass, "Arne Garborg, Mr Joyce, and Mr M'Diarmid" (September 1924) in MacDiarmid *RT1* (1996) 237.

[236] Committee to Inquire into the Position of Classics in the Educational System of the United Kingdom (1921) 247.

had been "more vital," for its "influence" had come at a time "of special moment and importance" for the country, a time when "Welsh scholars" had for "some years" been engaged in "a continuous movement towards the revival of a national literature."[237] During the final thirty years of the nineteenth century, education in Wales had undergone a dramatic reformation marked by a rising institutional interest in Welsh language and literature. This growth of interest in the 'native' ran parallel to the broad expansion of classical education both in secondary schools and at universities in Wales.[238] As Ceri Davies has observed, the "network of 'county' schools" in Wales, officially systemized by the Welsh Intermediate Education Act of 1889, were required to include in their curriculum "instruction in Latin, Greek, the Welsh and English language and literature" as well as other "modern languages, mathematics, natural and applied science."[239] The codification of curriculum and spread of new educational opportunity across Wales also began to transform regional university life. While the federated University of Wales was not founded by Royal Charter until 1893, its three constituent colleges had been established at Aberystwyth, Bangor and Cardiff between 1872 and 1881, and scholars of both Greek and Latin played a critical role early on in cementing the academic reputation of Welsh higher education – ensuring that the colleges of Wales would contribute to "the cultural life of their communities."[240] However, even as the establishment of the "University of Wales and the growth of intermediate schools appeared to augur well for the languages of antiquity," the precise nature of the wider contributions that these institutions were making to Welsh-speaking communities was disputed.[241] Indeed, the value of the Welsh tongue itself still seemed highly contestable not only with respect to Greek and Latin but perhaps, most controversially, with respect to English. For many, both the county grammar schools and the newly established colleges in Wales were seen as further "instruments" of Anglicization directed against Welsh-speaking areas.[242] Modeled on their

[237] Committee to Inquire into the Position of Classics in the Educational System of the United Kingdom (1921) 248.

[238] On the importance of classics for measuring "the tensions of a people" then beginning to "come to terms with the claims of two languages on their allegiance," see Davies (2009) 35–47, as well as Davies (1995) 115–55.

[239] Davies (1995) 116; The Welsh Intermediate Education Act (1889) can be accessed at: www.educationengland.org.uk/documents/acts/1889-welsh-intermediate-education-act.html.

[240] Davies (1995) 117. On the role of classics in the early history of the University of Wales, see Ellis (1972) 31–41, as well as J. Gwynn Williams (1985) 130–32.

[241] J. Gwynn Williams (1985) 130.

[242] Davies (1995) 118.

institutional counterparts in England, what these schools were thought to offer was not the advancement of Welsh cultural interests but only a means rather – a worldly way – to further alienate the 'native' Welsh from their local language and civilization. "Doubtless," Davies suggests,

> many teachers of Latin, false imitators of the traditions of the English public schools, behaved in a contemptuous way towards Welsh. D. Tecwyn Lloyd drew a brilliant portrait of his Latin master in Bala in the 1920s, always 'stubbornly English', without a word of Welsh heard from his lips, although he was brought up a Welsh-speaker in Penllyn.[243]

Fearing that the reforms in Welsh education might sow only further division and a deepening resentment towards the native language, advocates of Welsh Home Rule – principally members of the *Cymru Fydd*, the Young Wales movement founded by T. E. Ellis (1859–99) in 1886, and later led by David Lloyd George – vowed to counter the "strong antinational tendencies" present in Welsh schools.[244] Although "astonishing strides" had been made on behalf of the native language and literature, its "educational interests" had yet to be pushed forward "to the highest possible degree."[245] Outlining a vision for Wales in the 1895 manifesto *Cymru Fydd Gymru Rydd*, Young Wales insisted that it was essential for the Welsh language to be "intelligently taught and made a medium of instruction in our schools."[246] No Welsh university ought, they argued, be "other than national in its character and policy," for otherwise Wales would then have merely a "grotesque anomaly" for a university, a "weak imitation of Oxford, Cambridge, or London" copying "too closely" English curricula and failing to give "an honoured place" in its own matriculation syllabus to "Welsh ideals ... our language, literature and history."[247] Welsh, as they saw it, was not to be "regarded as a foreign language" but a required language like Latin: essential to the curriculum and not to be "placed amongst the optional subjects with Hebrew, Greek, French and German."[248] Encouragement of its study was bound to improve not only "education *in excelsis*," but the fortunes of Welsh literature at large.[249] For though the people of Wales had been "endowed with natural aptitude for writing and speaking," though there had been

---

[243] Davies (1995) 118.
[244] A Celt, *Cymru Fydd Gymru Rydd, or The National Movement in Wales,* Carnarvon: Welsh National Press Company (1895) 23.
[245] A Celt, *Cymru Fydd Gymru Rydd* 23, 19, 22.
[246] A Celt, *Cymru Fydd Gymru Rydd* 22.
[247] A Celt, *Cymru Fydd Gymru Rydd* 25.
[248] A Celt, *Cymru Fydd Gymru Rydd* 27, 26.
[249] A Celt, *Cymru Fydd Gymru Rydd* 28.

recently a "revival of artistic taste in Wales," many of the country's "best poets and preachers" remained at that time "men who have risen from the ranks of the people, and who might be described as almost entirely self-taught."[250]

In 1921 the Prime Minister's Committee on Classics also observed the growth of interest in Welsh literature and insisted that its revival seemed to show "every sign of further progress in the future."[251] However, the committee also suggested that Welsh literature had yet to "attain its full development," for new writing in the language had not explicitly learned, "like other western literature," to "base itself largely on the Classics," to learn what the committee called "the same lesson which England, France, and Italy studied at the Renaissance."[252] Moreover, by the time the Crewe Report was issued, the state of classical studies in Wales had diminished by some degree, for "the present position of Latin in the Welsh educational system" was noted as "satisfactory" while the status of Greek seemed far worse, indeed even "precarious in the extreme."[253] Nevertheless, the committee felt that the Welsh people still possessed "greater aptitude and desire" for the study of ancient languages, a preparation made possible by their own "bardic tradition" and the "keen literary spirit" kept alive by the modern Eisteddfod.[254]

> A Welshman bred in this tradition takes in language for its own sake a delight which is rare among other peoples, and is therefore, more likely to be alive to the attractions of the classical languages, and particularly Greek, with which his own has noteworthy similarities. Where the pupils are Welsh-speaking, we would take full advantage of this fact.[255]

Thus while the contemporary "co-existence in Wales of two-home languages," English and Welsh, had resulted in curricular competition at intermediate schools and at university, with less time being given to the study of other languages, the committee's report observed the benefits of

---

[250] A Celt, *Cymru Fydd Cymru Rydd* 29.

[251] Committee to Inquire into the Position of Classics in the Educational System of the United Kingdom (1921) 248.

[252] Committee to Inquire into the Position of Classics in the Educational System of the United Kingdom (1921) 248–49.

[253] Committee to Inquire into the Position of Classics in the Educational System of the United Kingdom (1921) 241.

[254] Committee to Inquire into the Position of Classics in the Educational System of the United Kingdom (1921) 244, 245.

[255] Committee to Inquire into the Position of Classics in the Educational System of the United Kingdom (1921) 245.

bilingualism: "where Welsh was taught ... an able pupil who already spoke both Welsh and English was at an advantage when he began Latin and particularly when he began Greek."[256] The native tongue, it seemed, offered suitable preparation from which one could begin instruction in the classics, so much so that the committee suggested it was best that "the Welsh boy ... not be taught to pronounce Greek after the traditional English fashion when his own Welsh instincts would in some respects bring him nearer to what we believe to be the original pronunciation."[257] Thus, despite the then "deplorable" condition of Greek in secondary schools, the committee remained convinced that the "genius of the Welsh people, its love of beauty and its keen sense of scholarship" were "pledges that the study of the Classics, if duly encouraged and supported, will permeate the whole course of its literature, and through this will enhance its contribution to the civilisation of western Europe."[258]

The committee's willingness to privilege the apparent revival of Welsh – a privilege their report denied to other Celtic language movements in both Ireland and Scotland – lay in what the committee saw as the "close connexion between the Welsh language and the languages of Greece and Rome."[259] For those sympathetic to Welsh nationalism and Home Rule, this "close connexion" was not merely a linguistic reality but a historical fact with contemporary political consequences: for even though no Romance language had ever achieved dominance on the British Isles, Welsh language and culture had taken on, it was thought, much of the broad and "many-sided influence" that the Romans had left during their ancient occupation of Britain from roughly AD 43 to 410.[260] As the historian Owen Morgan Edwards (1858–1920) claimed, whatever the state of Welsh education in classics was, the "persistence of Rome" could still be felt in contemporary Wales, not simply "in its political thought" but "in its language, and in its literature" as well.[261] Nationalist enthusiasm for claiming a classical inheritance in Wales had roots in the Welsh language

---

[256] Committee to Inquire into the Position of Classics in the Educational System of the United Kingdom (1921) 241.

[257] Committee to Inquire into the Position of Classics in the Educational System of the United Kingdom (1921) 245.

[258] Committee to Inquire into the Position of Classics in the Educational System of the United Kingdom (1921) 242, 249.

[259] Committee to Inquire into the Position of Classics in the Educational System of the United Kingdom (1921) 249.

[260] Committee to Inquire into the Position of Classics in the Educational System of the United Kingdom (1921) 249, 235.

[261] Edwards (1901) 24, 26.

movements of the nineteenth century, movements that drew strength not only from the Victorian expansion of classical education in Wales but from the "explosive rise of nonconformity" as well.[262] These forces helped precipitate a world wherein the Methodist educator Rev. Lewis Edwards (1809–87) would insist that contemporary writers of Welsh "demonstrate the possibilities of doing in Welsh what English translators of the classics had been doing since the days of Dryden and Pope."[263] Welsh nationalists of the 1920s – principally Saunders Lewis, Lewis Valentine (1893–1986) and H. R. Jones (1894–1930) – were eager, however, to exploit classics to even greater political advantage, and upon establishing *Plaid Cymru* at the Eisteddfod of 1925, they seized on the alleged likeness of the Roman and the Welsh to shape a new right-wing, agrarian vision of Welsh-Wales ideology. Believing the country's languages, literature and culture had to be kept from becoming "provincial and unimportant," Saunders Lewis set the Roman colonization of Wales as the historical turning point in a movement for Welsh self-determination and greater national recognition.[264] As the nationalist historian A. W. Wade-Evans (1875–1964) later put it, there was no "uncertainty" as to "when Welsh national life begins": the people of Wales first understood themselves to be Welsh when as "*filii Romanorum*, sons of the Romans, of the stock of Troy," they "tumbled to it in their Roman surroundings."[265] For Lewis the reputedly 'classical presence' that remained in Wales – its essential *Romanitas* – could be used not just to encourage greater study of the 'native' at schools and universities but as an explicitly conservative ideological weapon; it could defend Wales' "traditional social life" against the encroachments and economic debasement brought on by the "extension of English ... everywhere."[266] Welsh remained worthy of preservation and promotion, as it alone was, he once defiantly declared, "the direct heir in the British Isles of the literary discipline of classical Greece and Rome."[267] Within this strident political, linguistic and historical fabric, David Jones' polyglot experiments – specifically those that emerged in the 1952 poem *The Anathemata* – began to take shape. In Chapter 4 of this book I examine the nature of these experiments within the wider reception of *Romanitas*

---

[262] Morgan (1971) 156.
[263] Davies (2009) 41. See also Davies (1995) 111–14.
[264] Lewis (1930) 4.
[265] Wade-Evans (1950) 1.
[266] Lewis, "The Caernarfon Court Speech (13th October 1936)," in Lewis (1973) 115; Lewis (1939) 10. For further discussion of Lewis (1939), see Chapter 4, pp. 164–67.
[267] Lewis (1973) 115.

in Wales at this time. Although David Jones felt at times a certain sympathy for the nationalism espoused by Saunders Lewis and *Plaid Cymru*, he struggled to define in his work the *ingenium* left by Rome in Wales. No literature or politics bent on achieving greater linguistic or cultural purity could be authenticated by classical invocation, he felt, for the persistence of Romanity had not provoked a purity – a "predecessor culture" worthy of preservation in Wales – but instead a profound cultural hybridity born from complex networks of linguistic exchange across time.[268] Rather than build from a foundation of Welsh-Wales purism, Jones envisioned a stratigraphic *lingua macaronica* for his work, one that cross-fertilized his English with polyglot intromissions from Wales' *immensa tessitura*, a "vast fabric" of foreign cultural deposits drawn from across its history.[269] Drawing on recent historiographical work on Roman Britain, Jones represented *Romanitas* as a transformative force, one whose metamorphosis had transcended, not eradicated, the "purely 'natural' bonds" of race, language and religion.[270]

Across Ireland, Scotland and Wales, as the impulse to employ receptions of classical antiquity became a means to promote nationalist interests and the revival of Gaelic and Brythonic language, the field of contemporaneous literature composed in English in these countries was sown with seeds of foreign linguistic and cultural interference. These seeds sometimes flowered creatively, the allying of the Celtic and the classical being used to revolt against the "ascendancy" of English in Irish and British literature – most notably in, among others, the work of Yeats, Joyce, Jones and MacDiarmid.[271] Yet, though these authors emerged from a fraught context in which allusions to the ancients carried a powerful political charge and many-sided reception, their writing did not take on political manipulations of classical antiquity in a naive or conventional fashion. At only seventeen years of age, James Joyce had already intimated the contested space that classics then occupied in the literature and politics of the period. Thinking it time to stop paying homage to rigid presentations of the classical, Joyce boldly struck out against the pervasive orthodoxy of contemporary Irish literati when discussing modern drama at University College, Dublin, in January 1900. He insisted then that the "conditions of the Attic stage," that "syllabus of

---

[268] On the allure of "predecessor culture," see MacIntyre (2007) 36–50.
[269] "*Un'immensa tessitura*," a term taken from Joyce's "Ireland, Island of Saints and Sages" (1907) in Joyce *CWJJ* (1989) 165. See Chapter 2, pp. 91–97.
[270] Cochrane (1940) 73.
[271] See MacDiarmid *SP* (1992) 61–80. See Chapter 5, pp. 198–215.

greenroom proprieties and cautions" carried down from one generation
to the next in Europe, were in fact no longer useful for the present,
having been "foolishly set up as the canons of dramatic art, in all
lands."[272] Since the formal establishment of the Irish Literary Theatre in
early 1899, Yeats, Lady Gregory and Edward Martyn had been encouraging the emulation of Attic drama, hoping to show that modern Dublin
was "not the home of buffoonery and of easy sentiment, as it has been
represented" but in fact "the home of an ancient idealism."[273] Yet Joyce
questioned their approach, insisting that, while "the Greeks handed
down a code of laws," further generations had "with purblind wisdom"
falsely advanced these 'ideal' ancient conventions "to the dignity of
inspired pronouncements."[274] "It may be a vulgarism, but it is literal
truth to say," he argued, "that Greek drama is played out. For good or
bad it has done its work, which, if wrought in gold, was not upon lasting
pillars."[275] The reputedly uncritical reception of the Greeks prevalent on
the Dublin literary scene roused Joyce's wit, and slowly he turned his
antipathy for that enthusiasm towards creative endeavor. That antipathy
abounded in the self-consciously stylized pell-mell of the *Odyssey* enacted
throughout *Ulysses* (1922), where the "continuous parallel between
contemporaneity and antiquity" openly mocked the classical correspondences Joyce had experienced in the writings of Yeats and other advocates
of Revival;[276] and as he and Yeats began, so others followed. David Jones
and Hugh MacDiarmid possessed nothing close to fluency in ancient
Greek, Latin, Welsh or Scottish Gaelic, but both – in part by looking
back to the language politics and stylistic achievements of the Irish
Literary Revival – began to envision their own ways of bringing the
foreign pressures of a 'classical imaginary' into further expressions of
Celtic modernism in Wales and Scotland.

---

[272] Joyce, "Drama and Life" (1900) in Joyce *CWJJ* (1989) 39.
[273] Gregory (1913) 9.
[274] Joyce *CWJJ* (1989) 39.
[275] Joyce *CWJJ* (1989) 39.
[276] Eliot (1923) 483.

CHAPTER I

"A Noble Vernacular?"
Yeats, Hellenism and the Anglo-Irish Nation

With "the failure of the Irish people in recent times" on his mind, Douglas Hyde, an Irish translator and later the first president of the fledgling Gaelic League, took the stage at the Leinster Lecture Hall in Dublin late in the autumn of 1892.[1] Having been well publicized weeks before in *The Freeman's Journal* and in *United Ireland,* Hyde entitled the address he planned to make before the newly formed National Literary Society, "The Necessity for De-Anglicising Ireland." In anticipation, Hyde had spent days revising the lecture, believing he could illustrate Ireland's present cultural crisis, namely why it was that a "nation which was once, as every one admits, one of the most classically learned and cultured nations in Europe, is now one of the least so."[2] As Hyde saw it, Irish civilization had declined to such an extent that "one of the most reading and literary peoples has become one of the *least* studious and most *un*-literary," and on that account, the aesthetic sensibilities of the country at large had been degraded, "the present art products of one of the quickest, most sensitive, and most artistic races on earth" having become "only distinguished for their hideousness."[3] The erosion in learning and the arts in particular, he claimed, had emerged from a paradox plaguing popular "sentiment," sentiment that, he explained, "sticks in this half-way house ... imitating England and yet apparently hating it. How can [Ireland] produce anything good in literature, art, or institutions as long as it is actuated by motives so contradictory?"[4] For Hyde, the "half-way house" was most evident in the dominant yet alien language he saw spoken across nearly all social classes of contemporary

---

[1] Hyde (1986) 153. Hyde's speech was later published in the 1894 monograph *The Revival of Irish Literature, Addresses by Sir Charles Gavan Duffy, K.C.M.G., Dr. George Sigerson, and Dr. Douglas Hyde.* The quotation in the chapter title is taken from Hill (1998) 62.

[2] Hyde (1986) 153. See Dunleavy and Dunleavy (1991) 182–86.

[3] Hyde (1986) 153.

[4] Hyde (1986) 154.

society. The prominence of English in Irish public life had, he believed, served one purpose alone: to advance the cultural supremacy of England while fostering in the Irish confusion about what he called "the principle of nationality, rightly understood."[5] Pressed by strange customs and a tongue that was never fully familiar, the Irish people had learned to deny their own native genius, a genius Hyde thought most prominently expressed within their own language, Irish Gaelic. Now, Hyde argued, having tacitly exchanged a native language for a foreign one, the Irish were slowly adopting "pell-mell, and indiscriminately, everything that is English, simply because it *is* English."[6] While many nationalist sympathizers bemoaned the political dominance of England, too few, Hyde thought, had proved bold enough to scrutinize the linguistic origin of their own cultural captivity.[7] With no forceful action taken against the spread of English, there was little reason to expect anything but the further entrenchment of British control in Irish affairs. Soon, he lamented, the last remnants of Irish would be extinct, the language compromised by too many factors, not least among them its unofficial prohibition in the national schools and the devastation brought by the Great Famine, 1845–52.

While the stylistic character of Douglas Hyde's own English translations of Irish folklore was largely conventional for the period, the claims he made in "De-Anglicising Ireland" proved intellectually provocative and creatively suggestive to his contemporaries. As Michael Cronin has observed, Hyde saw "translation as an agent of aesthetic and political renewal" capable of not only bearing "witness to the past" but actively shaping the future of Ireland as a nation as well.[8] That desire for sweeping renewal pervaded Hyde's address of 1892, enmeshing his radical reflections about the growth of English with the varied historical receptions then given to both Gaelic and Greek antiquity during the era of Revival. In so doing, Hyde pushed other scholars and writers sympathetic to his views – Yeats above all – to consider the invention of any so-called Hiberno-English vernacular comparatively, in the wider contexts of not only other literary traditions that were living but those that were then dying and dead as well.[9] Indeed it was Yeats' own powerful responses to

---

[5] *Gaelic League Pamphlet* no. 13 [1901?] 5. See Introduction, pp. 17–24.
[6] Hyde (1894) 117.
[7] See Hyde (1986) 155–60.
[8] Cronin (1996) 136.

Hyde's address – with its implication that Ireland remained ghost-ridden, haunted by what Laura O'Connor has called "idealized notions of lost organic unity" – that came to engage these contexts broadly.[10] Eager to develop a new, suitably 'classical' body of contemporary Irish writing – one that could ably compete with modern literatures of Europe – Yeats strove to untether his own idiom of Hiberno-English from the 'main line' of English literature, thereby "unfolding and developing ... an Irish tradition" that would give "perfect expression to itself in literature."[11] In so doing, Yeats' early work also began, in oblique fashion, to sow in 'Anglo-Celtic' literary expression the seeds of further multilingual interference and greater stylistic experiment. These seeds would later flower demonstrably in the eccentric forms of Celtic literary modernism by James Joyce, David Jones and Hugh MacDiarmid.

As fluency and the broad social and political fortunes of the Irish language declined throughout the 1800s, many remained aware of "the leakage, the internal translation" that still was at work "between the island's two languages," English and the manifold varieties of demotic Irish.[12] That very leakage was, moreover, further subject to "parallel social and linguistic hierarchies" that made classical Greek and Latin ascendant among the country's educated elite.[13] Fertile contact between English and Irish fostered growth in bilingualism, and that phenomenon offered to those fluent among the "porous and interactive" language communities of Ireland what Nicholas Wolf has called "a mastery of the linguistic landscape not available to either Irish or English monoglots."[14] However, as the institutional power of both the state and the Catholic Church

---

[9] As O'Connor notes, the "close proximity of English to Gaelic and Scots (and Welsh ...) ... and the long history of their interaction, generated substantial direct and oblique discourse about the impact of Anglicization on British multilingual culture." O'Connor (2006) xvii.

[10] O'Connor (2006) xvii. See also Cronin (1996) 185–88.

[11] Yeats, "Irish National Literature, I: From Callanan to Carleton" (1895) in Yeats *CW9* (2004) 264.

[12] Cronin (1996) 4. On the various 'leakages' between Irish and other languages, see also Ó Dochartaigh (2000) 6–36.

[13] Stray (1998) 74. On the complex narratives of decline that have long surrounded scholarly accounts of Irish in the nineteenth century, and the fact that for the "Irish-speaking community of this period, decline and obsolescence were not the all-encompassing considerations that they have been for modern historians," see Wolf (2014) 20. Throughout the eighteenth and nineteenth centuries Irish never comprised "a single language" but rather a number of "regional variations." On this point, see O'Higgins (2017) 2–12.

[14] O'Higgins (2017) 3. Wolf (2014) 18. On the politics of translation in late nineteenth-century Ireland, see Cronin (1996) 131–46.

expanded, prominent national leaders and some clergymen, men such as Daniel O'Connell (1775–1847); James Warren Doyle (1786–1834), bishop of Kildare; and Paul Cardinal Cullen (1803–1878), archbishop of Dublin, deliberately ignored promoting the Irish language and instead encouraged the taking up of English, anglicization having become central to a broadly held vision of a new and powerful Irish Catholic middle class.[15] In much the same way as knowledge of Latin and Greek had once offered Victorian men of Britain and Ireland the possibility of greater civic entitlement in the empire, English was then presented as a central means by which greater social and political capital could be acquired. For that very reason, though, Douglas Hyde feared its spread, decrying the adoption of English as a mass form of cultural debasement and imitation. "[E]very external that at present differentiates us from the English" will be, he insisted,

> lost or dropped; all our Irish names of places and people turned into English names; the Irish language completely extinct; the O's and the Macs dropped; our Irish intonation changed, as far as possible by English schoolmasters into something English; our history no longer remembered or taught; the names of our rebels and martyrs blotted out; our battlefields and traditions forgotten; the fact we were not of Saxon origin dropped out of sight and memory, and let me now put the question – How many Irishmen are there who would purchase material prosperity at such a price?[16]

Knowing that many Irish might, in fact, buy material prosperity at this price, Hyde rejected the claim of some that an authentic national literature for Ireland could be forged in the common language of Spenser, Shakespeare, Pope and Shelley.[17] Even an English hybridized or cross-fertilized with Irish Gaelic, a reputedly Anglo-Irish vernacular would, he believed, betray the roots of Ireland's history and polity.[18] Traffic in English in any form could only enfeeble the last vestiges of "our once great national tongue," he argued, and further corrupt Ireland along

---

[15] On the evolution of the Roman Catholic Church's regard for Irish, see Wolf (2014) 223–67, and Ellis (1972) 96–121.

[16] Hyde (1986) 155.

[17] "I have often heard people thank God that if the English gave us nothing else they gave us at least their language. In this way they put a bold face upon the matter, and pretend that the Irish language *is* not worth knowing, and has no literature." Hyde (1986) 160.

[18] Hyde (1986) 158.

"racial lines," encouraging English imitation, the phenomenon Hyde called "West-Britonism."[19]

> [W]e must create a strong feeling against West-Britonism, for it – if we give it the least chance, or show it the smallest quarter – will overwhelm us like a flood, and we shall find ourselves toiling painfully behind the English at each step following the same fashions, only six months behind the English ones ... We will become, what, I fear, we are largely at present, a nation of imitators, the Japanese of Western Europe, lost to the power of native initiative and alive only to second-hand assimilation.[20]

Unless Ireland was willing to accept the irrevocable loss of its Gaelic past, and at present the further degradation of the race itself, English could have no place in public life. On this ground, Hyde predicated the development of a new national literature for Ireland on the revitalization of its native language as well as the annihilation of all further anglicizing impulses in Irish society.[21]

On hearing Hyde speak, W. B. Yeats confessed he was moved by his "learning," "profound sincerity" and the "passionate conviction" with which his words had been delivered.[22] On leaving the lecture hall that day, he reportedly overheard great enthusiasm for a speech that some there had thought "the most important utterance of its kind since '48."[23] Yet, though Hyde's words seemed "the best possible augury for the success of the movement we are trying to create," Yeats was "depressed" by the translator's suggestions regarding the revitalization of a new modern literature in Ireland.[24] The next month, he responded with a letter of his own to the editor of *United Ireland*, in which Yeats admitted that the extinction of Irish seemed an inevitable but regrettable fact: "Alas, I fear he spoke the truth," he observed, "and that the Gaelic

---

[19] Hyde (1986) 160, 169. On Hyde's view of "West-Britonism," see Crowley (2005) 136–40; and O'Connor (2006) 39–53.

[20] Hyde (1986) 169.

[21] Looking back in 1905, Hyde remained unmoved: any attempt at an English vernacular in Ireland, no matter how hybridized, could not sustain a national literature. "English gum is no substitute," he declared, "and never can be a substitute for Irish sap. Fifty years of bitter experience have taught us that the Young Ireland heroes did not arrest, and to my thinking could not arrest, the denationalization of Ireland by a literature which, rousing and admirable as it was, was still only a literature written in the English language and largely founded upon English models." Douglas Hyde, "The Gaelic Revival" (1905) in Hyde (1986) 184–85.

[22] Yeats, "To the Editor of *United Ireland*, 17 December 1892," in Yeats *CL1* (1986) 338. On Yeats' reaction to Hyde's address, see Foster (1997) 125–27.

[23] Yeats *CL1* (1986) 338. See also Dunleavy and Dunleavy (1991) 182–83.

[24] Yeats *CL1* (1986) 338.

language will soon be no more heard, except here and there in remote villages, and on the wind-beaten shores of Connaught."[25] At all costs, what remained of the language needed preservation, for Irish was still, he thought, "a fountain of nationality in our midst."[26] However, as the common vernacular for the country's emerging "hopes of nationhood," Yeats felt Irish would not do.[27] Therefore, rather than encourage a form of language purism, Yeats insisted that the best chance for inventing a new national literature lay in the development of an Anglo-Irish hybrid, a literary vernacular rooted in the translation and creative adaptation of ancient Gaelic poetry and Irish folklore.

> Is there, then, no hope for the de-Anglicising of our people? Can we not build up a national tradition, a national literature, which shall be none the less Irish in spirit from being English in language? Can we not keep the continuity of the nation's life, not by trying to do what Dr. Hyde has practically pronounced impossible, but by translating or retelling in English, which shall have an indefinable Irish quality of rythm [sic] and style, all that is best of the ancient literature?[28]

According to Yeats, the success of Hyde and other contemporary writers in anglicizing Irish folklore had demonstrated the viability of this new idiom. Modern literary work, he explained, work that sounded distinctively Irish (though in English), could be forged with an Anglo-Irish vernacular, a vernacular that would build "a golden bridge between the old and the new."[29]

> Mr. Hyde, Lady Wilde in her recent books, and Mr. Curtin, and the editor of the just-published "Vision of M'Comaile," are setting before us a table spread with strange Gaelic fruits, from which an ever-growing band of makers of song and story shall draw food for their souls.[30]

The English employed throughout these stories and translations had laid the foundation for new creative work, which Yeats envisioned as a "great school of ballad poetry in Ireland."[31] "I thought one day," he recalled years later,

---

[25] Yeats *CL1* (1986) 338.
[26] Yeats *CL1* (1986) 340.
[27] Yeats *CL1* (1986) 340.
[28] Yeats *CL1* (1986) 338. See Introduction, pp. 2–3; Chapter 2, pp. 105–08, Chapter 4, pp. 163–65.
[29] Yeats *CL1* (1986) 338.
[30] Yeats *CL1* (1986) 339.
[31] Yeats, "What Is 'Popular Poetry'?" (1901) in Yeats *CW4* (2007) 5.

I can remember the very day when I thought it – "If somebody could make a style which would not be an English style and yet would be musical and full of colour, many others would catch fire from him." ... I set to work to find a style and things to write about that the ballad writers might be the better.[32]

Since beginning the narrative poem, *The Wanderings of Oisin* (1889), Yeats himself had been at work on such a style, believing his poetic idiom could be submerged in "that wild Celtic blood, the most un-English of all things under heaven."[33] Yet, possessing no fluency in the Irish language, Yeats faced a practical difficulty in achieving the fusion between Irish and English that he had admired in Hyde's *The Love Songs of Connaught* (1893). Its "prose parts" were, he confessed, "the coming of a new power into literature."[34] Unlike Hyde, however, Yeats had, from a young age, failed to master any foreign language, whether ancient or modern. Although he was exposed to French, German, Greek and Latin, especially at The High School at Harcourt Street, Dublin, from 1881 to 1883, he was considered "constitutionally incapable of learning" these languages.[35] Now, however, he was undeterred by ignorance. Yet if an Anglo-Irish idiom were to be forged without actual interference from Irish, Yeats had to invent other ways of approximating a syntax and diction that could sound, by impression at least to readers of English, ancient, foreign and persuasively Celtic. With or without knowledge of Irish, the moment had come, he believed, for Irish poetry to separate from the mainstream of English literature – for writers to make their own mark as the country's hope for nationhood gained popular favor. The country was "at the outset of a literary epoch" and the movement he envisioned would not be seen, he hoped, as "merely a little eddy cast up by the advancing tide of English literature."[36]

Yet a sense of unease persisted for Yeats. Concerned that a national revival of Irish writing in English might be regarded as a fraudulent invention, a 'neo-romantic' movement born from the popular taste for the 'Celtic note' in England, Yeats set out in Dublin in May 1893 to lecture on "Nationality and Literature" and to establish a categorical

---

[32] Yeats *CW4* (2007) 5, 6.
[33] Yeats *CL1* (1986) 339. On the poem's composition and publication, see Yeats (1994a) vol. 2: 3–10.
[34] Yeats, "*Samhain:* 1902," in Yeats *CW8* (2003) 16.
[35] Foster (1997) 74. On Yeats' inadequate knowledge of foreign languages, see Arkins (1990) 2–5, Liebregts (1993) 7–21 and Foster (1997) 33–34. See Introduction, pp. 5–7, especially n28; Chapter 3, pp. 131–32, especially n60.
[36] Yeats, "Nationality and Literature" (May 19, 1893) in Yeats *UP1* (1970) 273.

difference in the contemporary character of Irish writing.[37] With no recourse – indeed, no desire – to use the Irish language as the defining trait for a new national movement, Yeats did not savage the influence of West-Britonism, nor did he condemn the English language with the expectation of restoring Gaelic purity. Instead, he intended to classify both Irish and English letters, comparing them against the most exalted literary traditions of the past, most notably that of Greek antiquity. Drawing on a critical method once employed by Matthew Arnold, Yeats hoped to "talk a little philosophy," to rationalize from Greek history a "general law" of literary development that might, in turn, be used to upset a central tenet in Arnold's criticism.[38] In his inaugural 1857 lecture as Oxford Professor of Poetry – a lecture Arnold entitled, "On the Modern Element in Literature" – he contrasted the present moment in English writing with what he called "the absolute, the enduring interest of Greek literature, and, above all, of Greek poetry."[39] In Arnold's view, the literature of Greece, specifically the work of fifth-century Athens, had emerged in a parallel modernity: Athens was a highly developed society marked by what he called the "manifestation of a critical spirit, the endeavour after a rational arrangement and appreciation of facts."[40] "[T]he culminating age in the life of ancient Greece" was, Arnold declared,

> beyond question, a great epoch; the life of Athens in the fifth century before our era I call one of the highly developed, one of the marking, one of the modern periods in the life of the whole human race. It has been said that the "Athens of Pericles was a vigorous man, at the summit of his bodily strength and mental energy." There was the utmost energy of life there, public and private; the most entire freedom, the most unprejudiced and intelligent observation of human affairs.[41]

---

[37] Yeats himself first used the term 'neo-romantic' to describe the ambitions of his early work: "we shall have a school of Irish poetry," he told Katharine Tynan (1861–1931) in 1887, "founded on Irish myth and History – a neo-remantic [sic] movement." See Yeats, Letter to Katharine Tynan (27 [April 1887]) in Yeats CL1 (1986) 10–12. Fraud and the 'Celtic note' had been popularly linked in Britain, at least since James Macpherson falsified his discovery of the Gaelic bard, Ossian (Irish: Oisín) in Scotland in 1761. Macpherson's finding of this 'Northern Homer', the epic poet of the ancient Gaelic world, was met with great fanfare at the time, but it was soon exposed as a hoax, first by the antiquarian Charles O'Conor (1710–91) and then by Samuel Johnson (1709–84). On the Ossian controversy, see Curley (2009) as well as Simonsuuri (1979) 108–42. More than a century later, Yeats remained anxious about Celtic forgery in English, fearing that contemporary poets might follow a path similar to the one Macpherson first cut. On the impact of the Ossian controversy on the Literary Revival, see Curley (2009) 123–55 and Watson (1998) 216–25.
[38] Yeats UP1 (1970) 268.
[39] Arnold (1960) 37.
[40] Arnold (1960) 25.
[41] Arnold (1960) 23.

Despite the allegedly parallel modernities of Greece and England, contemporary writers had thus far failed, Arnold claimed, to interpret English modernity "unprejudiced" in the same way their Athenian predecessors had done so effectively for their own time: England possessed no "comprehensive," "commensurate" or "adequate literature" that could meet the demands of "a copious and complex present, and behind it a copious and complex past."[42] There was no "intellectual deliverance" on offer in modern English literature, no relief from that "spectacle of a vast multitude of facts" that awaited, invited and indeed demanded "comprehension."[43] With that in mind, Arnold encouraged writers of English to study Attic literature – a literature he thought "commensurate with its epoch," most especially in "the poetry of Pindar, Aeschylus, Sophocles, Aristophanes" – and to apply "to other ages, nations, and literatures the same method of inquiry" so as to clarify the "intellectual history of our race."[44] To apprehend "the legitimate demands of our age," he insisted, "the literature of ancient Greece is, even for modern times, a mighty agent of intellectual deliverance; even for modern times, therefore, an object of indestructible interest."[45]

Far from Oxford and well over thirty years later, Yeats laid claim to something of the "same method of inquiry" that Arnold had urged on his contemporaries, stressing in his own lecture the "indestructible interest" of Greek literature in Ireland – not expressly to find an intellectual deliverance from modernity but rather to expose the broad chasm he saw between Irish literature and the diminishing intensity of English letters.[46] With Greece as a model, Yeats wished "to separate the general course of literary development," he wrote,

> and set it apart from mere historical accident and circumstance, and having so done, to examine the stages it passes through, and then to try and point out in what stage the literature of England is, and in what stage the literature of Ireland is. I will have to go far a-field before I come to the case of Ireland, for it is necessary, in this first instance, to find this general law of development.[47]

Scrutiny of classical antiquity, he thought, was essential to establishing a universal account of literary history, a history somehow raised above the

---

[42] Arnold (1960) 23, 22, 20.
[43] Arnold (1960) 20.
[44] Arnold (1960) 31, 37.
[45] Arnold (1960) 20.
[46] Arnold (1960) 37, 20.
[47] Yeats *UP1* (1970) 268.

vicissitudes of taste, language and changing fashion. Even a cursory examination of ancient history showed that Greek literature and civilization was divided into "three clearly-marked periods" of political and artistic development, each of which had been defined by the rise of a dominant literary genre.[48] These periods were, Yeats contended, "the period of narrative poetry, the epic or ballad period; next the dramatic period; and after that the period of lyric poetry."[49] Success in any of these forms, he argued, was dependent not solely on the talent of an individual writer but rather on the way in which that writer's work met the contemporary moment in national history, each genre expressing aspects of the nation's evolution. "In Greece," he explained,

> the first period is represented by Homer, who describes great racial or national movements and events, and sings of the Greek race rather than of any particular member of it. After him come Aeschulus [*sic*] and Sophocles, who subdivide these great movements and events into the characters who lived and wrought in them. The Siege of Troy is now no longer the theme, for Agamemnon and Clytemnestra and Oedipus dominate the stage. After the dramatists come the lyric poets, who are known to us through the Greek anthology. And now not only have the racial events disappeared but the great personages themselves, for literature has begun to centre itself about this or that emotion or mood, about the Love or Hatred, the Hope or Fear which were to Aeschulus and Sophocles merely parts of Oedipus or Agamemnon or Clytemnestra, or of some other great tragic man or woman.[50]

As discrete shifts in the political evolution of a country emerged, literary expression changed in a similar fashion, developing slowly to reflect the collective consciousness of the nation. Over time it was clear, Yeats argued, that formal expression always became less expansive, moving from the broad themes and grandeur of epic to the subtlety and refined emotion of lyric. As the national character itself underwent transformation, the particular genius expressed in a country's literature became ever more subdivided, he explained, turning "from unity to multiplicity, from simplicity to complexity."[51] "The poets had at the beginning for their material," Yeats declared,

> the national character, and the national history, and the national circumstances, and having found an expression of the first in the second, they

[48] Yeats *UP1* (1970) 269.
[49] Yeats *UP1* (1970) 269.
[50] Yeats *UP1* (1970) 269.
[51] Yeats *UP1* (1970) 268.

divided and sub-divided the national imagination, for there was nought
else for them to do. They could not suddenly become Turks, or
Englishmen, or Frenchmen, and so start with a new character and a new
history. They could but investigate and express ever more minutely and
subtly the character, and history, and circumstance of climate and scenery,
that they had got.[52]

When applying this law of development to English history, Yeats believed
it was plain: England had long been mired in an "age of lyric poetry"
where "every kind of subtlety, obscurity, and intricate utterance
prevails."[53] English writers employed "an ever more elaborate language,"
to express a "growing complexity of language and thought."[54] Yet, because
of that, the idioms of Byron (1788–1824), of Keats and, above all, of
Shelley appeared "too fine, too subjective, too impalpable" and broken, as
though "scattered into a thousand iridescent fragments, flashing and
flickering" to articulate only bits of the general life then alive in
England.[55] Stressing "ideas and feelings apart from their effects upon
action," the Romantics had explored aspects of subjective existence in
their work – what Yeats called "every phase of human consciousness no
matter how subtle, how vague" – rather than the broad collective themes
of race, nation and heroic action.[56] For this reason, he thought, English
poetry had stepped "out of the market-place, out of the general tide of
life" and become instead "a mysterious cult, as it were, an almost secret
religion made by the few for the few."[57]

Eager that Ireland would not imitate that "almost secret religion,"
Yeats insisted that national development across both countries had
been different, so much so that a central generic difference could easily
be discerned in their respective literary histories. "[N]ot only is this
literature of England different in character from the literature of
Ireland," he wrote, "as different as the beach tree from the oak ... the
two literatures are in quite different stages of their development."[58] As
Yeats envisioned it, Ireland's growth into a nation had been abruptly
halted during the Middle Ages. "[W]hen the day of battle came," he
wrote, Ireland

---

[52] Yeats *UP1* (1970) 269–70.
[53] Yeats *UP1* (1970) 271.
[54] Yeats *UP1* (1970) 271.
[55] Yeats *UP1* (1970) 271, 270.
[56] Yeats *UP1* (1970) 271.
[57] Yeats *UP1* (1970) 271.
[58] Yeats *UP1* (1970) 271, 269.

could not combine against the invader. Each province had its own assembly and its own king. There was no focus to draw the tribes into one. The national order perished at the moment when other countries like Germany and Iceland were beginning to write out their sagas and epics in deliberate form.[59]

Mired in political disarray the country had no outlet in which to express its national imagination. Rather than see its folklore emerge as the foundation for a developing literary tradition in Irish, the tales of early Irish myth and history never found their first necessary form in the "epic or ballad period."[60] Instead, the country's legends languished in relative obscurity and soon became what Yeats called

> a vast pell-mell of monstrous shapes: huge demons driving swine on the hill-tops; beautiful shadows whose hair has a peculiar life and moves responsive to their thought; and here and there some great hero like Cuchulain, some epic needing only deliberate craft to be scarce less than Homer. There behind the Ireland of to-day, lost in the ages, this chaos murmurs like a dark and stormy sea full of the sounds of lamentation.[61]

With no deliberate craft, there had been no Irish Homer. After 700 years of colonial subjugation – subjugation that Yeats and Hyde both regarded as political, linguistic and cultural – fragments of the country's folklore had survived; but where once a tree might have emerged, there were only "seeds that never bore stems, stems that never wore flowers, flowers that knew no fruitage," he lamented.[62] "The literature of ancient Ireland is a literature of vast, half-dumb conceptions ... Instead of the well-made poems we might have had, there remains but a wild anarchy of legends."[63]

Yet from the anarchy of Ireland's Gaelic past, Yeats believed that modern Irish literature needed merely formal rigor, indeed "only deliberate craft" for its work "to be scarce less than Homer."[64] A new national epic composed in Anglo-Irish would emerge, for "we are a young nation," Yeats explained,

> with unexhausted material lying within us in our still unexpressed national character, about us in our scenery, and in the clearly marked outlines of our life, and behind us in our multitude of legends. Look at our literature

---

[59] Yeats, "Bardic Ireland" (January 4, 1890) in Yeats *CW9* (2004) 111.
[60] Yeats *UP1* (1970) 269.
[61] Yeats *CW9* (2004) 112.
[62] Yeats *CW9* (2004) 112.
[63] Yeats *CW9* (2004) 112.
[64] Yeats *CW9* (2004) 112.

and you will see that we are still in our epic or ballad period. All that is greatest in that literature is based upon legend.[65]

Already the 1865 publication of *Lays of the Western Gael, and Other Poems*, Samuel Ferguson's "truly bardic" versions of Irish ballads, had helped advance the cause of a national vernacular in Ireland, a literature composed in the hybrid writing of Anglo-Irish.[66] Unlike his contemporaries in England, Ferguson was, Yeats insisted, "like the ancients; not that he was an imitator, as Matthew Arnold in *Sohrab and Rustum*, but for a much better reason; he was *like* them – like them in nature, for his spirit had sat with the old heroes of his country."[67] Rather than mimic the neoclassical impulse that had motivated Arnold, Ferguson cultivated in translation the original genius of the Irish language, and in so doing had begun to clear "the pathway" towards a new discovery of Irish epic, unearthing in his poem, *Deirdre*, what Yeats called "a fragment of the buried Odyssey of Ireland."[68] Through Ferguson's work "living waters for the healing of our nation" were rising, Yeats alleged, and if modern poets were to follow his example, gathering the remaining ballads and folk legends scattered throughout the country, they too might employ these in composing a new national poem.[69]

By the end of the nineteenth century, it had long been theorized across the academy in Europe that Homeric epic had first emerged in archaic Greece not as the work of a single creative genius but rather as a synthetic invention, an amalgamation of disparate songs, legends and folk ballads slowly emended and arranged into form by later rhapsodists and grammarians. "Habemus nunc Homerum in manibus, non qui viguit in ore Graecorum suorum," the German philologist, Friedrich August Wolf (1759–1824) declared in 1795,

> sed inde a Solonis temporibus usque ad haec Alexandrina mutatum varie, interpolatum, castigatum et emendatum. Id e disiectis quibusdam indiciis iam dudum obscure colligebant homines docti et sollertes; nunc in unum coniunctae voces omnium temporum testantur, et loquitur historia.[70]

---

[65] Yeats *UP1* (1970) 273.

[66] Yeats, "The Poetry of Sir Samuel Ferguson – II" (November 1886) in Yeats *CW9* (2004) 24.

[67] Yeats *CW9* (2004) 14.

[68] Yeats, "The Poetry of Sir Samuel Ferguson – I" (October 9, 1886) in Yeats *CW9* (2004) 4; Yeats *CW9* (2004) 14.

[69] Yeats *CW9* (2004) 4.

[70] Wolfius (1795) 264–65. "The Homer that we hold in our hands now is not the one who flourished in the mouths of the Greeks of his own day, but one variously altered, interpolated, corrected, and emended from the times of Solon down to those of the Alexandrians. Learned and clever men have long felt their way to this conclusion by using various scattered bits of evidence; but now the voices of all periods joined together bear witness, and history speaks." Wolf (1985) 209.

With the publication of Wolf's *Prolegomena Ad Homerum*, a historicist approach to Greek epic – based specifically around the notion that both the *Iliad* and *Odyssey* first existed simply as a series of songs or folk ballads – "swept the field."[71] Over time the poems had taken shape, Wolf argued, adapted by scholiasts whose task "in emending the text" was not "to consider what Homer sang, but what he ought to have sung."[72] Wolf's unorthodox views – his *abweichenden Gedanken über den Homer* – gave credence to the view that the poet's work was much less a monument to a single era in ancient Greek civilization and more, in fact, "like an archaeological site, with layers of history built into them in a palpable stratigraphy: the disparate effects of multiple compositional layers (some, including Jebb, would actually call them 'strata') and the intrusive hands of editors could all be felt in the poems."[73] In the Anglophone world, this view influenced not only further scholarly inquiry into the Homeric world but the practice of translation and composition of new English poetry as well. It was thought that if "the *Iliad* and *Odyssey* had been produced by a preliterate oral culture, then there might be similar cultural monuments preserved in obscure manuscript collections or still alive in oral traditions in remote parts of Europe."[74] Already, antiquarians, scholars and writers had for some time been searching for monuments of classical significance in the broadly Celtic past of the British Isles, hoping the achievements of some 'northern' bard might emerge, a bard whose genius paralleled the accomplishments of Homeric verse. James Macpherson's notorious and fraudulent discovery of Ossian in Scotland in 1760 – a third-century Gaelic poet whom the Scottish rhetorician Hugh Blair (1718–1800) proclaimed the "Homer of the Highlands" – was a watershed moment in that search, implicating folk ballads in what became a wider "romantic exploration of primitivity, modernity, and historicity."[75] With the publication of these translations, *Fingal* (1762) and *Temora* (1763), Ossian claimed a "resemblance to Homer," a similarity that was said to have proceeded from "nature, as the original from which both drew their ideas."[76] Having allegedly detected Homeric qualities in the ballad style and vulgar diction of "our rude Celtic bard," Macpherson transposed these elements in his

---

[71] Porter (2004) 336.
[72] Wolf (1985) 204.
[73] F. A. Wolf, Letter to Heyne, November 18, 1795, in Wolf (1797) 5; Porter (2004) 336.
[74] Graver (2007) 76.
[75] Hugh Blair, "Appendix to *A Critical Dissertation on the Poems of Ossian, The Son of Fingal*" (1765) 450, as in Macpherson (1996) 403; McLane (2001) 424.
[76] Macpherson (1805) vol. 2: 8, 9.

English forgery, a version whose "pervasive sense of melancholy for a lost past" was met with popular acclaim in Britain.[77] *Ossian*, as has been noted, allowed readers to indulge all at once "in the taste for the sentimentalism and gothicism that characterized contemporary poems and novels, in the grand style of melodramatic drama, in the solemnity of English Bible rhetoric, and in the epic seriousness of Dryden's Vergil and Pope's Homer."[78]

The impact of both Wolf and Macpherson was lasting.[79] There emerged throughout the nineteenth century the desire to see Homer translated into a ballad-style English comparable in texture and spirit to the original Greek. William Maginn's translation of sixteen ballads, *Homeric Ballads* (1838–1842, published again posthumously in 1850), Francis Newman's 1856 unrhymed version of the *Iliad* and, later, the criticism of Thomas Macaulay as well as the historical writings of England's most prominent Wolfian, George Grote (1794–1871), all helped advance the then unorthodox view that Homer was not an individual poet but rather representative of "the national genius of the Greek people itself, as it articulates its vision of its own experiences over the centuries."[80] To imitate that genius in English meant that "no English model" could be followed in translating Homer: the work required what Francis Newman called a "more antiquated style," one that was "fundamentally musical and popular" at the same time.[81] The "moral qualities of Homer's style" in the original, he argued, seemed "like to those of the English ballad."[82] For Newman, therefore, ballad meters would best replicate the "direct, popular, forcible, quaint, flowing, garrulous" qualities of Homeric verse, even if "those metres which, by the very possession of these qualities," might be "liable to degenerate into doggerel."[83]

Matthew Arnold, for his part, despised Newman's vision of Homer. Whatever caricature he made of the original Greek, the fact remained, Arnold thought, that Newman's translation had achieved little: the "eminently noble" qualities of the *Iliad* had no parallel in his English idiom.[84] Instead, Newman had joined "to a bad rhythm" what Arnold

[77] Blair (1763) 23; Curley (2009) 24.

[78] Curley (2009) 24.

[79] See Jenkyns (1980) 197–99, and Armstrong (2005) 177–78.

[80] Berlin (1976) 55.

[81] Newman (1856) x, ix, v.

[82] Newman (1856) v.

[83] Newman (1856) iv, v. See also Venuti (2008) 99–107.

[84] Matthew Arnold "On Translating Homer," in Arnold (1960) 102. See Venuti (2008) 107–20 and Reynolds (2006) 67–70. On Wolf's impact on Arnold's thinking, see Porter (2004) 338–41. See also Turner (1981) 178–81.

called "so bad a diction that it is difficult to distinguish exactly whether in any given passage it is his words or his measure which produces a total impression of such an unpleasant kind."[85] Maginn's work, he asserted, "just because they are ballads in their manner and movement," were "not at all Homeric," having nothing "in the world [of] the manner of Homer."[86] The journalist had constructed his *Odyssey* as twelve separate folk ballads, believing one could creatively roll back the evolution of the epic, returning the poem to its alleged origin as a set of loosely sequenced stories and myths. Arnold, however, believed that Maginn had managed only a "true ballad-slang" in his poem, a "detestable dance … jigging in my ears, to spoil the effect of Homer, and to torture me. To apply that manner and that rhythm to Homer's incidents, is not to imitate Homer, but to travesty him."[87] For Arnold, the *grand style* of Homeric verse was, practically speaking, inimitable in its plainness, directness, simplicity and nobility. Only a translator willing to immerse himself, to "penetrate himself with a sense of the plainness and directness of Homer's style; of the simplicity with which Homer's thought is evolved and expressed" might, he thought, avoid the seemingly inevitable dissolution of these qualities in English, a dissolution one could find even in the most sublime English versions of Homer.[88] Even George Chapman's seventeenth-century version was unfaithful in that regard; it was, Arnold argued, "*too* active," interposing on the original Greek a "mist of the fancifulness of the Elizabethan age, entirely alien to the plain directness of Homer's thought and feeling."[89] That fanciful character was, for its time, a significant literary achievement – certainly when compared with the lackluster ballad-style translations of the mid-nineteenth century – but still "a cloud of more than Egyptian thickness" remained over Homer, a thickness that had kept from English the four most notable qualities of his Greek.[90] Thus while the "proposition that Homer's poetry is *ballad-poetry*, analogous to the well-known ballad-poetry of the English and other nations, has a certain small portion of truth in it" – it being useful in discrediting "the artificial and literary manner in which Pope and his school rendered Homer" – Arnold insisted this view had been "extravagantly over-used."[91] Maginn's and Newman's failures proved that

[85] Arnold (1960) 132–33.
[86] Arnold (1960) 131.
[87] Arnold (1960) 131, 132.
[88] Arnold (1960) 111.
[89] Arnold (1960) 113, 103 (emphasis in the original).
[90] Arnold (1960) 103.
[91] Arnold (1960) 126.

one could not effectively anglicize Homer by simply equating the nobility and directness of his Greek with the ignoble and vulgar rusticity of English folk. "It is time to say plainly," Arnold declared, "that, whatever the admirers of our old ballads may think, the supreme form of epic poetry, the genuine Homeric mould, is not the form of the Ballad of Lord Bateman."[92]

With little to no fluency in Greek, Yeats himself showed no interest in translating Homer or weighing in on Arnold's opinion of Newman and Maginn. Yet the presence of the English 'ballad-style' Homer so despised by Arnold still held sway in his imagination, for Yeats believed – as he often discussed in his essays and private letters – that what still remained of Gaelic folklore was akin to the source material Homer himself had used when composing the *Iliad* and *Odyssey*. "[T]he celtic races love the soil of their countries vehemently," Yeats told a friend in 1897,

> & have as great a mass of legends about that soil as Homer had about his … the true foundation of literature is folklore, which was the foundation of Homer & of <more than half> Shakespeare but has not been the foundation of more modern writers … The life of drawing rooms will be altogeather [sic] changed in a few years the life of the poor, & the life that is in legends is still the life of Homers [sic] people.[93]

The "mass of legends" still present in contemporary Ireland was evidence, Yeats thought, that the country was now – like archaic Greece had been before Homer – on the cusp of articulating its genius in its first literary form.[94] Ready for a national epic, the Irish possessed the necessary folk stories, those "tales which are made by no one man, but by the nation itself through a slow process of modification and adaption, to express its loves and its hates, its likes and its dislikes."[95] With this abundance of folklore, its "unexhausted material," the modern poet could write collectively, Yeats thought, drawing on myth and history to define the racial character of a new Irish nation.[96] Already he explained,

---

[92] Arnold (1960) 126. A popular song sung in taverns and pubs, *The Loving Ballad of Lord Bateman* was published in an 1839 edition with illustrations by George Cruikshank (1792–1878) and a preface written anonymously by Charles Dickens (1812–70).

[93] Yeats, "To Richard Ashe King, 5 August [1897]," in Yeats *CL2* (1997) 129–30. Elsewhere Yeats claimed in like fashion that, "There is still in truth upon these great level plains a people, a community bound together by imaginative possessions, by stories and poems which have grown out of its own life, and by a past of great passions which can still waken the heart to imaginative action. One could still, if one had the genius, and had been born to Irish, write for these people plays and poems like those of Greece." Yeats, "The Galway Plains" (1903) in Yeats *CW4* (2007) 158.

[94] Yeats *CL2* (1997) 129.

[95] Yeats *UP1* (1970) 273.

[96] Yeats *UP1* (1970) 273.

> Our best writers, De Vere, Ferguson, Allingham, Mangan, Davis, O'Grady, are all either ballad or epic writers, and all base their greatest work, if I except a song or two of Mangan's and Allingham's, upon legends and upon the fortunes of the nation. Alone, perhaps, among the nations of Europe we are in our ballad or epic age.[97]

Though Ireland stood in its epic period, Yeats was quick to insist that Homeric poetry and Greek mythology were worthy only of emulation, not imitation, adaptation or direct translation. As he saw it, writers could only effectively compose an Irish epic by employing in verse native myths, stories of Ireland's own invention. The centuries-long tedium of recycling in English the same heroes, gods and goddesses from Greek and Roman antiquity was over. "The folk-lore of Greece and Rome lasted us a long time," he wrote,

> but having ceased to be a living tradition, it became both worn out and unmanageable, like an old servant. We can now no more get up a great interest in the gods of Olympus than we can in the stories told by the showman of a travelling waxwork company.[98]

To use such 'waxwork' across Irish literature would be tantamount, Yeats argued, to imitating the Romantic poets, in particular Shelley who, rather than cultivate Britain's own native folk life, had saturated his verse with mythological elements drawn from the classics. It was for this reason that Shelley "lacked the true symbols and types and stories," Yeats explained.[99] Engrossed in the foreign, his verse did not have "adequate folk-lore" so "as to unite man more closely to the woods and hills and waters about him, and to the birds and animals that live in them."[100] "Shelley had but mythology," Yeats wrote,

> and a mythology which had been passing for long through literary minds without any new inflow from living tradition loses all the incalculable instinctive and convincing quality of the popular traditions. No conscious invention can take the place of tradition, for he who would write a folk tale, and thereby bring a new life into literature, must have the fatigue of the spade in his hands and the stupor of the fields in his heart.[101]

In cultivating classical sources – the knowledge of which would be understood largely by only an educated elite in Britain and in Ireland – Shelley

---

[97] Yeats *UP1* (1970) 273.
[98] Yeats *CW9* (2004) 210.
[99] Yeats *CW9* (2004) 212.
[100] Yeats *CW9* (2004) 212.
[101] Yeats *CW9* (2004) 212–13.

had, according to Yeats, traded folklore for a foreignizing substitute whose tenuous connection to Britain's native character had made it impossible to ventriloquize what Yeats called "the voice of some race celebrating itself, embalming for ever what it hated and loved."[102]

With that in mind, Yeats eschewed allusions to Greek and Roman antiquity in his earliest published poetry: to adopt that material would not advance the kind of undeniable Irish epic he hoped to invent in Anglo-Irish; and yet, though he heaped scorn on the classicism of Shelley's poetry, Yeats insisted that Irish poets still had "to go where Homer went if we are to sing a new song."[103] That discipleship, however, demanded no abandonment of Irish for Greek but rather a return to the native, to the "great banquet on an earthen floor and under a broken roof" where Homer himself had likewise found inspiration.[104] That return, Yeats thought, would bring about an authentic rediscovery of the Homeric in Ireland, for by 1893 many notable Celtic philologists – scholars such as Marie Henri d'Arbois de Jubainville (1827–1910), John Rhys (1840–1915) and Alfred Trübner Nutt – believed that Gaelic folklore and the mythology of Homeric Greece had emerged from a common Indo-European source.[105] That "Greek kinship," as Synge later defined it, was at work in Ireland's folk culture; it was a kinship that had made the Celtic past indispensable to understanding the primitive world out of which Homer and the Greek classics had been born.[106] "Celtic legends are," Yeats wrote (when praising *The Voyage of Bran*, edited by Kuno Meyer and Alfred Nutt),

> according to certain scholars, our principal way to an understanding of the beliefs out of which the beliefs of the Greeks and other Europeans races arose ... "Greek and Irish alone have preserved the early stages of the happy other world conception with any fulness" and ... Ireland has preserved them "with greater fulness and precision" than the Greeks.[107]

---

[102] Yeats *CW9* (2004) 3.

[103] Yeats, "'Thoughts on Lady Gregory's Translations': Prefaces" (1902, 1903; rev. 1905, 1908, 1912) in Yeats *CW6* (1989) 132.

[104] Yeats *CW6* (1989) 131.

[105] The popularity surrounding d'Arbois de Jubainville's scholarship led to the 1903 translation, *The Irish Mythological Cycle & Celtic Mythology*, by Richard Irvine Best (1872–1959).

[106] Synge, "Celtic Mythology" (April 2, 1904) in Synge (1966) 365.

[107] Yeats *CW9* (2004) 416. In a like manner, the scholar of Irish, Richard Henebry, often insisted that, while "all civilizations in Europe to-day" represented "a development from a Roman or Latin source, Irish civilization, or what remains of it, goes back to a Keltic original," an original commonly thought to have preserved more fully primitive beliefs shared with ancient Greece. Henebry (1902) 295.

Still untapped, the potency of the Gaelic appeared to Yeats and to many advocates of revival as Greek in essence, classical at heart. The accuracy of such claims mattered little: scholarly sources positing a common origin of the Greek classics and the unexpressed potential latent in Irish could be used successfully to advance Yeats' vision of Anglo-Irish, a hybrid vernacular whose connection to classical antiquity remained unbroken, thus promising a return to what Yeats called "the habit of mind that created the religion of the muses."[108] Amid the ruin of English Romanticism, with the extinction of Irish Gaelic impending, Irish writers still held "ancient salt" in their grasp, a salt with which they could pack and preserve the past while still inventing the future in vernacular.[109] Forged by the creative adoption of folklore, and reputedly infused with the foreign accent of Irish, this new style of writing would sustain, Yeats believed, the exceptional kinship the Gael had long shared with the Greek.[110]

Years later, as he looked back on his youth, Yeats admitted that, despite his reservations, he aspired – like many other poets of his circle then – to the vision that Shelley had forged from the ancient Greek world. "Might I not," he reflected,

> with health and good luck to aid me, create some new *Prometheus Unbound*; Patrick or Columcille, Oisin or Finn, in Prometheus' stead; and, instead of Caucasus, Cro-Patrick or Ben Bulben? Have not all races had their first unity from a mythology that marries them to rock and hill?[111]

Although Yeats disliked the artificial character of Shelley's classicism, he did admire the *Prometheus Unbound*, the 1820 lyrical drama that he once declared the "sacred book" of his youth.[112] What attracted Yeats was not the use of Greek mythology but rather Shelley's attempt to translate and reinvigorate the ancient world in an English context. The *Prometheus Unbound* had been unsuccessful, he thought, only because its story was too inadequately married to the "rock and hill" of Britain, to the known imaginative landscape present in British literature.[113] "[I]f Shelley had nailed his Prometheus," Yeats explained,

> or some equal symbol, upon some Welsh or Scottish rock, [his] art would have entered more intimately, more microscopically, as it were, into our

---

[108] Yeats *CW9* (2004) 467.
[109] Yeats, "Introduction" (1937) in Yeats *CW5* (1994) 213.
[110] Synge (1966) 365.
[111] Yeats *CW3* (1999) 166–67.
[112] Yeats *CW3* (1999) 95.
[113] Yeats *CW3* (1999) 167.

thought and given perhaps to modern poetry a breadth and stability like that of ancient poetry.[114]

With no native setting, Shelley had failed to recapture the pathos, the passionate authority of Aeschylean tragedy in English. Moreover, through his dependence on foreign myth, Shelley's work could not speak for the whole race in Britain: *Prometheus* appealed only, Yeats argued, to an elite educated in the classics. In these failures, however, Yeats still recognized a model of composition that would steer his own first attempts to forge an Anglo-Irish epic, an epic powered by his own adaptation and re-stylization of Gaelic legend. From an early age, Yeats admired Shelley, confessing later that he had written many bad imitations of him all through youth.[115]

With the 1889 publication of his narrative poem *The Wanderings of Oisin*, Yeats believed he had at last freed his verse from juvenile flaws and grasped something of the "breadth and stability" that previously eluded Shelley.[116] In *Oisin*, he was intent on reclaiming what Herbert Tucker has called

> two originary moments in the history of Western epic: first, the Ossianic matter that Macpherson had confiscated for Scotland a century earlier; then, back behind that ... the primitive of glory of Homer, the bard of archaic wanderings whose pre-classical vigor metropolitan Victorians like W. E. Gladstone and Matthew Arnold had done their best to recruit into the institutional service of an imperial Englishness.[117]

When beginning work on *Oisin*, Yeats consulted two prior English versions of the legend, translations that, while conveying the substance of the hero's journey to the Celtic Otherworld, were stylistically conventional. Simple and literal, Bryan O'Looney's 1859 translation, *Lay of Oisin on the Land of Youths*, did not sacrifice clarity in English for the strange nuances of Irish.[118] Yeats' second source, David Comyn's *Laoidh Oisín air Thír na n-Óg* (1880), was likewise prepared as an "exactly literal rather

---

[114] Yeats *CW3* (1999) 137.

[115] "I had begun to write poetry in imitation of Shelley and of Edmund Spenser, play after play – for my father exalted dramatic poetry above all other kinds – and I invented fantastic and incoherent plots. My lines but seldom scanned, for I could not understand the prosody in the books, although there were many lines that taken by themselves had music. I spoke them slowly as I wrote and only discovered when I read them to somebody else that there was no common music, no prosody." Yeats *CW3* (1999) 81. See also Bornstein (1970) 13–27.

[116] Yeats *CW3* (1999) 137.

[117] Tucker (2008) 541.

[118] O'Looney (1859) 227–80.

than elegant" translation to be used especially for instruction in Irish Gaelic.[119] Comyn possessed a certain regard for the art of translation, believing it could be used to enrich and expand the semantic register of the target language. "Translation from one language into another," he wrote,

> enriches the language into which the translation is made, in ways other than by the actual worth of the work translated. The language is rendered more copious and pliable by being, as it were, put through a process of expansion to render it more capable of transmitting clearly the ideas conceived and expressed at first in a different idiom. English has been enriched in this way from many sources.[120]

Nonetheless, Comyn's own anglicization of Oisin did little to infuse English with expressly Gaelic strains, his verse being a crib for students and readers ignorant of the Irish original. Where he could not easily produce an English rendering of the Gaelic, Comyn marked the passage with parentheses and then employed "words required to bring out clearly in English the meaning of each clause … and when, in addition to this, the literal meaning requires still further to be idiomatically explained, a second version of the clause is given in italic."[121] This method, he claimed, gave preeminence to the aesthetic achievements of the original text, offering in English no stylistic surrogate, no ornate substitute for the Irish it replaced. Yeats, however, was dissatisfied with the uninspired vision of the Celtic Otherworld in these versions, and he would not, moreover, adopt the literalist approach of Comyn and O'Looney. Instead, he drew on recent English verse, mixing conventions from the Romantic and Victorian poetry he knew well with the Arcadian themes he had admired in Spenser.[122] To further advance the "new power" of 'Irish Gaelic-in-English' that Yeats had first seen coming in Hyde's *The Love Songs of Connacht* (1893), Yeats disguised conventions that Arnold and Shelley had earlier used to register the impression of Greek interference in English.[123] With no knowledge of Irish, he adopted these, believing he could evoke an 'ancient' resonance in his verse, replicating a 'stability' whose seemingly Gaelic accent would, moreover, distinguish Anglo-Irish epic from the recent subjectivism of English Romanticism.

---

[119]　Comyn (1880) vii.
[120]　Comyn (1881) 14.
[121]　Comyn (1880) viii.
[122]　Yeats *CW3* (1999) 98.
[123]　Yeats *CW8* (2003) 16.

Yeats' aspirations notwithstanding, contemporary critics were largely unimpressed with the finished poem. On publication, *Oisin* met mixed critical success: early reviews noted the apparent confusion, the "besetting sins" from which Yeats had suffered as he formulated the poem's elaborate style.[124] "Mr. Yeats has yet to rid his mind of the delusion," one critic wrote in *The Freeman's Journal*,

> that obscurity is an acceptable substitute for strenuous thought and sound judgment. People who desire to occupy their time in solving riddles and similar exercises can buy riddle books or mechanical puzzles; Mr. Yeats does justice neither to himself nor to his readers when he hides a jumble of confused ideas in a maze of verbiage and calls it all "The Wanderings of Oisin."[125]

Even sympathetic reviewers, like Oscar Wilde (1854–1900) and John Todhunter (1839–1916), also noted "strange crudities and irritating conceits" present in *Oisin*'s syntax and diction.[126] The poem possessed, Todhunter exclaimed, "real flaws of execution – slovenly lines, awkward and uncouth constructions, exuberances which are not beauties, concentrations of expression which are crude and stiff rather than powerful."[127] Yet, in spite these of imperfections, Yeats had achieved, Wilde argued, "at least something of that largeness of vision that belongs to the epical temper," even if the poem as a whole failed to effect "the grand simplicity of epic treatment."[128]

Oisin's "epical temper" was also not lost on Yeats' friend, the classicist and poet Lionel Pigot Johnson (1867–1902), who in praising "his ability to write Celtic poetry, with all the Celtic notes of style and imagination" suggested further that a "classical manner" was at work in Yeats' style.[129] "Like all men of the true poetical spirit, he is not overcome by the apparent antagonism of the classical and the romantic in art. Like the fine

[124] "Literature: Some Recent Poetry," *The Freeman's Journal* (February 1, 1889) 2.

[125] "Literature: Some Recent Poetry," *The Freeman's Journal* (February 1, 1889) 2.

[126] Oscar Wilde, "Three New Poets: Yeats, Fitzgerald, Le Gallienne," *Pall Mall Gazette* (July 12, 1889), as in Jeffares (1977) 73.

[127] John Todhunter, Review of *The Wanderings of Oisin and Other Poems. The Academy* 882 (March 30, 1889) 216, as in Jeffares (1977) 69.

[128] Wilde (July 12, 1889), as in Jeffares (1977) 73. Other reviews complained of the poem's failure to provide a "bardic treatment." An unsigned review (by George Coffey [1857–1916]) for the *Evening Telegraph* (February 6, 1889) noted how the "principal poem, 'The Wanderings of Oisin,' runs to some fifty pages" but was, "perhaps, the least satisfactory; we had looked for a more bardic treatment." *The Manchester Guardian* likewise deemed Yeats "a rough and sometimes a rather inharmonious bard." "Books of the Week," *The Manchester Guardian* (January 28, 1899) 6.

[129] Lionel Johnson, Rev. of *The Countess Kathleen and Various Legends and Lyrics*, by W. B. Yeats. *The Academy* 1065 (October 1, 1892), as in Jeffares (1977) 79.

Greeks or Romans," Johnson wrote, Yeats "treats his subject according to its nature. Simple as that sounds, it is a praise not often to be bestowed."[130] Yeats had taken on "a Celtic theme, some vast and epic legend," but he did not display what Johnson called "the mere confused vastness" of Ireland's folk culture.[131] Instead, he had formed a poem "full of reason" from the ancient past, "a masterpiece of severe art" that set the "monstrous, barbaric frenzy" of primitive Ireland "in verse of the strictest beauty."[132] Though the poem had nothing of the "*gravitas*, that *auctoritas*, which belongs to the poetry of Rome and of England," *Oisin* possessed a reputedly 'classical' manner in its "beautiful childishness and freshness," its "quickness and adroitness in seizing the spiritual relations of things."[133] That quickness reflected, Johnson argued, the "gift of simple spirituality," one born of what the French historian Jules Michelet (1798–1874) had called the profound sympathy of "le genie celtique … avec le genie grec."[134] The *Clonmel Chronicle* reached a similar conclusion about *Oisin*, calling the poem "a genuine product of what is called the Classical School of English Literature."[135] Remarkably, the reviewer wrote, Yeats managed to avoid the "flat, stale, and unprofitable idea of imitation" even while working with

> a classical subject … [he] has submitted that subject to a purely classical design and treatment. In his imitation of the Celtic Homer's lays, Mr. Yeats is, no doubt, following the true bent of his genius: he exhibits many of the intrinsic attributes of true art, a refined sense of beauty, an imagination of vast range and considerable power, and a diction of exquisite felicity and elegance.[136]

Unlike those classically minded writers who possessed an "unconquerable disrelish to admit of sensible progress, and in many instances even a morbid belief in the retardation of poetic genius," Yeats tried, if not to overcome the "ill-timed unsympathetic ways" of the classical school, then to only admit them while "making his story interesting by picturesque descriptions and some pretty lays."[137]

---

[130] Johnson (October 1, 1892), as in Jeffares (1977) 79–80.
[131] Johnson (October 1, 1892), as in Jeffares (1977) 80.
[132] Johnson (October 1, 1892), as in Jeffares (1977) 80.
[133] Johnson (October 1, 1892), as in Jeffares (1977) 82.
[134] Johnson (October 1, 1892), as in Jeffares (1977) 82. See also Michelet (1835) 1:121.
[135] Acoe (1889). Yeats admired this review. For many years, he kept a newspaper clipping of it among the papers later bequeathed to the National Library in Dublin. See Yeats Papers, MS 31087, National Library of Ireland, Dublin (NLI).
[136] Acoe (1889).
[137] Acoe (1889).

Praise aside, the classical manner that Lionel Johnson and others detected in *Oisin* had little to do with its "vast range," "severe art" or Yeats' treatment of a "subject according to its nature" and more to do with stylistic techniques that English poets had sometimes used to convey the pressure of ancient Greek. Over the course of the nineteenth century, two divergent 'Hellenic' styles emerged in English poetry, and both exerted influence on Yeats' efforts to dislocate his Anglo-Irish from conventional English.[138] The first 'Greek' style has been described as a "new and stricter neo-classicism largely derived from Winckelmann and his idealization of the 'noble simplicity and tranquil grandeur' of the Greeks; in literature, this corresponded to a style which emphasized swiftness and clarity, simplicity, crystalline transparency."[139] By mid-century, Matthew Arnold had become the foremost advocate of this style in English letters, writing in the preface to *Poems* (1853) that the "clearness of arrangement, rigour of development, simplicity of style" once achieved by ancient Greek poetry was needed in English, for at present the "multitude of voices counselling different things bewildering" was too great.[140] To clarify the "confusion of the present times," English required the "eternal objects of poetry, among all nations, and at all times," objects that the "Greeks understood far more clearly than we do."[141] Because Greek poets had not subordinated "great action treated as a whole" to more impermanent aspects of literary expression, Greek literature remained rooted in what the "cultivated Athenian required," namely that the "permanent elements of his nature should be moved."[142] Such movement had been expressed most eloquently and most lucidly, Arnold argued, in Sophocles and in Homer whose work reflected "intense significance," "noble simplicity" and "calm pathos": both were therefore "excellent models" to shape new commensurate forms of writing in an otherwise rudderless modernity.[143]

Arnold himself tried to recast this 'Greek' form of permanence in his own idiom, fashioning in the narrative poem *Sohrab and Rustum* (1853) what Coventry Patmore (1823–96) called "a vivid reproduction of Homer's manner and spirit."[144] Drawing a story from Persian myth, he

---

[138] On these poetic stylizations of Greek, see Haynes (2003) 104–37.
[139] Haynes (2003) 115.
[140] Matthew Arnold, "Preface to Poems" (1853) in Arnold (1960) 12, 8.
[141] Arnold (1960) 8, 3, 5.
[142] Arnold (1960) 12, 6.
[143] Arnold (1960) 12, 8–9.
[144] Patmore (1854) 495. On the poem as evidence of the "direct influence of Greek upon English," see Clark (1923) 3–7, and Holloway (1967) 34–37.

set out to anglicize the "perfect plainness and directness" of Homeric Greek through parataxis and often literal translations of Greek similes, two conventions that Arnold believed could help anglicize "noble simplicity" and a "baldness of expression."[145] Yet, while influential, the classical ideals articulated by Arnold did not resemble Yeats' view of ancient civilization in Ireland, a primitive folk world that possessed, he thought, little clarity and less restraint – ancient Ireland was a fractured civilization, best represented by what Yeats called its "wild anarchy of legends."[146] Where Arnold found a grand style, a nobility, an order in Homeric epic, nothing of a *genus sublime dicendi* had yet to emerge in Irish; there remained instead a scattered collection of folk tales still in need of aesthetic stability.[147] "There behind the Ireland of to-day," Yeats explained, "lost in the ages, this chaos murmurs like a dark and stormy sea full of the sounds of lamentation. And through all these throbs one impulse – the persistence of Celtic passion."[148] Accordingly, in *Oisin* Yeats hoped to bring that passion and chaos into stricter form. Though he saw in Irish antiquity nothing of the order Arnold ascribed to Homer – and though Yeats also commonly ridiculed the English critic's influence in contemporary debates about modern poetry – he found the paratactic style of Arnold's Homeric imitation compelling;[149] and just as Arnold had done and as William Morris had attempted with his own 1887 ballad-style version of the *Odyssey*, Yeats too employed parataxis to pace *Oisin*, to give Anglo-Irish something of an epic, grand treatment.[150] Throughout *Sohrab and Rustum*, Arnold used the convention to mimic the "eminently rapid" quality, the plainness and directness he found in both the *Iliad* and the *Odyssey*.[151] In a similar way, Yeats sought to keep *Oisin* free from embedded clauses and unfettered by subordinate

---

[145] Arnold (1960) 116, 12, 6.

[146] Yeats *CW9* (2004) 112.

[147] Quintilian, *Institutio Oratoria* 11.1.3. See also Saint-Girons (2014) 1091–96.

[148] Yeats *CW9* (2004) 112.

[149] Yeats often derided Arnold's belief that poetry was a "criticism of life." "Great poetry does not teach us anything," he wrote in 1886, "it changes us ... Heroic poetry is a phantom finger swept over all the strings, arousing from man's whole nature a song of answering harmony. It is the poetry of action, for such alone can arouse the whole nature of man. It touches all the strings – those of wonder and pity, of fear and joy. It ignores morals, for its business is not in any way to make us rules for life, but to make character. It is not, as a great English writer has said, 'a criticism of life', but rather a fire in the spirit, burning away what is mean and deepening what is shallow." Yeats *CW9* (2004) 6. On Yeats' regard for Arnold, see Kelleher (1950) 197–221, Watson (2006) 36–58, Grene (2008) 197–204, and Schuchard (2008) 191–97.

[150] On William Morris and the reception of classical epic, see Tucker (2008) 511–12.

[151] Arnold (1960) 102.

complexities, preferring instead simple phrases linked with coordinating conjunctions – a hallmark of parataxis – as in this passage excerpted from the poem's first book.[152]

> And then I mounted and she bound me
> With her triumphing arms around me,
> And whispering to herself enwound me;
> But when the horse had felt my weight,
> He shook himself and neighed three times:
> Caoilte, Conan, and Finn came near,
> And wept, and raised their lamenting hands,
> And bid me stay, with many a tear;
> But we rode out from the human lands.
>
>   (1.106–14)[153]

Resolved to marry Niamh, "daughter of the King of the Young," Oisin rides to the strange, earthly paradise of *Tír na nÓg*, the homeland of his fairy bride and a safe haven for everlasting youth. On route, the poem's syntactic similarities to *Sohrab and Rustum* and other Victorian versions of Homer become apparent: sequenced with simple independent clauses and linked by coordinating conjunctions, Yeats forges a heroic measure, one parallel to the reputedly Greek rapidity Arnold attributed to Homer. Yet, however evocative its syntax may seem, the action of *Oisin* is slowed by a further complication, the syntax mired in what Oscar Wilde derided as the "out-glittering" effect of Yeats' diction.[154] One after another, Yeats elaborates the polysyndetonic images of *Tír na nÓg* in a florid, pictorial fashion, stressing the painted strangeness in the Celtic Otherworld – as in the passage that follows, where Niamh entices Oisin, invoking all the pleasures that will soon consume him, bit by bit, on the Island of Youth.

> "O Oisin, mount by me and ride
> To shores by the wash of the tremulous tide,
> Where men have heaped no burial-mounds,
> And the days pass by like a wayward tune,
> Where broken faith has never been known,
> And the blushes of first love never have flown;
> And there I will give you a hundred hounds;
> No mightier creatures bay at the moon;
> And a hundred robes of murmuring silk,
> And a hundred calves and a hundred sheep

---

152 On the "breaking of hypotaxis," see Adamson (1998) 630–46.
153 Yeats *VE* (1987) 9–10.
154 Wilde (July 12, 1889), as in Jeffares (1977) 73.

Whose long wool whiter than sea-froth flows;
And a hundred spears and a hundred bows,
And oil and wine and honey and milk,
And always never-anxious sleep;
While a hundred youths, mighty of limb,
By knowing nor tumult nor hate nor strife,
And a hundred ladies, merry as birds,
Who when they dance to a fitful measure
Have a speed like the speed of the salmon herds,
Shall follow your horn and obey your whim,
And you shall know the Danaan leisure;
And Niamh be with you for a wife."

(1.80–102)[155]

Niamh's enumeration of pleasures in this excerpt typifies the *enargeia*, the "extravagant picturesqueness" of *Oisin* whose "grotesque machinery" so irritated the poet William Watson (1858–1935) that he dismissed Yeats' Celtic "fantasies" as "stage-properties of the most unillusive kind."[156] Their visual intensity overburdened the poem and robbed it not only of excitement but also of the plainness that Arnold thought fitting for authentic Homeric poetry. Though they left the reader with elaborate impressions of "luxuriant fancy," *Oisin's* "beautiful fantasies" had nonetheless made the heroic struggle in *Tír na nÓg* seem dull and without drama.[157]

Though Arnold's principles for anglicizing Homer may have provided some model for Yeats to structure *Oisin*, he did not think plainness of diction, a diction marked with "baldness of expression," would best reflect or translate ancient Irish myth into the 'hybrid' vernacular he desired.[158] For Yeats, Ireland's folk stories had emerged in an altogether primitive world far from modernity, a foreign world "full of restless energies … as might be said of Greece."[159] That civilization possessed little of the "calm pathos" Arnold attributed to Homeric poetry, and so Yeats instead aimed to articulate in his Anglo-Irish idiom the so-called restlessness at work in the untamed Gael, whose "persistence of Celtic passion" had given birth to ancient Ireland's "wild anarchy of legends."[160] Accordingly, a competing form of Greek reception in English poetry

[155] Yeats *VE* (1987) 8–9.
[156] William Watson, A Review of "The Countess Kathleen and Various Legends and Lyrics," *Illustrated London News* (September 10, 1892), as in Jeffares (1977) 77.
[157] Francis Thompson, "A review of 'The Wanderings of Oisin and Other Poems'," *Weekly Register* (September 27, 1890), as in Jeffares (1977) 74.
[158] Arnold (1960) 6.
[159] Yeats *CW9* (2004) 111.
[160] Arnold (1960) 12; Yeats *CW9* (2004) 112.

made an indelible impact on the diction of *Oisin*.[161] An altogether different fashioning of Greek influence – a "rough high style, modelled especially on Aeschylus," a style that stressed disorder in English through "agglutination, and abruption rather than lucidity, translucence, and clarity" – features prominently in the poem, having been mediated to Yeats by the English Romantic he admired most in his youth, Shelley.[162] Shelley, Yeats believed, had portrayed in his *Prometheus Unbound* (1820) a strange archaic world, a world overrun with untrammeled energy, chaos and divine strife. The *Prometheus* showed a "grotesque, un-hellenic, unglorified" Greece, a dark Greece whose reception in the Anglophone world did not receive critical explanation until Walter Pater's essays on "The Myth of Demeter and Persephone" emerged in 1876.[163] Tracing the development of Demeter across the religious imagination of the Greeks, Pater suggested that a radical transformation was at work. At one time the veneration of the goddess

> belonged to that older religion, nearer to the earth, which some have thought they could discern behind the more definitely national mythology of Homer. She is the goddess of dark caves, and is not wholly free from monstrous form ... She is the goddess then of the fertility of the earth, in its wildness; and so far her attributes are to some degree confused with Thessalian Gaia and the Phrygian Cybele.[164]

Slowly, however, he observed, her monstrous, chthonic form had given way to the marmoreal image of the new classical world, the representation of the goddess becoming "replaced by a more beautiful image in the new style, with face and hands of ivory ... in tone and texture, some subtler likeness to women's flesh ... the closely enveloping drapery being constructed in daintily beaten plates of gold."[165]

Eager to portray Irish antiquity as full of "monstrous form," Yeats perhaps found the darker, anarchic vision expressed in *Prometheus* commensurate with the "vast pell-mell" of Gaelic folklore.[166] In *Oisin*, therefore, Shelley's stylization of the Greek is discernible in his diction in two specific ways. First, in imitation of Shelley, Yeats saturated the poem with privatives. In *Prometheus*, Shelley had used these generously, hoping to translate the common, alpha-privative construction found in ancient

---

[161] Haynes (2003) 104–37.
[162] Haynes (2003) 153.
[163] Pater (1876b) 269.
[164] Pater (1876a) 92.
[165] Pater (1876b) 270.
[166] Pater (1876a) 92; Yeats *CW9* (2004) 112.

Greek. Compared with other Indo-European languages, classical Greek has been said to possess what one study has called "a richer variety of forms of the negative prefix in compounds," and so Shelley exploited these, inventing neologisms, negative adjectives in English with the prefix 'un-' and the suffix '-less'.[167] He did so not simply to register the foreign presence of Greek in his work but to generate also an "obscuring effect" in his imagery, an effect that enacted within each privative a withdrawal, a Platonic stripping away of the "sensuous character of experience."[168]

> For Shelley the veil was the interposition of the material world between finite mind and Platonic idea; it was also the obscuring effect of concrete imagery, with its appeal to our senses, which his negative epithets were intended to remove. They withdraw the veil of sense-perception.[169]

The force of Shelley's negative adjectives helped drive the *Prometheus* from the familiar, "sensuous character" of native English, pushing the poem instead to a foreign ideal, to an anglicized Greekness whose strange, alien sound in English stressed "the intellectual, ideal world of Platonic forms" more than the 'native Doric'.[170]

At the time of writing *Oisin*, Yeats had little interest in the Platonic resonance of the *Prometheus*, but nevertheless Shelley's manner of manipulating Greek in English offered a suggestive model of composition, perhaps even an escape from his ignorance of Irish. "It is markedly in the Shelleian vein, or rather in one Shelleian vein," declared one contemporary critic of *Oisin*, "He is a fay hopped out of a corner of Shelley's brain."[171] Hoping to dislocate, to foreignize his own idiom, Yeats mimicked Shelley's practice to mask his English with apparent interference from Irish. In this way, the Celtic Otherworld Yeats sketched out in *Oisin* was also a conscious attempt at a *lingua dissimilitudinis*, a language of unlikeness pressed to evoke the ancient and Gaelic. To this end, as in this excerpt, Yeats' use of the privative did significant work:

> "Flee from him," pearl-pale Niamh weeping cried,
> "For all men flee the demons"; but moved not
> My angry king-remembering soul one jot.
> There was no mightier soul of Heber's line;
> Now it is old and mouse-like. For a sign

---

[167] Moorhouse (1959) 47.
[168] Buxton (1978) 159.
[169] Buxton (1978) 159, as quoted in Haynes (2003) 129.
[170] Buxton (1978) 159. On Shelley's use of negatives, see Webb (1983) 37–62.
[171] Thompson (September 27, 1890), as in Jeffares (1977) 74.

I burst the chain: still earless, nerveless, blind,
Wrapped in the things of the unhuman mind,
In some dim memory or ancient mood,
Still earless, nerveless, blind, the eagles stood.

(2.92–100)[172]

Here, the negatives obscure the psychic reverie of Oisin's adversaries, the "two old eagles, full of ancient pride," servants of the sea-god, Manannán mac Lir.[173] Transfixed by the Celtic past and wrecked by unseen "ancient things," their "unhuman" minds are now kept from both sight and sound in the present.[174] Denying the "presence of the attribute, which the positive describes," Yeats' privatives rupture the past and the present, stressing separation, not simply the passing of time but the passing from language to language as well. The negatives strip from the description the material "sensuous experience" of English, pushing Yeats' diction to denial: haunted by the absence of Irish Gaelic, his idiom possessed with its radical unlikeness to 'native' English expresses itself, paradoxically, through negative invention.[175]

The influence of Shelley's 'grecified' English is discernible also in Yeats' manipulation of numerous compound epithets throughout *Oisin*. A prominent feature of Shelley's *Prometheus*, compounds were widely regarded, from as early as the late sixteenth century, as evidence of ancient Greek interference in English. In his *Defence of Poesy* (1595), Philip Sidney (1554–86) praised English for being "particularly happy in compositions of two or three words together, near the Greek, far beyond the Latin: which is one of the greatest beauties can be in a language."[176] Likewise, George Puttenham's 1589 handbook on rhetoric, verse and prosody, *The Arte of English Poesy*, noted how "happy" the Greeks were with the "freedom and liberty of their language," a language that, Puttenham argued, had allowed them "to invent any new name that they listed and to piece many words together to make of them one entire, much more significative than the single word."[177] With the rise of Romanticism in Britain, growth in the poetic use of the compound followed, and its prominence in the work of Keats and of Shelley was greeted "with a whole-hearted enthusiasm not known before."[178] Shelley,

[172] Yeats *VE* (1987) 35–36.
[173] Yeats *VE* (1987) 34.
[174] Yeats *VE* (1987) 34, 36.
[175] Buxton (1978) 159. On the influence of *Prometheus* in Yeats' early work, see Bornstein (1970).
[176] Sidney (1983) 155.
[177] Puttenham (2007) bk 3, chap. 9, 241.
[178] Groom (1937) 309–10.

in particular, was drawn to the convention in his attempts to anglicize
the agglutinated "heavy compounds" of Aeschylean Greek.[179] Once satirized by Aristophanes in the *Frogs*, Aeschylus was known for his boldness
in employing a "multitude of long words."[180] As one scholar has put it,
the Greek poet "constantly builds an iambic trimeter out of four words
and not rarely out of three; and of those long words heavy compounds
form a large part ... Aeschylus in fact grows bolder in the formation of
new compounds, not, like Sophocles, more cautious."[181] Shelley, though
he confessed to taking "licence" with the received myth of Prometheus –
one which "supposed reconciliation of Jupiter with his victim" – set out
to replicate the verbal saturation that Aeschylus had mastered.[182] The
results, however, troubled contemporary critics of his work, who felt that
the macaronic idiom of the *Prometheus* was "intolerable," ruined, as one
writer put it, by "the very exaggeration, copiousness of verbiage, and
incoherence of ideas."[183]

> If the poet is one who whirls round his reader's brain, till it becomes dizzy
> and confused; if it is his office to envelop he knows not what in huge folds
> of a clumsy drapery of splendid words and showy metaphors, then,
> without doubt, may Mr. Shelley place the Delphic laurel on his head. But
> take away from him the unintelligible, the confused, the incoherent, the
> bombastic, the affected, the extravagant, the hideously gorgeous, and
> *Prometheus*, and the poems which accompany it, will sink at once into
> nothing.[184]

According to James Russell Lowell (1819–91), *Prometheus* embodied
"Shelley at his worst period," the poem possessing what he called an
"unwieldy abundance of incoherent words and images, that were merely
words and images without any meaning of real experience to give them
solidity."[185] No matter the reception, Shelley's aim had been an "elaborate
and grandiose diction" of verbal and visual depth whose roots were not
set in the familiar conventions of English poetry but outcrossed rather
with what Aristophanes had once satirized in *Frogs* as an "ungated
mouth, uncircumlocutory, a big bombastolocutor" – the ἀπύλωτον

---

[179] Earp (1948) 6.
[180] Earp (1948) 6.
[181] Earp (1948) 6, 9.
[182] Shelley, "Author's Preface" to *Prometheus Unbound* in Shelley (2002) 206.
[183] W. S. Walker, *The Quarterly Review* 26 (October 1821–January 1822) 177, as in Barcus (1975) 263.
[184] Walker (October 1821–January 1822) 177, as in Barcus (1975) 264.
[185] James Russell Lowell, Review of *The Life and Letters of James Gates Percival*. *North American Review* 104 (January 1867) 281, as in Barcus (1975) 269.

στόμα, ἀπεριλάλητον κομποφακελορρήμονα (*Fr.* 838–39) – of Aeschylean Greek.[186]

Though the reception of the *Prometheus* was tepid on publication, Yeats still thought it his "sacred book";[187] and, when in 1894 the London firm, T. Fisher Unwin offered to print a "new and corrected edition" of all of his previous poetry, Yeats used the opportunity to significantly revise *The Wanderings of Oisin*. Under Shelley's influence, he continued to use the *Prometheus* as a model for defamiliarizing, 'de-anglicizing' his idiom. Infusing the 1895 revision of *Oisin* with elaborate compound epithets, Yeats complicated the paratactic syntax inherited from Arnold's *Sohrab and Rustum*. In so doing, he hoped to strengthen the poem's visual character, to keep it from the bland literalism of previous versions. The journey to the Celtic Otherworld was to be saturated in fantastical poeticisms, as in this passage where Oisin and Niamh ride on to *Tír na nÓg*.

> And passing the Firbolgs' burial-mounds,
> Came to the cairn-heaped grassy hill
> Where passionate Maeve is stony-still;
> And found on the dove-grey edge of the sea
> A pearl-pale, high-born lady, who rode
> On a horse with bridle of findrinny;
> And like a sunset were her lips,
> A stormy sunset on doomed ships;
> A citron colour gloomed in her hair,
> But down to her feet white vesture flowed,
> And with the glimmering crimson glowed
> Of many a figured embroidery;
> And it was bound with a pearl-pale shell
> That wavered like the summer streams,
> As her soft bosom rose and fell.[188]
>
> (1.16–30)

Yet, though Yeats believed his compounds would stress the foreign character and strangeness of the Celtic world, the 1895 revision appears more derivative than its predecessor of 1889. Yeats' exaggerated word choice never reached the radical heights of Shelley's *Prometheus*: his "stony-still," "dove-grey," "high-born" and "pearl-pale" expose not a maturity of vision

---

[186] Earp (1948) 10. The translation is that of Jeffrey Henderson from the Loeb Classical Library edition, *Aristophanes: Frogs, Assemblywomen, Wealth* (Henderson 2002, 139).

[187] Yeats *CW3* (1999) 95.

[188] Yeats *VE* (1987) 3–4.

but rather an imitative foreign-ness, a fanciful epic that absorbed – largely naively – recent stylistic innovations of nineteenth-century England. Perhaps Yeats was aware of this, perhaps not; but in either case he would admit a certain discouragement with the poem in the preface to an 1895 revision of his poems. Though he had

> revised, and to a large extent re-written, *The Wanderings of Usheen* and the lyrics and ballads from the same volume … He has, however, been compelled to leave unchanged many lines he would have gladly re-written, because his present skill is not great enough to separate them from thoughts and expressions which seem to him worth preserving.[189]

Oisin, it seemed, had failed, and Yeats' dissatisfaction with the poem only increased as the years passed. His rising discontent became a standard feature in his discussions of further stylistic reinvention later in his work. In the memoir of 1922, *The Trembling of the Veil*, Yeats again faulted *Oisin* as "too elaborate, too ornamental," marred by a "vagueness of intention, and the inexactness of its speech."[190] Nonetheless, it was that vagueness – what he called the "sentimental sadness" and "womanish introspection" of his early verse – that would drive him, he often alleged, to a poetry of "prose directness" and "hard light."[191] "[W]hen I had finished *The Wanderings of Oisin*," he explained,

> dissatisfied with its yellow and its dull green, with all that overcharged colour inherited from the romantic movement, I deliberately reshaped my style, deliberately sought out an impression as of cold light and tumbling clouds. I cast off traditional metaphors and loosened my rhythm, and recognizing that all the criticism of life known to me was alien and English, became as emotional as possible but with an emotion which I described to myself as cold.[192]

The narrative of a leaner poetic idiom, a revised 'modernist self-fashioning' that Yeats advanced across his autobiographical writing, is compelling, and it did profoundly impact the negative reception that *Oisin* long endured. A work of "tortured symbolism, Pre-Raphaelite diction, and Romantic sensibility," it is said to have fallen "[f]ar from aspiring to an authentic Irish identification," a recent critic notes, "the exotic Celtic names and settings are mere decoration for the real

---

[189] Yeats (1895) v. On the 1895 revision, see Parkinson (1971) 1–50.
[190] Yeats *CW3* (1999) 279, 127.
[191] Yeats, "Letter to George Russell (Æ) [April 1904]," in Yeats *CL3* (1994) 577. Pound (1914) 66, 67. See Chapter 3, pp. 135–38.
[192] Yeats *CW3* (1999) 86.

substance of the poem: the allure of the imagination and the insatiable pursuit of desire."[193] However, taken without qualification, this can still obscure the intense "neo-romantic" impulse of Yeats' earliest revisions to his *oeuvre*: *Oisin*'s elaborate, seemingly Pre-Raphaelite fusion of Hellenisms was made all the more ornamental in the first attempted rewriting of the epic. Dissatisfied with the poem, however, Yeats had become demoralized by what he called "this endless war with Irish stupidity" in matters both political and literary, and as such he grew increasingly skeptical of his own epic ambitions for Ireland (that distrust would later be powerfully mediated through his reception of Sophoclean tragedy).[194] From as early as 1894, though, Yeats was already questioning whether any Irish writer could compose a poem that would "awaken or quicken or preserve" a coherent sense of nationality.[195] "My experience of Ireland, during the last three years," he explained,

> has changed my views very greatly, & now I feel that the work of an Irish man of letters must be not so much to awaken or quicken or preserve the national idea among the mass of the people but to convert the educated classes to it on the one hand to the best of his ability, & on the other – & this is the more important – to fight for moderation, dignity, & the rights of the intellect among his fellow nationalists. Ireland is terribly demoralized in all things – in her scholourship [*sic*], in her criticism, in her politics, in her social life.[196]

As Yeats saw it, what Ireland needed was not excess – neither in literary style nor in politics where new forms of anti-intellectual extremism threatened to restrict the country's poets and artists. What was required, he believed, was a creditable literary tradition, a national literature written with "laborious care" and "studied moderation of style."[197] *Oisin* had been tepidly received, and having failed to "convert the educated classes," the poem did little to rouse the kind of "national idea" Yeats hoped to mobilize across Irish society – to distinguish Ireland with a new epic and with the invention of a hybrid vernacular.[198] As such, Yeats began to purge his work of what he perceived as the note of 'false' Celticism; and yet, nevertheless, *Oisin*, even with its "overcharged colour," brought to bear on his early verse the ghostly pressures of

[193] Gomes (2014) 376.
[194] Yeats, "To Katharine Tynan Hinkson, 7 April [1895]," in Yeats *CL1* (1986) 458.
[195] Yeats, "To Alice Milligan, 23 September [1894]," in Yeats *CL1* (1986) 399.
[196] Yeats *CL1* (1986) 399.
[197] Yeats *CL1* (1986) 399.
[198] Yeats *CL1* (1986) 399.

languages lost, both those of the classical world and those of the Celtic.[199] Though Yeats had had no Irish, no Greek and very little Latin, the imaginative weight of these absences would later flourish across the British Isles in other responses to revival – not only in the work of Joyce's *Ulysses* but in the epic ambition of both Hugh MacDiarmid and David Jones as well. Their polyglot forms gained greater prominence as attempts to untether Anglophone expression from English 'ascendancy' led to new modes of modernist linguistic hybridity. These forms of experimental writing, however, sometimes stood in clear opposition to the nationalization of a Celtic 'classics', and as such questioned and satirized the very ground on which Yeats and others had forced a marriage between the Hellenic past and the desire for a de-anglicized future.

[199] Yeats *CW3* (1999) 86.

CHAPTER 2

"Hellenise It"
Joyce and the Mistranslation of Revival

"I am distressed and indignant," declared T. S. Eliot (1888–1965).[1] "[D]iscreet investigations" were warranted, he told Sylvia Beach (1887–1962), for a "conspiracy" against James Joyce's newly published novel, *Ulysses*, seemed to be afoot in England.[2] In the months since the book's 1922 printing in Paris, a number of English literary critics had come forward seeking press copies, but few actual reviews of the novel had appeared in British magazines and journals. Disheartened, Joyce himself explained to Harriet Shaw Weaver (1876–1961) that "certain critics" seemed keen to obtain the novel if only to then "boycott the book."[3] Eager to promote Joyce, Eliot interceded on his behalf, offering to "give publicity to the affair, if that were possible and desirable" while promising to review *Ulysses* himself.[4] Eliot saw in Joyce a sympathetic mind, for his "moulding a contemporary narrative upon an ancient myth" was "of interest to Yeats, Pound and myself," he explained, "though I have not yet found that it interests anyone else!"[5] His review, "*Ulysses*, Order, and Myth," appeared in *The Dial* in November 1923, but Eliot became despondent over what he had written for Joyce, believing his essay provided little "reason to be proud."[6] "I shall simply lose my reputation," he told the *Dial*'s editor, Gilbert Seldes (1893–1970), "and disgrace the periodicals for which I write."[7] Nevertheless, Eliot's "badly written" review, specifically its discussion of the "mythical method," left a lasting impression on Joyce.[8] "I like it and it comes opportunely," he told

---

[1] T. S. Eliot, "To Sylvia Beach, 4 April 1922," in Eliot *LTSE1* (2009) 658.
[2] Eliot *LTSE1* (2009) 658.
[3] James Joyce, "To Harriet Shaw Weaver, 10 April 1922," in Joyce *LJJ* (1957) 183.
[4] Eliot *LTSE1* (2009) 658.
[5] Eliot, "To Gilbert Seldes, 6 February 1923," in Eliot *LTSE2* (2009) 39.
[6] Eliot, "To Gilbert Seldes, 31 December 1923," in Eliot *LTSE2* (2009) 289.
[7] Eliot *LTSE2* (2009) 289.
[8] Eliot *LTSE2* (2009) 289; Eliot (1923) 483.

Harriet Weaver, "I shall suggest to him when I write to thank him that in alluding to it elsewhere he use or coin some short phrase, two or three words, such as one he used in speaking to me 'two plane'."[9] The "two plane" style at work in *Ulysses*, as Eliot saw it, was part of a small but influential movement, a movement that embraced a new way of composing poetry and narrative fiction in English: the "mythical method" drew on psychology, ethnology and, above all, the mythologies of ancient civilizations and their long reception histories. These elements Joyce had fused together in the collage of *Ulysses*, all to give "a shape and a significance" to the "immense panorama" of anarchy and unrest Eliot believed present in modernity.[10]

For Eliot, the influence of Homeric epic over *Ulysses* was unmistakable. However, too few critics, he thought, had taken Joyce's use of the Greek poet seriously, failing "to appreciate the significance of the method employed – the parallel to the Odyssey, and the use of appropriate styles and symbols to each division."[11] Many had been aware, no doubt, of the Homeric parallels at work in each episode of the novel, but too often these parallels were dismissed as "an amusing dodge, or scaffolding erected by the author for the purpose of disposing his realistic tale, of no interest in the completed structure."[12] Even Richard Aldington's article for *The English Review* had mistaken the novel's stylistic complexity for an "invitation to chaos," born from a "great undisciplined talent ... more dangerous than a ship-load of Dadaistes."[13] Eliot, for his part, however, was unwilling to ship Joyce out with the Dadaistes: *Ulysses* was no invitation to new forms of "vulgarity and incoherence" but the result rather of something admirably "classical in tendency" at work in Joyce and other modern writers.[14] That tendency, he explained, had not pushed him "like some contemporary writers" to turn "away from nine-tenths of the material which lies at hand ... selecting only mummified stuff from a

---

[9] Joyce, "To Harriet Shaw Weaver, 19 November 1923," in Joyce *LJJ3* (1966) 83.

[10] Eliot (1923) 483. On Eliot's mythical method and its reception, see Nikopoulos (2017) 292–311.

[11] Eliot (1923) 480.

[12] Eliot (1923) 480.

[13] Eliot (1923) 481; Aldington (1921) 339. Having outgrown his "fine precise prose" and the "Naturalisme of *Dubliners*," Joyce had chosen, Aldington insisted, to squander "his marvellous gifts" on a "more bitter, more sordid, more ferociously satirical" book intended only "to disgust us with mankind." A "tremendous libel on humanity," *Ulysses'* considerable influence was bound to be bad. "Young writers," Aldington claimed, "will be dominated by his personality; they will copy his eccentricities instead of developing their own minds. If only we could treat Mr. Joyce as Plato recommends; give him praise and anoint him with oil, and put a crown of purple wool on his head, and send him to the United States." Aldington (1921) 335, 336, 338, 336, 338, 336, 339–40.

[14] Aldington (1921) 341; Eliot (1923) 482.

museum."[15] Joyce was classical rather by having done "the best one can with the material at hand," by having been "responsible" to the "living material" born of the contemporary moment, a moment that encompassed what Eliot called a "whole complex of interests and modes of behaviour and society of which literature is a part."[16] Rather than reduce that complexity, Joyce employed a collage of experimental techniques to recast the "futility and anarchy" of the present, drawing on Homeric mythology and the reception history of the *Odyssey* to forge what Eliot called "a continuous parallel between contemporaneity and antiquity."[17] In advance of his time, he had not slipped into labyrinthine chaos but used rather prior receptions of antiquity to evolve new styles, to break down the English novel's obsolescent frame in pursuit of a "deep memorial palimpsest", one where various traces of Homeric receptions – fragments drawn up from the "penumbral zone residua of past impressions" – could be overwritten through Irish modernity.[18]

However, in so doing – contrary to Eliot's insistence upon order and structure – Joyce did not principally engage receptions of Homer to stabilize the so-called chaos or futility of the contemporary world. Rather, he felt what Steven Yao has called the "radical inability of established artistic forms and genres to confront and accurately represent the new realities of the world."[19] The classical past and the present moment were drastically incommensurate, and in his work Joyce sought to break the chain of recent Homeric receptions as sutured together in Ireland – to upset a philhellenic insistence on the coming of a new 'epic' order. Recent scholarship has stressed how pervasive the phenomenon of so-called non-translation – the "deliberate refusal to provide translations of foreign words, phrases and quotations" – was across prominent works of Anglo-American and Irish modernism.[20] While Joyce's refusal of Irish Hellenism did indeed employ the effects of multilingual collage, it was not built purely of 'non-translations' but also of intentional mistranslations, or slanted retranslations, of the Homeric. The "aesthetics of irreverence" Joyce cultivated not only challenged standardization, literalism and

---

[15] Eliot (1923) 482.
[16] Eliot (1923) 482.
[17] Eliot (1923) 483.
[18] De Quincey (1845) 742; *United States v. One Book Called "Ulysses."* 5 F.Supp. 182 (1933) – District Court, S. D. New York, December 6, 1933. See also Davenport (1987) 53–63.
[19] Yao (2002) 7.
[20] Harding and Nash (2019) 7. On the "theory of mistranslation" as an "aesthetics of irreverence," see Sergio Waisman's study of Jorge Luis Borges (1899–1986), *Borges and Translation: The Irreverence of the Periphery* (2005).

readerly expectation of translation but also made comical notions of broad semantic equivalence across languages and clear cultural correspondence between the ancient and the modern.[21] "[S]trategies of deliberate mistranslation," as Vera Kutzinski suggests, often enact "an aesthetics of theft and infidelity, in which even a so-called original can betray its translation."[22] As Joyce saw it, unwitting theft and infidelity had reigned over Revival-era receptions of the Homeric, but in that imaginative space – a space rife with mistranslation, misreading and misconstruction – he too saw possibilities for intentional acts of stylistic larceny in *Ulysses*. Words mistranslated, Irish receptions retranslated – though perhaps void of any literal fidelity to the Greek – could be turned to ironize the Revival's bold claims of "authoritative originality" and Homeric likeness.[23] To expose such claims – to attack what Gregory Castle has called "the ambivalent social position of Anglo-Irish Revivalists pursuing a project of cultural redemption" – *Ulysses* transposed the Revival's "obsessive alignment" with the Homeric world, mocking its incongruities and the distinctive authority Homer possessed among Joyce's contemporaries.[24] Rather than manipulate a correspondence with antiquity to bring on an Irish vision of Homeric order, Joyce drew on partial knowledge of ancient Greek, on classical scholarship and on recent 'Wardour-Street' styles of translationese to misalign mythological types and mistranslate the novel's correspondence with the *Odyssey*. With this hybridized, 'imperfect' idiom, *Ulysses*' irreverent aesthetic not only spurned neoclassical imitation but questioned the very authority of Greek in Ireland. No aggressive appropriation of classics or its prestige – no reading them "in the original" – could resuscitate an authentic past or somehow bring about a more Celtic future.[25]

According to Eliot, the mythical method as practiced by Joyce was not an entirely new phenomenon: the novelist, he claimed, had been drawn to it aware of it being "already adumbrated by Mr Yeats."[26] As Denis

[21] Waisman (2005) 124.
[22] Kutzinski (2012) 100–1.
[23] Kutzinski (2012) 100.
[24] Castle (2001) 30–31; Platt (1998) 110. The novel's use of mistranslation in 'corresponding' with Homer is present at the outset of the book when Buck Mulligan comically renders οἶνοπα ('winedark') as both "scrotumtightening" and "snotgreen" while admonishing Stephen Dedalus to read the Greeks "in the original." Joyce *Ulysses* (1986) 4–5 (1.77–81). See Chapter 2, pp. 115–19.
[25] Joyce *Ulysses* (1986) 4–5 (1.79–80).
[26] Eliot (1923) 483.

Donoghue has suggested, Eliot believed that, on reading the 1910 collection *The Green Helmet and Other Poems*, Joyce may have taken note of both "A Woman Homer Sung" and "No Second Troy," two poems in which Yeats had "presented a personage distinct from himself; and did so precisely by relating that personage to a legendary or mythic figure more distant still."[27] Although Ezra Pound had praised "No Second Troy" as emblematic of "the spirit of the new things" in literature, whether Joyce held that poem in high regard is unclear.[28] What is clear was Eliot's desire to cast Joyce as 'classical' and to set *Ulysses'* Homeric contours in a line of descent emerging from Yeats. That, however, obscures more than it reveals, for from as early as 1901, when Joyce published his pamphlet "The Day of the Rabblement" in protest against the Irish theatre, he questioned the genius of Yeats.[29] Later, on first meeting the poet, he told Yeats "his own little book" of poems, *Chamber Music*, was a greater achievement than Yeats' recent work, because it "owed nothing to anything but his own mind which was much nearer to God than folklore."[30] Yeats retorted that "one gets great art, the art of Homer, and of Shakespeare, and of Chartres Cathedral" when the life of the artist is married to the collective will and popular imagination of a nation's "folk life."[31] However, for Joyce, the notion of making art wholly reliant "on emotions or stories" taken from folklore and mythology seemed passé.[32] No conscription of antiquity, Celtic or classical, could make the Literary Revival worthwhile – no matter how often Yeats insisted that he could

> make the land in which we live a holy land as Homer made Greece, the Anciant [*sic*] Indians India & the Hebrew Prophets Judea ... for the celtic races love the soil of their countries vehemently, & have as great a mass of legends about that soil as Homer had about his ... the life that is in legends is still the life of Homers [*sic*] people.[33]

---

[27] Donoghue (1997) 215. See Introduction, pp. 33–34, Chapter 3, pp. 135–38, and the Conclusion, pp. 248–50.

[28] Ezra Pound, "23: Ezra Pound to Margaret Cravens, 27 November [1910]," in Pound (1988) 61.

[29] Joyce, "The Day of the Rabblement" (1901), in Joyce *CWJJ* (1989) 68–72.

[30] Ellmann (1950) 625.

[31] Ellmann (1950) 626.

[32] Ellmann (1950) 625.

[33] Yeats, "To Richard Ashe King, 5 August [1897]," in Yeats *CL2* (1997) 129, 130. Yeats often reiterated this view of Greek antiquity during the Revival. Lecturing in 1901 before the Literary Society of Dublin, he likened Irish legends to those of Greece: "The Greeks looked within their borders, and we, like them, have a history fuller than any modern history of imaginative events; and legends which surpass, as I think, all legends but theirs in wild beauty, and in our land, as in theirs, there is no river or mountain that is not associated in the memory with some event or legend ... I would have Ireland recreate the ancient arts, the arts as they were understood in Judaea, in India, in

Despite Joyce's skepticism, however, Yeats had persuaded many nationalist sympathizers to believe in Ireland's "correspondence with classical
Greece."[34] As Fiona Macintosh has observed, "many efforts to 'celticise'
Ireland from the 1880s onwards were ... veiled attempts to 'hellenise'
Ireland by aligning the burgeoning nation with what was perceived to be
the ideal nation-state."[35] Suggested first perhaps in the popular histories
of Standish James O'Grady (1846–1928), the insistence upon an essential
likeness – on a close analogical link – between the Gael and the Greek
had become by the turn of the century "a standard feature" in "the
jargon of contemporary critical approval amongst revivalists," so much
so that Yeats felt in hearing "my own unfinished *On Baile's Strand* ...
Greek tragedy, spoken with a Dublin accent."[36] Joyce, however, had no
desire to imitate that accent. While still an undergraduate, he denigrated
those who believed that ancient Greek poetry still held sway over
modern letters, whether in Ireland or elsewhere. Speaking at University
College, Dublin, in 1900, Joyce warned that blind adherence to antiquity's "code of laws," the "syllabus of greenroom proprieties and cautions
to authors" that had emerged on the Peloponnese, would only kill the
coming of new genius.[37] "[P]urblind wisdom," he explained, had
advanced the conventions of Greek poetry "to the dignity of inspired
pronouncements," but so far as these pronouncements pertained to
modern theatre at least, Joyce insisted it was the "literal truth to say that

Scandinavia, in Greece and Rome, in every ancient land; as they were understood when they moved
a whole people and not a few people who have grown up in a leisured class and made this understanding their business." Yeats, "Ireland and the Arts" (August 1901), in Yeats *CW4* (2007) 151–52.
See Chapter 1, pp. 57–61, 65–67. Yeats inherited this 'folk' view of Homer not only from William
Maginn's ballad-style translations but also from his devotion to Samuel Ferguson, whose critical
reception was often framed with Homeric comparisons. Ferguson's *Congal* (1872) was widely praised
as a work possessing "Homeric felicity." "No poem," one contemporary wrote, "so Homeric in the
march of the narrative, in the character of the heroes, or in the resonant majesty of the versification,
has appeared in our time, and withal it is thoroughly and in essence Celtic." Ferguson (1888) 5. See
also O., "The Poetry of Sir Samuel Ferguson, The Epic of 'Congal'" *The Irish Monthly* 12 (1884) 218.

[34] Platt (1998) 113.
[35] Macintosh (1994) 4.
[36] Platt (1998) 112, 113. Yeats *CW3* (1999) 331. In *History of Ireland: Critical and Philosophical* (1881),
O'Grady claimed for Ireland a history deeper than that of Greek civilization. "I cannot help," he
wrote, "regarding this age and the great personages moving therein as incomparably higher in
intrinsic worth than the corresponding ages of Greece. In Homer, Hesiod, and the Attic poets,
there is a polish and artistic form, absent in the existing monuments of Irish heroic thought, but
the gold, the ore itself, is here massier and more pure, the sentiment deeper and more tender, the
audacity and freedom more exhilarating, the reach of imagination more sublime, the depth and
power of the human soul more fully exhibit themselves." O'Grady (1881) vol. 1: 201. See also Platt
(1998) 111–13.
[37] Joyce, "Drama and Life" (1900) in Joyce *CWJJ* (1989) 39.

Greek drama is played out. For good or for bad it has done its work, which, if wrought in gold, was not upon lasting pillars."[38] Like the ghostly Michael Furey – whose "partial darkness ... standing under the dripping tree" tormented Gabriel Conroy – ancient *exempla* were nostalgic enticements, a menace to artistic invention.[39] No past moment, no past form could be effectively resurrected, and to saddle contemporary writers with the burden of revival, whether it be of Gaelic Ireland, Homeric Greece or any other ancient civilization, was to invite not new achievement but an insidious romanticism.[40] For this reason, "Hellenism" itself, he declared in 1904, was a "European appendicitis" – one whose advent in Irish literature would nurse only "regressive dreams of a return to the past."[41]

Nevertheless, Joyce remained attracted to the difficulties presented by Hellenism in European literature, and in early 1907, as he was trying to summon Dublin's "ingenuous insularity and its hospitality" in writing "The Dead," his focus turned again to its assertion in Ireland.[42] Though living abroad, Joyce was then engrossed with recent news from Dublin. Late that January, John Synge's new play, *The Playboy of the Western World* (1907), had premiered at the Abbey Theatre to riots and violent protest. According to the *Irish Independent*, those "who had the opportunity of seeing, and hearing, the play on its first production, with few exceptions, left the Abbey Theatre with a sense of having been fooled" by what the newspaper called an "act of inexplicable stupidity" and a "perpetration of this gross offence against Art and Truth."[43] *The Freeman's Journal*, similarly, pronounced the *Playboy* an "unmitigated, protracted libel upon Irish peasant men, and worse still, upon Irish peasant girlhood," whose "squalid, offensive production, incongruously styled a comedy in three acts" made its repulsiveness "quite plain."[44] Although the Abbey was "seriously and widely recognised as a home of drama" possessing "culture and thoughtfulness," there was then a "need for a censor."[45] In the face of these accusations, Synge himself reportedly "had little to say" (though he did sarcastically allude to "having at last got something like a fair

---

[38] Joyce *CWJJ* (1989) 39.
[39] Joyce *Dubliners* (1993) 383.
[40] On Joyce's view of romanticism, see Power (1974) 98–99.
[41] Joyce (1965) 91; Kiberd (1996) 329.
[42] Joyce, "To Stanislaus Joyce, 25 September 1906," in Joyce *SLJJ* (1975) 110.
[43] "The 'National' Theatre," *Irish Independent* (January 31, 1907) 4.
[44] "The Abbey Theatre, *The Playboy of the Western World*," *The Freeman's Journal* (January 28, 1907) 10, in Kilroy (1971) 7, 9.
[45] *The Freeman's Journal* (January 28, 1907) 10, in Kilroy (1971) 7, 9.

hearing").[46] Yeats, however, was eager to use the dispute to further advance his vision of the theatre. The week following the premiere, Yeats led a public debate at the Abbey on "the Freedom of the Theatre."[47] According to *The Freeman's Journal*, its arguments were "noisy, farcical, and at one period disgusting."[48] Taking stage with the journalist P. D. Kenny (1862–1944), the poet was met with a "very mixed reception" that evening, "cheers and hisses" rising from an audience that was, in part at least, "in favour of the creation of a censorship in Ireland."[49] The poet, however, was adamant that the "dispute" that

> lay between them [between the Abbey and the public] was one of prin-
> ciple (A Voice – 'That won't wash'). There was one thing no one there
> would say he flinched from his fight (cheers). He was not a public enter-
> tainer (laughter), he was an artist (renewed laughter), setting before them
> what he believed to be fine works (hisses and laughter), to see and insist
> that they shall receive a quiet and respectful attention (laughter, hisses, and
> cheers).[50]

Writing to his brother from Rome, Joyce delighted in imagining the Abbey convulse under public pressure. Synge's "very gross and wanton insult to the Irish people" and the ensuing discussion "must have been very funny," he quipped, for the "pulpit Irishman is a good fellow to the stage Irishman ... As I told you before I think the Abbey Theatre is ruined. It is supported by the stalls, that is to say, Stephen Gwynn, Lord X, Lady Gregory etc., who are dying to relieve the monotony of Dublin life."[51] The support Yeats had thrown behind the Abbey Theatre had long been a source of both wonder and loathing for Joyce. Years earlier, he had implored Yeats to break "with the half-gods" of the Dublin stage; otherwise how could it be known, he exclaimed, whether or not Yeats, in fact, "has or has not genius."[52] What Yeats did have, he argued, was "a floating will," as well as a "treacherous instinct of adaptability" for which one could blame his association with the Abbey Theatre, "a platform from which even self-respect should have urged him to refrain."[53] 'Self-respect'

[46] "Mr. Synge 'Beaming'," *Evening Herald* (February 1, 1907) 5.
[47] "The 'Freedom of the Theatre'," *The Freeman's Journal* (February 5, 1907) 7. On the debate, see Yeats *CL4* (2005) 862–85.
[48] "Parricide and Public – Discussion at the Abbey Theatre," *The Freeman's Journal* (February 5, 1907) 6.
[49] *The Freeman's Journal* (February 5, 1907) 6.
[50] *The Freeman's Journal* (February 5, 1907) 6.
[51] *The Freeman's Journal* (January 29, 1907) 6; Joyce, "To Stanislaus Joyce, 11 February 1907," in Joyce *LJJ2* (1966) 211–12.
[52] Joyce *CWJJ* (1989) 71.
[53] Joyce *CWJJ* (1989) 71.

once again did not keep Yeats from defending the Abbey, and courting "the favour of an Irish mob and its leaders" before whom he appeared, Joyce thought, "a tiresome idiot ... quite out of touch with the Irish people."[54] The poet's disaffection was perhaps most evident in the exaggerated claims he made trying to persuade others of Synge's worth. As the philologist, R. I. Best (1872–1959) later recalled, Yeats did not merely think Synge equal with the greatest of Greek tragedians; he was convinced that he possessed no less than "all the talent of Aeschylus and Sophocles combined."[55] For that reason, Synge seemed, to Yeats at least, the ideal playwright to advance in Ireland "a dramatic art which the Englishman of the time of Shakespeare and the Greek of the time of Sophocles and the Spaniard of the time of Calderon and the Indian of the time of the Kaladasa would have recognised as akin to their own great art."[56] Joyce himself made few remarks on the essential quality of Synge's work, except to say that by 1907 he had "read only one play of his *Riders to the Sea*," but even then he amusedly noted that that play had "made Yeats first think of the Greeks (who are always with us)."[57]

For the rest of the winter, the crisis roiling the Abbey Theatre hung over Joyce. "This whole affair has upset me," he told his brother, "I feel like a man in a house who hears a row in the street and voices he knows shouting but can't get out to see what the hell is going on."[58] To clear his mind, he turned to preparing a series of lectures he had been asked to give at Trieste's Università del Popolo. Yet rather than directly address the present controversy in Dublin, he chose instead to scrutinize the political and cultural history of Ireland, examining in part the ground on which claims of an alleged "Greek kinship" might be based.[59] "Is this country destined," he wondered, "to resume its ancient position as the

---

54 S. Joyce (2003) 181; Joyce, "To Stanislaus Joyce, (11 February 1907)," in Joyce *LJJ2* (1966) 211; on Yeats' behavior during the debate, see Kilroy (1971) as well as Kavanagh (1950) 53–60. See also A. Murphy (2017) 94–96.

55 Rodgers (1973) 104.

56 Yeats, "To the Editor of the *United Irishman*, c. 21 April 1902," in Yeats *CL3* (1994) 179. See also Flannery (1976) 65–67.

57 Joyce, "To Stanislaus Joyce, 11 February 1907," in Joyce *LJJ2* (1966) 212.

58 Joyce, "To Stanislaus Joyce, 11 February 1907," in Joyce *LJJ2* (1966) 212.

59 The phrase "Greek kinship" was used by John Synge in a 1904 review of Marie Henri d'Arbois de Jubainville's *The Irish Mythological Cycle and Celtic Mythology* (1903), translated from the French by Richard Irvine Best. Synge praised the book, arguing that it demonstrated how "Irish mythology has been found to give, with the oldest mythology that can be gathered from the Homeric poems, the most archaic phase of Indo-European religion." Synge, "Celtic Mythology" (April 2, 1904) in Synge (1966) 365. On Synge's view of "Homeric realism" and Ireland's relation to the "classics of Greece," see also Stephens (1974) 65–67. See also Chapter 1, pp. 67–68.

Hellas of the north some day?"[60] The irony of Joyce's question masked the antipathy for revivalism and certain forms of cultural nationalism that motivated the first lecture, "Ireland, Island of Saints and Sages." There, he suggested that nations all too often eagerly cultivate their own "ego," quickened by the desire to "attribute to themselves qualities and glories foreign to other people."[61] "[F]rom the time of our ancestors, who called themselves Aryans and nobles," he explained, this tendency was all too common, pervasive even among "the Greeks, who called all those who lived outside the sacrosanct land of Hellas barbarians. The Irish, with a pride that is perhaps less easy to explain, love to refer to their country as the island of saints and sages."[62] Rather than recall antiquity to commend the nationalist fervor at work in Ireland, Joyce drew on the alleged likeness with ancient Greece to cast a cold eye on the broad practice of cultural appropriation rife within the Literary Revival. "We Irishmen," he declared, quoting a statement Yeats often attributed to Oscar Wilde, "have done nothing, but we are the greatest talkers since the time of the Greeks."[63] Yet no matter how "eloquent" – how 'talkatively' Hellenic the Irish seemed – Joyce insisted that "a revolution is not made of human breath and compromises."[64] Though Ireland's "fountain of nationality" was said to be classical at its source – the "root-stories of the Greek poets are told to-day at the cabin fires of Donegal," Yeats asserted – Joyce felt such claims were a "convenient fiction" for a country and people that could endure no more "equivocations and misunderstandings."[65] If Ireland were again "to enrich the civil conscience with new discoveries and new insights," if 'she' were "truly capable of reviving, let her awake, or let her cover up her head and lie down decently in her grave forever."[66] An authentic revival could neither be predicated on nostalgia for past achievements nor be realized by heaping "insults on England for her misdeeds in Ireland."[67] So long as Joyce's contemporaries were content to confront English influence with "bitter invectives" and "empty boasts," he asserted, no "revival of this

---

[60] Joyce, "Ireland, Island of Saints and Sages" (1907) in Joyce *CWJJ* (1989) 172.

[61] Joyce *CWJJ* (1989) 154.

[62] Joyce *CWJJ* (1989) 154.

[63] Cited in Joyce *CWJJ* (1989) 174.

[64] Joyce *CWJJ* (1989) 174.

[65] Yeats, "To the Editor of *United Ireland*, 17 December 1892," in Yeats *CL1* (1986) 340; Yeats *CW9* (2004) 210. See also Joyce *CWJJ* (1989) 166, 174. See Chapter 1, pp. 53–63.

[66] Joyce *CWJJ* (1989) 173, 174.

[67] Joyce *CWJJ* (1989) 166.

race" would come.[68] Even though "the art of miniature in the ancient Irish books, such as the *Book of Kells*, the *Yellow Book of Lecan*, the *Book of the Dun Cow*" was said to "date back to a time when England was an uncivilized country," being "almost as old as the Chinese," appropriating that past guaranteed little for Ireland's future.[69] "If an appeal to the past in this manner were valid," Joyce explained, "the fellahin of Cairo would have all the right in the world to disdain to act as porters for English tourists."[70] Joyce associated this naive, romantic view of national history not only with cultural nationalists in Ireland but, later, with the Italian irredentism he encountered in Trieste as well. As John McCourt has noted,

> the Triestine irredentists turned a blind eye to the complexities of the past in order to present a mythical vision of it which they hoped to re-create in the future ... Joyce would never accept this use of history, whether it was written by [Attilio] Tamaro or [Pádraig] Pearse, whose version of patriotism, as enunciated in 1914, was close to what the irredentists sought from their supporters in Trieste.[71]

Yet to disavow the "pejorative conception of Ireland" would not be easy, Joyce thought; the past was not a repository for the "old national soul" of Gaelic Ireland, a place from which one could recover a purity of Celtic race and language.[72] Because the Revival had popularized fear of further mongrelization, the language movement had been eager to rediscover a 'classical' integrity in Irish – the 'purer' tongue whose revitalization would help rid Ireland of what D. P. Moran (1869–1936), the founder of the nationalist paper *The Leader*, once called the "English-speaking, English-imitating mongrel."[73] As Joyce saw it, however, the languages and histories of Irish civilization had always been marked by continual infusions and repeated intrusions from a variety of foreign influences: "What race, or what language," he exclaimed, "can boast of being pure today? And no race has less right to utter such a boast than the race now living in Ireland."[74] The linguistic, racial, religious and indeed the cultural complexities of the Irish had never been "pure and

---

[68] Joyce *CWJJ* (1989) 173.
[69] Joyce *CWJJ* (1989) 173.
[70] Joyce *CWJJ* (1989) 173.
[71] McCourt (2000) 99.
[72] Joyce *CWJJ* (1989) 171, 173.
[73] Moran (2006) 35. On Irish Gaelic as a "repository of Irishness," see Crowley (2005) 128–63 as well as the Introduction, pp. 12–27 and Chapter 1, pp. 49–53.
[74] Joyce *CWJJ* (1989) 165–66.

virgin" but especially hybridized – what he called "a vast fabric, in which the most diverse elements are mingled, in which nordic aggressiveness and Roman law, the new bourgeois conventions and the remnant of a Syriac religion are reconciled."[75] Thus any attempt to extract a pure thread, an authentic or original thread that might "exclude from the present nation all who are descended from foreign families," was both intellectually bankrupt and socially repugnant.[76] "[T]o deny," he declared, "the name of patriot to all those who are not of Irish stock would be to deny it to almost all the heroes of the modern movement."[77] A figure no less powerful and compelling than Charles Stewart Parnell (1846–1891) had "not even a drop of Celtic blood," though he appeared to Joyce, at least, "the most formidable man that ever led the Irish."[78] No resurgence of nationality could take place if the "backward and inferior" people now dwelling in the country held intractably to a time, place and language beyond reach of resurrection.[79] "Ancient Ireland is dead," he asserted, "just as ancient Egypt is dead. Its death chant has been sung, and on its gravestone has been placed the seal."[80]

If an authentic sense of nationality were to emerge, it had to "find its reason for being rooted in something that surpasses and transcends and informs changing things like blood and the human word."[81] Paraphrasing Pseudo-Dionysius' *De Coelesti Hierarchia* – that Ἔστησε γὰρ ὁ ὕψιστος ὅρια ἐθνῶν κατὰ ἀριθμὸν ἀγγέλων θεοῦ (9.2), (in Joyce's translation, "God has disposed the limits of nations according to his angels") – Joyce suggested that nationality could be better aligned with the Greek notion of ἔθνος.[82] Broadly signifying – though not indisputably so – "a number of people living together," ἔθνος was preferable to γένος because "in Ireland the Danes, the Firbolgs, the Milesians from Spain, the Norman invaders, and the Anglo-Saxon settlers have united to form a new entity."[83] That new entity, that "new Celtic race ...

---

[75] Joyce *CWJJ* (1989) 165. See also Platt (1992) 259–66.

[76] Joyce *CWJJ* (1989) 161–62.

[77] Joyce *CWJJ* (1989) 162.

[78] Joyce *CWJJ* (1989) 162.

[79] Joyce *CWJJ* (1989) 166.

[80] Joyce *CWJJ* (1989) 173. On Joyce's "exposé of an Ireland frozen in servitude," see Kiberd (1996) 334–38.

[81] Joyce *CWJJ* (1989) 166.

[82] For *De Coelesti Hierarchia*, see Heil and Ritter (1991) 37; Joyce *CWJJ* (1989) 166. See also Deuteronomy 32:8.

[83] Joyce *CWJJ* (1989) 166; on Greek notions of race and ethnicity, see Jones (1997); Cohen (2009) as well as Hall (1997) and Jones (1996) 315–20. Joyce gave partial expression to this view of nationality in Leopold Bloom's generous though waffling definition of a nation in *Ulysses*. See Joyce *Ulysses* (1986) (12.1419–1431) 271–72.

compounded of the old Celtic stock and the Scandinavian, Anglo-Saxon, and Norman races," needed collective expression, but one that embraced all aspects of Ireland's cultural hybridity, better articulating the many complexities in its "national temperament."[84] Weakened by "centuries of useless struggle and broken treaties," Ireland's poor "economic and intellectual conditions" had increasingly left the prospects for "individual initiative ... paralysed."[85] For that reason, he explained, "[n]o one who has any self-respect stays in Ireland, but flees afar as though from a country that has undergone the visitation of an angered Jove";[86] and no appropriation of Greek antiquity, he insisted, could dim that anger or further mend the "old national soul that spoke during the centuries through the mouths of fabulous seers, wandering minstrels, and Jacobite poets."[87]

Following the lecture, Joyce grew, it seems, more reluctant to publicly address matters of national significance.[88] Even as armed attempts at revolution broke out in Ireland over the next decade, even as war erupted across Europe, he wrote comparatively little on these matters. That reticence led Yeats to assume that Joyce wanted little "to do with Irish politics, extreme or otherwise."[89] "I think he disliked politics," the poet told Edmund Gosse (1849–1928):

> He always seemed to me to have only literary and philosophic sympathies. To such men the Irish atmosphere brings isolation, not anti-English feeling. He is probably trying at this moment to become absorbed in some piece of work till the evil hour is passed. I again thank you for what you have done for this man of genius.[90]

Joyce was indeed "absorbed in some piece of work" at that time, but Yeats mistook his relative silence on political matters for a lack of civic commitment.[91] In March 1914, Joyce had in fact approached the publisher Angelo Formiginni (1878–1938) of Modena about collecting nine essays on contemporary politics in Ireland, essays that he had written for the Triestine newspaper *Il Piccolo della Sera* over the previous

[84] Joyce *CWJJ* (1989) 161.
[85] Joyce *CWJJ* (1989) 171.
[86] Joyce *CWJJ* (1989) 171.
[87] Joyce *CWJJ* (1989) 173–74.
[88] Joyce was asked to deliver three lectures at Trieste's Università del Popolo in 1907, but after completing a draft of a second lecture on the poet James Clarence Mangan he gave only the first. See Ellmann (1982) 258–60.
[89] Yeats, "To Edmund Gosse, 28 August [1915]," in Yeats *LWBY* (1955) 601.
[90] Yeats *LWBY* (1955) 601.
[91] Yeats *LWBY* (1955) 601.

decade. "[T]he Irish problem has reached an acute phase," he explained, and "England, owing to the Home Rule question, is on the brink of civil war."[92] Though Joyce felt the essays possessed "absolutely no literary value," he was convinced they still set out current problems facing Ireland "sincerely and objectively."[93] Yet the book *L'Irlanda alla Sbarra* never went to press.[94] Nonetheless the energy Joyce intended for the revision of these essays he began to rechannel into what Georgio Melchiori has character-ized as a recovery of his "creative powers."[95] That recovery eventually found radical expression in "Cyclops," where Joyce expanded the critique of revivalism he had begun in 1907, working it into the episode's contorted manipulation of perspective, pleonasm and hyperbolic description – elements Joyce drew, in part, from his complex reception of Homer and Greek antiquity.

In the summer of 1919, as reports of social unrest and violence against the Royal Irish Constabulary reached Joyce (by then living in Zurich), he began to break his silence. He had long been disabused of the notion that a peaceful, legislative solution to the question of Irish sovereignty would come about, but as Richard Ellmann observed, these "recent events" did not please him "even though they represented the triumph of the Sinn Féin principles which in Rome and Trieste he had vigorously espoused."[96] With the election of December 1918, the fortunes of the moderate Irish Parliamentary Party (IPP) had been crushed: of the sixty-seven seats the IPP held before the election, only six remained.[97] In their stead, Sinn Féin prevailed, promising both to withdraw "Irish Representation from the British Parliament" and to oppose "the will of the British Government or any other foreign Government to legislate for Ireland."[98] By refusing to stand in Westminster, Sinn Féin intended to establish in Dublin a "counter-state," the first *Dáil Éireann* on January 21, 1919.[99] The country was soon declared a nation free to take action "in arms against foreign usurpation," against English rule that "always has been, based

---

[92] Joyce, "To Angelo Formiginni" (March 25, 1914) in Melchiori (1981).

[93] Melchiori (1981).

[94] Melchiori suggests that Joyce's letter to Formiginni was "never answered" due to the outbreak of the First World War, which complicated pathways for communication for those living in Trieste.

[95] Melchiori (1981).

[96] Ellmann (1982) 533.

[97] The election proved to be a decisive defeat not only for the IPP but for moderates within Sinn Féin as well. See Townshend (2014) 58–63, as well as Knirck (2006) 45–48.

[98] Éamon De Valera, *The Testament of the Republic* (c. 1924) 4. On Sinn Féin's post-election strategy, see Townshend (2014) 64–66.

[99] See the chapter "Building the Counter-State" in Mitchell (1995) 43–119.

upon force and fraud and maintained by military occupation against the declared will of the people."[100] Amid these circumstances, Joyce tried to begin "Cyclops," aware perhaps that the sweeping historical change and political turmoil then taking place in Ireland would make stylizing an episode focused on 'one-eyed' nationalism difficult.[101] For "the changing styles of *Ulysses*," as W. J. McCormack writes,

> do not so much chronicle the events of one specific day as they seek to come to terms with the changing perspectives upon a 'fixed' day which a revolutionary period generated. *Ulysses* is thus historical in two senses, first in that it takes as its setting a date which is progressively seen as historical; and second, as a stylistic consequence, the process of composition itself is historicized.[102]

Complicating matters further was the fact that the experimental character of *Ulysses* had increasingly divided opinion among both friends and critics. The recently completed episode, "Sirens," had been received tepidly in London, where Ezra Pound complained of Joyce's "*obsessions arseore-ial.*"[103] One could "fahrt with less pomp & circumstance," he argued, "any obsession or tic shd. be very carefully considered before being turned loose. Besides. Bloom has been disproportionately on ??? or hasn't he. Where in hell is Stephen Tellemachus?"[104] Further, Joyce, it seems, found himself mired in a "state of blank apathy out of which it seems that neither I nor the wretched book will ever more emerge ... If the *Sirens* have been found so unsatisfactory I have little hope," he told Harriet Shaw Weaver, "that the *Cyclops*, or later the *Circe* episode will be approved of: and, moreover, it is impossible for me to write these episodes quickly. The elements needed will only fuse after a prolonged existence together."[105] Though progress was halting, Joyce did fuse a draft of "Cyclops" together by September 1919, in part by revisiting his 1907 lecture and the scrutiny he gave to Irish Hellenism. Intent on exposing its absurdities, Joyce manipulated the structure of "Cyclops" broadly, misaligning the 'high' and 'low' idiomatic registers that had been used to stylize – to hallow even – Ireland's 'Greek kinship' in revivalist writing.

---

[100] Éamon De Valera, *The Testament of the Republic* (c. 1924) 8.
[101] McCormack (1985) 280–81.
[102] McCormack (1985) 280.
[103] Ezra Pound, Letter to James Joyce (June 10, 1919) in Pound (1970) 158. See also Ellmann (1982) 459.
[104] Pound, Letter to James Joyce (June 10, 1919) in Pound (1970) 158.
[105] Joyce, "To Harriet Shaw Weaver (20 July 1919)," in Joyce *LJJ* (1957) 128.

It has been widely noted – by Hugh Kenner and by Ron Bush – that *Ulysses* was composed at a time when scholarship on the ancient Greek world rapidly altered not only popular perceptions of Homeric antiquity but artistic engagements with Homer as well.[106] The once provocative controversy that had engulfed the Homeric question in the nineteenth century – namely whether the *Iliad* and the *Odyssey* were works, as F. A. Wolf had argued, of multiple authors or whether the epics were, as Matthew Arnold insisted, the work of a grand style and very likely one noble mind – had given way, as Bush notes, to a greater consideration of the "Trojan cycle's social world."[107] The Victorian debate over authorship exerted significant influence in Yeats' and others' efforts to rework ballads drawn from Irish folklore into a new national epic.[108] By the turn of the century, though, the dominant questions surrounding the nature of Homeric epic had shifted, as wide-ranging scholarly speculation into the concrete, 'real' conditions of archaic Greece took hold – namely, speculation into the geography, topography, demography and historical character of the epics' so-called "sticks and stones."[109] These areas of inquiry were derived in part from recent archaeological discoveries surrounding Troy and Ithaca, principally Heinrich Schliemann's excavation at Hissarlik and Wilhelm Dörpfeld's work at Lefkada, but also, by parallel course, from the "mythological bias" espoused by the Cambridge Ritualists, namely E. B. Tylor (1832–1917), F. M. Cornford (1874–1943), Jane Harrison (1850–1928) and, popularly, Gilbert Murray (1866–1957).[110] Collectively, the "heavy food" from these new forms of "historical and scientific knowledge," as Eliot once called them, had brought the findings of ethnography, archaeology and cultural anthropology "to the aid of philology" and thereby "superannuated in a stroke the Victorian Homer, whose noble outline rendered details unimportant."[111] According to Eliot, if antiquity were to have a "vitalizing effect" once again – to be "as present to us as the present" – poets and translators had to do more than "pick up some of the more romantic crumbs of Greek literature."[112]

---

[106] Kenner (1969) 285–98. Bush (2019) 322–57. See also Bush (1976) 125–34. On the broader influence of primitivism in Joyce's work and within the Revival at large, see Castle (2001), Mattar (2004), as well as McGarrity (2009) 133–52, 17–39.
[107] Bush (2019) 322.
[108] See Chapter 1, pp. 65–76.
[109] Kenner (1969) 285.
[110] Bush (1976) 125. See also Kenner (1978) 109–10. On modernist attraction to primitive myth and religion, see Gere (2009), Carpentier (2016) 69–99, as well as Gere (2019) 200–25.
[111] Eliot (1920) 70; Bush (1976) 125. See also Kenner (1969) 296–97.
[112] Eliot (1920) 66, 70, 69.

"[M]uch greater exertions" were to be given over to recent scholarly considerations, not merely to the increase in "historical knowledge" but to the then pervasive "curious Freudian-social-mystical-rationalistic-higher-critical interpretation of the Classics."[113]

Joyce, it seems, anticipated this admonition, for, as Bush notes, he was already by then bringing to bear in the "extraordinarily dense texture ... and willed obscurity" of *Ulysses* the "complexity insinuated by late nineteenth-century theories about the *Odyssey's* geographical, demographic and archaeological strata."[114] The background to his vision of the Homeric world was indebted not merely to Samuel Butcher and Andrew Lang's 1879 version of the *Odyssey* – a version imbued with Arnoldian notes stressing Homer's "charm, his bright and equable speed" – but also to turn-of-the-century scholarship and translations, principally Samuel Butler's renditions and his treatise *The Authoress of the Odyssey* (1897) and Victor Bérard's *Les Phéniciens et l'Odyssée* (1902–1903) as well as the ritualist thought of Tylor, Murray, and Harrison.[115] Coupled with Joyce's exposure to a variety of Anglicized Homers – his "museum of Homers" as Kenner called it – these analyses of Greek religion and mythology and their place in archaic epic helped mold the 'mistranslated' styles of correspondence Joyce developed across "Cyclops."[116] Before finishing the episode in 1919, he had also been trying to further remedy his ignorance of ancient Greek, hoping to improve his ability to read Homer. The Zurich copybooks dating from 1916 demonstrate, rather crudely, his increasing interest in practicing the language and the difficulty of mastering it, whether ancient or modern. Scrawling long notes and vocabulary lists in the language, Joyce marked down, in addition, two short passages from the *Odyssey* in careful handwriting (though with inaccurate accentuation).[117] Yet, despite such eagerness, "insufficient knowledge" of

---

[113] Eliot (1920) 70, 68.
[114] Bush (2019) 324.
[115] Butcher and Lang (1879) vii. On the eccentricity of Butler's commentary, see Bush (2019) 323–24.
[116] On Joyce's knowledge of Harrison's thought, see Carpentier (2016) 71–76.
[117] These notebooks are reproduced in facsimile in the Garland edition: "Greek (Buffalo VIII.A.6.a–j, 4, 2, 1)." See Joyce (1979) 288–352. At this time Joyce also annotated interlinear Greek–Italian editions of *The Odyssey*, notably the third edition of *L'Odissea: Testo, costruzione, versione letterale e argomenti. Libro I*, published in 1905 by Societá Editrice Dante Alighieri di Albrighi, as well as a version of book 14 entitled, *Il libro XIV dell'Odissea* (1915). Schork notes: "this school edition of book 1" contained "copious notes of every sort and a line-by-line translation into grotesquely literal Italian. On several pages of this book Joyce wrote occasional notes, almost all of them involving a mechanical transfer of a vocabulary word from the commentary into the text." Schork (1998) 85. See also Gillespie and Stocker (1986) 120–21. Rodney Wilson Owen dates Joyce's Greek notebooks, Buffalo VIII.A, to late 1916 through early 1917. See Owen (1983) 96–104.

Greek continued to plague him, and the fact "he was not a Greek scholar by high academic standards" became, as Frank Budgen (1882–1971) later recalled, a "sore point with him."[118]

> I told him that I left school and went to work in my thirteenth year, but that the only thing I regretted about my lack of schooling was that I was never able to learn Greek. He thereupon regretted his insufficient know-ledge of that language but, as if to underline the difference in our two cases (or so I interpreted it), he said with sudden vehemence: "But just think: isn't that a world I am peculiarly fitted to enter?"[119]

Although Joyce never learned enough Greek to read Homer without the crutch of translation, his reliance on translation proved especially critical for "Cyclops," where parodic imitations of English 'translationese' were drawn from the Englished Homers he knew very well.[120] Amusing passages such as "And lo, as they quaffed their cup of joy, a godlike messenger came swiftly in, radiant as the eye of heaven" were, Kenner noted, what seemed like "a fair approximation to the rhetoric" of Samuel Butcher and Andrew Lang's version, and perhaps also that of Charles Lamb.[121] Yet it was not only these translations that mattered. In contrast to Butcher and Lang's unapologetic use of "Biblical English" – a "language which" though it "does not come spontaneously to the lips" was nonetheless considered by them as "nearly analogous to the Epic Greek, as anything that our tongue has to offer" – Joyce admired also Samuel Butler's prose versions of Homer and found in *The Iliad* of 1898 and *The Odyssey* of 1900 compelling alternatives to Butcher and Lang's approach.[122] Butler had attempted to modernize Homer's epics in a "plain

---

[118] Budgen (1972) 359.

[119] Budgen (1972) 359. On whether this statement betokens a common "nostalgia" for Greek on Joyce's part, see Farrell (2012) 60–61.

[120] Kenner (1969) 297. See also Kenner (1978) 110–12. It is unclear precisely how many translations of Homer Joyce consulted when writing *Ulysses*. Kenner notes Samuel Butcher and Andrew Lang's 1879 version, a finding that is supported by the recollection of Frank Budgen. Joyce's brother, Stanislaus, also recalled that the author knew Charles Lamb's 1808 adaptation of George Chapman's translation as well as William Cowper's 1791 version. On Joyce's use of translation as well as his knowledge of Greek, see Ames (2005) 15–48; Schork (1998) 118–23; McCleery (1994) 557–63; and McCleery (1990) 635–39.

[121] Joyce *Ulysses* (1986) 245 (12.244–45); Kenner (1969) 288. It is notable that one of the earliest scholars of Joyce's work, Stuart Gilbert (1883–1969), contributed greatly to the reception of Butcher and Lang's edition in subsequent analyses of *Ulysses*. He did so, however, not because of clear substantive links to the composition of the novel but because he thought their Wardour Street English "better to convey the spirit of the original" Greek "than any of the more modern versions." Gilbert (1950) ix.

[122] Butcher and Lang (1879) ix.

prose," a colloquial and seemingly contemporary idiom that possessed what he called "the same benevolent leaning, say, towards Tottenham Court Road that Messrs Butcher and Lang have shewn towards Wardour Street."[123] The Homeric originals were for Butler "so luminous and so transparent," so much so that he saw little point in further elevating or distancing Homer from "English readers."[124] Instead he aimed "fearlessly and without taint of affectation at making a dead author living to a generation other than his own."[125]

> Shakespeare tells us that it is Time's glory to stamp the seal of time on aged things. No doubt; but he will have no hands stamp it save his own; he will rot an artificial ruin, but he will not glorify it; if he is to hallow any work it must be frankly secular when he deigns to take it in hand – by this I mean honestly after the manner of its own age and country.[126]

Just as some of the very places in which the dramatic action of the *Iliad* and the *Odyssey* had unfolded had been dug out and rediscovered recently, so too, he thought, could the language of Homer be dug out in English – transfused into the lived experience of a contemporary idiom.

The incongruities that resulted from these rival approaches to translation, to say nothing of their contrasting visions of the Homeric – Butcher and Lang's elevated, antique and noble Homer versus Butler's "accessible, domestic, realistic, and robust" Homer – suggested a powerful solution for fusing "Cyclops," namely to develop, by counterpoint, divergent narrative styles of correspondence across the episode.[127] One largely reflected the Victorian pose encouraged by Arnold, Butcher and Lang, while the other stressed the coarse demotic realities of Dublin. The importance of Butler's "many gifts" in this solution – his "resurrection of the *Odyssey* precedes *Ulysses*" – cannot be underestimated, but they are inflected also by the significant influences of both Victor Bérard and Jane Harrison.[128] Bérard's "minute exploration of Homer's geography" spoke to Joyce's "temperamental fascination with topographical detail," but perhaps more attractive was his insistence that the *Odyssey*

---

[123] Butler (1893) 2. On Wardour Street English, see Ballantyne (1888) 585–94 as well as Venuti's discussion in *The Translator's Invisibility* (2008) 117–18.
[124] Butler (1893) 1; Butler (1898) xi.
[125] Butler (1898) vi.
[126] Butler (1898) vi.
[127] Raby (1991) 240.
[128] Davenport (1997) 41.

constituted *un périple phénicien (de Sidon, de Carthage ou d'ailleurs), transposé en vers grecs et en légendes poétiques* – a Phoenician/Semitic collection of earlier stories later Hellenized and transposed into Homeric Greek.[129] This evoked, by parallel, something akin to Joyce's reflections on the cultural hybridity of Ireland itself, his belief that the country had no center of civilizational purity but was instead a "vast fabric, in which the most diverse elements are mingled."[130] Moreover, the idea that the very *periploi* of Homer were not original but rather readapted versions of earlier Semitic tales or legends bolstered Joyce's desire to forge in *Ulysses* a stylized evolution of the Homeric. Both Butler and Butcher and Lang had presented divergent idiomatic expressions of Homer, and their influence could be employed to overwrite the 'original' Greek and develop a kaleidoscopic layering across the novel, a collage of competing receptions. This interest in stylistic stratification resonated also with the scholarship of Jane Harrison whose 1903 book *Prolegomena to the Study of Greek Religion* had claimed that "a theological stratification" existed within the religious practices of the ancient Greeks.[131] Despite the "superficial serenity" often attributed to Greek religion, Harrison insisted that "within it and beneath it" there remained "elements of a darker and deeper significance."[132] "[T]wo diverse, even opposite, factors" were present in its rites and rituals: the Olympian and the Chthonic, elements that could be characterized in turn by "*service* (θεραπεία)" and "*aversion* (ἀποτροπή)."[133] "The rites of *service*," she explained,

> were connected by ancient tradition with the Olympians, or as they are sometimes called the Ouranians: the rites of *aversion* with ghosts, heroes, underworld divinities. The rites of service were of a cheerful and rational character, the rites of aversion gloomy and tending to superstition.[134]

As Harrison saw it, the rites of "burnt-sacrifice, of joy and feasting and agonistic contests" were linked to the *do ut des* ("I give that you may give"), transactional mode of prayer and sacrifice to the Olympians.[135] That "cheerful and rational" model of relative divine beneficence bore very little likeness, she maintained, to the *do ut abeas* rites of the "gloomy

[129] Bush (2019) 324. Bérard (1902) 4. On Bérard's influence in *Ulysses*, see Seidel (1976).
[130] Joyce *CWJJ* (1989) 165.
[131] Harrison (1903) 11.
[132] Harrison (1903) 10.
[133] Harrison (1903) 10.
[134] Harrison (1903) 10.
[135] Harrison (1903) 11, 7.

underworld."[136] Its ceremonies of aversion fostered "a lower and more 'fearful' stratum of religion" whose purpose was largely employed for "the promotion of fertility by the purgation of evil influences."[137]

> The formula of that religion was not *do ut des* "I give that you may give," but *do ut abeas* "I give that you may go, and keep away." The beings worshipped were not rational, human, law-abiding *gods*, but vague, irrational, mainly malevolent δαίμονες, spirit-things, ghosts and bogeys and the like, not yet formulated and enclosed into god-head.[138]

Because the contrast between these elements seemed "so marked," Harrison concluded that the 'rational' rites of the Olympian had been progressively "superimposed" on an "underlying stratum," a "primitive, barbarous, even repulsive" order of worship.[139] By parallel, Joyce stratified idiomatic mistranslations across "Cyclops," casting the episode with competing styles of expression, principally two rival ways of presenting a correspondence with Greek antiquity. Putting a "bloody mangy mongrel" demotic on the lips of the drunks at Barney Kiernan's, he then overwrote that chthonic vernacular of the Dublin underworld with an exaggerated 'Olympian' translationese, an idiom Joyce mimicked with conventions he knew from recent translations of Homer and from popular 'classicized' versions of Irish folklore as well.[140] The dissonance generated in setting an allegedly barbarous form of speech against this noble idiom animates the satire in "Cyclops": the bloody, "sudden reality" of barroom obscenities smashing to "a pulp" the high-minded "romanticism" with which Homer had been embraced.[141]

Despite Joyce's use of classical scholarship and a variety of anglicized Homers in "Cyclops," these were never the principal targets of the episode's humor. With Yeats' 1893 declaration that Ireland was still in its "epic or ballad period" of literary development – ready for a 'Northern Homer' to appear – many revivalist writers had insisted that Irish folklore could be best 'Englished' with an idiom infused by allegedly archaic, Homeric grandiloquence.[142] The Greek poet's "perfect ... lovely grandeur," as Arnold once called it, also had life in ancient Irish legend, it was thought, and thus the task of the translator was to articulate that life

---

[136] Harrison (1903) 10, 11.
[137] Harrison (1903) 7, ix.
[138] Harrison (1903) 7.
[139] Harrison (1903) 11, ix, 29.
[140] Joyce *Ulysses* (1986) 242 (12.119–20).
[141] Joyce, as quoted in Power (1974) 98.
[142] Yeats *UP1* (1970) 273. See also Chapter 1, pp. 55–61.

in an English reminiscent of the style used to elevate the Victorian nobility of Homer.[143] However, from as early as 1890, prominent scholars of Irish warned their contemporaries: the difficulty of making "a good translation from Irish into English," let alone one that could be justly thought Homeric, was profound, for "no two Aryan languages" were, as Douglas Hyde argued, "more opposed to each other in spirit and idiom."[144] Richard Henebry, Professor of Irish at University College, Cork, went further, claiming that Irish was practically untranslatable. Ancient Irish remained the "one literature that was never Hellenised" amid the other literatures in Europe whose "standard is the Hellenic," and for that reason it was said to have a primitive, strange force lingering from the period of "Indo-Keltic unity," a time before England and the rest of Europe had sought to imitate "the fundamental canon of Greek art."[145] The comparative unlikeness of the "Keltic standard" to that of Hellenic under whose influence English had fallen meant that translation from Irish into English would be difficult.[146] The reader "whose mind is charged with English," Henebry argued, would hear in Irish only sounds

> strange, uncouth and foreign. To one reared in Irish it is the same tune he always heard: he knows it. But how define its tone, its atmosphere for the foreigner? It cannot be done, it is the other way, it differs in everything and entirely from the way of the strange people. Nor can it be translated.[147]

Nonetheless, Yeats, Hyde and others still insisted that an "unidiomatic English" might approximate some Irish effects in the target language, and possibly help even "build up a national tradition, a national literature ... none the less Irish in spirit from being English in language."[148] Poets and translators could therefore be less careful about philological accuracy: "more literary, less scholarly works" of translation and adaptation, like those of P. W. Joyce (1827–1914), Standish O'Grady, A. H. Leahy (1857–1928) and Eleanor Hull (1860–1935), rested on "two largely unspoken premises: that the old stories should not merely be translated – for the scholars ... but reshaped according to modern fictional criteria and

---

[143] See Matthew Arnold's lecture "On Translating Homer" (1860–61) in Arnold (1960) 168.
[144] Hyde (1890) xlvii.
[145] Henebry (1909) 522, 524. See Introduction, pp. 16–19.
[146] Henebry (1909) 524.
[147] Henebry (1909) 524.
[148] Hyde (1890) xlviii; Yeats CL1 (1986) 338. See Introduction, pp. 2–3; Chapter 1, pp. 53–55; and Chapter 4, pp. 163–65.

expectations; and second, that the new-told tales ... should promote the cause and redound to the glory of modern Ireland."[149] These expectations pushed Yeats and Lady Gregory to new stylistic extremes. As discussed in the previous chapter, drawing on influence from Shelley, Swinburne as well as William Morris and other recent English poets, Yeats' early 'Celtic' work employed a decadent English, infused with neologism, unconventional syntax and archaisms. As one critic later noted, "the lavish foreground of the Pre-Raphaelites" present in his "fragments of the Ossianic cycle" spun out "bright tapestries of legendary figures" and "decorative pictures of imaginary lands ... into dyeshot gossamer with Tennysonian heroics and Swinburnian rhetoric."[150] Lady Gregory, by contrast, believed that a more unadorned, alliterative idiom could capture something authentic from Gaelic legend. Her translation of the Ulster cycle *Cuchulain of Muirthemne* (1902) claimed the "plain and simple words" of her Kiltartan parish, words she recalled "in the same way my old nurse Mary Sheridan used to be telling stories from the Irish long ago."[151] Eschewing the far-flung aestheticism of Yeats' early Celticism, her "wonderfully simple and powerful language" garnered praise for resembling "a good deal the peasant dialect of the west of Ireland," but Gregory too had not dispensed with the ambition of inventing a suitably epic style for Irish literature.[152] Rather than simply imitate a rustic dialect, she balanced "plain and simple words" with what Geraldine Higgins has called "an amenable nineteenth-century idiom and mode" bearing some likeness to the pseudo-archaic Butcher and Lang.[153] Her translation was "made venerable by archaism" but seasoned as well with the apparent "spontaneity of storytelling and speech patterns."[154] The result impressed Yeats, who boldly declared Gregory's work "the best that has come out of Ireland in my time. Perhaps I should say it is the best book that has ever come out of Ireland."[155] "As she moved about among her people," he effused,

> she learned to love the beautiful speech of those who think in Irish, and to understand that it is as true a dialect of English as the dialect that Burns

[149] Foster (1987) 23.
[150] Bullough (1934) 29.
[151] Gregory (1970) 5. On the mixed reception of Gregory's work within the wider network of the Gaelic language revival, see O'Leary (1994) 223–79 as well as Higgins (2012) 47–48. On some of the "virtues of Gregory's style," see Kiberd (2001) 399–419.
[152] J. M. Synge, "An Epic of Ulster," *The Speaker* (June 7, 1902), in Synge (1966) 367.
[153] Gregory (1970) 5; Higgins (2012) 47.
[154] O'Connor (2006) 76.
[155] Yeats, "Preface" (1902), as in Gregory (1970) 11.

wrote in. It is some hundreds of years old, and age gives a language authority. We find in it the vocabulary of the translators of the Bible, joined to an idiom which makes it tender, compassionate, and complaisant, like the Irish language itself. It is certainly well suited to clothe a literature which never ceased to be folk-lore even when it was recited in the Courts of Kings."[156]

As Yeats saw it, the Revival, it seems, finally had the balanced literary vernacular it needed: Gregory had generated a "kind of English that fitted" Ireland's legends "as the language of [William] Morris's prose stories – the most beautiful language I had ever read – fitted his journeys to woods and wells beyond the world."[157] As the "book of the National Stories of Ireland," *Cuchulain of Muirthemne* was "meant for everybody the Iliad of a people," a book that promised to do "great service to the nation."[158]

Despite Yeats' endorsement, questions about the book's value abounded, and no claims of Homeric likeness dispelled these questions, especially among hardline devotees of Irish Ireland and the Gaelic Revival. *The Freeman's Journal* did admit that Gregory's *Cuchulain* was "in truth, the Irish Homer, done into that division of the Anglo-Irish dialect which still preserves many of the forms of the Gaelic idiom," but the paper eviscerated Yeats' promotion of the book.[159]

> [I]t is pitiable that a work like Lady Gregory's should be introduced by such a statement as that "to us Irish these personages should be more important than all others, for they lived in the places where we ride and go marketing, and sometimes they have met one another on the hills, that cast their shadows upon our doors at evening. If we will but tell these stories to our children the Land will begin again to be a Holy Land, as it was before men gave their hearts to Greece and Rome and Judea." Literary blaspheming of this kind is not only repulsive but silly. The Land has never ceased to be a Holy Land to the Irish or their children, and it is only the Anglo-Irish blindness that may miss the fact.[160]

---

[156] Yeats, "Preface" (1902), as in Gregory (1970) 12.
[157] Yeats, "Preface" (1902), as in Gregory (1970) 12. By contrast, Douglas Hyde was skeptical of Gregory's idea of "harmonising Cuchulain" in English. She reported in December 1900 that "Hyde rather snubs my idea of harmonising Cuchulain – I think his feeling is a scholar shd do it – & he is bewildered at my simple translations ... 'Of course an epic should not be translated in colloquial style' he says – which accounts for his translations of epic bits being heavy & formal, quite different from his folk tales & peasant poem translations – However he gave his consent, which is all I wanted." Gregory (1996) 293.
[158] Yeats, "To the Editor of the *United Irishman* [May 23, 1902]," in Yeats *CL3* (1994) 188.
[159] Donovan (1902) 5.
[160] Donovan (1902) 5.

Yeats was "wholly at sea" in his view of the translation, too prone, the paper argued, "to read into the Irish peasant mind the notes of his own."[161] His extravagance seemed "anything but Irish" but instead rather the product of his "affectation of neo-Paganism ... a corruption of the French decadent school," corruption that if left unchecked might do serious injury to the Revival.[162] The "polite condescension" of W. P. Ryan (1867–1942) from *The Leader* was less generous.[163] While *Cuchulain of Muirthemne* seemed to him a "temporary and incidental good,"

> we may trust that in ten or twenty years' time it will be regarded as entirely out of date, or as possessing a sort of historical interest as a specimen of the contrivances that served a useful purpose as Ireland returned from the desert. Lady Gregory means well by Irish Ireland, and as we know, works well for it, and so no one will be gladder than she herself at the outcome in question.[164]

While Gregory's Kiltartan "idiom now and then has an Irish turn and flavour," he continued, the dialect she had largely invented could serve no enduring literary purpose for "[p]eople cannot make true speech or literature out of languages that they do not understand, nor should they attempt new 'dialects' in foreign tongues ... [s]he treats a half-way house as a goal, and we have too much of such compromise in Ireland."[165] Despite Yeats' praise, Ryan saw the book as a place "[w]here information and knowledge failed," a place rife with "imaginings or conjectures ... hence we have had much that is fantastic. We have had a little of Cuchulain and a deal of modern fancy and phantasm. The folk in question have not been able to re-create that older Ireland as it existed in the daytime."[166]

Joyce, for his part, wrote little of Gregory's translation, but he cared less for the commendations Yeats had made. Yet *Cuchulain of Muirthemne* and its Homeric acclaim presented a further opportunity for satire. With Yeats in mind, Joyce set Buck Mulligan on the poet's pretension, imitating the "Yeats touch ... mopping, chanting with waving graceful arms" while intoning that *Cuchulain* was without doubt, of course, "The most beautiful book that has come out of our country in

[161] Donovan (1902) 5.
[162] Donovan (1902) 5.
[163] O'Leary (1994) 226.
[164] Ryan (1902) 297–98.
[165] Ryan (1902) 298.
[166] Ryan (1902) 299.

my time. One thinks of Homer."[167] Whether or not others were induced
to think of Homer, Gregory's translation had made Yeats think of the
Greek or, perhaps more accurately, the Englished Homer he admired
most. Fifteen years earlier, William Morris (1834–1896) – England's "only
true story-singer since Chaucer" according to Oscar Wilde – had
published "the most perfect and the most satisfying" version of the
Odyssey in English.[168] As Wilde put it, Morris was "best qualified by
nature and by art to translate for us the marvellous epic of the wanderings of Odysseus" with "lovers of Greek literature … so eagerly" looking
forward to his version.[169] *The Odyssey of Homer Done into English Verse*
(1887–1888) did not disappoint: its "use of archaic words and unusual
expressions" had made tangible for the modern reader what the
"Athenian of the fifth century B.C." would have experienced on first
hearing Homer's "old-world romance and old-world beauty" in Greek.[170]
Yeats likewise esteemed the style of Morris, finding that his "little tricks
of speech" exuded "spontaneity and joy."[171] Yet to others Morris' liberal
use of "old words" felt forced, as though they had robbed his version of
"true Homeric simplicity," a quality Matthew Arnold had described as
"the pure lines of an Ionian horizon, the liquid clearness of an Ionian
sky."[172] As the critic Archibald Ballantyne observed, Morris' English – an
idiom of such an "antique and archaic cast" – did little to clarify Homer's
Greek but showed instead only the "strange linguistic ways" of Morris
himself.[173] Criticism from *The Quarterly Review* likewise suggested that its
"clumsy travesty of an archaic diction" was "an extreme form of that
affectation which plumes itself on despising the thoughts, manners, and
needs of its own time."[174] "[S]ham Saxon" was not "literary English of
any date" but rather what Ballantyne mocked as "Wardour-Street Early
English – a perfectly modern article" born from a contemporary
"linguistic craze" for the archaic.[175] Too often, he insisted, modern readers

---

[167] Joyce *Ulysses* (1986) 178 (9.1161–65).
[168] "Mr. Morris's Odyssey," *Pall Mall Gazette* (April 26, 1887) in Wilde (1909) 153, 154. On Wilde's
       view of classical translation and regard for Morris, see Ross (2013) 90–96.
[169] Wilde (1909) 153, 154.
[170] "Mr. Morris's Completion of the *Odyssey*," *Pall Mall Gazette* (November 24, 1887) in Wilde
       (1909) 216, 218.
[171] Yeats *CW3* (1999) 131.
[172] Wilde (1909) 217, 216; Arnold (1960) 168. On the demand for idiomatic simplicity in English
       poetry, see Ruthven (1979) 33–50 as well as Emerson R. Marks' chapter "Matthew Arnold" in
       Marks (1998) 197–215.
[173] Ballantyne (1888) 588.
[174] Morris (1888) 407.
[175] Ballantyne (1888) 588, 589, 592.

had been subjected to hearing stories in which heroes from antiquity cavorted "among the men-folk, and the god-folk, and the thrall-folk, and the sheep-kind; here servants are swains of service, and butlers are wine-swains."[176] The fabrications wrought in these "mock Anglo-Saxonisms" mirrored a common practice in the London trade of fake antiques, where "one of the well-known tricks," he explained,

> is the production of artificial worm-holes in articles of modern manufacture. The innocent amateur, seeing the seemingly worm-eaten chair or table, is filled with antiquarian joy, and wonders how so precious a relic of the past can be so exceedingly cheap. So in the Wardour Street of literature. Take whole handfuls of dights and cow-kinds and men-folk; season, according to taste, with howes and mayhappens and smithying-carles: and you have an English literary article which – well, which the professional dealer knows is not in genuine English language of any period at all.[177]

Nevertheless "antiquarian joy" and the desire for "artificial worm-holes" were sweeping across the British Isles where a growing "industry" had emerged, as one critic put it, to make accessible "these heroic tales ... to a public hungry for the ancient literature of Ireland."[178] With its 'Hiberno-English' and its claims on being classical, no book, it seems, fed such popular demand more than *Cuchulain*.[179] The poet Æ confessed to "have long wanted a book of these legends," and Lady Gregory had "acted the fairy godmother to me and to many Irish people by bringing the good gift our hearts desired. The prose seems wonderfully fitted for the purpose."[180] The *Tuam Herald* agreed. Gregory presented the ruggedness of ancient Irish life in a "plain Chaucerian English" whose "simple Saxon style" possessed a "fitness" for translating Gaelic legend.[181] Synge, however, was more circumspect in his remarks – disappointed by Gregory's arrangement of legends as well as her omission of "certain barbarous features" from the original Irish text.[182] Nonetheless he admitted that *Cuchulain* remained "a part of my daily bread," though

---

176 Ballantyne (1888) 588.
177 Ballantyne (1888) 590, 589–90.
178 Ballantyne (1888) 589. "An Irish Epic," *Dundalk Democrat* (June 4, 1904) 8.
179 "Within ten years four editions were sold out, and even through the twenties, the book continued to make money." Daniel Murphy, Foreword to Augusta Gregory, *Cuchulain of Muirthemne* (1902) in Gregory (1970) 10.
180 As quoted in Murphy, Foreword to Augusta Gregory, *Cuchulain of Muirthemne* in Gregory (1970) 10.
181 "Lady Gregory on Cuchulain," *Tuam Herald* (May 17, 1902) 4.
182 J. M. Synge, "An Epic of Ulster," *The Speaker* (June 7, 1902) 285, as in Synge (1966) 370; see also Valente (2011) 179.

even he could not shake a strong distaste for the "needlessly archaic" English by which many contemporary writers had stylized Irish legend.[183] The Wardour Street industry had gone far enough, and nothing seemed "quite so worthless" as the "tawdry commonplace jingle" made "from it in Ireland during the last century."[184] In his own writing, therefore, Synge eschewed archaicism and aimed not at a high-minded Homeric or classical grandiloquence but "a nearer appreciation of the country people, and their language."[185]

Unlike Synge, however, Joyce found the "worm-holes" of Wardour Street compelling, if absurd, and in 1919 its industry standards proved especially useful in "Cyclops."[186] As Michael Groden has noted, the composition of this episode marked a radical departure from *Ulysses'* previous narrative experiments: Joyce resolved "to drop the monologue technique, which he had already distorted practically beyond recognition in 'Sirens'," but initially he lacked a straightforward idea of what might replace it.[187] In the earliest drafts, Joyce did not begin with the one-eyed pub argot of "[b]arney mavourneen's" but instead with a parody of James Clarence Mangan (1803–1849), whose "Prince Aldfrid's Itinerary Through Ireland" recalled something of the faux world of Wardour Street.[188] Eager to expose its conventions – the "verbal paraphernalia" that aligned the Victorian Homer with the nobility of a folk Gaelic past – Joyce kept nothing sacred.[189] He grossly amplified Mangan's idiom, embellishing the bounty of "Inisfail the fair" while enumerating, list upon list, the dense varieties of all its pleasures.[190]

> In ~~green Erin of the west~~ <Inisfail the fair> there lies a land, the land of holy Michan. There rises a watchtower beheld from afar. There sleep the dead as they ~~slept in life~~ <in life slept>, warriors and princes of high renown. There wave the lofty trees of sycamore; the eucalyptus, giver of good shade, is not absent: and in their shadow sit the maidens of that land, the daughters of princes. They <sing and> sport with silvery fishes, caught in silken nets; their fair white fingers toss the gems of the <fishful>

[183] As quoted in Gregory (1976) 403; J. M. Synge, "A Translation of Irish Romance," *Manchester Guardian* (December 28, 1905) 5, as in Synge (1966) 373.

[184] Synge (1966) 372.

[185] Synge (1966) 367.

[186] Ballantyne (1888) 589.

[187] Groden (1977) 118.

[188] Joyce *Ulysses* (1986) 241 (12.59). Mangan based his own version of the poem on John O'Donovan's unrhymed translation of a seventh-century Irish ballad, first published in the *Dublin Penny Journal* (September 1832).

[189] "Nineteenth-century translations from Irish sources – except for the proper names – would have been replete with the same verbal paraphernalia as is the Butcher and Lang rendition of the Odyssey." Schork (1998) 122.

[190] Joyce *Ulysses* (1986) 241 (12.68).

sea, ruby and purple of Tyre. And men come from afar, heroes, the sons of kings, to woo them for they are beautiful and all of noble stem.[191]

As Leah Flack observes, the vision of Gaelic antiquity forged by Mangan reappears ironically: its "abundant apparel," its interminable catalogues of the "ornaments of the arboreal world" and the "fishful streams ... too numerous to be enumerated" lampoon Butcher and Lang's extravagant account of all "the splendid gifts of the gods in the palace of Alcinous."[192] In addition to mistranslating Mangan, Joyce's mock heroic idiom repositions the poem's setting, moving it from an idyllic pastoral landscape to the dirty byways of contemporary Dublin, specifically the city Corporation's Fruit, Vegetable, and Fish Market. Bound to the west by St. Michan's Street and to the north by Mary's Lane, the market had once been described by Joseph Meade, Lord Mayor of Dublin (1839–1900), as "'second to none in the empire.'"[193] First opened in December 1892, its completion became a "lasting symbol" of the city's broad efforts to enact municipal regulations to improve the quality of urban life, not least of which was the imposition of new "safety standards on food offered for sale";[194] and it was the market's local reputation as a place of plenty that pushed Joyce to the exaggerations of Wardour Street. He would 'English' its venerable place, rendering its phenomena as faux archaic while mimicking the very stylistic conceits by which many revivalists of the previous generation had aligned Irish and Greek antiquity. In so doing, Joyce held up to scrutiny a Wardour Street style once said to be so full of "eccentricities and caprice" that it appeared as "the most odious shape that false culture can assume."[195]

Throughout *Cuchulain of Muirthemne* Lady Gregory had sought to merge a reputedly peasant idiom with a higher style born, in part at least,

---

[191] Groden (1977) 130–31. See also Herring (1977) 152–53. The selection drawn from this poem also recalls the opening of Joyce's 1907 lecture, "Ireland, Island of Saints and Sages." There he began with an Italian rendition of the poem's opening quatrain. The corresponding passage in Mangan's version:

> I found in Innisfail the fair,
> In Ireland, while in exile there,
> Women of worth, both grave and gay men,
> Many clerics and many laymen.
> I travelled its fruitful provinces round,
> And in every one of the five I found,
> Alike in church and in palace hall,
> Abundant apparel and food for all.
> Gold and silver I found, and money;
> Plenty of wheat and plenty of honey;
> I found God's people rich in pity
> Found many a feast and many a city. Mangan (1846) 61–62.

[192] See Flack (2015) 108–13; Joyce *Ulysses* (1986) 241–42 (12.68–86); Butcher and Lang (1879) 105–07.
[193] Joseph Meade, as quoted in Lysaght (1996) 43.
[194] Dickson (2014) 415.
[195] Morris (1888) 408, 407.

from the conventions of recent classical translation. Joyce, by contrast, was
not so eager to fuse styles in "Cyclops" as to exploit a clear stylistic divergence between high and low registers of English, between the affectations of
sermo nobilis and the coarse ejaculations of *sermo vulgaris*. Thus the episode's
comic pith was developed largely by juxtaposition – the lofty extravagance
of Wardour Street set against an equally "colossal vituperativeness" that
Joyce drew not from the idealized Hiberno-English of Ireland's country folk
but from the working-class, Irish-infused slang of local drunks, most
notably that of the Citizen.[196] His invidious delusions about nationality are
outdone only by his hatred of those "bloody brutal Sassenachs and their
patois."[197] Combining the muscular, Irish Ireland rhetoric of D. P. Moran
(1869–1936) with the brutal nativism of Michael 'Citizen' Cusack, founder
of the Gaelic Athletic Association (1847–1906), the Citizen's outsized,
"vigorous and manly" speech offers through guttural insults "giant work for
the preservation of the Irish race."[198]

> – Their syphilisation, you mean, says the citizen. To hell with them! The
> curse of a goodfornothing God light sideways on the bloody thicklugged
> sons of whores' gets! No music and no art and no literature worthy of the
> name. Any civilisation they have they stole from us. Tonguetied sons of
> bastards' ghosts … They're not European, says the citizen. I was in Europe
> with Kevin Egan of Paris. You wouldn't see a trace of them or their
> language anywhere in Europe except in a *cabinet d'aisance*.[199]

As the Citizen unburdens "his soul about the Saxo-Angles in the best
Fenian style," Joyce offset his vulgarity with bloodless passages of epic
parody, passages he thought appeared "explanatorily 'He spoke
of the English, a noble race, rulers of the waves, who sit on thrones of

---

[196] Joyce, "To Frank Budgen, 19 June 1919," in Joyce *LJJ* (1957) 126.
[197] Joyce *Ulysses* (1986) 266 (12.1190–91).
[198] [Michael Cusack], "The G.A.A. and the Future of the Irish Race," *The Celtic Times* (February 19,
       1887) 4. Cusack was also editor of the short-lived newspaper *The Celtic Times*, where he insisted
       on the necessity of sport to the racial well-being of Ireland, drawing parallels between Ireland and
       ancient Greece, a practice Joyce made use of in "Cyclops." See Joyce *Ulysses* (1986) 260 (12.897–
       926). "Ancient Ireland, like ancient Greece," wrote Cusack in 1887, "was universally known as a
       home of athletics. Hurling – pre-eminently the national game – was indulged in to an extraordi-
       nary extent, and we read that at one time a war was caused by a disputed hurling contest
       between two provinces, so great was the interest taken in that manly game by the highest as well
       as the humblest in the land. The name of Ireland, like that of Greece, then, and indeed through
       succeeding ages, was synonymous with bravery. This characteristic of two of the most celebrated
       nations of antiquity is directly attributable to the nature and extent of athletic practices."
       [Michael Cusack], "The G.A.A. and the Future of the Irish Race," *The Celtic Times* (February 19,
       1887) 4. On Cusack's contributions to the Gaelic Athletic Association and his complicated rela-
       tionship with nationalist politics of the period, see Mandle (1987) 20–31, 153–55.
[199] Joyce *Ulysses* (1986) 266–67 (12.1197–1201, 1203–05).

alabaster, silent as the deathless gods'."[200] Although both styles are set in dueling opposition, both creatively transpose the episode through circumlocutory mistranslation. Stylistically this only sharpens the division between Bloom and the Citizen. Neither 'one-eyed' idiom through which the reader sees Barney Kiernan's conveys the humane and ambiguous contours of Bloom's character or registers the considered debate about nationality he might at first like to have. One idiom aggrandizes the matter at hand into legendary conflict, while the other debases it into *ad hominem*, anti-Semitic attack. Where the 'best Fenian style' shows clear deficiencies in advancing understanding, the epic parody – as translation – merely amplifies that inadequacy through its verbose forms of explanation, its "loanwords or loan-translations, neologisms" and "circumlocutions."[201] In this sense, the exploitation of translation in "Cyclops" does not free the episode "from obsessive concerns with continuity and purity" but instead mocks that very "Cyclopean fixation," one that would regard "culture as static and immutable."[202]

Although "Cyclops" marked a further stylistic expansion of Joyce's Homeric satire, its stress on mistranslating Homeric parallels and mixing high and low registers of language has antecedents early in *Ulysses*, most notably at the novel's opening in "Telemachus." Atop the Martello Tower, Buck Mulligan gazes over Dublin Bay, blurting out:

> – God! he said quietly. Isn't the sea what Algy calls it: a great sweet mother? The snotgreen sea. The scrotumtightening sea. *Epi oinopa ponton.* Ah, Dedalus, the Greeks! I must teach you. You must read them in the original. *Thalatta! Thalatta!* She is our great sweet mother. Come and look ... God, Kinch, if you and I could only work together we might do something for the island. Hellenise it.[203]

Mulligan's vision brings together not merely an accurate transliteration of the Greek but the deliberate misapplication of οἶνοπα's literal significance "in the original." Where one might perhaps have expected something literally translated, or even a poeticism reflecting the somber character of "what Algy calls it" – a mother "fed with our dead" in whom Swinburne once hoped to "hide ... with all thy waves" – Buck Mulligan traces the epithet with scatological abandon.[204] Joyce had written out

[200] Joyce, "To Frank Budgen, 19 June 1919," in Joyce *LJJ* (1957) 126.
[201] Jakobson (1959) 234.
[202] Cronin (1996) 168.
[203] Joyce *Ulysses* (1986) 4–5, 6 (1.77–81, 157–58).
[204] See Swinburne (1904) 34–47.

verses from the *Odyssey* containing the phrase επι οἶνοπα πόντον ("on the wine-dark sea") in his Greek copybooks dating from Zurich 1916–18. He did so, however, less than carefully. Compare this transcription (a) with the *Odyssey*'s established text (b):

(a) τοῖσιν δ'ικμενον οὖρον ἵει γλαυκῶπις Ἀθήνη
    ἀκραῆ Ζέφυρον, κελαδοντ'επι οἶνοπα πόντον.[205]

(b) τοῖσιν δ' ἴκμενον οὖρον ἵει γλαυκῶπις Ἀθήνη,
    ἀκραῆ Ζέφυρον, κελάδοντ' ἐπὶ οἶνοπα πόντον. (*Od.* 2.420–21)

And grey-eyed Athena sent them a favourable gale, a fresh West Wind, singing over the wine-dark sea.[206]

What began, no doubt, as common student mistakes in Greek transcription – some missing accents and incorrect breathings – developed into a fraught 'betrayal' of the original Greek in "Telemachus." Mulligan's impromptu anglicizing of οἶνοπα thwarts readerly expectation, ironically usurping Homer and the wine-dark 'purity' of the *Odyssey* with "snot-green" and "scrotumtightening" conscription. This moment of intentional mistranslation prefigures something of the *agon* that Joyce later expanded across "Cyclops." Here the novel foregrounds the broad pendulum on which *Ulysses* set the dynamic forms of its engagement with Homeric translation, its oscillation between the vulgar and reputedly noble, between vernacular slang and a 'classical' mode. Throughout Joyce was eager to show slanted exchanges between reverential approaches to English translation and their cruder, more self-conscious counterparts. For his own part in the episode, the figure of Joyce's youth, Stephen Dedalus – roiled by grief for his "beastly dead" mother – gives Mulligan's Hellenic ejaculations no immediate reply.[207] Instead he draws attention to the imperfections of mimetic representation, seizing on a so-called "symbol of Irish art" nearby – the stolen mirror "cleft by a crooked crack" that Buck draws to his face.[208] Its "cracked lookingglass" suggests not only Stephen's growing self-awareness but the inability of artifice to imitate reality in its fullness or complexity.[209] Art and precedent remain incommensurate to the moment. Yet Mulligan gives little heed to Stephen's

---

[205] Joyce, Buffalo VIII.A.4–29, in Joyce (1979) 331.

[206] Butcher and Lang (1879) 29.

[207] Joyce *Ulysses* (1986) 7 (1.198–99). On the rivalry of Joyce and Oliver St John Gogarty (1878–1957) – of Dedalus and Mulligan – as rivalry of competence in classical languages, Latin and Greek, see Schork (1991) 76–92, and Senn (1992) 215–17.

[208] Joyce *Ulysses* (1986) 6 (1.146, 135–36).

[209] Joyce *Ulysses* (1986) 6 (1.146).

thought, and instead aggressively locks Dedalus' arm in his own. Leading him on, he insists plainly that "if you and I could only work together we might do something for the island. Hellenise it."[210] No explanation of what that Hellenizing would entail is given. Nonetheless, though, with little resistance, Stephen begins to passively reflect on a parallel incongruity, the poor 'translation' of a friend here presented to him in Mulligan's embrace and, bitterly, the loss of his 'original' companion – "the noblest and truest friend a man ever had" – Cranly.[211] Like the Greek, the warmth of that friendship, however imperfect, is usurped, poorly imitated by the presence of a vulgar surrogate: "Cranly's arm. His arm."[212] Mulligan deliberately usurps the Homeric text with crudely Hellenized English, but so too is Stephen's receptive capacity for 'authentic' human understanding stunted by parallel mistranslation: Mulligan himself becomes the novel's blunt weapon of debased appropriation, a mere 'usurper' of Stephen's friend "in the original."[213]

Broadly speaking, the irreverence with which Joyce treated commonplace notions of the 'authentic' or 'original' Homer did not end, of course, in "Telemachus." Expanding the novel, he was eager to examine further whether translation, or other forms of cultural correspondence, could in fact provide semantic equivalence across languages or a greater understanding of nationality. In "Cyclops" that kind of interrogation is enacted through the serial mistranslations of Leopold Bloom's presence, principally at the hands of its 'one-eyed' narrator and his drinking companions. With no recourse to the inner recesses of Bloom's imagination – the seat of his seemingly authentic self – Bloom becomes a metamorphic enigma, a shape-shifting site of translation enmeshed in the episode's competing idioms of correspondence. When Bloom first enters the episode, the Olympian narrator dramatically hails his

---

[210] Joyce *Ulysses* (1986) 6 (1.157–58).

[211] Joyce *Portrait* (1993) 276. Cranly was based largely on the person some consider Joyce's closest friend from his days at University College Dublin, namely John Francis Byrne (1880–1960). From 1908 to 1910 Byrne lived at 7 Eccles Street in Dublin, the fictional home of Leopold and Molly Bloom. It was at this address in August 1909 that Joyce arrived in "utter perturbation," believing that his companion, Nora Barnacle (1884–1951), had been unfaithful to him during the initial months of their romance five years earlier. "Never in my life have I seen a human being more shattered," Byrne reported. Byrne helped persuade Joyce that both he and Nora had been victims of a malicious plot by Joyce's old acquaintances, Oliver St John Gogarty and Vincent Cosgrave – who had lied to Joyce about Nora's alleged infidelity to settle a bet. On the profound anguish caused, see Joyce's letters to Nora Barnacle of August 1909, in Joyce *LLJ2* 231–33. On Byrne's life and friendship with Joyce, see his memoir, *Silent Years: An Autobiography with Memoirs of James Joyce and Our Ireland*. Byrne (1953) 156.

[212] Joyce *Ulysses* (1986) 6 (1.159).

[213] Joyce *Ulysses* (1986) 19, 4–5 (1.744, 79–80).

approach, transforming Bloom's character with a form of nativizing appropriation: "Who comes through Michan's land, bedight in sable armour? O'Bloom, the son of Rory: it is he. Impervious to fear is Rory's son: he of the prudent soul."[214] No longer simply Leopold Bloom, cuckold and canvasser for *The Freeman's Journal*, he is O'Bloom, knight of faith armored in mock translation and possessed of a noble, yet faux Gaelic lineage. In this guise Bloom's national origin and heroic character are in little doubt, having been deliberately mischaracterized with idiomatic fragments drawn from Irish folklore. However, when faced with the blistering Anglophobia of the Citizen, Bloom becomes a "*Throwaway*" (like the horse who wins the Gold Cup), a "rank outsider" whose name and breeding are increasingly difficult to 'translate' into the chthonic Irish prized by the Citizen.[215] With no further Wardour Street clichés to render him native, Bloom soon appears with a "dunducketymudcoloured mug on him and his old plumeyes rolling about."[216] His tongue-tied vacillation when discussing nationality, race and ethnicity do little, moreover, to help him with the pub's patrons ("A nation is the same people living in the same place ... Or also living in different places"), and they begin to wonder aloud "what the hell is he," whether

> a jew or a gentile or a holy Roman or a swaddler ... says Ned. Or who is he? No offence, Crofton.
> – Who is Junius? says J. J.
> – We don't want him, says Crofter the Orangeman or presbyterian.
> – He's a perverted jew, says Martin, from a place in Hungary and it was he drew up all the plans according to the Hungarian system. We know that in the castle.
> – Isn't he a cousin of Bloom the dentist? says Jack Power.
> – Not at all, says Martin. Only namesakes. His name was Virag, the father's name that poisoned himself. He changed it by deedpoll, the father did.
> – That's the new Messiah for Ireland! says the citizen. Island of saints and sages![217]

As Myron Schwartzman has observed, Joyce deliberately chose to present Bloom in "Cyclops" with "every trace of interior monologue" removed.[218]

---

[214] Joyce *Ulysses* (1986) 245 (12.215–17).
[215] Joyce *Ulysses* (1986) 267 (12.1219).
[216] Joyce *Ulysses* (1986) 271 (12.1415–16).
[217] Joyce *Ulysses* (1986) 272 (12.1422–23, 1428), 276–77 (12.1631–43).
[218] Schwartzman (1974–1975) 65.

Seen only from without, Bloom thereby becomes a troubling enigma, a character whose ideological significance and absolute 'ethnic value' cannot be measured by the purisms of debate at Barney Kiernan's. As such, he is subject to competing reconstructions of his character from the patrons at the pub, mistranslations that elevate and debase him – all, in effect, diminishing the cultural, religious and linguistic hybridity of Bloom's past and present life. The "vast fabric" of his identity is stretched by opposing idioms, and Bloom becomes, by turns, a canvas on which the desirable and undesirable can be written and rewritten.[219]

The "semantic sweep" of the Odyssean epithet, πολύτροπος (*Od.* 1.1;10.330), with its "notions of much-traveled, much-wandering, turning many ways, versatile, shifty, wily," gave Joyce "manifold leverage" to enlarge the aesthetic range of Homeric reception in *Ulysses* and to "not depend on particular echoes" alone.[220] πολύτροπος performs "multifariously" across the novel, he writes, pushing its diverse styles *multis modis* "to speak in many ways."[221] In "Cyclops," however, Joyce's polytropic depiction of Bloom specifically had roots in Odysseus' struggle with Polyphemus, an encounter that included, he once explained, some of Homer's most "delicious humor."[222] In the Greek copybooks he kept in Zurich, Joyce had copied out Odysseus' famous proclamation to the Cyclops, his adoption (or mistranslation) of the name, οὖτις.

> Οὖτις ἐμοί γ' ὄνομα. Οὖτιν δέ με κικλήσκουσιν
> μήτηρ ἠδέ πατὴρ ἠδ' ἄλλοι πάντες ἑταῖροι.
> (*Od.* 9.366–67)[223]

Noman is my name, and Noman they call me, my father and my mother, and all my fellows.[224]

The minor mistakes Joyce made in transcribing the Greek (specifically in the accentuation of οὖτις and οὖτιν) show little of his fondness for classical wordplay. Yet elsewhere in the copybooks – emulating the spirit of Odyssean fabrication and forgery – he toyed with the phonetic qualities of οὖτις itself, suggestively linking the pseudonym to Ὀδυσσεύς with the false etymology of οὐδείς.[225] However, unlike in *A Portrait of the Artist As*

---

[219] Joyce *CWJJ* (1989) 165.
[220] Senn (1987) 34. See also Senn (1984) 121–37.
[221] Senn (1987) 34.
[222] Borach (1954) 326.
[223] Joyce, Buffalo VIII.A.4–29, in Joyce (1979) 331.
[224] Butcher and Lang (1879) 145.
[225] Separating the name Odysseus, into two parts, Joyce set it among "*outis* and *oudeis* (nobody, no one); directly opposite this pair of synonyms he added, also in Greek, the name Zeus.

a Young Man ("Stephanos Dedalos! Bous Stephanoumenos! Bous Stephaneforos!"), none of that homophonous paronomasia made its way into the final draft of "Cyclops."[226] Nonetheless the allure of Odysseus' false name is still felt powerfully across the episode, specifically in the unstable, untranslatable essence Joyce injected into Bloom himself. As Joyce's longtime friend John Francis Byrne (1880–1960) observed, "the totality of Mr. Bloom" is

> a concoction dished up by a skillful chef. After partaking of this concoction some more or less initiated tasters have declared their recognition of one or other of the ingredients, and have given names to them. But happily, no one has named either the constituents of the concoction or its essence, and it is most unlikely that anyone ever will. This is as James Joyce wanted it to be, although he himself sailed more than once pretty close to the wind.[227]

In setting Leopold Bloom up as a Homeric οὖτις, Joyce presented him as a 'nobody' entangled in the nets of "nationality, language, religion" that Stephen Dedalus once sought to evade.[228] His surname having been changed from Virag, Bloom becomes both "entity and nonentity" in the episode, mediated through mistranslations that permit him to be "Assumed by any" but "known to none. Everyman or Noman."[229] He is a sometime Protestant, a once and still Hungarian, a then and now Jew, an unwelcome stranger in Ireland, and yet also at times a hero of Irish legend. It is precisely the multivalent "concoction" of these many complex aspects that drive the episode's conflict: none of the 'one-eyed' narrative forms can find a suitable epithet, a proper form with which to ensnare, to translate the full scope of Bloom's 'authentic self.' At the end, what the reader learns is that Bloom remains, above all, an enigma of culturally hybrid aspect. The object of heightened xenophobic obsession, he is conscripted across both the 'high' and the 'low' styles of Homeric reception employed within the pub. First, as the native "O'Bloom," he appears as a domestic invention, the product of aggressive nationalist attempts to ennoble the present with Wardour Street dress.[230] Yet unease

---

Immediately preceding this entry Joyce provided a translation/interpretation of his exercise in etymology: NO/GOD, Odys/seus." See Joyce (1979) 332, as well as Schork (1998) 87.

[226] Joyce *Portrait* (1993) 194. For discussion of this passage in *Portrait*, see the Introduction, pp. 34–36.

[227] Byrne (1953) 160.

[228] Joyce *Portrait* (1993) 230.

[229] Joyce *Ulysses* (1986) 598 (17.2006–08).

[230] Joyce *Ulysses* (1986) 245 (12.216).

persists at the coming of a "bloody jewman" into "holy Michan," a place where Bloom's queer habits and intellectual curiosity seemingly have no home.[231] Thus exposed to the Irish-inflected, anti-Semitic obscenities of the Citizen, Bloom no longer remains a rightful "son of Rory" – the son of Ruaidrí Ua Conchobair, High King of Gaelic Ireland (1116–1198) – but becomes rather a dispossessed intruder whose national loyalties and religious persuasion are far too suspect to be trusted.[232] Like Odysseus hiding "bound beneath the breasts of his thick-fleeced flocks," he is deemed a "wolf in sheep's clothing ... That's what he is. Virag from Hungary! Ahasuerus I call him. Cursed by God."[233]

Fritz Senn has noted how thoroughly *Ulysses* confronts the "question of experiencing great literature merely through the medium of restrictive translations."[234] Perhaps nowhere is such restrictiveness – the partial nature of all translation – at once more apparent, and more useful to Joyce, than in the 'one-eyed' narrative idioms of "Cyclops."[235] By the end of the episode, Leopold Bloom has been so refracted by the irreverent artifice of mistranslation – an aesthetic that both demonizes and glorifies all his apparent affiliations – that his 'authentic' self slips away from Barney Kiernan's, much like the corresponding events from the *Odyssey* itself. For Joyce – as for *Ulysses* at large – translation entailed error, a wandering from and an elusive misalignment with only partially exposed sources that could not be known in full. No style, no approach to the source could grasp, or faithfully receive, the character of what Borges called "las imaginaciones de Homero, a los irrecuperables hombres y días que él se representó" – "Homer's imaginations and the irrecoverable men and days he portrayed."[236] The contextual details – the eccentricities of place, language, idiom and particular culture – that differentiated the originary moment of the source text with that of the target language were too vast, "an immeasurable labyrinth" too impossible to bridge.[237] Yet, for all of the apparent restrictions translation might impose, Joyce reveled in this labyrinth, treating the notion of the original not as an object whose

---

[231] Joyce *Ulysses* (1986) 280, 241 (12.1811, 12.68).

[232] Joyce *Ulysses* (1986) 245 (12.216).

[233] Butcher and Lang (1879) 148; Joyce *Ulysses* (1986) 277 (12.1666–67).

[234] Senn (1992) 216.

[235] "Translations are a partial and precious documentation of the changes the text suffers." See "The Homeric Versions," in Borges (2001) 69. On Borges and Joyce, see Waisman (2005) and Novillo-Corvalán (2011). See also Laura Jansen's discussion of "classics as a rumour" in Jansen (2018) 3–5 as well as 52–75.

[236] Borges (1932); Borges (2001) 74.

[237] See "The Homeric Versions," in Borges (2001) 69.

order had to be retrieved but as a kaleidoscopic center radiating creative errancy and mistranslation.[238] If Joyce possessed a 'mythical method,' it was no doubt linked to the profound interest Yeats and others had expressed in developing a Homeric pattern for Irish literature – but Joyce satirized that obsession, reconfiguring it again and again throughout the dense stylistic variety of *Ulysses*. His 'errant' styles did not so much as structure, or bring contemporary anarchy to order, as ironize the "chain of receptions" by which the "continued readability" of an Irish Homer had been forged.[239] *Ulysses* was, he confessed, the "work of a sceptic" – for whatever claims had been made about the coming of a Homeric age in Ireland, the Revival had brought no credible epic, no 'northern Homer' to the nation.[240] "[T]oday other bards," Joyce observed, "animated by other ideals, have the cry."[241]

[238] "James Joyce's passion for literature and languages was also a passion for translation." Cronin (1996) 161.
[239] Martindale (1993) 7.
[240] Budgen (1972) 156.
[241] Joyce *CWJJ* (1989) 174.

CHAPTER 3

"Straight Talk, Straight As the Greek!"
Ireland's Oedipus *and the Modernism of Yeats*

"For the last few days I have been longing for the quiet of the boat," declared W. B. Yeats.[1] As Yeats boarded the RMS *Lusitania*, bound for New York on January 31, 1914, he welcomed the journey. The previous month had seen him ridiculed in the English press. George Moore (1852–1933), the novelist and his sometime adversary, had published an excerpt from his memoir, *Hail and Farewell*, where he skewered Yeats, recalling a tantrum the poet had thrown in 1904. Speaking for Hugh Lane (1875–1915) and his exhibition of Impressionist paintings, Yeats had appeared "with a paunch, a huge stride, and an immense fur overcoat."[2]

> We were surprised at the change in his appearance, and could hardly believe our ears when, instead of talking to us as he used to about the old stories come down from generation to generation, he began to thunder like Ben Tillett himself against the middle classes, stamping his feet, working himself into a great passion, and all because the middle classes did not dip their hands into their pockets and give Lane the money he wanted for his exhibition.[3]

As Yeats sailed from Liverpool, he hoped Moore's "mere novel writing" would not dog him across the Atlantic,[4] but the crossing brought him little pleasure and less peace. On board he found the voyage "villainous" – "only one calm day yesterday & we are much behind time," he told Lady Gregory: "I spent three days on my back, not actually sick but sufficiently miserable."[5] Adding to his misery was the fact he could not escape discussion of Moore's memoir. Some passengers, however, were sympathetic.

---

[1] Yeats, "To Lady Gregory" (January 31, 1914) in Yeats *CLWBY*, entry no. 2394.
[2] Moore (1914a) 167. This excerpt was published in the third volume of Moore's memoir, *Hail and Farewell! Vale*. See Moore (1914b) 160.
[3] Moore (1914a) 167.
[4] Yeats *Mem* (1972) 269.
[5] Yeats, "To Lady Gregory" (February 5, 1914) in Yeats *CLWBY*, entry no. 2396.

One in particular, "a very strange man that introduced himself … in the smoking room," he recalled, "came up with a low bow & asked me to write something in his diary for his wife as his wife 'thought me the greatest poet in the world'."[6] Although pleased by the praise, Yeats soon tired of the man, thinking him one of those Americans who "display their personalities at once."[7] The eager American was Fenton Benedict Turck (1857–1932), a doctor who had recently been appointed director of a medical laboratory financed by the Pearson Research Fund.[8] Having attained a "position of eminence and authority" in his profession, Turck was admitted to the practice of medicine in New York without customary examination.[9] Yet Turck had little interest in discussing his research with Yeats. Instead he spoke mostly of what Yeats called his "one other subject," the civilization of ancient Greece.[10] "When he talks of his science," Yeats told Lady Gregory,

> he is careful & precise but he has one other subject Greece. On that he is a rhetorician of the wildest kind. He talks American journalese, & constantly talks of 'moral uplift' & has the gestures of a public speaker. He sees the whole world as a war between all sorts of evil - in which the Church of Rome is the main sort – & the spirit of Greece … the moment the restraint of his science was off him he would break out into phrases such as 'Oh all conquering power of love' & ejaculations about 'moral uplift.'[11]

Despite, or perhaps because of Turck's enthusiasm for defending the Greeks' "traditions from the barbarians" – "We must become Greek" he quipped – Yeats thought the doctor an "incoherent & prepostorous [sic]" man, a man who seemed "to mispronounce every Greek name he uses."[12]

When Yeats boarded the *Lusitania* in 1914, Greek antiquity was once again becoming a fertile but contested site in his life and imagination, a site marked not only by a long-standing desire to see the promise of the Irish Literary Revival fulfilled – a phenomenon whose Homeric

---

[6] Yeats, "To Lady Gregory" (February 5, 1914) in Yeats *CLWBY*, entry no. 2396.

[7] Yeats, "To Lady Gregory" (February 5, 1914) in Yeats *CLWBY*, entry no. 2396.

[8] Passenger Manifest for the RMS *Lusitania*, sailing from Liverpool to New York City, January 31, 1914, list 4, line 29. See *Passenger Lists of Vessels Arriving at New York, New York, 1820–1897*. Microfilm Publication M237, 675 rolls. NAI: 6256867. Records of the U.S. Customs Service, Record Group 36. National Archives at Washington, D.C. On Turck's reputation, see Garland (1926).

[9] Garland (1926) 54.

[10] Yeats, "To Lady Gregory" (February 5, 1914) in Yeats *CLWBY*, entry no. 2396.

[11] Yeats, "To Lady Gregory" (February 5, 1914) in Yeats *CLWBY*, entry no. 2396.

[12] Yeats, "To Lady Gregory" (February 5, 1914) in Yeats *CLWBY*, entry no. 2396.

dimensions have been discussed in the preceding chapters – but also by a desire to dramatically refashion both his poetry and his political vision. Though Yeats had once, like many writers of the Revival, eschewed direct allusion and use of Greek and Roman mythologies early in his creative work, thinking they had become "worn out and unmanageable" having "ceased to be a living tradition," he nonetheless regarded Greek literature as an important model on which a 'classical' form of contemporary Anglo-Celtic literature might be established – unchained from the dominant stream of English literature.[13] John Synge's death, however – as well as Yeats' growing frustration with the Irish "Pulpit and the Press" – prompted a shift in approach.[14] Amid that shift, the literature of Greek tragedy, especially Sophocles' *Oedipus Rex*, attracted greater interest from Yeats. Put crudely, his attention turned from Homer and the epic ambition of Revival to the dramatic and a self-critical look back over his past endeavors. The reception given to Sophocles in Yeats' work, however, was not mediated, on the whole, by direct engagement with source texts in Greek. His fascination emerged rather from a multivocal chain of transmission in English, his *King Oedipus* (1926) being not so much the result of a "discrete solo operation" with the original Greek as a self-conscious work of conglomerated retranslation, an aggressive re-stylization of the Victorian vision of Sophocles.[15] The retranslated idiom Yeats built for *King Oedipus* was largely adapted from earlier English versions of the play – even as he eviscerated the poetic affectations that had made these, he thought, hopelessly passé and inauthentic. By bringing Sophocles out of England, and into the orbit of Irish revivalism, however, Yeats carried the Greek across significant "cultural and temporal boundaries," and, because of that, the governing principles of his translating, his stylizing of Sophocles, evolved too.[16] Retranslations of this kind, Lawrence Venuti has observed, are unique in that they create significance "doubly bound to the receiving situation, determined not only by the receptor values which the translator inscribes in the source text, but also by the values inscribed in a previous version."[17] As such, retranslations may often come to "reflect," Venuti writes, "changes in the values and institutions of the translating culture" that may, in some

---

[13] Yeats *CW9* (2004) 210. See Introduction, pp. 31–33; Chapter 1, pp. 67–68.
[14] Yeats, "*Samhain*: 1903 – The Theatre, The Pulpit and the Newspapers," in Yeats *CW8* (2003) 36.
[15] Washbourne (2016) 169.
[16] Lowe (2014) 413.
[17] Venuti (2013) 96.

cases, inspire "new ways of reading and appreciating the source texts."[18] In the doubly bound case of Yeats and *Oedipus*, however, Venuti's point may be taken further – not least because the story behind Ireland's *Oedipus Rex* is not solely one of Yeats repackaging specific Victorian versions of Sophocles. His encounter with the tragedian also forms part of a more complex story, that of Yeats' so-called modernist reinvention. As Ezra Pound (1885–1972) observed in 1914, Yeats had already begun a radical metamorphosis in his style and in his politics – even as he strove, with difficulty, to work through a version of *Oedipus*. His writing appeared, Pound wrote, "at *prise* with things as they are and no longer romantically Celtic."[19] Throughout this transformation, Yeats returned, often self-critically, to revise and retranslate parts and fragments of the Oedipus cycle over time. These acts of continual revision did not just invigorate "new ways of reading" the ancient Greek tragedy; they also helped push Yeats to reform the aesthetic and political dynamism of his creative work at large.[20] The reception of Sophocles thus became a "complex collectivity" on which he could draw, one which did indeed help him produce the Abbey Theatre's *King Oedipus* in 1926 but which also drew out a wide-ranging stylistic revolution.[21] *Oedipus* spoke powerfully to Yeats – in equal parts to his lingering belief in the Revival's Hellenic ambitions and to his growing doubt that any 'classical' ideal would ever come to pass in Ireland. In *Oedipus* Yeats examined that dream and that doubt, skeptically renegotiating many of the "debates and identities" that had been central in his early reception of ancient literature.[22] The important role that classics played in modernist renegotiations of Celtic revival is, of course, not exclusive to Yeats' dramatic work with Sophocles alone but can be traced also in the mock Homeric world of Joyce's *Ulysses* and later in the epic divergence of multilingual collage that both Jones and MacDiarmid derived from Scottish and Welsh movements.

Given Yeats' shifting approach to Greek reception, it is perhaps unsurprising that Fenton Turck's superficial moralism, his desire to elevate the Greeks as paragons of perennial virtue, upset him. Two weeks after the *Lusitania* docked, Yeats savaged Turck's vision of Greece in an extensive

---

[18] Venuti (2013) 107.
[19] Pound (1914) 68.
[20] Venuti (2013) 107.
[21] Washbourne (2016) 169.
[22] Hardwick (2000) 80.

interview with the *New York Times*. Without naming him, he attacked at length his phrase "moral uplift" and argued that American taste for the arts was stuck in a bygone age. "In many ways, in this country," he told the newspaper, "I think you still live in the Victorian epoch, so far as literature is concerned. Your very phrase 'moral uplift,' implies it. I think all that sort of thing a misunderstanding of literature."[23] The concept of 'moral uplift' had possessed some relevance in America during the 1890s in curricular discussions about the place of classical literature in state-sponsored education. In 1898 the president of Vassar College, James Monroe Taylor (1848–1916), had argued that secular education could effectively instill a sense of civic morality without reference to specific religious dogma. "[S]ound education has never been separable from ethical training," he explained: "By a sketch of the principal periods of Greek and Roman education it was shown that the reform movements in education came in connection with moral uplift. A neglect of moral teaching always involves the degradation of education, the debasement of society, the destruction of the school and the state."[24] Taylor's belief in the moral utility of classics was part of a wider phenomenon that stressed the "moral genius of the Greeks."[25] As Frank Turner observed, the desire to find in classical antiquity "prescriptive patterns for a literature of moral uplift and sanity" was widespread at the end of the nineteenth century when the "metaphor of Greece" had opened up, popularly speaking, "a humanistic path toward the secular – a path along which most traditional religious landmarks were absent but from which other traditional values still able to address the problems of society and art could be dimly perceived."[26] This "selective portrayal of Greece" proved useful in making tangible a "sense of cultural and ethical confidence about the possibility of a life of dignity, decency, and restraint outside the intellectual and moral boundaries of religion."[27] Surveys of Greek literature from this period were therefore clotted with "prescriptions of traditional English humanist values," values directed against "commercialism, pluralistic,

---

[23] "'American Literature Still in Victorian Era' – Yeats," *New York Times* (February 22, 1914) SM10.
[24] Taylor (1899) 41.
[25] Livingstone (1912) 24.
[26] Turner (1981) 34, 35.
[27] Turner (1981) 35. Granville Stanley Hall (1846–1924), a psychologist and one-time student of William James (1842–1910), argued likewise in *Educational Problems* (1911): "moral uplift" in literature was to be sought above all other "supernal elements." All "English literature studied in the high school," he argued, was to be selected neither with religious doctrine in mind nor according to "the dangerous principle of art for art's sake," but "primarily with reference to moral values." Hall (1911) vol. I, 271.

liberal politics, and subjective morality."[28] As a "conservative ideological weapon," ancient Greek literature was thus appropriated to consolidate conventional tastes for an educated middle class, confirming what R. W. Livingstone (1880–1960) called "our moral sympathies," not "the morbid pathology and the charming affectations of modern literature."[29] Ancient writers were not motivated by avant-garde aims, he thought, by "Art for Art's sake," or even "Intellect for Intellect's sake ... its writers do not lead us, like Mr. Yeats, into the bypaths of the human soul, to travel by dark and enchanted ways," but to a consideration of the "deliberate, laborious, and triumphant battle for virtue."[30]

For Yeats, however, the value of Greek literature had little to do with secular virtue or reinforcing conventional codes of social conduct. Greek poets had explored, he thought, the depths of the human mind without restriction – refusing to "deny expression to any profound or lasting state of consciousness."[31] No "state of consciousness" ever appeared "morbid and exaggerated" in their literature, for the "Greeks had no exaggerated morbidity of sex, because they were free to express all. They were the most healthy of all peoples. The man who is sex-mad is hateful to me, but he was created by the moralists."[32] If contemporary poets were to eschew "morbidity" and exaggeration in their own work, they had to embrace the desire "to express all" and reject moralism.[33] "It is," Yeats told the *Times*,

> the history of the more intense states of consciousness that a great artist expounds, and it is necessary to his very existence as an artist that he should be free to make use of all the circumstances necessary for the expression of any permanent state of consciousness; and not only is this necessary to the artist, but to society itself.[34]

During his tour of America that winter, Yeats continued to praise the Greeks as exemplars of artistic freedom while attacking the "commercial theatre" whose "damnable system of morals" had brought a "great deal of money for a great many people" but had sacrificed "great realistic art" for "purely topical sentiment."[35] Despite that theatre's popularity with the

[28] Turner (1981) 33.
[29] Turner (1981) 33; Livingstone (1912) 167, 168.
[30] Livingstone (1912) 163, 24.
[31] "'American Literature Still in Victorian Era' – Yeats," *New York Times* (February 22, 1914) SM10.
[32] "'American Literature Still in Victorian Era' – Yeats," *New York Times* (February 22, 1914) SM10.
[33] "'American Literature Still in Victorian Era' – Yeats," *New York Times* (February 22, 1914) SM10.
[34] "'American Literature Still in Victorian Era' – Yeats," *New York Times* (February 22, 1914) SM10.
[35] Yeats, "The Theatre and Beauty" (c. December 1913), as in O'Driscoll (1971) 68, 70, 68.

public, Yeats was convinced that a new "revival of poetry" was nonetheless on the rise.[36] "Art for art's sake," he declared, "the disinterested service of the Muses, passed away for a time, and everywhere now it is coming back. Paris, like London, is ceasing to be commercial in literature."[37] The roots of this revival lay in a new "violent realism ... dragging into the light what is hidden, before it can return to a literature of beauty and peace."[38] Just as the Greeks had embraced the freedom to express all, poets were again drawn to "the inner life, the life of our emotions," for in the exploration of one's mind, even the contemporary writer could become "the spectator of the ages."[39] "The Tale of Troy is quite near to me," he declared,

> probably much nearer than anything I read in this morning's paper ... when I am going to express my own mind, the things I think of when alone, the things I feel as a solitary man – then I want all culture. I cannot know too much. I want a vast symbolism, a phantasmagoria going back to the beginning of the world, and always the Tale of Troy, of Judea, will be nearer to me than my own garden, because I am not limited by time. I am as old as mankind.[40]

Yeats' tenacious defense of artistic freedom stretched back to bitter disputes he had with both the Irish press and the country's Catholic hierarchy. Ten years prior, when Synge's play *In the Shadow of the Glen* (1903) was vilified as a work whose "libel on womankind" was tantamount to "staging a Lie," Yeats denounced the criticism.[41] "Extreme politics in Ireland were once the politics of intellectual freedom also," he wrote, "but now, under the influence of a violent contemporary paper, and under other influences more difficult to follow, even extreme politics seem about to unite themselves to hatred of ideas."[42] As he saw it, the press and the pulpit feared "the imagination of highly-cultivated men, who have begun that experimental digging in the deep pit of themselves, which can alone produce great literature."[43] Paralyzed by the "enemies of life, the chimeras of the Pulpit and the Press," writers were pressured to produce work "full of personified averages, partisan fictions, rules of life

[36] "'American Literature Still in Victorian Era' – Yeats," *New York Times* (February 22, 1914) SM10.
[37] "'American Literature Still in Victorian Era' – Yeats," *New York Times* (February 22, 1914) SM10.
[38] "'American Literature Still in Victorian Era' – Yeats," *New York Times* (February 22, 1914) SM10.
[39] Yeats, as in O'Driscoll (1971) 70–71.
[40] Yeats, as in O'Driscoll (1971) 71.
[41] Griffith (1903) 1.
[42] Yeats, "To the Editor of the *United Irishman*, 24 October 1903," in Yeats *CL3* (1994) 451.
[43] Yeats *CL3* (1994) 451.

that would drill everybody into the one posture, habits that are like the pinafores of charity-school children."[44] Audiences had thus become less inclined "to care for a play because it is a play" but rather only "because it is serviceable to some cause."[45] Fearing new efforts might place the Irish theatre under an official censor – perhaps England's Lord Chamberlain, then Edward Hyde Villiers, the 5th Earl of Clarendon (1846–1914) – Yeats set out to defy the "rough-and-ready conscience of the newspaper and the pulpit," to bait those who were eager "to make the bounds of drama narrower."[46] In what was an unlikely place, he discovered a tragedy controversial enough to show that Dublin was indeed "a place of intellectual excitement – a place where the mind goes to be liberated as it was liberated by the theatres of Greece and England and France at certain great moments in their history."[47]

While on tour in North America in 1904, Yeats visited the University of Notre Dame, and found, to his surprise, a "general lack of religeous [sic] prejudice" among the priests and students in South Bend.[48] "I have been entirely delighted by the big merry priests of Notre Dame – all Irish & proud as lucifer of their success in getting Jews & non-conformists to come to their college."[49] Given the recent maltreatment Synge's work had received, Yeats was shocked to learn also that in 1899 a group of undergraduates had been allowed to translate and stage Sophocles' Oedipus

---

[44] Yeats CW8 (2003) 36.

[45] Yeats, "Samhain: 1904 – The Dramatic Movement," in Yeats CW8 (2003) 44.

[46] Yeats, "Samhain: 1903 – Moral and Immoral Plays," in Yeats CW8 (2003) 29; Yeats, "To the Editor of the United Irishman, 10 October 1903," in Yeats CL3 (1994) 440. Since the Licensing Act of 1737 and the subsequent Theatre Regulation Act of 1843 – a law that adapted censorship to serve "the taste of the emergent Victorian bourgeoisie" – theatrical productions in England were required to seek a formal license from the government. The Lord Chamberlain retained the right to alter the title, dialogue, or general character of scripts submitted for review. According to Yeats, this requirement had helped create a theatre stained by commercial interests and marred with a "pretended hatred of vice and a real hatred of intellect." In Ireland, by contrast, stage production remained outside English jurisdiction and largely free from external review. "[W]e are better off so far as the law is concerned than we would be in England," Yeats wrote. "The theatrical law of Ireland was made by the Irish Parliament ... we must be grateful to that the ruling caste of free spirits, that being free themselves they left the theatre in freedom." Nevertheless, "the prevailing standards for acceptable stage productions in Ireland drew heavily," as one scholar has suggested, "upon the British model, especially in restricting the representation of living or recently deceased people as stage characters and in prohibiting obscenity and blasphemy. The majority of plays performed in Ireland at the end of the nineteenth century were works licensed by the Lord Chamberlain." Green and Karolides (2005) 568; Yeats CW8 (2003) 45; Dean (2004) 11, as well as Fowell and Palmer (1913) 372–74.

[47] Yeats, "Samhain: 1903 – The Reform of the Theatre," in Yeats CW8 (2003) 26.

[48] Yeats, "To Lady Augusta Gregory [18 January 1904]," in Yeats CL3 (1994) 520.

[49] Yeats CL3 (1994) 520.

Rex.[50] At the time, producing *Oedipus Rex* was censored in England, where it was thought the play's frank exploration of incest and parricide would induce viewers to "gratify unclean and morbid sentiment."[51] Sophocles was widely studied at British schools and universities – Matthew Arnold had praised his poetry for showing "human nature developed in a number of directions, politically, socially, religiously, morally developed – in its completest and most harmonious development" – but *Oedipus* was thought too scandalous to stage, too likely to foment "a vitiated public taste solely in the cause of indecency."[52] It was precisely that indecency, however, that power to offend which intrigued Yeats. Eager to distinguish Ireland's theatre from England's, eager also to resist any threats that might "limit our freedom from either official or patriotic hands," Yeats returned from America motivated to produce *Oedipus Rex* in Dublin.[53] Yet to bring Sophocles to the Irish stage Yeats felt that *Oedipus* would have to be anglicized in a new idiom that would clear the play of any impulse to bowdlerize its scandalous nature. The conventions of "those great scholars of the last century" had often produced a language "too complicated in its syntax for the stage," a language that obscured the tragedy with a "Latin mist."[54] He wrote, "I think" those

> who translated Sophocles into an English full of Latinised constructions and Latinised habits of thought, were all wrong–and that the schoolmasters are wrong who make us approach Greek through Latin. Nobody ever

[50] The performance at Notre Dame took place on May 15, 1899. It was commemorated with the publication of *The Oedipus Tyrannus of Sophocles, Translated and Presented by the Students of Notre Dame University*. The book contained the Greek text of the play alongside an English translation. Introducing the tragedy, the students noted that in producing the *Oedipus* "nothing should be farther from our minds than idolatry or superstition. Although we will introduce you, next Monday, into a pagan temple, in the very hour of sacrifice, we beg that our actions and our sayings be not considered, in any way, as idolatrous.

> We do not mean to pray to pagan gods,
> And if we swear in Greek, the harm is less."

[51] Stanley Buckmaster, Member of the Advisory Board on Stage Plays, Letter to the Lord Chamberlain, Charles Spencer (November 23, 1910). Lord Chamberlain's Plays Correspondence File: *Oedipus Rex* 1910/814, British Library Archive.

[52] Arnold, "On the Modern Element in Literature" (1857) in Arnold (1960) 28; Sir John Hare, Member of the Advisory Board on Stage Plays, Letter to the Lord Chamberlain, Charles Spencer (November 21, 1910). Lord Chamberlain's Plays Correspondence File: *Oedipus Rex* 1910/814, British Library Archive.

[53] Yeats, "*Samhain*: 1903 – The Reform of the Theatre," in Yeats *CW8* (2003) 34. On Yeats' interest in the play, see also Arkins (2005) 156–58 as well as Lauriola (2017) 273–74.

[54] Yeats, "Oedipus the King" (September 8, 1931) in Yeats *CW10* (2000) 221; Yeats, "Plain Man's Oedipus" (15 January 1933) in Yeats *CW10* (2000) 244, 245.

trembled on a dark road because he was afraid of meeting the nymphs and satyrs of Latin literature, but men have trembled on dark roads in Ireland and in Greece.[55]

Because, as Yeats saw it, the kinship of the Irish and the ancient Greek ran deeper even than the bond of Latin and Greek, the Irish theatre was well placed to make men dread again Oedipus' κλύδωνα δεινῆς συμφορᾶς, the "breakers of misfortune" (*OT* 1527).[56] Drawing on the scholarship of the French philologist Marie Henri d'Arbois de Jubainville (1827–1910), who had insisted that "an old foundation of Graeco-Celtic legends" existed prior "to the separation of the two races," Yeats believed that Sophoclean tragedy would "seem at home" in Ireland.[57] "No man has ever prayed to or dreaded one of Vergil's nymphs," he declared, "but when Oedipus at Colonus went into the Wood of the Furies he felt the same creeping in his flesh that an Irish countryman feels in certain haunted woods in Galway and in Sligo."[58] Though the Irish were equipped to strip *Oedipus* of that "half Latin, half Victorian dignity" laid on it by the nineteenth century, Yeats himself, however, had little Greek.[59] Being a poor student of the language, his headmaster at the Erasmus Smith School in Dublin (a school he attended from 1881 to 1883) once reported that his "taking up French and German simultaneously with Latin and Greek" had been "ruinous."[60] Age did not improve his ability – still unable to read classics in the original, Yeats could only gaze, he wrote, "in useless longing at books that have been, through the poor mechanism of translation, the builders of my soul."[61]

Despite this fact, Yeats still pursued *Oedipus* vigorously, seeking help from Greek scholars and amateur enthusiasts. He first approached Gilbert Murray, then of New College, Oxford, who had recently translated Euripides' *Hippolytus*. "Will you translate Edipus Rex for us? We can offer you nothing for it but a place in heaven," Yeats told him, "but if you do, it

---

[55] Yeats *CW10* (2000) 221–22.
[56] Grene (1942) 154.
[57] d'Arbois de Jubainville (1903) 69; Yeats *CW10* (2000) 245.
[58] Yeats *CW10* (2000) 245.
[59] Yeats *CW10* (2000) 244.
[60] Murphy (1978) 133. On Yeats' knowledge of Greek, see Arkins (1990) 2–5: "Yeats refused to go to Trinity because he felt he would fail the entrance examination: 'neither my Classics nor my mathematics were good enough for any examination' (A 79–80). This statement shows clearly that on leaving the High School Yeats had some knowledge of Latin and Greek, but that it was inadequate." See Foster (1997) 33–34, Liebregts (1993) 7–21 as well as the Introduction, p. 6n28; Chapter I, p. 55n35.
[61] Yeats *CW3* (1999) 76.

will be a great event. Our company are excited at the idea ... There is no censor here to forbid it as it has been forbidden in England."[62] In spring 1904 Murray's *Hippolytus* had a successful production under Harley Granville-Barker's direction at London's Lyric Theatre. The production triggered a minor revival of Attic drama in England that began to make Greek tragedy "no longer the exclusive preserve of the private theatres in the English-speaking world."[63] To Yeats, however, Euripides' London success exemplified the lack of stylistic daring he associated with the commercial interests of the English theatre. Thus he pleaded with Murray to "not ask us to play Euripides instead, for Euripides is rapidly becoming a popular English dramatist, and it is upon Sophocles that we have set our imaginations."[64] Staging *Oedipus* would, he assured him, make a great mark on the public mind in Ireland, persuading the country

> that she is very liberal, abhors censors delights in the freedom of the arts, is prepared for anything. When we have performed Edipus the King, and everybody is proud of having done something which is forbidden in England, even the newspapers will give [up] pretending to be timid.[65]

Although he believed Murray would agree, Yeats underestimated how the scholar's aims were shaped by a desire to democratize and popularize the classics.[66] As Christopher Stray has noted, central to Murray's "vision of Hellenism" was the notion that classics possessed a "reforming and educative mission" in the modern world, a mission to maintain "in an ocean of barbarism" what Murray later called "a large and enduring island of true Hellenic life."[67] As he saw it, Sophocles did not neatly fit

---

[62] Yeats, "To Gilbert Murray, 24 January [1905]," in Yeats *CL4* (2005) 22–23.

[63] Hall and Macintosh (2005) 496.

[64] Yeats *CL4* (2005) 23. It is likely that Yeats' distaste for Euripidean tragedy came by way of Nietzsche's condemnation of *frevelnder Euripides* ("wicked Euripides") in *The Birth of Tragedy* (1872). Unlike Sophocles and Aeschylus, Euripides' "aesthetic maxim," Nietzsche insisted, "that 'to be beautiful everything must be known,' is parallel to the Socratic principle that 'to be good everything must be known.' We may thus regard Euripides as the poet of aesthetic Socratism. Like himself, Socrates was also a spectator at the theatre, who did not comprehend, and therefore did not appreciate the old tragedy; in alliance with him, Euripides ventured to be the herald of a new artistic activity. If then the old tragedy was destroyed, it follows that aesthetic Socratism was the murderous principle." Nietzsche (1901) 4.

[65] Yeats *CL4* (2005) 23.

[66] Though Murray was regarded as the "most popular Hellenist of his time," the "most conspicuous Greek propagandist of the day," some like T. S. Eliot doubted whether he had had the "slightest vitalizing effect on English poetry." The "quite dead" attempts that Murray had made in translating Euripides showed that he had no "creative eye," no "creative instinct," only an ability to compose an English "masquerading as a vulgar debasement of the eminently personal idiom of Swinburne." Eliot (1920) 66, 70, 66.

[67] Stray (2007b) 3; Murray (1954) 58.

this mission. When considering the "historical growth" of his drama, Murray noted Sophocles' apparent "lack of speculative freedom" and was moreover "offended by what seem to be inexplicable pieces of conventionalism."[68] Murray therefore refused Yeats:

> O Man, I will not translate the Oedipus Rex for the Irish Theatre, because it is a play with nothing Irish about it: no religion, not one beautiful action, hardly a stroke of poetry. Even the good things that have to be done in order to make the plot work are done through mere loss of temper. The spiritual tragedy is never faced or understood: all the stress is laid on the mere external uncleanness. Sophocles no doubt did many bad things in his life: I would not try to shield him from just blame … Seriously, I rather hope you wont do the Oedipus. It is not the play for you to cast your lot with. Do the Prometheus … or even the Persae with a seditious innuendo. Or the Antigone.[69]

Without his help Yeats approached Oliver St John Gogarty (1878–1957) and his former classmate, William Kirkpatrick Magee (1868–1961), better known as John Eglinton. However, before either could complete their versions, Yeats complained about their use of archaisms, fearing that that a "language highly artificial and conscious" would "not prove vocal" on stage.[70] Though Yeats could not find a scholar prepared to translate an unadorned *Oedipus*, the prospect of flouting the authority of the Lord Chamberlain remained irresistible, and, by late 1911, his plan to stage *Oedipus* in Dublin began to dovetail with a desire to transform his own style, to move from "dreamy languorousness towards concrete vigorousness."[71] Abandoning the idea of performing someone else's version, Yeats

---

[68] Murray (1897) 203, 239, 203. On Murray's view of Greek drama, see Griffith (2007) 51–80.

[69] Murray (1977) 145–46.

[70] Oliver St John Gogarty, Letter to G. K. A. Bell (April 7, 1905) in Gogarty (1971) 88; Yeats, "To John Millington Synge, 3 October [1906]," in Yeats *CL4* (2005) 509. Gogarty observed that Yeats considered archaism "only admissible when one had discovered it for oneself: there was no defence for the continuance of mere metrical conventions: '*Hast*', '*shalt*', '*thou*', '*thee*', '*wert*', '*art*' etc." Gogarty (1971) 88.

[71] Longenbach (2010) 322. In August 1909, amid a new censorship crisis stirred up by George Bernard Shaw's play *The Shewing-Up of Blanco Posnett* (1909), Yeats once again reaffirmed his desire to produce *Oedipus* on Irish soil. When the under-secretary of Dublin Castle threatened to abolish the patent of the Abbey Theatre for its planned staging of Shaw's play, Yeats insisted that not only would he proceed with the production of *Posnett* but his theatre would also perform the Oedipus Rex that year. Thinking that the suppression of a "performance of the greatest masterpiece of Greek drama" might be too much for the Castle to risk, Yeats again held up the staging of Sophocles as illustrative of both Ireland's liberal-mindedness and its bold ingenuity in theatre: "We will put Oedipus the King (also censored in England) on with Posnett, & allow them to take away our Patent. We consider ourselves the guardians of the liberties of the Irish National Theatre of the future, of its political freedom for one thing." Yeats, "A. E. F. Horniman [15 August 1909]," in Yeats *CL5* (2018) 577; Yeats, "To John Quinn [15 August 1909]," in Yeats *CL5* (2018) 577.

set out to adapt Richard Jebb (1841–1905) and A. W. Verrall's (1851–1912) *The Oedipus Tyrannus of Sophocles As Performed at Cambridge November 22–26, 1887. With a Translation in Prose by R. C. Jebb, And a Translation of the Songs of the Chorus in Verse adapted to the Music of C. Villiers Stanford, M. A., by A. W. Verrall.*[72] He was aided by Walter Nugent Monck (1877–1958), the founder of the Norwich Players and later a director of the Maddermarket Theatre. Though neither had much Greek, they began overwriting Jebb and Verrall in January 1912 with a translation of a translation. This transformation plunged the polarizing reception of *Oedipus* into both the nationalist aspirations of the Abbey Theatre and also Yeats' desire to develop "a manifestly new note" in his poetry.[73] With *Oedipus* as a testing ground for "compression and rhythmical invention" – elements that were to become "so characteristic of Modernist verse" – Yeats worked at a Sophoclean aesthetic of "prose directness" and "hard light."[74]

From as early as October 1902 Yeats had professed admiration for "the regulated declamation of the Greeks," a practice "we are trying to get back to."[75] The "secret" to the "greatest of all the arts ... the art of speech," he argued, had been bequeathed to the civilized nations of Europe by the Greeks, but that secret had been "lost for centuries."[76] Without it poetry often drifted into an "exageration [*sic*] of sentiment & sentimental beauty which," he wrote, "I have come to think unmanly."[77] For Yeats, the 'weak' poetry of the *fin de siècle*'s prevailing "decadence" exemplified the height of sentimental abstraction and exaggeration.[78] Even his "own early subjective verse" with its "shadows & hollow images" had come from a "region of brooding emotions full of fleshly waters & vapours which kill the spirit & the will, ecstasy & joy equally."[79] Having

[72] "The text was without doubt the edition of Jebb mentioned earlier, *The Oedipus Tyrannus of Sophocles as Performed at Cambridge.*" See Yeats (1989b) 20, 6n5. Jebb and Verrall's (1887) edition printed the English in a column across from the original Greek on each page. Yeats' copy with annotations is held in the Yeats' archive at the National Library of Ireland, MS 40,568/224. Edward O'Shea notes in *A Descriptive Catalog of W. B. Yeats's Library* (1985) that "This is the basic text, the point of departure for WBY's *King Oedipus.* This copy has been extensively edited by WBY, mostly to delete passages of archaic diction, but there are occasional very brief rewritings or additions as well." See O'Shea (1985) 254n1962.

[73] Pound (1914) 65.

[74] Yao (2002) 135; Pound (1914) 66, 67. See also Pound's praise for "hard Sophoclean light" in his poem, "Xenia." Pound (1913) 60.

[75] "Speaking to Musical Notes," *The Freeman's Journal* (October 31, 1902) 4.

[76] "Speaking to Musical Notes," *The Freeman's Journal* (October 31, 1902) 4.

[77] Yeats, "To George Russell (Æ), [April 1904]," in Yeats *CL3* (1994) 577.

[78] Yeats *CL3* (1994) 577.

[79] Yeats *CL3* (1994) 577.

grown "weary of that wild God Dionysius [*sic*]," Yeats needed "the
Far-Darter," Apollo, instead, and drawing on a distinction he had
encountered in Nietzsche's *The Birth of Tragedy* (1872), Yeats rationalized
as Apollonic his desire for more concrete, more formal invention in
poetry.[80] George Moore observed at this time the aspersions Yeats cast on
the 'Dionysian' character of contemporary poetry, the "softness, the
weakness, the effeminacy of modern literature [which he thought] could
be attributed to ideas."[81] By contrast, "Yeats said," Moore recalled,

> that the ancient writer wrote about things ... "There are no ideas in
> ancient literature, only things," and in support of this theory, reference
> was made to the sagas, to the Iliad, to the Odyssey, and I listened to him,
> forgetful of the subject which we had met to discuss. "It is through the
> dialect," he said, "that one escapes from abstract words, back to the sensa-
> tion inspired directly by the thing itself."[82]

The longing to see poetry return from the "region of shadows" to "the
thing itself" prefigured not only Pound's Imagist doctrines of 1913 – his
insistence on "[d]irect treatment of the 'thing' whether subjective or
objective" – but also T. E. Hulme's assertion that "after a hundred years
of romanticism" a "classical revival" was afoot in modern poetry, a revival
marked by "dry, hard, classical verse" where writers could again remind
man of "finiteness ... that he is mixed up with earth. He may jump, but
he always returns back; he never flies away into the circumambient gas."[83]
For Hulme, the "new classical spirit" differed from the "strange light" of
Romanticism, a movement whose view of humanity as an "infinite reser-
voir full of possibilities" had "debauched us" with "round metaphors of
flight ... always flying, flying over abysses, flying up into the eternal
gases. The word infinite in every other line."[84] The classical vision, by

---

[80] Yeats, "To John Quinn, 15 May [1903]," in Yeats *CL3* (1994) 372. Yeats' interest in Nietzsche's analysis of Greek tragedy was reported on in *The Daily Chronicle* of May 13, 1903. Lecturing at
Clifford's Inn in London, the poet then extolled "the Dionysic and the Apollonic moods of
poetry, which went to make up the perfection of the Greek drama." These moods were also, he
alleged, operative in the literature of ancient Ireland, where Gaelic "folk poetry" corresponded to
"the Greek chorus," its "extravagant cry" being what Yeats called "the utterance of the greatest
emotions possible, the heartfelt lyric of an ancient people's soul." Ireland's heroic poetry, by
contrast, reflected the "Apollonic" mood, possessing "the sense of form, the dramatic or epic
portion of the work of art, the heroic discipline, which, of course, has no relation to morality as
generally understood or to service to the State and mankind." See P. G. W. (1903) 7.

[81] Moore (1911) 348.

[82] Moore (1911) 348.

[83] Yeats *CL3* (1994) 577; Moore (1911) 348; Pound (1918) 95; see the essay "Romanticism and
Classicism," in Hulme (1924) 113, 133, 120.

[84] Hulme (1924) 113, 127, 116, 127, 120.

contrast, accepted the "sane classical dogma of original sin" and saw the human being as "an extraordinarily fixed and limited animal" that needed "accurate description," not the "bringing in of some of the emotions that are grouped around the word infinite."[85]

To free his own writing from "round metaphors of flight," Yeats had once looked to Synge whose "peasant dialect and dialogue" had enacted something of "the elemental staging of the primitive, unelaborate stage" at the Abbey.[86] Yet where Synge had employed a knowledge of Irish Gaelic as a corrective to the decorative excess of aestheticism, Yeats had no such recourse. As he began to adapt *Oedipus*, he had no Greek, no Irish, nor even Synge himself to rely on any longer.[87] What Yeats did have, however, was a belief that his "lyric faculty" was perhaps finally returning.[88] After publishing his eight-volume *The Collected Works of William Butler Yeats* (1908), the poet had wondered whether his talent would "ever recover from the heterogeneous labour of these last few years," labor that included advocacy for the Abbey as well as his involvement in the disputes of contemporary nationalism.[89] However, by the time Yeats turned to Sophocles, his responsibilities at the Abbey had diminished and his recovery was underway, due in part to his collaboration with Ezra Pound. In 1910 it was Pound who suggested that Yeats had "come out of the shadows & has declared for life … Yeats has found within himself spirit of the new air which I by accident had touched before him."[90] His poem "No Second Troy," with its stark vision of Helen – "beauty like a tightened bow, a kind / That is not natural in an age like this"– impressed Pound and intimated that a new kind of Hellenic perfection might be possible.[91] The poem exemplified, Pound wrote, "the spirit of the new things as I saw them in London."[92] As he saw it, Yeats was beginning to move away from abstraction, drawn to the *quidditas* of ancient Greek. To articulate in English the 'whatness' of reality – just as the Greeks had

---

[85] Hulme (1924) 117, 116, 127.

[86] Hulme (1924) 120; J. M. Synge, Letter to Spencer Brodney (December 10 and 12, 1907), as noted in Synge (1966) 47n1; *Weekly Freeman* (May 23, 1903) 9, as cited in Schuchard (2008) 130.

[87] For advice about ancient Greek, Yeats and Nugent Monck sometimes called on Rev. Rex Rynd, the preceptor of Norwich Cathedral, and a young scholar named Charles Stewart Power (1892–1950).

[88] Yeats *Mem* (1972) 172. On Yeats' poetic transformation in this period, see James Longenbach, *Stone Cottage: Pound, Yeats and Modernism* (1988) 14–16.

[89] Yeats *Mem* (1972) 171.

[90] "16: Ezra Pound to Margaret Cravens" (June 30, 1910) in Pound (1988) 41.

[91] Yeats *VE* (1987) 256–57. See Introduction, pp. 33–34, Chapter 2, pp. 88–91, and the Conclusion, pp. 248–50.

[92] "23: Ezra Pound to Margaret Cravens" (November 27, 1910) in Pound (1988) 61.

expressed things and not ideas in verse – soon became a shared ambition for both writers, one which pushed Pound to seek in contemporary work: "no slither; direct – no excessive use of adjectives, no metaphors that won't permit examination. It's straight talk, straight as the Greek!"[93] Yeats similarly stressed a desire for the simplicity and directness of speech. In a diary entry dated December 1912, he elaborated on the "First Principles" then guiding his work:

> Not to find ones art by the analysis of language or amid the circumstances of dreams but to live a passionate life, & to express the emotions that find one thus in simple rhythmical language ~~which never shows the obviously studied vocabulary~~. The words should be the swift natural words that suggest the circumstances out of which they rose ~~of real life~~. One must be both dramatist and actor & yet be in great earnest.[94]

The extent to which Yeats' work on Sophocles helped clarify these principles is unclear, but it is clear that in the year prior to articulating this rationale Yeats had been adapting Jebb and Verrall's *Oedipus*, convinced that the ancient Greeks had perfected a plain "impassioned speech" that spoke of things, and not abstractions.[95]

As Yeats saw it, Jebb and Verrall's failure with *Oedipus* lay in their desire to keep strictly to "every minutest feature in the Greek structure, every *nuance* of meaning."[96] They thereby blunted the play's pathos, drowning the tragedy in unspeakable literalism and scholarly abstraction, and so, in January 1912, Yeats began to break down their idiom "from the point of view of speech," thinking he might rescue Sophocles from the "old, learned, respectable bald heads" of the scholars.[97] Jebb was, of course, widely regarded as one having "sympathetic insight" into what Samuel Henry Butcher (1850–1910) once called "the niceties of Sophoclean language," its "deflections from ordinary usage" and its "pregnant expressions."[98] His seven-volume edition of "perfectly literal" Sophoclean translations, published between 1883 and 1896, showed evidence of a "remarkable and, so far as I know, a unique, faculty of infusing poetry into

---

[93] Pound, "7: To Harriet Monroe" (October 1912) in Pound (1971) 11.

[94] Yeats, "First Principles." Maud Gonne Xmas Notebook, 1912 (NLI 30, 358). Yeats Archive, Box 88.2, SUNY Stony Brook. See also Foster (1997) 476–77. Yeats' obsession with "natural order," "swifter dialogue a more direct syntax," was a long-standing fixation. See, for example, Yeats, "Letter to Gordon Bottomley" (January 8, 1910) in Yeats *CL5* (2018) 679–80.

[95] "Speaking to Musical Notes," *The Freeman's Journal* (October 31, 1902) 4.

[96] Review of R. C. Jebb, *Sophocles: The Plays and Fragments, with Critical Notes, Commentary, and Translation in English Prose* in *Journal of Education* 6.178 (n. s.) (May 1, 1884) 180.

[97] Yeats, "To Lady Gregory" (6 January 1912) in Yeats *CLWBY*, entry no. 1794; Yeats *VE* (1987) 337.

[98] Butcher (1884) 796.

grammar, of leading his readers, through particles, moods, and tenses, vividly to realise the dramatic situation and enter into the feelings of the speaker."[99] To Yeats, however, Jebb's literalism made for poor dialogue and utterly un-Hellenic stagings of Sophocles. Jebb himself set little store by claims of stylistic or dramatic merit for his versions of Sophocles, once saying of his *Electra* (1870) that "Nothing is staked upon it; it pretends to be nothing more than a school & college book, & if thought useful in that character, it will have fulfilled its purpose."[100] Yeats, though, needed more than a schoolbook *Oedipus*: he wanted an unmitigated, 'pure' *Oedipus* for the Abbey stage, one that could capture for a modern audience the felt passion of spoken Greek. The play's directness was not clouded by the "elaborate diction" of Sophocles' "original and complex" Greek.[101] However, when Jebb and Verrall had sought a bare equivalence in English, Sophocles' "unusual words and phrases" were confused in a new and foreign context: words and phrases once thought to "escape notice" in Greek "because they harmonize so perfectly with other factors in their context" became almost unreadable.[102] Yeats therefore put "readers and scholars out of [his] mind," retranslating his own version "to be sung and spoken. The one thing that I kept in mind was that a word unfitted for living speech, out of its natural order, or unnecessary to our modern technique, would check emotion and tire attention."[103]

For Jebb, expressing the literal nuances of Greek had presented both stylistic problems for English and more substantive thematic difficulties as well. Sophocles was a "model of serenity and restraint, and the perfect representative of 'the best Greek time'," and his work moreover demonstrated "evidence of true faith and morals."[104] Thus Jebb sought to present him in an exacting manner not only to show "the higher moral and mental side of the age of Pericles" but to provide sanctuary to those eager to "retreat from civilization."[105] Unlike Aeschylus and Euripides (whose "irrationality and pathos" Jebb thought modern), Sophocles exemplified

---

[99] Review of R. C. Jebb, *Sophocles: The Plays and Fragments. With Critical Notes, Commentary, and Translation in English Prose* in *The Athenaeum* 2948 (April 26, 1884) 531; Butcher (1884) 796–97.

[100] Jebb, as in Stray (2013) 47. For its time, though, Jebb's 'Englished' Sophocles was considered "different from the cumbrous translationese which was then so common." Stray (2007a) 79. See also Yeats *CW10* (2000) 221–22.

[101] Earp (1944) 147; Long (1968) 3.

[102] Long (1968) 3.

[103] Yeats, "Notes" for *Sophocles' King Oedipus: A Version for the Modern Stage,* as in Yeats (1966) 851. See also Morash (2020) 218–34.

[104] Stray (1998) 219; Turner (1981) 102.

[105] Jebb (1877) 88; Stray (1998) 219.

"balance and poise, grandeur and grace combined."[106] His "noble tone of
conciliation between sacred tradition and a progressive culture, between
authority and reason, between the letter and the spirit of religion,"
opposed much of the modern spirit, and thus Sophocles could not "easily
come home" to contemporary readers.[107] "If Sophocles has been," he
explained,

> on the whole, less popular in the modern world than either Aeschylus or
> Euripides, one reason may be this – there is no other Greek poet whose
> genius belongs so peculiarly to the best Greek time. Aeschylus has an
> element of Hebrew grandeur, Euripides has strong elements of modern
> pathos and romance ... But in order fully to appreciate Sophocles, we
> must place ourselves in sympathy with the Greek mind in its most charac-
> teristic modes of thought and with the Greek sense of beauty in its highest
> purity.[108]

To put a reader in touch with Sophocles' "union of power with purity of
taste," Jebb disavowed verse translation and sought to show in prose
"fully and exactly how the work of Sophocles is understood by me, both
in its larger aspects, and at every particular point."[109] To this end he
asserted an "absolute fidelity to the original," not adherence "to the letter
of the original, at the cost of the spirit, but to the spirit as expressed in
the letter," and prose, he maintained, was preferable to metrical verse for
that would possess "a more or less modern spirit of its own, due to its
very form."[110] For Jebb, translation was to be approached "solely from the
stand-point of the *commentator*, as an indispensable instrument of lucid
interpretation," to aid those who might be induced to "read a play of
Sophocles as they would read a great poem of a modern poet, – with no
such interposing nightmare of τύπτω as at Athens came between
Thackeray and his instinctive sense of what was admirable in the nature
and art around him."[111] The interpretation that Jebb gave to *Oedipus*

---

[106] Stray (1998) 220, 219–220.
[107] Jebb (1877) 88.
[108] Jebb (1877) 88.
[109] Jebb (1893) 189; Jebb (1883) vi.
[110] Jebb (1883) vi.
[111] Jebb (1883) vi, vii–viii. Citing Thackeray's view that Athens was "a humbug," Jebb refers to the
       fierce, physical disciplinary methods by which some British students were made to learn Greek
       and Latin. Thackeray's visit to Athens had confirmed his "doubts about the classics," doubts that
       he first experienced while a student at the London Charterhouse in the 1820s. There he was made
       to learn Greek at the hands of a "brute of a schoolmaster, whose mind was as cross-grained as any
       ploughboy's in Christendom ... whose lips, when they were not mouthing Greek or grammar,
       were yelling out the most brutal abuse of poor little cowering gentlemen." "Fancy the brutality,"

Tyrannus (1884) was no such "interposing nightmare" but a prose rendering considered "perfectly literal ... more literal than one of Bohn's, yet written in the clear, racy idiomatic English in which Mr. Jebb has no superior."[112] Lauded for its "literary merits," Jebb's work was a "treat of the very highest kind," one composed by not only a "scholar and critic of the largest attainments" but one of "great literary ability" as well.[113]

> [A]nd again and again, in unraveling the manifold subtleties of his author, [Jebb] gives us brilliant exemplifications of this true literalness, this triumph of the living spirit over the dead letter.[114]

Although some still doubted that Sophocles possessed "the Greek sense of beauty in its highest purity," Jebb was not alone in claiming "grand moral effects" for his work.[115] Not only Matthew Arnold but Edward Hayes Plumptre (1821–91) – the effusive translator, professor and chaplain of King's College, London – also believed that in Sophocles and "[n]owhere" else, "even in the ethics of Christian writers, are there nobler assertions of a morality divine, universal, unchangeable, of laws whose dwelling is on high."[116] Though the Greek poet had lived with "the absence of a higher knowledge" with "a veil over the central truth," he had not composed "half rhetorical sophistry," but wrote instead of the "true principles of all morality," timeless principles "of prior obligation to all conventional arrangements of society, or the maxims of political expediency."[117] "We may well rest in the belief that the name of Sophocles stands as clear and unblemished," Plumptre claimed, "as that of one against whom like charges were brought in the very recklessness of slander, the noble and true-hearted Socrates."[118] The characterization of

he declared, "of a man who began a Greek grammar with 'τύπτω, I thrash'! We were all made to begin it in that way." Jebb hoped, it seems, his translation could mollify the methods by which English speakers learned the classics. See Thackeray (1845) 45. See also Adams (2015) 63–68.

[112] Jebb (1883) vii; Review of R. C. Jebb, *Sophocles: The Plays and Fragments. With Critical Notes, Commentary, and Translation in English Prose* in *The Athenaeum* 2948 (April 26, 1884) 531.

[113] "Mr Jebb's 'Sophocles'," *The Spectator* 57.2913 (April 26, 1884) 555.

[114] Review of R. C. Jebb, *Sophocles: The Plays and Fragments. With Critical Notes, Commentary, and Translation in English Prose* in *The Athenaeum* 2948 (April 26, 1884) 531.

[115] Jebb (1877) 88; "Nay in Sophocles what is valuable is not so much his contributions to psychology & the anatomy of sentiment, as the grand moral effects produced by *style*. For the style is the expression of the nobility of the poet's character, as the matter is the expression of the richness of his mind." Arnold, "To Arthur Hugh Clough" (c. 1 March 1849), in Arnold (1993) 53; on the views of Arnold and Jebb, see Stray (1998) 218–21, Turner (1981) 28–33 as well as Vance (2015) 187–88.

[116] Plumptre (1867) lxxvi. See also Turner (1981) 102.

[117] Plumptre (1867) lxxvii, lxxvi.

[118] Plumptre (1867) lxxiv.

Sophocles as a Socratic, magnanimous victim "free from the alloy of baser metal" reflected the desire to see his drama "provide, within limits, instruction for human beings in a later time and place."[119]

Despite this characterization, however, controversy still swirled around the prospect of publicly producing *Oedipus*. When stage licenses were sought, the censor refused them, thinking there was little way of conveying *Oedipus* "in such a manner as not in any way to involve immoral teaching."[120] Even when Gilbert Murray's version was considered in 1910, the criterion for approval remained clear: a production would be allowed when it was shown that its translation "modifies rather than accentuates anything in the language which would cause offence."[121] Sensitive to *Oedipus*' reception, Yeats took up the tragedy – not to burnish Sophocles' reputation as a moral poet (after the fashion of Arnold, Jebb and Plumptre) – but to shock the public and to provoke newfound respect for the national theatre he had founded in Dublin. As Steven Yao has observed, "Yeats conceived of translation not just as a literary exercise, but as a form of political action as well; and the extraordinarily drawn-out process that finally issued in his 1928 version of *King Oedipus* began, fittingly enough, with an expressly and perhaps even crudely political desire to stage the play."[122] Intent on making his audience tremble with the "same creeping" as Oedipus himself had felt, Yeats sought to pry Sophoclean reception from conventional Christian notions, the so-called "unwritten ... eternal law of purity," with which Greek literature had then been broadly painted.[123] Working from

---

[119] Plumptre (1867) lxxiv; Turner (1981) 15–16. See also Jenkyns (1980) 60–73, and Stray (1998) 235–70.

[120] Sir John Hare, Letter to the Lord Chamberlain, Charles Spencer (November 21, 1910) Lord Chamberlain's Plays Correspondence File: *Oedipus Rex* 1910/814, British Library Archive. Disputes over the character of *Oedipus* reflected a "wider public debate concerning consanguineous sexual relations, which culminated in the passing of The Punishment of Incest Act (1908)." Before 1908 incest in England and Wales had been prosecuted in "ecclesiastical courts, despite numerous attempts to make it a criminal offence. When a Joint Select Committee of the House of Lords and the House of Commons was set up to investigate the state of theatre censorship in Britain, the anxieties concerning incest and the opposition to the Lord Chamberlain's Office came together in the discussions of Sophocles' proscribed play." Macintosh (2008) 529.

[121] Stanley Buckmaster, Letter to the Lord Chamberlain, Charles Spencer (November 23, 1910). Another member of the Lord Chamberlain's Advisory Board commented at this time that Murray's manner of translating the Greek had toned down the depiction of that "most horrible evil" – incest – "in one or two places he softens the language a little to save susceptibilities." Walter Raleigh, Member of the Advisory Board on Stage Plays, Letter to the Lord Chamberlain, Charles Spencer (November 22, 1910). Lord Chamberlain's Plays Correspondence File: *Oedipus Rex* 1910/814, British Library Archive.

[122] Yao (2002) 126.

[123] Yeats *CW10* (2000) 245; Jebb (1877) 88.

manuscripts on which Monck had already made revisions during the autumn of 1911, Yeats strove to free Jebb and Verrall of hypotactic constructions, relying on short phrases, repetition, apposition and asyndeton to achieve an "idiomatic fragmentation … modeled on normal patterns of English speech."[124] He was, he told Lady Gregory, taking Jebb and turning

> him into simple speakable English dictating the result. Yesterday I had Rynd's help he took the Greek text and looked up the literal meaning of passages for me. The choruses I am putting into rough unrhymed verse. I am of course making it very simple in fact turning it into an Abbey play. Monck had already made his cuts.[125]

The end results in 1912, though far less experimental and less conversant with the original Greek, could nonetheless be regarded as a forerunner of modernist bricolage in translation, a form Pound later perfected in *Homage to Sextus Propertius* (1919), where he employed collage, emendation and outright mistranslation to upset the common conventions of a more scholarly approach.[126] By contrast, roughly contemporaneous attempts to render *Oedipus* – not only by Jebb and Verrall but also by Gilbert Murray as well as his teacher, Francis Storr (whose Loeb translation was published in 1912) – had domesticated Sophocles with an English style that elided Greek's "different organization of language," an organization "for which there are no precise, or constant, equivalents."[127] Storr, in particular, was eager to draw Sophocles into the canon of English masters. In the introduction for his translation of *Oedipus the King, Oedipus at Colonus* and *Antigone*, he not only compared Sophocles' life to that of Tennyson but assigned him Ben Jonson's epitaph for Shakespeare as well:

> "His life was gentle." *Gentle* is the word by which critics ancient and modern have agreed to characterize him. The epitaph is Shakespeare's, and Ben Jonson applies it to Shakespeare himself, but it fits even more aptly the sweet singer of Colonus, in whom "the elements were so mixed" as to form what the Greeks expressed by εὔκολος.[128]

---

124 Baker (1967) 94. On Yeats' desire "to make the language of poetry coincide with passionate, normal speech," see Earle (1988) 19–48, Parkinson (1964) 181–231, and Arkins (1994) 3–26. See also Yeats, "Introduction" (1937) in Yeats *CW5* (1994) 212.

125 Yeats, "To Lady Gregory" (January 7, 1912) in Yeats *CLWBY*, entry no. 1796.

126 On the Homage, see Sullivan (1964), Bush (1983) 61–79, Hooley (1988), Rudd (1994) 117–58, as well as Thomas (1983) and Willett (2005) 173–220.

127 Carne-Ross (2010) 238.

128 Storr (1912) ix. *Liddell-Scott-Jones* glosses the range of meaning for εὔκολος as "easily satisfied," or "content," when of persons; when of things, "easy" or "easy to understand" and when of mind, "at peace," "contented," "good-natured" or even ready "ready" or "agile."

Yeats, by contrast, was driven by a desire to atomize and reconfigure literal equivalence, to disrupt the *eukolic* vision of Sophocles, which had made the Greek poet seem 'native' for broader public consumption. Yet, as David Clark and James McGuire observe, this did not come easily. Yeats had thought *Oedipus* could be ready for production in early winter 1912 – "Jan 18 we play Oedipus," he confidently told Lady Gregory – but his progress with the play was slower than expected.[129] "I am merely putting the dialogue into prose and choruses into rough unrhymed verse," Yeats explained, "I'm not trying to make a serious work of it. I haven't time for that, but something had to be done for the existing translations won't speak."[130] Though his *Oedipus* began as no "serious work," the difficulty of making Sophocles speak is evident in the manuscripts. Where, in the tragedy's opening lines – beginning ὦ τέκνα, Κάδμου τοῦ πάλαι νέα τροφή – Jebb and Verrall had been prolix,

> My children, latest-born to Cadmus who was of old, why are ye set before me thus with wreathed branches of suppliants, while the city reeks with incense, rings with prayers for health and cries of woe? I deemed it unmeet, my children, to hear these things at the mouth of others, and have come hither myself, I, Oedipus renowned of all. Tell me, then, thou venerable man ...[131]

Yeats felt their archaizing language awkward. He began compressing their version, making the nominal clause "latest-born to Cadmus who was of old" into the short apposition "descendants of Cadmus." Despite his efforts, however, the earliest revisions – those dating from 1912 in a manuscript known as "Rex 2" – still kept much of Jebb and Verrall's version. When compared with the stark and sober questions from the final published version of *King Oedipus* (1928), "Rex 2" shows a gradual modification.[132]

> My children '} descendants of Cadmus that was of old ~~time,~~ why do you come before [me] ~~me thus~~? [with] ~~With~~ the wreathed branches of suppliants, while the city smokes with incense and murmurs ~~with~~ [and] cries ~~and prayers~~ of sorrow; [with] prayers for health. I would not ~~hear~~ [learn] ~~these~~ from another's mouth, and therefore I have questioned you myself. Answer me, old man.[133]

[129] Yeats, "To Lady Gregory" (December 20, 1911) in Yeats *CLWBY*, entry no. 1786.
[130] Yeats, "To A. H. Bullen" (January 7, 1912) in Yeats *CLWBY*, entry no. 1795.
[131] Jebb and Verrall (1887) 1.
[132] Yeats (1989b) 28–34.
[133] Yeats (1989b) 189.

King Oedipus (1928):

> Children, descendants of old Cadmus, why do
> you come before me, why do you carry the branches
> of suppliants, while the city smokes with incense
> and murmurs with prayer and lamentation? I would
> not learn from any mouth but yours, old man, there-
> fore I question you myself.[134]

A curious effect of Yeats' 'double retranslation' of this passage – his retranslation of "Rex 2" – is the rendering of ὦ τέκνα. Had he kept Jebb and Verrall's "My children" (rather than simply choosing to begin with "Children"), less of the allusivity implicit in the Greek source text would have been lost. The invocation of "My children" for ὦ τέκνα signals, rather forcefully, the irony surrounding Oedipus' claims to parenthood and rightful leadership in Thebes. The hermeneutic discretion employed – to add words (in this case a simple possessive pronoun) – makes explicit what is more obscure in the Greek, foreshadowing the twisted realities of kinship Oedipus later confronts. Yeats' further alteration to "Children" in the 1928 version blunts the suggestiveness of Jebb and Verrall's version for a greater formality in address. Furthermore, where Sophocles expressed the opening question with a single verb, θοάζετε, Jebb and Verrall rendered the Greek literally, reduplicating the verb and also the participle, ἐξεστεμμένοι, as "with wreathed branches of suppliants." Yeats' 1928 text, by contrast, broke down the original into a vigorous repetition of questions, questions that dissolved the complexity of syntax introduced by the Greek participle, and allowed for an urgent staccato of interrogatives: "why do you come ... why do you carry ..." According to Clark and McGuire's exhaustive account of the play's development, it was, in part, Paul Masqueray's French translation, *Oedipe-Roi* (1922), which helped Yeats to alter "every sentence" of the first revision.[135] A better understanding of passages in French "freed" him to use a "more idiomatic English," to rid Jebb and Verrall of anything "that might not be intelligible on the Blasket Islands."[136]

Although Yeats completed a draft of the dialogue in February, having "made a fine version," the motivating force behind his interest in Sophocles was, by then, removed: the Lord Chamberlain lifted the ban

---

[134] Yeats (1966) 809.
[135] Yeats *CW10* (2000) 244. See Yeats (1989b) 37–39.
[136] Yeats (1989b) 38; Yeats *CW10* (2000) 245.

for Max Reinhardt's January 1912 production of Gilbert Murray's *Oedipus, King of Thebes* (1911).[137] Murray was initially hesitant to take on the task, but he decided at last to translate the "great stage masterpiece of Sophocles" with "English rhyming verse," convinced by what he called "the fascination of this play, which has thrown its spell on me."[138] *Oedipus* did contain "a few points of unsophisticated technique," but it seemed to Murray then "drama of amazing grandeur and power."[139] Murray still preferred the "philosophic reflections," "subtleties of technique" and "tremendous choric effects" of Euripides, but he admitted that in "respect of plot, no Greek play comes near [*Oedipus*]."[140] Murray's apparent 'about-face' was indebted, in part, to his "old master, Francis Storr," with whom Murray had read Sophocles at the Merchant Taylors' School.[141] For Yeats, however, the Lord Chamberlain's acquiescence diminished the polemic of Irish *Oedipus*, and yet it was only in hindsight that Yeats attributed his loss of interest to the ban's removal.[142] The immediate cause was the fact that his efforts to make the choruses of *Oedipus* seem spoken had been tested by the odes' metrical variation and syntactic complexity.[143] From as early as 1904, Yeats anticipated that the Greek chorus would present a challenge both in translation and on the stage, telling London's *Evening Mail* then that the "greatest difficulty" in performing Greek tragedy lay "in the management of the chorus."[144] Nonetheless, he was still confident then that "this little obstacle will be overcome," but managing the odes into a desirable 'straight talk' proved troublesome.[145] That trouble was manifested in the turgid archaisms he inherited from Jebb and Verrall, as in this passage, excerpted from their first chorus:

> O sweetly-speaking message of Zeus, in what spirit hast thou come from
> golden Pytho unto glorious Thebes? I am on the rack, terror shakes my

---

[137] Yeats, Letter to Lady Gregory (21, 22? February 1912), as in Yeats (1989b) 29. On Max Reinhardt's production, see Hall and Macintosh (2005) 538–54, Macintosh (1997) 298–301, as well as Purdom (1955) 129–33.

[138] Murray (1911) v, iii, v.

[139] Murray (1911) viii.

[140] Murray (1911) xi, x, viii.

[141] Murray (1911) xi.

[142] Yeats *CW10* (2000) 219–220. See also Yeats (1989b) 29–33, on Yeats' reaction to Max Reinhardt's London production of January 1912.

[143] Macintosh (2008) 530.

[144] R. M. (1904) 4.

[145] R. M. (1904) 4. When Yeats returned to working on "the material version of a chorus for a version of *Oedipus* intended for the stage" in February 1926, he reiterated that his verse had "more and more adopted – seemingly without any will of mine – the syntax and vocabulary of common personal speech." Yeats, "Letter to H. J. C. Grierson (21 February [1926])," in Yeats *LWBY* (1955) 710.

soul, O thou Delian Healer to whom wild cries rise, in holy fear of thee, what thing thou wilt work for me, perchance unfelt before, perchance returning in the fulness of the years: tell me, thou immortal Voice, born of golden Hope!"[146]

In imitation Verrall employed two questions in his version; but Yeats composed instead four syntactically similar questions that allowed him to eliminate many of the relative clauses and prepositional phrases.

> What message comes to famous Thebes from the Golden House?
> What message of disaster from that sweet-throated Zeus?
> What monstrous thing our fathers saw do the seasons bring?
> Or what that no man ever saw, what new monstrous thing?
> Trembling in every limb I raise my loud importunate cry,
> And in a sacred terror wait the Delian God's reply.[147]

The alliterative repetition articulated in these questions better suggested, Yeats believed, the syntactic cadence of spoken English.[148] Yet, though that cadence framed the ode for better dramatic treatment, Yeats' desire to mitigate the "Latin mist" of Jebb and Verrall also drastically reduced the thematic scope and metrical variation of the Sophoclean original.[149] In Greek the four odes of *Oedipus* comprised roughly 155 lines, lines that Jebb and Verrall expanded into 213 lines. Ignorant of Greek, Yeats shrank from the difficulties posed by the 'little obstacle' of chorale management and simplified them into a mere fifty-eight lines. Even the odes, he felt, had to appear closer to "the syntax and vocabulary of common personal speech."[150] "I spoke out every sentence, very often from the stage," he declared, "with one sole object that the words should sound natural and fall in their natural order, that every sentence should be a spoken, not a written, sentence."[151] In a sense, then, Yeats refused to engage deeply with the difficulty of the odes, with the foreignness the Greek enacts in the "sudden switch from statement to the cadence of daemonic possession."[152] Instead his odes were set to be only more

---

[146] Jebb and Verrall (1887) 5.
[147] Yeats (1966) 813.
[148] This dramatic repetition of interrogatives, modeled on contemporary English dialect, gained prominence in other works of contemporaneous poetry – perhaps most notably in Eliot's "A Game of Chess" from *The Waste Land* (1922), where, from lines 111 to 138, domestic ennui shifts into aggressive interrogation.
[149] Yeats *CW10* (2000) 245.
[150] Yeats *LWBY* (1955) 710.
[151] Yeats *CW10* (2000) 244.
[152] Carne-Ross (2010) 244.

speakable and, as such, their role in the tragedy was diminished. Nevertheless, the "strategic repetition" of interrogatives "functioning independently of narrative connection" became a syntactic hallmark of Yeats' lyric and dramatic verse, especially after the 1916 premiere of his Noh drama, *At the Hawk's Well.*[153] Repetition of questions had become a means for refusing clear "narrative connection," a way of centering dramatic action not on plot or character but on the accumulation of fragmentary perceptions, a fabric threaded around what Yeats saw as the cadence of a "single metaphor."[154] This approach exemplified what James Longenbach has called some of the "organizing principles that would ultimately distinguish so many modernist long poems, beginning with the early cantos and *The Waste Land.*"[155] Thus Yeats' atomization of Jebb and Verrall – the "intense unnatural labour" he exerted in doubly retranslating the 'Victorian' Sophocles with a "bare, hard and natural" idiom – while not as effective as he might have hoped, nonetheless played a role in developing forms of poetic collage that could weave together an "intricately reticulated fabric of multiple images."[156]

Having left the choruses unfinished in 1912, Yeats did not return again to work on *Oedipus* until early 1926 when – likely not by coincidence – the specter of official censorship had reemerged to cast its shadow over artistic endeavors in Ireland. When declared a dominion within the British Commonwealth in 1922, the Irish Free State effectively took on "the whole body of British statute law – and English common law tradition – with a few minor exceptions consequent on the terms of the Treaty."[157] No exception dealt directly with censorship and so with "regard to the legislation controlling obscene literature the establishment of the Irish Free State brought no change at all."[158] Various organizations began, however, to loudly insist that the new government take up new measures to "combat" what the Catholic Truth Society had called "the pernicious influence of infidel and immoral publications."[159] "However

---

[153] Longenbach (2010) 325.
[154] Longenbach (2010) 325.
[155] Longenbach (2010) 325.
[156] Yeats *LWBY* (1955) 710; Yeats, "To Olivia Shakespear" (December 7, 1926) in Yeats *LWBY* (1955) 720; Longenbach (2010) 326.
[157] Adams (1968) 13.
[158] Adams (1968) 13.
[159] A description of the Society's aims was advertised in the entry for the "Catholic Truth Society of Ireland" in *The Irish Catholic Directory and Almanac for 1920* (1920) 207.

we may differ in our political opinions to-day," wrote the Rev. R. S. Devane (1876–1951),

> and however bitter the feelings that have arisen in recent times may be, I think we may truthfully say that Republican and Free Stater, Capitalist and Worker, Protestant and Catholic, would all rejoice in the re-definition of 'indecency' or 'obscenity,' thereby setting up 'as high a standard as possible,' and so giving a moral lead to other nations.[160]

According to Devane, the nascent government of the Free State could perhaps best distinguish the character of Ireland by creating a "new legal definition of 'obscenity' and 'indecency' which would be in complete harmony with the religious ideals and moral standards of the people."[161] The clergy, he believed, were to have a critical role in shaping public opinion and policy within the Free State, for the "time is now ripe," he asserted,

> for the introduction of Social Legislation ... we are still dominated by old traditions, and by the hitherto prevailing legal standards of public morality. Can these be broken and replaced? This depends on the pressure brought to bear on the Government.[162]

In February 1926 the Minister of Justice, Kevin O'Higgins (1892–1927), responded and convened a "Committee of Enquiry on Evil Literature," which he tasked to explore "whether it is necessary or advisable in the interest of public morality to extend the existing powers of the State to prohibit or restrict the sale and circulation of printed matter."[163] On examining the matter, the committee recommended expanding censorship, proposing in its final report (dated December 28, 1926) the creation of a board "to advise the Minister for Justice as to any books, newspapers or magazines circulated in the Saorstat that, in the opinion of the Board, are demoralising and corrupting."[164] The Minister of Justice would then possess the "power to prohibit by notice" the circulation of immoral literature as well as the authority to punish by fine or imprisonment those "persons exposing for sale or circulating any prohibited book."[165]

---

[160] Devane (1925) 189–90.
[161] Devane (1925) 203.
[162] Devane (1925) 202.
[163] Committee on Evil Literature (1927) 3. On the committee, see Murphy (2017) 140–72.
[164] Committee on Evil Literature (1927) 18.
[165] Committee on Evil Literature (1927) 18.

As a member of the Irish Senate, Yeats often supported the policies of W. T. Cosgrave's government, but he abhorred the notion that the Free State would curtail intellectual freedom in so drastic a fashion (in a stricter form than had been enforced under British rule). As Elizabeth Cullingford observes:

> The censorship dispute marks a real diminution of Yeats's respect for the Cosgrave Government. It had betrayed its trust by bowing to mob fanaticism ... He left the Senate, then, a disillusioned man. During his term of office he had advocated order, unity, and liberty: the Government had supplied order but had infringed liberty and thus jeopardized unity.[166]

Yeats railed against this legislation. He believed that to "give one man, the Minister of Justice, control over the substance of our thought, for its definition of 'indecency' and such vague phrases as 'subversive of public morality'," would

> permit him to exclude *The Origin of Species*, Karl Marx's *Capital*, the novels of Flaubert, Balzac, Proust, all of which have been objected to somewhere on moral grounds, half the Greek and Roman Classics, Anatole France and everybody else on the Roman index, and all great love poetry. The Government does not intend these things to happen, the Commission on whose report the Bill was founded did not intend these things to happen, the holy gunmen and 'The Society of Angelic Warfare' do not intend all these things to happen; but in legislation intention is nothing, and the letter of the law everything, and no Government has the right, whether to flatter fanatics or in mere vagueness of mind to forge an instrument of tyranny and say that it will never be used.[167]

Decades earlier, Yeats had believed that poetry and drama produced for the cause of Irish nationhood – literature modeled on the classics even – might invigorate "a conception of the race as noble as Aeschylus and Sophocles had of Greece."[168] Yet with British rule largely cast off, Ireland's newfound freedom still remained threatened by "mob censorship."[169] Thus Yeats sometimes felt himself in "deep gloom about Ireland," still believing that "the extreme party may carry the country."[170] "I see no hope of escape from bitterness ... When men are very bitter, death & ruin draw them on as a rabbit is supposed to be drawn on by the dancing

---

[166] Cullingford (1981) 193.
[167] Yeats, "The Irish Censorship" (September 29, 1928) in Yeats *CW10* (2000) 215–16.
[168] Yeats *Mem* (1972) 184.
[169] Yeats *CW10* (2000) 216.
[170] Yeats, "To Olivia Shakespear" (December 22, 1921) in Yeats *CLWBY*, entry no. 4039.

of the fox."[171] "Fixed ideas" and "Nationalist abstractions" continued to rise unabated, but Yeats continued to define Ireland's literary potential with terms and examples drawn from classical antiquity, still envisioning "on occasions," as one scholar has observed, the country's "future as being allied to the pattern of the Greeks."[172] His understanding, however, of how that future could indeed fit any ancient Greek pattern had evolved dramatically throughout the many years it took to bring his *King Oedipus* to the stage.

At its first production on December 7, 1926, *King Oedipus* was hailed for being "simply and effectively set and dressed" – Yeats' language even receiving especial praise for its being "very clear in meaning and actable" – but Yeats had long since begun to seriously doubt whether any staging of Sophocles could, in fact, convince Ireland, as he once hoped, that "she is very liberal, abhors censors delights in the freedom of the arts."[173] His version had slowly become emblematic of a new, more embittered polemic instead – one whose self-critical force had doubly retranslated, in a sense, the romantic nationalism Yeats had first attached to the tragedy's staging in 1904. As he later explained on BBC Radio, Oedipus seemed to him "representative of human genius": blinded by belief in his own capacity for governing wisely and aggravated by "involuntary sin," Oedipus sought answers to ἀνόρθωσον πόλιν (*OT* 46) – "Uplift our State" – to save Thebes' citizens from plague.[174] The catastrophe of *Oedipus* lay not in the king's inability to rescue his subjects but rather in his failure to see that the 'uplift' he did provide was itself compromised and predicated on a severe and lasting cost: exile, blindness and internecine strife. Collective self-deception had reduced the city-state to a wasteland, for in willfully ignoring Oedipus' history, the Thebans had been

---

[171] Yeats, "To Olivia Shakespear" (December 22, 1921) in Yeats *CLWBY*, entry no. 4039. On leaving the Senate, Yeats felt he had "failed … and his advice to Pound, 'Do not be elected to the Senate of your country', reflects his feeling of inadequacy. Yet his despondency was the product as much of events in Ireland as of any personal failure. His high hopes for the Free State were never fulfilled, and when he relinquished his Senate seat he foresaw only further bitterness for his country." Cullingford (1981) 165.

[172] Yeats *CW3* (1999) 192. "That Yeats was not alone in his optimism is illustrated by a curious episode in 1924, after the foundation of the Free State, when Oliver St John Gogarty – the surgeon who had received a classical training at Trinity under Mahaffy – launched two swans in the River Liffey and wrote a poem to commemorate the occasion in which the myths of Leda and Fionnula are united. Greece and Ireland were now one." Macintosh (1994) 15. See Gogarty's poem, "To the Liffey with Swans," in Gogarty (2001) 67. On the alleged link between this episode with Yeats' own poem, "Leda and the Swan," see O'Connor (1964) 220–21.

[173] Holloway (1968) 20; Yeats *CL4* (2005) 23.

[174] Yeats *CW10* (2000) 221; Yeats (1966) 810. Yeats' use of 'uplift' recalls, ironically, his derision for 'moral uplift' detailed at the beginning of this chapter. See Chapter 3, pp. 123–30.

deceived by a heroic, authoritarian ideal, by a romantic vision whose presence brought home only plague and ruin. In performing that deception in Dublin – in staging what Friedrich Hölderlin (1770–1843) once called the undoing of Oedipus' *Allessuchende, Allesdeutende* – Yeats perhaps saw something of the same pattern at work in the Free State.[175] For Yeats, the high-minded vision of cultural and political independence espoused during the Revival had, in spite of all, led Ireland's "popular mind to its own lawless vulgarity."[176] The nation, like "every country" he thought, had passed "out of automatism" to a new state of "demoralization";[177] and in this state, Yeats, like many others, failed to inoculate himself against the politics of resentment. An overweening fetish for order saw him give in to an "over-heated" attraction to the authoritarianisms of the early 1930s.[178] The far-right 'fixed ideas' of Eoin O'Duffy (1890–1944) would not "promote the rule of the educated classes, nor indeed any of Yeats' cherished ideals," but still the presence of the "parafascism" of the Army Comrades Association, otherwise known as the Irish Blueshirts, allowed the poet to mime the heroic in "a fantasy world of action, drama, and self-aggrandizement, centred on the idea of the Blueshirts."[179] "Politics are growing heroic," he told Olivia Shakespear (1863–1938) in 1933: "A Fascist opposition is forming behind the scenes to be ready should some tragic situation develop. I find myself urging the despotic rule of the educated classes as the only end to our troubles. (Let all this sleep in your ear.) I know half a dozen men any one of whom may be Caesar – or Cataline."[180] The Irish had "no choice but to go on into intelligence," he thought, and his *Oedipus* was evidence of that turn, he thought: no longer simply Jebb's "masterpiece of Attic Tragedy," its translation and performance were proof that a "new satirical comedy" would rise with "a vision of the new Ireland."[181] Though hardened by war and demoralized by various attempts to "rock the cradle of a man of genius," the ideal of nationhood still appeared heroic: Ireland remained "so full of curiosity, so full of self-criticism ... sometimes so tolerant, sometimes so bitter in its merriment."[182]

---

[175] Hölderlin (1804) 107.
[176] Yeats *CW10* (2000) 217.
[177] Yeats *CW10* (2000) 217.
[178] Cullingford (1981) 207.
[179] Cullingford (1981) 204. Foster (2003) 472. On Yeats' links with the Blueshirts and European fascism, see Cullingford (1981) 197–213 as well as McCormack (2005) and Foster (2003) 468–83.
[180] Yeats, "Letter to Olivia Shakespear, 13 July [1933]," in Yeats *LWBY* (1955) 811–12.
[181] Yeats *CW10* (2000) 217; Jebb (1885) v; Yeats *CW10* (2000) 223.
[182] Yeats *CW10* (2000) 216, 223.

The national platform on which Yeats set Attic tragedy – and there debated the struggles of 'nation-building' – remained intact in the Irish theatre into the late twentieth century when adaptations of Greek drama slowly began to reflect a "postcolonial sensibility reflective of the cultural and critical priorities of their time."[183] "Greek tragedy, with its stark content and spare execution," no longer existed solely to examine the cultural politics behind bold claims of a national consensus but leapt inward to examine the harsher "social and political realities" of ethnic and religious division within specific communities, principally Ulster.[184] This meant, of course, that the range of the late twentieth-century Irish receptions were not crudely fixated on "oppositions of Britain/Ireland and coloniser/colonised. Other aspects of Irish identity have also been examined, for example constructions of gender and the impact of social change."[185] Nonetheless, specific Irish adaptations of Sophoclean tragedy did turn to examine more closely 'provincial' matters of social unrest and sectarian politics, not merely the "academic and critical discourse which predominated in Irish public life."[186] Nowhere was this more conspicuous, as Hardwick notes, than in "various attempts in the 1980s to appropriate Sophocles' *Antigone* to the conflict between Nationalists and Unionists in Northern Ireland."[187] Yet the usefulness of *Antigone* evolved beyond this moment as well; and by the turn of the twenty-first century – as the violence of the Troubles largely subsided, and as the Irish Republic started to grapple with its place as a member state of the European Union – Sophocles had become more than a 'provincial' poet. The reception of *Antigone*, in particular, reflected a preoccupation with collective nostalgia, contemporary international politics and the difficulty of public grieving in the wake of the September 11 terror attacks. Seamus Heaney (1939–2013) translated his version, *The Burial at Thebes* (2004), in this atmosphere, an atmosphere where the representation of "provincial strife" no longer seemed like a pejoratively 'local' matter but emblematic rather of an intractable problem, a "global reality" that urgently demanded new witness.[188]

---

[183] Mahony (2016) 655.
[184] Mahony (2016) 655.
[185] Hardwick (2000) 88.
[186] Mahony (2016) 670.
[187] Hardwick (2000) 88. On the use of *Antigone* in examining questions of provincial dispute, both in the Republic and in Northern Ireland, see Macintosh (2011) 90–103; Hardwick (2000) 79–95; Mahony (2016) 667–70; M. McDonald (2000) 16–26; P. McDonald (1995) 183–203, as well as Roche (1988) 221–50.
[188] Mahony (2016) 670.

Ben Barnes, the artistic director of the Abbey Theatre (2000–05), approached Heaney in December 2002 for a translation of the tragedy, thinking Sophocles recomposed by a major Irish writer would be key in commemorating the Theatre's 2004 centenary.[189] Heaney agreed – hoping to set *The Burial at Thebes* against work Yeats had already done. "One person who had not done a version [of *Antigone*] was W. B. Yeats," he wrote,

> Yeats had indeed made for the Abbey Theatre prose translations of Sophocles' other two Theban plays, but with the exception of a few lines entitled "From the 'Antigone'" (included in his sequence "A Woman Young and Old"), he had not put his trademark on this one. So to that extent at least the road was open.[190]

The road was clear, but still from the beginning the question of necessity plagued Heaney. "How many *Antigones* could Irish theatre put up with?," he wondered,

> Round about the time the idea was floated, Conall Morrison was touring his adaptation, setting the action in a Middle Eastern context, and a little earlier I had read in manuscript a scholarly and illuminating translation by Professor Marianne McDonald. And if that weren't enough, I had to face the fact that Brendan Kennelly, Tom Paulin and Aidan Carl Mathews had all done their own versions of this particular tragedy, so why take it up again?[191]

In the intervening years since Yeats' work, Sophocles had become a more domesticated animal in the Irish theatre, his reception and reputation having shifted, perhaps, from that of a controversial, incendiary truth-teller (worthy of censorship) to an approachable poet of socially respectable standing (worthy of appreciation). Moreover, while Yeats' versions, *King Oedipus* (1928) and later *Oedipus at Colonus* (1934), emerged in moments of apparent national urgency, both in Ireland's political history and in the reception history of Sophocles, Heaney's did not have that benefit. With Sophocles as midwife, Yeats had set out to flout censorship, to advance both a nationalist vision and a certain experimentalism in art. Heaney, by contrast, was asked to translate in a moment of a collective nostalgia for the achievements of the Abbey – the "abbeyonehundred" – a theatre that was by then mired in practical mismanagement and deep

---

[189] Seamus Heaney Literary Papers, 1963–2010, MS 49,493/242. National Library of Ireland, Dublin.
[190] Heaney (2004) 75.
[191] Heaney (2004) 75.

financial trouble.[192] As Macintosh observes, Heaney "was writing at the end of a particular tradition and at the dawn of a new one."[193] Creatively his *Antigone* was set to mark past glories, not to chart a future vision, a future theatre, nor even to examine the sectarian violence of the Troubles in the way Paulin's "stone us in the street" *Antigone*, *The Riot Act* (1985) – or even his *Philoctetes* entitled *The Cure at Troy* (1991) (to say nothing of Heaney's lyric adaptation of *Oresteia*, "Mycenae Lookout") – had done years earlier.[194] Nevertheless, Heaney still felt, as Yeats, Paulin and others had, that translating Sophocles possessed a political urgency beyond mere nostalgia. Translation remained for him "an instrument for political change."[195] Yet Sophocles no longer seemed especially useful for arbitrating the politics of cultural nationalism. Still Heaney insisted that his *Burial* did indeed provide new ground for political reflection on present-day global strife, namely the "War on Terror" waged by the United States in the years following the attacks of September 2001.[196] Comparing Creon's intransigence, his desire to punish Antigone for disobedience to the state, with the strong-arm strategies of the Bush administration's campaign for war in Iraq, Heaney saw the *Antigone* "reenacted in our own world. Just as Creon forced the citizens of Thebes into an either/or situation in relation to Antigone, the Bush administration in the White House was using the same tactic to forward its argument for war on Iraq."[197] However accurate the parallel may seem at present, the comparison is instructive: it broadly illustrates a complex evolution of Sophoclean reception in the Irish experience and, to a lesser extent, in

---

[192] Barnes (2008) 246. According to a 2014 report commissioned by Ireland's Arts Council, the Abbey endured a "major crisis in governance in 2004." Neither Heaney's *Antigone* nor Tom Murphy's translation of Chekhov, *The Cherry Orchard*, managed to save the theatre from coming close to financial insolvency. Despite being advertised to commemorate the centenary, both productions played to what *The Guardian* called "pitiful houses." The failure to generate much at the box office pushed the theatre's debt to 1.7 million euros. By the summer of 2005 Ben Barnes and the management board of the Abbey had been forced to resign, the debt of the theatre ballooning to nearly 3.4 million euros. See Arts Council of Ireland (2014) 1; Chrisafis (2004, 2005). See also Jordan and Weitz (2018) 20.

[193] Macintosh (2011) 102.

[194] Paulin (1985) 10. On Heaney's attraction to Aeschylus following the 1994 declaration of ceasefire in the North, see especially Lavan (2019) 50–68, as well as Impens (2018) 61–63.

[195] Hardwick (2000) 81.

[196] First published in *The Irish Times* on November 17, 2001, Heaney's free translation of Horace's Ode 1.34, "Anything Can Happen," not only marks the poet's response to the attacks of September 11, 2001, but is perhaps also the first instance of the more global approach Heaney took in adapting classical literature. Broadly speaking, the Greek and the Roman had clearly become sites for reflection on matters beyond the borders of the Republic and the North. On this translation, see Harrison (2019) 244–62.

[197] Heaney (2004) 76.

English literature at large. As Crawford notes, the evolving vision offered by Irish classicism seemed to slowly provide "a way of moving beyond contemporary national politics," to challenge the threat of "cultural incest which is an inevitable problem for small nations and communities whether in Ireland, Scotland, Wales or elsewhere."[198] Thus the translation of the Attic tragedian became no longer a means for compelling stylistic experimentation and the politics of national self-determination. Instead Heaney's Sophocles became a palimpsest over which the ancient *agon* of Antigone and Creon could be overwritten with a contemporary reflection on matters of international intrigue – a reflection whose rather 'basic' English weighed the effects of global terror and new imperial response.

[198] Crawford (2011) 141, 139. See also Impens (2019) 532–37.

CHAPTER 4

"Heirs of Romanity"
Welsh Nationalism and the Modernism of David Jones

Standing before a judge in the Welsh town of Caernarfon, Saunders Lewis, a playwright and the president of *Plaid Cymru*, defended the right of conscience. The offence for which he and his associates Lewis Valentine and D. J. Williams then stood accused

> is not in dispute. We ourselves were the first to give the authorities warning of the fire, and we proclaimed to them our responsibility. Yet we hold the conviction that our action was in no wise criminal, and that it was an act forced upon us, that it was done in obedience to conscience and to the moral law, and that the responsibility for any loss due to our act is the responsibility of the English Government.[1]

The men were under indictment for arson to His Majesty's property, a deed that "feloniously" violated sections 5 and 51 of the 1861 Malicious Damage Act.[2] Before dawn on September 8, 1936, the three had crept onto the grounds of a Royal Air Force Armament Training Camp on the Llŷn Peninsula. There they allegedly thrashed a one-armed night watchman and set fire to the aerodrome and military buildings. "It was an [*sic*] glorious fire: we didn't need lights," Lewis remarked; the blaze was kindled simply with "petrol and a syringe."[3] Later that morning, the conspirators turned themselves in at a police station in nearby Pwllheli, but before doing so, Lewis handed over a letter written in Welsh to the inspector on duty. There he declared the grave purpose he and his accomplices had in mind:

> Ever since the intention to build a Lleyn bombing camp was first announced we, and many of the leaders of the public life of Wales, did everything we could to get the English Government to refrain from

---

[1] Saunders Lewis, "The Caernarfon Court Speech (13th October 1936)," in Lewis (1973) 115.
[2] The 1861 Act is available at: www.legislation.gov.uk/ukpga/Vict/24-25/97/contents/enacted.
[3] As quoted in Jenkins (1998) 39, 41.

placing in Lleyn an institution which would endanger all the culture and traditions of one of the most Welsh regions in Wales. But in spite of our pleading, in spite of the letters and protests forwarded from hundreds of religious and lay societies throughout the whole of Wales, and although thousands of the electors of Lleyn itself signed a petition imploring prevention of this atrocity, yet the English Government refused even to receive a deputation from Wales to talk over the matter. Lawful and peaceful methods failed to secure for Wales even common courtesy at the hands of the Government of England. Therefore, in order to compel attention to this immoral violation of the sure and natural rights of the Welsh nation, we have taken this method, the only method left to us by a Government which insults the Welsh nation.[4]

In court over a month later, Lewis pressed his defense of the "one of the most Welsh regions in Wales." Before the trial commenced, he demanded that all jurors be competent in the Welsh language, but the judge, Wilfred Lewis (1881–1950), deemed his request a "farce," insisting that Lewis and the other defendants address the court in English.[5] However, when called to enter a plea, Lewis replied in Welsh, incensing the judge who then reputedly berated him into compliance with "the emphasis of a barrister cross-examining."[6] By attempting to enter his plea in Welsh, Saunders Lewis was not simply flouting the judge's authority but attacking the official proscription of the language in British courts – courts that had outlawed it since the Tudor-era dismantling of Wales' own legal system, *Cyfraith Hywel*. The Laws in Wales Acts, passed by the Parliament of Henry VIII between 1535 and 1542, had banned the language on the grounds that Welsh had allegedly provoked "some rude and ignorant people" to make "distinccion and diversitie betwene the Kinges Subiectes of this Realme and hys subiectes of the said dominion and Principalitie of Wales."[7] Because of such "dyvysion murmur and sedicion," the Crown established "like Fourme" for Wales, hoping to eliminate "sinister usages and customes" that differed from those of England: "all othes of officers iuries and enquestes and all other affidavithes verdictes and Wagers of lawe" were "to be geven and done in the

---

[4] "To the Chief Constable of Caernarvon," 7 September 1936, as in "Fire at R.A.F. Camp, Malicious Damage Charge, Welsh Nationalists Sent for Trial," *The Times* (September 17, 1936) 9.
[5] As noted on a trial ticket, Caernarvon Winter Assize, Winter, 1936 – County No. 5, by "Mr. J. Williams, Welsh Board of Health, Market Street," National Library of Wales, Aberystwyth. See also Jenkins (1998) 60.
[6] Jenkins (1998) 57.
[7] "The Act of Union of England and Wales, 1536," as transcribed in Rees (1938) 81.

Englisshe tonge."[8] Despite his many attempts to force the issue by testifying in Welsh, Lewis felt the court-provided translator was so inept that he made his closing statement in English. The destruction of the "monstrous bombing range in Lleyn," he told the court, had been done in "defence of Welsh civilization, for the defence of Christian principles, for the maintenance of the Law of God in Wales."[9] He and his accomplices were without guilt for the "universal Christian tradition" had pushed them "to preserve the life of a nation ... to defend it from any mortal blow, by all means necessary short of taking human life unjustly or breaking the moral law."[10] By refusing "the absolute power of the State-God," Lewis believed they had resisted a government whose aim was to "shatter the spiritual basis" of Welsh identity in its native language and literature.[11] Welsh, he insisted, was not simply a cherished native growth but in fact "the direct heir in the British Isles of the literary discipline of classical Greece and Rome. And it is a living, growing literature, and draws its sustenance from a living language and a traditional social life."[12] "[W]eaned on the milk of the West," Wales remained the only place in Britain to have been fully part of the Roman Empire:

> [T]he fact remains and obtrudes like a rock through the centuries – this nation of Wales stands today on the very territory it occupied – the *only* territory it occupied – when Wales was a part of the Roman Empire. You English call us Welsh, and the name Welsh means Romans. Please do not believe the comic old-fashioned idea that the word means *foreigners* and that your ancestors drove mine out of England into Wales and then dubbed us *foreigners* ... There never was any great drive of the Welsh out of England, and your name for us recognises that we are the only nation in the British Isles who were once a part of the Roman Empire.[13]

While the poet-painter David Jones viewed the actions of Lewis, Valentine and Williams in a largely sympathetic light, the influence that their Welsh-Wales nationalism exerted on his literary output – specifically the 1952 poem *The Anathemata* – was complex. Jones admired efforts to

---

[8] Rees (1938) 81, 95–96. Lewis had then recently savaged the Laws in Wales Acts in *The Listener*. See Lewis (1936) 915–16. On the sweeping change the Tudors brought to Welsh law, language and religion, see Williams (1993) 253–78; R. Brinley Jones (1970) 33–54; and Blank (1996) 130–35.

[9] Lewis (1973) 126. See also Chapman (2006a) 24–42.

[10] Lewis (1973) 123.

[11] Lewis (1973) 125, 126.

[12] Lewis (1973) 115. On classical allusions in the creative work of Saunders Lewis, see C. Davies (1995) 131–42.

[13] Saunders Lewis, *Y Ddraig Goch* (November 1927), trans. by Dafydd Glyn Jones in Lewis (1973) 33; Lewis (1936) 915.

preserve the Welsh tongue, but the notion that it comprised an untouched cultural or linguistic purity – one that could then be mobilized into more coercive forms of political action – did not persuade him. Compelled by the example of Joyce, Jones felt that the history of the British Isles' "Celtic hinterland" was too hybrid, too marked with "deposits" from many languages and cultures for its "complex heritage" to serve any ideology of demographic or linguistic purism.[14] Nevertheless, Jones was magnetized by Lewis' claims linking the classical discipline of Greece and Rome to Welsh. Drawn to contemporaneous scholarship on the matter of Rome and its reception in early British history, he too believed that *Romanitas* was present in Wales, but Romanity for Jones, broadly understood, represented not a purity to be preserved but a model of synoptic cultural translation – one that inhered in early Welsh civilization and there synthesized many fragments of cultures and languages together, each leaving their distinctive characteristics untouched by the whitewash of an imperial ideal. The classical legacy left by Rome was thus, as he saw it, no crude acculturating force: it required no "loppings off of meanings or emptyings out" of cultural or linguistic difference but instead provided the possibility of radically integrating diverse forms of genius across wide gulfs of variation.[15] As such, *The Anathemata* is a poem of mottled origin, one whose "sustained attention to detailed particularity" employs various linguistic forms to present "something richer than mere antiquarianism."[16] Its "metamorphic form," its "series of fragments, fragmented bits, chance scraps really," Jones shaped into an eccentric collage, a "displaced epic" whose linguistic hybridity he enmeshed with the rhythms of Catholic liturgical practice and his own complex reception of *Romanitas*.[17]

For Saunders Lewis, the assertion of a genealogical claim on the classical world was not simply a political maneuver.[18] Bolstered by recent scholarship on Roman Britain – such as the work of R. G. Collingwood (1889–1943), J. N. L. Myres (1902–1989) and Charles Norris Cochrane (1889–1945) as well as that of the nationalist historian Arthur Wade-Evans – Lewis felt that hard facts had indeed proved that the Welsh were

---

[14] Jones (1959) 305. Jones (2016) [10]. On Jones' debt to Joyce, see Staudt (1994) 129–38.
[15] David Jones, "Preface to *The Anathemata*" in Jones (1952) 24.
[16] Wray (2019) 420.
[17] Corcoran (1982) 86; Jones (1952) 34; Dilworth (1988) 152.
[18] On Welsh cultural identity and classical studies in the nineteenth century, see C. Davies (2009) 35–47.

"heirs of Rome," modern inheritors of classical antiquity with the so-called "blood of the West in their veins."[19] According to Nennius' *Historia Brittonum*, both peoples, that of Rome and that of Britain, could claim descent from Aeneas of Troy through Ascanius, his son.[20] As such, the Britons were kin of the archaic Roman kings at Alba Longa, and even the Latin epithet first used to describe those of Welsh descent, *Britanni*, had been given to honor, it was said, Britain's patriarch, Britto, the grandson of Aeneas.[21] With a shared lineage, the Welsh could assert what Arthur Wade-Evans called "the same high origin as the Romans, the Britons being, as one very early document puts it, *filii Romanorum*, sons of the Romans, of the stock of Troy."[22] Accordingly *Romanitas* took hold with ease in medieval Britain, for the Welsh were "already Romans," Wade-Evans argued, "before they realized that they were Britons."[23] However, by the beginning of the fifth century, the Western Empire began to deteriorate: imperial garrisons were abandoned across Britain, and new dangers emerged to threaten its Roman settlements. Germanic tribes – Angles, Saxons and Jutes – had invaded Britannia along its eastern shore, slowly driving the Britons west and forcing some to forsake their Christianity and their Romanity for "Barbaria and paganism."[24] "The mind of Roman Britain," was, he claimed, thus splintered then into "a Roman and Christian mind in the West, and a non-Roman and non-Christian mind in the East."[25] Yet, though Britannia's "Roman cities" lapsed into "a state of decay," some of the Britons were said to have clung to their classical identity.[26]

> They stood for Romanitas, 'Romanity', which was the 'conservatism' of the time. But they were set in the midst of a barbarized *Britanni*, who (now that they were free) were beginning to assert themselves, slackening

---

[19] "I believe that the Latin relations of Welsh are more important than the Celtic. Our language is partly Celtic; but our literature and culture and a great part of our speech are Latin. We too are the heirs of Rome, and for that reason it is deplorable that Latin is no longer compulsory throughout the Welsh University, and it is even ludicrous that there should be Welsh Honours graduates having no Latin." Saunders Lewis (September 10, 1925) Thomas Jones Papers, CH, H1/7, as in Chapman (2006b) 106.

[20] Wade-Evans (1938) 38.

[21] Banished from Italy for accidentally killing his father, Britto "arrived in this island, which took a name from his name, to wit, Britain, and he filled it with his own stock, and he dwelt there. From that day Britain has been inhabited even to this day." Wade-Evans (1938) 39.

[22] Wade-Evans (1950) 1.

[23] Wade-Evans (1950) 1.

[24] Wade-Evans (1950) 10.

[25] Wade-Evans (1950) 11.

[26] Wade-Evans (1950) 9.

in what attachment they felt towards Roman traditions, including Christianity, the official religion of the empire. In other words, Barbaria was gathering strength throughout the area governed by the Roman cities, and a prolonged tension set in between it and Romanitas.[27]

Despite the spread of *Barbaria*, Welsh loyalty to the "Roman way of life" went undiminished.[28] "Romanitas triumphed in Wales and Cornwall as against Barbaria," but "the opposite occurred in England" where, as Wade-Evans insisted, the natives had succumbed to an insidious foreign power brought from the east: they had become "barbarized or as the Romans might say 'Saxonized'."[29]

Although the historical revisionism of Welsh-Wales nationalists regarded the Roman character as safely preserved in the early medieval period, Wade-Evans, Lewis and others sympathetic to *Plaid Cymru* likened new more modern threats to the 'Saxonized' barbarism of late antiquity. The recent growth of industrial capitalism, particularly in South Wales, was considered a blight on the country's rural economy, devastating farming communities and furthering the spread of English. Such development had promised to raise the material fortunes of Wales, but throughout the 1920s and into the 1930s, a precipitous decline in the trade of coal and steel had depressed the economy in South Wales, producing what one historian has called "a fundamental decay in the entire fabric of the economic life of the coalfield, and in those communities that depended on it for their livelihood."[30] Saunders Lewis blamed modern industrialism writ large, casting it as an English import set to ravage the landscape and wean Wales from its native language.[31] While a lecturer at University College, Swansea, Lewis encouraged the eradication of English from the cultural, political and religious life of Wales. A new national consciousness could take shape, he thought, only in a Welsh-language national literature. Attempts to invent a hybrid vernacular, a so-called Anglo-Welsh dialect of English, had been unsatisfactory. Though such idioms – he wrote when reviewing the drama of John Oswald Francis (1882–1956) – could possess the "local colour that some Welsh interjections and emphatic repetitions may give," these generated "only tolerable English plays about Welsh life ... To read

---

[27] Wade-Evans (1950) 9.
[28] Wade-Evans (1950) 9.
[29] Wade-Evans (1950) 11, 12.
[30] Morgan (1981) 214. See also J. Davies (2007) 514–20.
[31] See Lewis (1939) 9. For further discussion of this lecture, see Chapter 4, pp. 164–67. See also Lewis (1975) (pamphlet first published in Welsh by *Plaid Cymru*, 1926; reprinted with an English translation).

them or see them acted would be fit penance for a soul in purgatory."[32] Marred by what Lewis saw as 'impure', exploitative origins in industry, labor unions and English journalism, the "awkwardness of Anglo-Welsh" was a poor fit for literary work of any kind.[33]

> Welshman have had to learn English in the worst of schools. Labour leaders of Cockney dialect, an army of unemployed who came from all industrial parts of England to help exploit the mineral wealth of South Wales, railways from Lancashire carrying the vowels and idioms of Manchester to the valleys of Snowdon, these have been our teachers of English. From these and the newspapers we have formed our Anglo-Welsh speech, and no feebler stuff is spoken in these islands.[34]

Despite his remarks Lewis had himself once tried to solve Wales' "problem of language" with his own Anglo-Welsh.[35] Enchanted by the desire to "find an English diction that would interpret the native speech of the Welsh," he admired the drama of Ireland's National Theatre, thinking "the works of Yeats, Synge, Patrick (*sic*) Colum, the Irish," had offered an idiom "close enough to the rhythms and grammatical patterns of Welsh to provide a possible and plausible English."[36] Certain factions within the Irish Literary Revival had effectively translated the essence of Irish Gaelic, creating an authentic Anglo-Irish hybrid based upon the speech of the "southern peasantry."[37] That success inspired Lewis, and in 1921 he sought to "suggest in English the rhythms and idioms of Welsh" with his own "Anglo-Celtic" drama, *The Eve of Saint John*.[38] Yet, before the play was published, he felt the work had become a conventional product of imitation rather than invention. "The fault of my own attempt to render that richness," he wrote, "is that it suggests too often a convention of Anglo-Celtic dramatists, – instead of something fresh and living. But perhaps thus to state the problem will rouse some other to its solution, and that shall be my excuse for publication."[39] Lewis would

---

[32] Lewis (1919) 4. See also Lloyd (1988) 100–14.

[33] Francis was said to use the "horrible jargon of men who have lost one tongue without acquiring another." Lewis (1919) 4.

[34] Lewis (1919) 4.

[35] Lewis (1919) 4.

[36] Lewis (1955) 12. A. T. Davies (1961) 9, as translated in Griffiths (1979) 4.

[37] Lewis (1919) 4.

[38] Lewis (1921) [1], [2].

[39] Lewis (1921) [2]. "I spoke of it as an Anglo-Celtic convention, and it was in that convention that I wrote *The Eve of Saint John*. This was my first play, and so far my last in English. I couldn't be satisfied with its diction and I settled the issue by turning and learning to write in Welsh. It was the logical thing to do." Lewis (1955) 12–13.

remain an ardent admirer of Synge, Yeats and others associated with the Irish Revival. Indeed he continued even to attribute something of his fervor for *ysbryd cenedl* – the Welsh "national spirit" – to the Irish, but no national writer in Wales, he thought, could follow their path for revival.[40] Anglo-Welsh would never raise the collective, national consciousness with a "rich, expressive, individual, powerful" literature in English – certainly not by the same measure that Anglo-Irish had forged what Yeats called "a national tradition, a national literature … Irish in spirit" though "English in language."[41]

Nevertheless, the history of English in Ireland proved useful in Lewis' attempts to analyze the contemporary problem of language in Wales. In a 1938 lecture entitled "Is there an Anglo-Welsh Literature?" he examined this matter at length, again praising Anglo-Irish as a language "rich in traditional idiom and folklore and folksong."[42] The English used by the modern Irish theatre had risen during the eighteenth century, he asserted, by way of the country's Protestant Ascendancy, a rural ruling class committed to fostering its spread among the peasantry. "[U]ncommercialised and untouched by industrialism," English flourished for more than 150 years in the "insulated environment of a separate and Catholic countryside," soon becoming a national tongue, an "English dialect, the English of Ireland."[43] By the turn of the twentieth century, with a decline in spoken Irish, Anglo-Irish became the dominant form of "native speech," its gestation having turned the tongue into something linguistically distinctive, "something rhythmically and emotionally and idiomatically separate from all the dialects of progressive and industrialised England."[44] Bled of its "echoes or rhythms of the English literary tradition," Anglo-Irish could be used effectively, he thought, not for "interpreting Ireland for English readers" but for "interpreting Ireland to herself."[45] In Wales, by contrast, the work of national interpretation was far different:

> English is to-day penetrating the Welsh countryside as never before, so that one might suggest that it may yet evolve as it evolved in Ireland, that "the best is yet to be." No. It is penetrating the countryside just at the

---

[40] A. T. Davies (1961) 9.
[41] Lewis (1921) [2]; Yeats, "To the Editor of *United Ireland*" (December 17, 1892) in Yeats *CL1* (1986) 338. See Introduction, pp. 2–3; Chapter 1, pp. 53–55; Chapter 2, pp. 105–08.
[42] Lewis (1939) 7.
[43] Lewis (1939) 7.
[44] Lewis (1939) 7.
[45] Lewis (1939) 7.

moment in history when the creation of dialect seems beyond the powers of the countrymen.[46]

Unlike the Irish, the Welsh were not learning their English from landed nobility, nor were they able to cultivate their dialect in a rural society largely sheltered from direct influence of English political and commercial interests. The English of Wales was instead the very "language of industrialism," and like the industry brought into the country, its inroads had a disastrous effect on Welsh-speaking peoples.[47]

> The extension of English has everywhere accompanied the decay of that culture, the loss of social traditions and of social unity and the debasement of spiritual values. It has produced no richness of idiom, no folksong, but has battened on the spread of journalese and the mechanised slang of the talkies. There is a Welsh accent on our English, – it is the mark of our foreignness, – but there is no pure dialect.[48]

For Lewis, the effect of English on Welsh had made impossible even the notion that "a separate literature, having its peculiar traditions and character" could be considered or "acknowledged as Anglo-Welsh."[49] Although English was spoken then with a "Welsh accent," Anglo-Welsh was not "the speech of an organic community," for "[w]hatever culture there has been in the mining valleys of South Wales has been the remnant of the social life of the countryside, and has been Welsh in speech."[50] Where Wales remained distinctively Welsh, it was so most in its own language, and where the country was becoming 'Saxonized', an alarming decay of the Welsh tongue was evident.[51]

> Every scholar who knows and cherishes the Welsh dialects is aware that in the last 20 years there has been an alarming deterioration in the standard of their purity and richness. Industrialism has invaded the countryside with the motor bus, the radio, the chain stores of the market towns, the schools and the cinemas. There is no longer a self-contained rural

---

[46] Lewis (1939) 10.
[47] Lewis (1939) 9.
[48] Lewis (1939) 10. On the history of Anglo-Welsh and its differences from Welsh in this period, see Morgan (1981) 241–71.
[49] Lewis (1939) 5.
[50] Lewis (1939) 10.
[51] As farming communities suffered in Wales, the Welsh language declined rapidly. In 1911 the British census suggested that roughly 43.5 percent of the population in Wales still spoke some Welsh. By 1931 this number had dropped to 36.8 percent. The 1951 census – the first taken since before the Second World War – reported a greater loss. Just 28.9 percent of the population reported being conversant in the language. On the decline of Welsh, see J. Davies (2000) 78–108, as well as Tanner (2004) 186–218.

community. There is only the outer fringe of industrialism. Farming is now merely ranching. Rural life has lost its independence and its creative powers. And as it grows anaemic it grows Anglicised.[52]

Because no legitimate vernacular, "no pure dialect," had yet taken the place of the native tongue, Lewis urged his contemporaries to abandon English entirely.[53] "We cannot therefore aim," he asserted, "at anything less than to annihilate English in Wales ... It is bad and wholly bad, that English is spoken in Wales. It must be deleted from the land called Wales: *delenda est Carthago*."[54] The language had allegedly devastated Welsh farming communities, and what was needed for restoration was not Anglo-Welsh but the purity of Welsh alone-an ancient language whose historic links with Roman literature could be touted to defy the encroaching influence of capitalism.

> To create a Welsh-speaking Wales is the surest way of building up a country within which the oppression of international capitalism cannot dwell. Of course, our socialist friends are quite unable to grasp this. So enmeshed are they in the coils of nineteenth-century materialism that they do not see that economic oppression will ultimately be defeated by spiritual forces.[55]

If, however, Welsh suffered extinction, the Britto-Romanic sources that had made the country "direct heir" to classical antiquity would be lost.[56] Such a reality would enfeeble not only Welsh but civilization across all of Britain – even that of the so-called "Anglo-English."[57] Citing J. W. Mackail's 1895 treatise *Latin Literature*, Lewis likened the contemporary linguistic crisis to the phenomenon of "new Latinity" that settled over the Roman Empire in the latter stages of its decay.[58] The "influx of provinces

---

[52] Lewis (1939) 10.
[53] Lewis (1939) 10.
[54] Saunders Lewis, excerpted from "Un Iaith i Gymru" (August 1931), translated as "One Language for Wales," in D. H. Davies (1983) 77–78. The Latin translation of the Greek original used by Lewis is the common, abbreviated form of the sententia: *Ceterum autem censeo Carthaginem delendam esse*. For Greek variation of the phrase, see Plutarch's "δοκεῖ δέ μοι καὶ Καρχηδόνα μὴ εἶναι", in *Plutarch's Lives, Marcus Cato*, chap. 27. See *Plutarch's Lives, with an English Translation by Bernadotte Perrin* (1914), Loeb edition, vol. 2: 382. Attributed to the Roman senator, Cato the Elder, its reception has been examined in Thürlemann (1974) 465–75. See also Gordon (2017) 31–32.
[55] Lewis, as quoted in Dafydd Glyn Jones, "His Politics," in Lewis (1973) 32. On language purism as political doctrine in Wales, see D. H. Davies (1983) 73–79 and Morgan (1981) 206–9. See also Darryl Jones (1996) 31.
[56] Lewis (1973) 115.
[57] Lewis (1939) 14.
[58] Lewis (1939) 14; Mackail (1895) 167.

into literature" had moved then with such "continually accelerating force" that literary strains from "Gaul, Spain, and Africa" appeared "side by side with Italy," just as Italy herself sunk "towards the level of a province."[59] Latin was thus transformed: no longer a pure *urbanus sermo*, it had evolved from "that austere and noble language which was the finest flower of her civilisation" to something that could "be written in another than the Roman manner."[60] By parallel, a loss of Welsh or other Celtic languages promised to generate a number of deleterious provincial dialects whose influence on 'purer' strains of English would mitigate the 'native' strength of "Anglo-English." To neglect the "national life" of Celtic countries, to leave their cultures and their languages subject to such "undirected drifting" posed a radical threat to English literature itself: Wales, so hybridized, Lewis thought, would "give no new colour to a borrowed tongue, nor any folksong. It will wear its English like a shroud."[61]

As Lewis pressed his defense in Caernarfon, the immediate question of whether the fire on Llŷn constituted arson and malicious damage went undecided. The trial ended in a hung jury, with legal officials transferring the case to the Central Criminal Court at London's Old Bailey. There, in January 1937, *y Tri* ("The Three") were found guilty. Their defense on grounds of conscience was rejected, the judge castigating them for acts of "common anarchy."[62]

> You three men – educated men – have resorted to a most dangerous and wicked method of calling attention to what you believe to be the propriety of your views. It is not for me to express any opinion. All I can say is that this a plain case of arson and malicious damage, not to houses in which people reside, but to empty places, and doing damage to a large amount. I must sentence you all, as it would be in ill accord with the legal history of this country if it should be understood for one moment that justice is not administered properly because of some reason put up by an accused person which is not a reason for doing what he did, but merely an opinion which he says is the basis of his offence.[63]

Though Lewis, Williams and Valentine were sentenced to serve nine months in prison in the second division, the spectacle the trial provided

59 Mackail (1895) 167; Lewis (1939) 14.
60 Mackail (1895) 168; Lewis (1939) 14.
61 Lewis (1939) 14, 10.
62 Fishlock (1976) 12.
63 Jenkins (1998) 115.

proved somewhat advantageous for *Plaid Cymru*. As John Davies has suggested, the fire and the ensuing legal battle "aroused deep feelings in Wales," feelings that were, on the whole, sympathetic to Lewis and his accomplices (though many had doubts about both Lewis' Catholicism and the conservatism he adopted in leading the party).[64] Membership in *Plaid Cymru* began to tick upward as "the circulation of the Party's papers rose," but even then rising enthusiasm and increased public exposure did not easily "translate itself into electoral success. The party organizer, J. E. Jones, making the best of a bad job, spoke of the late 1930s as a period of 'consistent strong slow progress'."[65] That slow progress did, however, instigate significant change five years later, when officials in Parliament – under further pressure from Lewis and William George (1912–2006) the nephew of the former prime minister David Lloyd George – reconsidered the Tudor-era language statutes governing British courts. In passing the Welsh Courts Act (1942), Parliament formally enfranchised Welsh as a legal language in the United Kingdom, providing what Saunders Lewis had sought, namely "the provision and employment of interpreters of the Welsh and English languages for the purposes of proceedings before courts in Wales."[66]

By this measure alone Lewis' legal fight was beneficial to the cause of Welsh Wales. The controversy surrounding the trial of *y Tri*, however, reverberated in circles well beyond barristers and policy makers. Among those who followed the story was the painter and poet David Jones. Reading the *Times* and *Catholic Herald*, Jones thought the Llŷn fire had been a courageous act, one which moved him so deeply that he attempted to contact Saunders Lewis while he was still incarcerated at Wormwood Scrubs in West London. In June 1937 Jones wrote to Lewis' wife, offering one of the six author's copies he had received of his first literary work, *In Parenthesis* (1937), a book which had then received praise for being an "epic of war ... like no other" composed of "words as hard and bright as the things they signify."[67]

> Dear Mrs Saunders Lewis, I wanted to send to your husband a copy of my
> book, just published called "In Parenthesis" ... I do not know your

[64] J. Davies (2007) 575–76.

[65] Jenkins (1998) xiv–xv; Chapman (2006a) 25.

[66] The Welsh Courts Act, 1942 may be accessed at: www.legislation.gov.uk/ukpga/Geo6/5–6/40/contents. The 1942 law has since been superseded by the Welsh Language Acts of both 1967 and 1993.

[67] Read (1937) 457.

husband personally but I very much wish to give him this copy of my book if he will accept it. It deals largely with Wales & might interest him.[68]

Margaret Lewis forwarded the message to Lewis, who had in fact already heard of *In Parenthesis*, having perhaps read James Agate's review of the "masterpiece" in the *Daily Express*.[69] Eager to read it, he asked her to keep the book for the time being, on account of prison rules (on release inmates were expected to leave behind books they had received while incarcerated).[70] Two weeks following his release from prison – an occasion that saw *y Tri* feted with "bonfires … lit in North Wales to celebrate their homecoming" – Lewis began *In Parenthesis* and wrote Jones the first letter in what became a lasting friendship.[71]

> We had our big show of welcome and speechifying yesterday, and from the moment of coming out of prison I had to be preparing for that. But now that it's over I propose at once to read "In Parenthesis". In fact I shall begin after posting this, because the mist and rain are surging towards me over Holyhead mountain, and only a near foreground of shining grass and much protruding grey rock and one grey-rock farm and one whitewashed cottage are visible. It's to be a soaked afternoon of Autumn. I'll write again to you when I've read it. Thanks seem inadequate.[72]

Throughout the next thirty-seven years, Jones and Lewis debated contemporary matters touching on the religion, art and politics in Britain and Wales, for in both being veterans of the First World War and converts to Roman Catholicism, they shared common experience, a common creed as well as similar artistic passions and cultural concerns.[73] As Geraint Evans notes, this friendship with Lewis helped sow curious

---

[68] David Jones, Letter to Margaret Gilcriest Lewis (June 21, 1937) MS File #22724E, folio 91, National Library of Wales (NLW), Aberystwyth. See "Mr. Saunders Lewis, an Appeal and an Explanation," *Catholic Herald* (June 4, 1937) 2, as well as Evans (1987).

[69] James Agate, as in Dilworth (2017) 190; See Saunders Lewis, Letter to Margaret Gilcriest Lewis (July 19, 1937) in Lewis (1993) 626.

[70] Dr. Gwent Jones, Letter to Margaret Gilcriest Lewis (July 4, 1937) in Lewis (1993) 619.

[71] "Welsh Nationalists Released," *Ballymena Observer* (September 3, 1937) 9; See also "Welsh Leaders, Released Professor on Their Action," *The Scotsman* (September 13, 1937) 11, as well as "Welsh Nationalist Welcomed Home, Speaks in English – and Tells Why," *Western Daily Press and Bristol Mirror* (October 18, 1937) 8.

[72] Saunders Lewis, Letter to David Jones (September 12, 1937) David Jones Papers, CT 1/4, folio 4. National Library of Wales (NLW), Aberystwyth. The "speechifying" to which Lewis alludes refers to the speech he gave at the Caernarvon reception of September 11, where he declared that, "The position is transparently clear; Wales is in slavery; it is treated as a subject race." "Welsh Leaders, Released Professor on Their Action," *The Scotsman* (September 13, 1937) 11.

[73] On Lewis and Jones' friendship, see Dilworth (2017) 279–81, and Dentinger (2004) 222–34.

yet crucial elements in Jones' creative work and, more broadly, in the emergence of literary modernism in Welsh writing at large – linking the metropolitan "London modernism of T. S. Eliot" with the "Welsh radicalism of Saunders Lewis."[74] Jones often wrote Lewis, wondering, as he once explained,

> how *you* are, not only because I wonder how you are in health as a friend naturally would, but because I wonder what you are thinking touching the matters ~~we ha in~~ in which we have a mutual involvement and understanding, – a sort of ~~eyd~~ *cydgyfarfyddiad* – (if that's the ~~right~~ right word) where those three highly complex & usually dissevered 'things': the *res Walliae*, the Catholic religion, culture and *ars*, are intermuddled. You are the only person among my various good & dear friends to whom I can share without any chance of misunderstanding ~~on those three matters~~ *where those three matters*, ~~conjoin~~ so to say, conjoin.[75]

Yet, though the two men were likeminded with regard to "dissevered 'things'," Jones never sought the role of being a public intellectual or a reputedly national poet; he was rather a reluctant figure, a creative recluse who, though he shared something of Lewis' scorn for the "modern, post-Methodist, petite bourgeoisie," assessed political matters in a mostly cautious manner. Jones did admire activism on behalf of saving Welsh, but he considered *Plaid Cymru* "very far from satisfactory."[76] "There's no real cutting edge," he once told Lewis.[77] The party's aims were like all "political things" "so boring & superficial, in fact, damned silly."[78]

---

[74] Evans (2019) 459.

[75] David Jones, Letter to Saunders Lewis (December 3, 1967) MS File No. 22724E, folio 50, NLW. The Welsh term *cydgyfarfyddiad* denotes a "meeting-together," a "concurrence" or a "conjoining." See its entry in Thomas (1967).

[76] Dilworth (2017) 280; David Jones, Letter to Saunders Lewis (23 December 1961) MS File #22724E, folio 37, NLW.

[77] Jones, Letter to Saunders Lewis (December 23, 1961) MS File No. 22724E, folio 37, NLW.

[78] Jones, Letter to Saunders Lewis (23 December 1961) MS File No. 22724E, folio 37, NLW. Nonetheless Jones' active support for the Welsh nationalist cause was often assumed by others. In November 1963 he was asked to stand for election as president of the London branch of *Plaid Cymru*. He "felt it an honour" to be considered, but Jones felt he was "wholly unsuited for such an office" especially since he "was not actually a member of *Plaid Cymru*, & could not speak Welsh." Jones, Letter to Saunders Lewis (November 23 [22?], 26, 1963) MS File No. 22724E, folio 46, NLW. It should also be noted that after stepping down as president of *Plaid Cymru* in 1939 (and later losing the University of Wales by-election in 1943), Saunders Lewis began to take a dimmer view of the party's left-leaning approach to Welsh politics and independence. Lewis would soon become, as Tudur Hallam writes, an "awkward father figure" for later generations of Welsh nationalists. In 1962 Lewis complained to David Jones of the leftward shift in the "nationalist party that I partly founded." It had become "a nest of Aldermaston Anglo-Welsh socialists, and I loathe them. I wish I could get back to Italy, stay there, and hear no more ever of Wales."

Jones' lack of enthusiasm was not born, however, from indifference or disregard for the condition of Wales. On the contrary, from a young age he possessed a certain nostalgia for Wales – what he later described as his "Welsh affinity," a devotion that drove him to begin a concentrated study of the myth, history and literature of Wales.[79] Many times, from as early as age sixteen, Jones had tried to teach himself Welsh but fluency eluded him. As he later complained,

> I ~~don't~~ can't speak or read Welsh & being inordinately stupid with regard to learning languages, find it hard to conquer – I *do* wish I had known ~~knew~~ it from when I was young – it's so awfully hard to learn any language – however much one's desires impel one to try – when one is middle-aged, at least I find it so. The more memory seems to get so faulty as one gets older.[80]

Jones failed to learn the language not because he was "inordinately stupid" but rather because Welsh had largely fallen out of use in his childhood home. His father, James Jones (1860–1943), did sing songs to him "in Welsh, and the clear-vowelled Cymraeg and perfect pitch without any sign of effort filled me with wonder, certainly with pride, and a kind of awe," but Jones grew up a "Londoner, brought up entirely in an English setting."[81] Nonetheless, he still felt the gravity of "that sense of 'otherness'," an otherness caught up in the reality in which the "Muse of History" had placed him, "one half Welsh, if one half Cockney, with a dash of Italian."[82] With this mixed ancestry Jones felt Welsh, but he also desired to express the cultural hybridity of his "immediate forbear's – *patria*."[83] "[T]hose of us who chance to be in some way 'Welsh' cannot

---

Saunders Lewis, Letter to David Jones (April 4, 1962) David Jones Papers, CT 1/4, folio 41, NLW. On Lewis' legacy and political influence, see Hallam (2019) 507–28.

[79] On this "affinity," see David Jones, "Some Notes on the Difficulties of One Writer of Welsh Affinity Whose Language Is English," as in Jones (1976) 55–65. On Jones' early encounters with Wales, both in his family and in his reading, see Dilworth (2017) 17–21, 29–30 as well as Dilworth (2012) 25. On Jones' interest in Wales as a historical site, see Dilworth (2000) 67–88.

[80] David Jones, Letter to Saunders Lewis (July 22, 1948) MS File No. 22724E, folio 1, NLW. Jones' failure to gain fluency in Welsh remained a source of bitterness throughout his life: "It is impossible to explain the sense of frustration, – genuine bitterness, grief is not too strong a word. Of course one can *feel* the way the language behaves and perceive its felicities and be read in Welsh history and the splendour of its *chwedlau* and realise the unique character of its complex metric. *But* that is not to *know* the language. It is a scientific fact that the ability to learn things by rote, begins to get more difficult from an early age and rapidly so after one is say 20, and learning by rote is virtually essential in the case of languages ... And I chance to be a dunderhead in languages and was wholly concerned with the visual arts of drawing and painting until 1928 when I began to make written works." Jones (1974) 4.

[81] Jones (1972) 8; Jones (1976) 56.

[82] Jones (1972) 8; Jones (2016) [4].

[83] Jones (1976) 56.

(except by total silence)," he explained, "do other than continue to draw upon such fragmentary bits and pieces of our national heritage as may be available to us in an alien tongue," to somehow convey "in English, what, at its subtlest & best and most incantational is locked up in the ancient tongue of Britain."[84]

It should be noted that Jones' regard for both the alleged purity of his father's Welsh ancestry and the "Welsh strains in the English genius" emerged in an all too precarious moment, when a variety of new mendacious forms of nationalism were fanning out across Europe throughout the 1930s – with devastating consequences.[85] Jones' growing interest, therefore, in both studying and reenvisioning the early history of the Welsh may be seen in the stark context of some of these new nationalist ideals; and Jones himself was not entirely unaware – or ignorant in the least – of the potential parallels: he unabashedly professed fascination with the rise of fascism across Italy and Germany, writing in May 1939 that there was indeed "much in both the Fascist and Nazi revolutions that demand our understanding and sympathy. They represent, for all their alarming characteristics an heroic attempt to cope with certain admitted corruptions in our civilization."[86] As Tom Villis has suggested, this approbation for Hitlerism echoed "many of his Catholic contemporaries, too, in viewing Nazism as the lesser of many evils. There is a suggestion that Nazism is not only a lesser evil than communism, but also a lesser evil than liberal capitalism."[87] Jones' statements on Hitler, however, were also marked by some reluctance and a bit of skepticism, too. *Mein Kampf* was "amazingly interesting in all kinds of ways," he explained to Harman Grisewood (1906–97) just weeks earlier,

> but pretty terrifying too. God, he's *nearly* right – but this *hate* thing mars his whole thing, I feel. I mean, it just misses getting over the frontier into the saint thing – he won't stand any nonsense or illusions or talk – but, having got so far, the conception of the world in terms of race-struggle (that's what it boils down to) will hardly do. But I do like a lot of what he says – only I must admit he sees the world as just going on *for ever* in this steel grip. Compared with his opponents he is grand, but compared with the saints he is bloody. And I think I mean also by saints – lovers, and all kinds of unifying makers. Anyway, I back him still against all this currish,

---

[84] Jones (1976) 58, 61.
[85] Jones (1976) 59.
[86] Jones, as quoted in Villis (2018) 79.
[87] Villis (2018) 50.

leftish, money thing, even though I'm a miserable specimen and dependent upon it.[88]

By contrast, Saunders Lewis and those sympathetic to *Plaid Cymru* were more unequivocal, if generally unspecific, about the rising threat of fascism: Wales' national interests had to be defended against any form of "bureaucratic control and Fascist totalitarianism … Some corners of the continent may escape this fate, Ireland, perhaps, and Portugal; it would be splendid if we could say Wales too, but that depends on the success of the Nationalist movement in Wales."[89] Lewis' opposition to fascism remained conservative, motivated by his own decidedly eccentric, right-wing brand of Catholic communitarianism. Thinking Nazism essentially anti-Christian (an ideology of Marxist origin no less), he was convinced that it would be destroyed neither "by revolution" nor by a "return to the Liberalism of the last century" but rather "by patiently and laboriously building up new ideals in small communities and some small countries. Men will have to develop anew," he wrote, "and, at first, on a small scale, new communities in the shadow of the industrialism of the modern State. And that is a task that cannot be accomplished without a faith, as strong as the faith of the Nazis. But a different faith."[90]

Despite Jones' dalliance with fascism, he largely sought to evade the contemporary political struggles of Europe and remained more interested in exploring and immersing himself in various historiographical and aesthetic representations of early Welsh Romanization. Convinced that the first strains of Welsh genius had received an enduring shape in late antiquity, Jones insisted that a "Brythoneg-Rhufeinig link" had been cultivated throughout the "three or four centuries of Roman occupation" during the *Provincia Britannia* (AD 43–410), a time when "the deposits of the Hellenistic-Roman world" were said to have "infiltrated the indigenous 'Celtic' culture."[91] The infiltration had been so complete, so effective, he thought, that even in the twentieth century, Wales could not "escape the via Romana."[92] "[O]wing to a vast complex of causes," the country still possessed a "*direct* connection" with the ancient Greeks – one which

---

[88] David Jones, "To H. J. G., 24 April 1939" in Jones *DG* (1980) 93.

[89] Lewis (1941–42) 2, 3. On *Plaid Cymru's* disavowal of European fascism, see R. W. Jones (2014).

[90] Lewis (1941–42) 8, 3, 8.

[91] "Brythoneg-Rhufeinig" meaning in Welsh: "Brythonic-Roman." David Jones, Letter to Saunders Lewis (October 12 [11?], 1971) MS File No. 22724E, folio 73, NLW. David Jones, Letter to Michael Richey (April 19–27, 1965), David Jones Archive, Burns Library, Boston College.

[92] David Jones, "The Eighth Letter" (November 13, 1961) in David Jones (1996) 40.

had been enmeshed "through Rome."[93] "Even at the lowest level of mere debate," he told Lewis,

> it was possible to say to the anglicizers: "We emerged from within the Roman *imperium* & are the *only* people left in this island who did. In fact our native princes ~~spring~~ sprung from a line of Latin officials, &, in contrast to Gaul the Brittonic speech continued side by side of Latin throughout the 4 centuries of Roman occupation. – we are the heirs of romanity. How can we think of Meirionnydd without thinking of Marianus, or *Padarn Beis Rhudd* without recalling Paternus, etc."[94]

Yet, though Jones felt Romanity still remained palpable, there existed across Britain "an astounding disregard of the historic roots of the Cymry."[95] For more than 1,500 years the "Brythoneg-Rhufeinig link" had linked Wales with a Roman source, but growing Anglicization and ever encroaching modernity seemed, to his mind at least, to threaten that classical patrimony.[96] Intent on lessening his own ignorance, Jones devoted himself to the study of these historic roots, reading both recent works by R. H. Hodgkins (1877–1951) and other histories of the period published in the previous century. He admired Hodgkins' *History of the Anglo-Saxons* – calling it a "really beautifully done book, some lovely illustrations in it, and proper *maps*" – but he did feel that Hodgkins' writing had done little to upset the dominant (but wrong) Victorian

---

[93] Ancient Greece, as Jones saw it, could only be grasped through the "via Romana": "I love Greek art better than anything, almost," he wrote, "but, owing to a vast complex of causes, our *direct* connection with it comes through Rome. It's rather like the business of religion. *Quite apart* from the truth or untruth of it, it seems to me that only by becoming a Catholic can one establish continuity with Antiquity. I've put this *badly*, but you'll see what I mean. We *can't* escape the via Romana – not if we are Western men." David Jones, "Eighth Letter to Richard Shirley Smith" (November 13, 1961) in David Jones (1996) 40 (emphases in the original).

[94] Jones, Letter to Saunders Lewis (October 12 [11?], 1971) MS File No. 22724E, folio 73, NLW. Saunders Lewis later addressed their mutual interest in Wales' Roman inheritance in a televised interview on the BBC on March 15, 1965. Noting the inspiration Jones took from "Roman antiquity and Roman art," Lewis insisted that he thought "the Welsh are Romans," a notion – which though then not widely recognized – Jones had "done a great deal to help to get it recognized." "[T]hat is a great contribution of yours, not to Wales so much, as to the whole of the British Isles and its memory of its own past." Hunter-Evans (2014) 29. See also Evans (2019) 460–61.

[95] Jones, Letter to Saunders Lewis (October 12 [11?], 1971) MS File No. 22724E, folio 73, NLW.

[96] Jones, Letter to Saunders Lewis (October 12 [11?], 1971) MS File No. 22724E, folio 73, NLW. For Jones' extensive discussion of "vernacularization," see his letters to Saunders Lewis (January 4, 1962) folio 38–39, (October 3, 5, 1964) folio 47, (December 3, 1967) folio 50–51, (October 12 [11?], 1971) MS File No. 22724E, folio 73, NLW. Jones was fond of using the phrase *Fuit Ilium*, from *Aeneid* (2.325) to express a certain cultural pessimism about the historical fortunes of Wales. See, for example, David Jones, Letter to Saunders Lewis (December 11, 22, 25, 1955) MS File No. 22724E, folio 11, NLW. See also his notable watercolor lettering, *Cara Wallia Derelicta* (1959), which contains a reference to the same line.

understanding of Roman Britain.[97] His history, like previous accounts, still saw largely only progressive movement – the upward path of social and political development from the annihilation of Roman Britain to the present day, with distinctive periods passing "from the Roman culture of the later Empire through sub-Romanism to a Celtic and a Christian renaissance."[98] The nineteenth-century English historians Edward Augustus Freeman (1823–92) and John Richard Green (1837–83) had likewise insisted on the success of the "English conquest" of Britain after the fall of Roman rule.[99] According to Green, proof of the sheer "completeness of this destruction of all Roman life" was evident everywhere, Britain having become

> the only province of the Empire where Rome died into a vague tradition of the past. The whole organization of government and society disappeared with the people who used it. Roman roads indeed still led to desolate cities. Roman camps still crowned hill and down. The old divisions of the land remained to furnish bounds of field and farm for the new settlers. The Roman church, the Roman country-house was left standing, though reft of priest and lord. But Rome was gone ... Its law, literature, its manners, its faith, went with it.[100]

Freeman similarly insisted that, as Rome perished, the influence of its language and religion dissipated as well; even its legal tradition was thought to have exercised "no influence upon our insular jurisprudence, until, in times after the Norman Conquest, the civil law was introduced as something utterly exotic ... The municipal institutions of the Roman towns in Britain utterly perished."[101] As Jones saw it, Hodgkins had not effectively altered the gross imperial narrative of his predecessors, for though his "most scholarly piece of work" had indeed "enormously developed the details" of the period with "new archaeological evidence," it left "the *main pattern*" of Victorian historiography "much unchanged."[102] He also was

> too much of the Teutonic school to please me – but all the same in a nice kind of way ... He is unable to be anything but a bit superior about the Welsh; it comes out in the oddest ways. But at *least* he admits that with

97   David Jones, "To H. J. G., 20 July 1935," in Jones *DG* (1980) 75.
98   Hodgkins (1935) vol. 1: 72.
99   Green (1878–80) vol. 1: 7; Freeman (1867–76).
100 Green (1878–80) vol. 1: 32.
101 Freeman (1867–76) vol. 1: 17–18.
102 David Jones, Letter to Saunders Lewis (October 3, 5, 1964) MS File No. 22724E, folio 47, NLW.

the loss of the Island to the 'steady', prudent etc. Teutons, they in their hills wove, as he would say, a web of magic and imagination round the story of their defeat, which in turn gave to the world the Arthurian cycle.[103]

Though Jones found little of sympathy in Hodgkins' work, he felt a new historical consensus was slowly coalescing against the pervasive 'Teutonic' understanding of Roman Britain. No longer could the link between the 'native' Briton and invading Roman be characterized through the "traditional English view," namely that "between Britons and Romans there was an initial cleavage of race, language, and culture which to the last was never really bridged."[104] On the contrary, the recent scholarship of R. G. Collingwood (1889–1943) offered a more nuanced theory, one that admitted the possibility of greater overlap or cultural hybridity:

> [T]he two cultures, Roman and British, were not absolutely foreign to one another, just as the two physical types were not really distinct. One of the strongest reasons for the success of the Roman Empire is that it included a number of peoples who were so far homogeneous both in race and in civilization that they could blend into a single whole without doing violence to anything in their natures.[105]

Unlike the imperial regimes of contemporary Europe, the Roman Empire possessed the power to legitimize a broad range of cultural and linguistic differences within its territories. For that reason, Collingwood believed that the Britons had not sacrificed their 'native' character while in the grip of Roman colonial power: "the Britons did not remain a mere subject race, held down by a Roman army. They became Romans; Romans in speech, in habits, and in sentiment. But this Romanization did not involve an unnatural warping of the British character."[106] Having taken unto themselves "a full share in the Roman civilization and a flourishing Romanized life of their own," they became inheritors of what Charles Cochrane later called *Romanitas*, a phenomenon that somehow

---

[103] Jones, "To H. J. G. 20 July 1935," in Jones *DG* (1980) 75.
[104] Collingwood (1924) 12.
[105] Collingwood (1924) 14–15. Collingwood's view, though markedly different, built upon that of his teacher, Francis John Haverfield (1860–1919). His book, *The Romanization of Roman Britain* (1905), cast Romanization as a "complex process with complex issues." "It did not everywhere and at once destroy all traces of tribal or national sentiments or fashions." Though those traces did eventually dissipate, "the process worked with different degrees of speed and success in different lands." Elements of the tribal under Roman rule "remained at least for a while and in certain regions, not in active opposition, but in latent persistence, capable of resurrection under proper conditions." Haverfield (1905) 22.
[106] Collingwood (1924) 14.

"transcended all purely 'natural' bonds."[107] "Amid the wreckage of empires founded on tyranny and exploitation," Rome "stood alone," he asserted, "as the project of a world-community united by ties of the spirit. As such, it was genuinely *political*; it went beyond race, beyond colour, and, in all but a few exceptional instances, beyond religion as this was envisaged by antiquity."[108] Yet, even as Rome encouraged all to rise above racial, ethnic and religious differences, *Romanitas* did not demand that local "heterogenous elements" be repudiated; they were organized rather "in support of the imperial idea. Under the aegis of Eternal Rome, Greek and Latin, African, Gaul, and Spaniard remained free to lead their own lives and achieve their own destiny."[109]

More recent scholarly work has complicated or dispensed with the concept of Romanization altogether, noting that a greater emphasis on diverse regional expressions, social variability and the "infinitely varied" forms of cultural hybridity are as important to the analysis of "the Roman cultural package found around the empire" as seeking to identify "elements of homogeneity."[110] "[M]uch of what we identify as 'Roman' culture in provinces like Britain," David Mattingly observes, "in fact came from the other provinces in northern and western Europe, rather than from Italy or even the Mediterranean region."[111] Moreover, Romanization is itself "not a Roman concept" of the period but is often employed as a more contemporary "unilateral, unidirectional and progressive" notion that tends to crudely reduce "the question of cultural identity to a simple binary opposition: Roman and native."[112] A critical difficulty with this approach is, as Richard Hingley notes, its denial of the many multivocal negotiations of the so-called native/Roman dynamic prevalent across the empire, not only among the archaeological traces left by provincial elites but more widely in the so-called non-elite aspects of local material culture, where variations in acculturation and Roman reception, in the "hints of ways of life ... are far too complex to be cate-gorized through the use of Romanization theory."[113]

---

[107] Collingwood (1924) 14. Cochrane (1940) 73. Cochrane developed his views regarding the "formal discipline of *Romanitas*" in *Christianity and Classical Culture* (1940) 114–76, 179–80, a book Jones saw as a "most illuminating" study. See David Jones, Letter to Rev. Desmond Chute (February 3, 1953) in Jones *IN* (1984) 43.
[108] Cochrane (1940) 72–73.
[109] Cochrane (1940) 115, 73.
[110] Mattingly (2006) 15. See also Millet (1990) 1–8.
[111] Mattingly (2006) 14–15.
[112] Mattingly (2006) 14.
[113] Hingley (2005) 93.

The Roman world did not operate according to simple and well established rules, and the ideas that we use to study it may sometimes collide and contradict. In other words, we need to think further than the useful but simplistic image of 'Roman' identity. The combination of a number of competing approaches enables us to keep a focus upon the power-relations that were used to the create empire, while considering its character as a variety of overlapping networks of power and identity.[114]

Too often "a tension between the local context of individual societies and the creation of Roman cultural coherence" is still said to dominate scholarly discussions – with Rome's "civilizing mission" among the 'native' provinces of empire lurking in the background.[115] The history of that tension in scholarship, Mattingly suggests, was likely conditioned by the late nineteenth- and early twentieth-century "involvement of European scholars at the time in their own world of colonization and empire."[116] The stress often laid upon the "benign aspect" of Rome's colonial reach might therefore be read as implicit encouragement at the time that imperial states of Europe imitate its apparent "accommodation with local cultures," perhaps even to further advance what Collingwood had called "a society of peoples in which intercourse was nowhere checked by barriers such as separate races or even nations."[117]

Nonetheless, Collingwood's notions surrounding the complex transmission of classical culture, the synthetic fusion of Roman and Briton, attracted Jones' interest in aesthetic representations of civilizational hybridity. In *Roman Britain and the English Settlements* (1936), an extensive study Collingwood coauthored with the archaeologist J. N. L. Myres (1902–89), Jones found a more appealing vision of Roman Britain than he had yet encountered. Its ancient civilization was one marked by competing cultural and linguistic forces – forces native, foreign, Briton, Roman and Anglo-Saxon – through which common syntheses slowly appeared, an essential hybridity that Jones would later describe as Britain's "complex heritage."[118] What he admired in Collingwood and Myres was not simply their belief that the Britons were not "a mere subject race" but the insistence rather that Roman Britain's collapse was born of conflicts too complex, too local for the linear narratives of

[114] Hingley (2005) 93.
[115] Hingley (2005) 48; Mattingly (2006) 14.
[116] Mattingly (2006) 14.
[117] Mattingly (2006) 14, 13. Collingwood (1924) 15–16. On Collingwood's 'Roman' and 'anti-exceptionalist' vision of history, see Browning (2004) 73–96.
[118] Jones (2016) [10].

contemporary historiography.[119] These times, "the darkest centuries in English history," they wrote,

> were times whose quality cannot be portrayed without serious distortion in those broad and rational sequences of cause and effect so beloved by the historian. The conflicts are too complex, issues too obscure, the cross-currents too numerous, and the decisions too local, to make possible the application of any single formula to their solution; and it is at least reassuring sometimes to remember that, if we found such a formula, we should unquestionably be wrong. *Uno itinere non potest perveniri ad tam grande secretum.*[120]

Inadequate evidence had kept the ruin of early Britain from sight, and little of "the flotsam and jetsam left by the ebb tide of Roman imperialism" could help historians craft a credible narrative of social progress.[121] The "character of the times" was too obscure, so much so if one were left "with little more than a blurred impression in our minds," that blurred impression would represent "more faithfully than any clear-cut picture the spirit of the age."[122] For Jones, the work of Collingwood and Myres marked an important shift of approach among a growing number of historians and linguists.[123] That which began "in Myers [*sic*] contribution to *Roman Britain*," he told Saunders Lewis, introduced "a more definite change in [F. M.] Stenton, & in Peter Hunter Blair's Cambridge paperback *An Introduction to A. S. [Anglo-Saxon] England* [where] some of the fruits of re-questioning show themselves."[124] Both Stenton and Blair accepted as axiomatic that obscurity clouded early British history; that

---

[119] Collingwood (1924) 14.

[120] Collingwood and Myres (1937) 455–56. This passage is partially excerpted (and slightly misquoted with Jones writing "appreciation" instead of "application") in a letter "To T. F. B, 16 May 1942," in Jones *DG* (1980) 119. Jones noted the quotation as "jolly nice to end a book of great learning and sweat like that." The Latin phrase contained therein – translated roughly as "not by one pathway alone can one come to so great a secret" – is taken from the appeal Quintus Aurelius Symmachus made to Valentinian II in AD 384. Symmachus wrote the emperor pleading that the pagan Altar of Victory be restored to the Roman Curia. His petition was denied and later rebutted by Ambrose, Bishop of Milan. See section 3.10 of *Symmachi Relatio III* in *Der Streit um den Victoriaaltar. Die dritte Relatio des Symmachus und die Briefe 17, 18 und 57 des Mailänder Bischofs Ambrosius*, trans. and ed. Richard Klein (Darmstadt: Wissenschaftliche Buchgesellschaft, 1972), 104–6.

[121] Collingwood and Myres (1937) 451.

[122] Collingwood and Myres (1937) 455, 456.

[123] On the evolving reception of Anglo-Saxon history at this time, see Keynes (2003) xvii–xxxv. See also Mattingly (2006) 3–20.

[124] Jones refers to Stenton (1943) and Blair's *An Introduction to Anglo-Saxon England* (2003), first published in 1956. Jones, Letter to Saunders Lewis (October 3, 5, 1964) MS File No. 22724E, folio 47, NLW.

fact alone disproved what Freeman, Green and Hodgkins assumed, namely that "Rome was gone" from the religion, law and literature of Britannia.[125] It suggested rather – as Myres claimed – that contemporary methods of historiography were too coarse, too crude to detect the traces of Romanity that remained following the Western Empire's collapse. The "pro-'Anglo-Saxon'" bias of previous research – its devotion to the "broad and rational sequences of cause and effect so beloved by the historian" – could not untangle the forces that, in driving Roman civilization to ruin, still somehow translated something essentially Roman into Welsh.[126] "[W]e shall never now know the truth," Jones confessed, "for instead of more recent specialist research making the 'pattern' or 'lack of pattern' clearer it makes it much more complex."[127]

Though "that chaos" of the fifth and sixth centuries seemed too obscure to elucidate in historical form, its concealment still stirred Jones' imagination;[128] and precisely because he was ignorant of this key moment – because he was denied a more exacting knowledge of the acculturating forces at work in Welsh identity – Jones began to envision a poetic style that would 'document' the multilinguistic hybridity of early British history. Though drawn somewhat superficially to the advocacy of *Plaid Cymru*, he thought no native purity – whether racial, ethnic or linguistic – had ever existed on "*ynys hon*, 'this island'": British civilization was too "subtly meshed indeed," he argued, "intricated (very much so) with our common Western deposit, the mythos of Hellas and of Rome, together with the Aramaean mythos of the Mabinog Iesu."[129] Even when the Saxons, Angles and Jutes had invaded, their migration had not compromised the "mythos of Wales" in any sense.[130] It was not so much Anglo-Saxon civilization, Jones maintained, as those "blasted Vikings and the Isamlic [*sic*] assault of the 7th–8th–9th centuries that really destroyed the *romanitas* of the West rather than the Germanic invasions of the 5th & 6th centuries."[131] Roman civilization had once fused with the Celts; so too could it have "assimilated" the Anglo-Saxon.[132] Thus Jones found himself

[125] Green (1878–80) vol. 1: 32.

[126] Jones, "To H. J. G. 20 July 1935," in Jones *DG* (1980) 75; Collingwood and Myres (1937) 455.

[127] Jones, Letter to Saunders Lewis (October 3, 5, 1964) MS File No. 22724E, folio 47, NLW.

[128] Jones, Letter to Saunders Lewis (October 3, 5, 1964) MS File No. 22724E, folio 47, NLW.

[129] Jones (2016) [10], [7–8]. Jones often elaborated on the broadly hybridized character of Celtic identity, insisting that the "early deposits of Wales are intricated with those of Ireland as well as with the Romanic thing so one has to be very cautious in trying to disentangle the *materia*." Jones, Letter to Michael Richey (April 19–27, 1965) Boston College, Burns Library.

[130] Jones (2016) [7].

[131] Jones, Letter to Michael Richey (April 19–27, 1965) Boston College, Burns Library.

[132] Jones, Letter to Michael Richey (April 19–27, 1965) Boston College, Burns Library. On Jones' view of Anglo-Saxon culture, see Johnson (2010) 89–109.

out of step with contemporaneous calls for greater Welsh purity, for "*at every possible level*," he once told Saunders Lewis, "'Englishness', in a thousand small ways, penetrates what remains of 'Welshness'."[133] The animus of politicized Anglophobia was an ahistorical phenomenon, an equal threat even to Welsh bilingualism. "[T]he English," he observed, "have been with us for about a millennium and a half, so they can be regarded as naturalized by now."[134] No obliteration of English nor indeed of Welsh was needed but rather a greater awareness of "those chancy twists and meanders of history and of quasi-history" that had formed Britain's culturally mixed character.[135] It was the sheer ignorance of this "complex heritage," this hybrid linguistic and cultural history, that had to be rooted out for "none of us, whoever we are," he asserted, "should neglect to recall those things which have determined what we are."[136]

With such understanding contemporary poets could "under certain circumstances and given a perceptive response, vitalise the things of England."[137] In recent literature, Jones noted, no lesser invention than the sprung rhythm of Gerard Manley Hopkins (1844–89) had been forged from traces of Welsh, from his "study of *cynghanedd* and his stay in Gwynedd."[138] Fascinated with the "instress and charm of Wales," Hopkins learned of *cynghanedd*, or "consonant-chime" as he called it, at St. Bueno's College in North Wales.[139] There in 1875 he began composing *The Wreck of the Deutschland*, using "certain chimes suggested by the Welsh Poetry [he] had been reading (what they call cynghanedd)."[140] Yet, because of that, Hopkins came to think *The Deutschland* possessed "a great many more oddnesses [that] could not but dismay an editor's eye."[141] For Jones, however, those oddnesses reflected Hopkins' creative imagination, his desire to expose English prosody to the linguistic charge

---

[133] Jones made this remark when discussing Emyr Humphreys' novel *A Toy Epic* (1958). He admired the book for its realism and alternating perspectives on growing up in "the four corners of Wales." David Jones, Letter to Saunders Lewis (June 2, 1959) MS File No. 22724E, folio 14, NLW. See also Humphreys (1958) 7. Humphreys' novel has been said to set forth a "tribal view of Welsh identity as a linguistic community – rooted in farming and Nonconformism – that continues to survive under the surface of an ever-encroaching, English-speaking modernity." Webb (2019) 546.

[134] Jones (2016) [9].

[135] Jones (2016) [4].

[136] Jones (2016) [10], [4].

[137] Jones (2016) [11].

[138] Jones (2016) [10].

[139] Gerard Manley Hopkins, "Journal for 1874," in Hopkins (2015) 601; Gerard Manley Hopkins, "26–7 November 1882 to Robert Bridges," in Hopkins (2013b) 551. On Welsh influence in Hopkins, see Lilly (1943) 192–205.

[140] Hopkins, "5–10 October 1878 to Richard Watson Dixon," in Hopkins (2013a) 317.

[141] Hopkins (2013a) 317.

and foreign timbre of Welsh poetry. Of his use of Welsh, Jones wrote, "sometimes, hundreds of years later, things that have become formulae, provide a renewal of life in some unexpected context perhaps in another language, & of this Hopkins is a most outstanding example."[142] Without fully understanding the "exacting but invigorating nature of Welsh metrical forms," Hopkins set off a "creative explosion" in English, one to which most readers – even his confidant Robert Bridges (1844–1930) – had remained "totally blind," even "to the nature of the possible *cyd-gysylltiad* ['interconnection'] of *the causes*" behind it.[143] His "English metric," however, became one "of very great felicity, subtlety and strength," and not because he cultivated mere convention but because he had sought out a foreign world – the "hidden things of Wales" to "vitalise the things of England."[144]

Yet, though Hopkins had already manipulated Welsh to expand the poetic range of English writing, Jones felt that he could still delve more deeply into the "entailed inheritance" of British history to fertilize new literature.[145] Drawn from the country's complex linguistic history, a new multilingual style might demonstrate

> basic things: the early mixed racial deposits, the myth (mythus) that is specifically of this Island, and the Christian Liturgy, and the Canon of Scripture, and the Classical deposits ... a great complex of influences and interactions which have conditioned us all.[146]

However, as a self-described "'English monoglot'," Jones was not fluent in any other language – not in Welsh nor even in Greek or in Latin, languages whose reception he thought especially critical to the Welsh "mythos."[147] Unlike some of his contemporaries, he had not enjoyed a rigorous university education in classics, nor had he read Latin or Greek intensively at either the Camberwell School of Art (1910–14) or the Westminster School of Art (1919–21).[148] By middle age, as he composed

---

[142] David Jones, Letter XXIII to Aneirin Talfan Davies (November 27, 1962) in Jones (1980) 86.

[143] Jones (1980) 87, 86. For Jones' view of Hopkins, see Berenato (2018) 101–267, as well as Staudt (2018) 321–25.

[144] Jones (2016) [10], [11].

[145] Jones (2016) [11].

[146] Jones (1952) 40.

[147] Jones (1952) 11. See Jones (2016) [7].

[148] While living at Ditchling and Capel-y-Ffin during the 1920s, Jones regularly associated with many others who had received greater formal education in classics. His friend René Hague (1905–81) had gone up to Oriel College, Oxford, on a classics scholarship, but as Dilworth notes, Hague was "sent down for spending (and being unable to repay) the funds of a drama society." Jones' associate, Douglas Cleverdon (1903–87) likewise studied classics at Jesus College, Oxford,

The Anathemata, Jones often complained about his lack of a "public school or university background," believing that he might be "a good writer, if I knew all about these root languages but it's hard otherwise."[149] Like the Welsh he had so often tried to learn, the Latin and the Greek he retained were largely self-taught, but Jones longed for a capable tutor: "I do wish I knew Latin," he told his friend Louis Bussell in 1945, "I've been trying to conjugate the verbs 'to come' & 'to adore' but it's all too complicated at 50!"[150] His ancient Greek, however, was worse. In 1952, when thanking Rev. Desmond Chute (1895–1962) for sending him an engraved Greek inscription, Jones noted that, "I can't read Greek but someone staying in this house translated it for me and I like the sound of it and what it says very much."[151] As he aged, Jones regularly upbraided himself over his lack of fluency in both languages as well as Welsh, believing that his ignorance had, lamentably, been marred by collective amnesia – some aspect of a "memory-effacing Lethe" – afflicting contemporary civilization.[152] "'Only as you get older,'" he complained in an interview for *The Guardian*,

> "you get so much slower. I hate it – taking twelve times as long to try to say something, and then not getting it right. And there's this terrible ignorance one is trying to make up all the time. I can't command even one

while Rev. Martin D'Arcy (1888–1976), a Jesuit priest whom Jones befriended in 1922, excelled in Greek and Latin, having taken a first in 'Greats' from Campion Hall, Oxford (1912–16). See Dilworth (2017) 90–91, 94–95, 76–77.

149 Johnston (1964) 321. David Jones, Letter to Harman Grisewood (March 19, 1940), as cited in Staudt (1994) 130.

150 David Jones, Letter to Louis Bussell (March 14, 1945) Burns Library, Boston College. On Jones' Latin, see Miles (1990) 45.

151 David Jones, Letter to Rev. Desmond Chute (December 29, 1952) in Jones *IN* (1984) 25.

152 Jones (1952) 16. Jones often linked the diminishment of Welsh with the decline of Greek and Latin, perhaps most notably when complaining at length about the decrease of Latin in the liturgies of the Catholic Church. He lamented the preference for the vernacular as the dominant liturgical language (see Second Vatican Council, *Sacrosanctum Concilium* (1963) chap. 1, 3.36.2): "I think our boys are making the same mistake as those classical dons who used to say that the teaching of the Greek and Latin languages was maintained because it taught men to think clearly, to write clear English, to become competent civil servants or what not. Apart from being largely balls, the reasons are utile and so-called 'practical'. What the dons ought to have said was that the classics were an integral part of our Western heritage and should be fought for on that ground alone. Our Church leaders have even more reason to guard that heritage – for it is saturated with the sacral. It's not a matter of knowledge but of love. It's a terrible thought that the language of the West, of the Western liturgy, and inevitably the Roman chant, might become virtually extinct … I believe it's only part of the Decline of the West. Perhaps I'm talking balls, I don't know. But the *kind* of arguments used I find highly unsatisfactory, and they have just that same tang that distresses me so over the language of my father's *patria*. They prove by statistics that the Welsh language is dying and that it has no practical value anyhow. Damn such bloody arguments." Jones, "To H. J. G. 6 July 1964," in Jones *DG* (1980) 209.

language besides English" (he has taught himself to read a little Welsh but not to speak it). "If I'd gone to school, at least they'd have taught me Greek and Latin."[153]

Despite such "terrible ignorance," Jones remained committed, however, to test his fragmentary knowledge of Welsh and the classics in a polyglot style whose density would resemble the "shape in words" he first made in *In Parenthesis* (1937).[154] There the soldiers' experience of the Great War, its "complex of sights, sounds, fears, hopes, apprehensions, smells, things exterior and interior," had been drawn together as though it were the "landscape and paraphernalia of that singular time and of those particular men."[155] Using some material he had started in 1939, he began drafting *The Anathemata* in earnest in January 1948.[156] Convinced by Collingwood's dictum that to "study history" was a means "to attain self-knowledge," Jones was eager that his new work traverse not simply "a singular time" as *In Parenthesis* had but cut across a broad trajectory of British history, language and mythology; it would illustrate therein something of the "whole argosy of mankind."[157] He therefore drew on "the Welsh and Latin languages and a great many concepts and motifs of Welsh and Romanic provenance," phenomena that remained still part, as he put it, of the present "writer's *Realien*, within a kind of Cockney setting."[158] Additionally, he used Greek, French, German and Anglo-Saxon for an effective ἀνάμνησις of late Roman Britain, a multilingual *prosimetrum* that enacted in collage the "extraordinary mix-up of the break-up of the phenomenally mixed mess-up of Celtic, Teutonic & Latin elements in the Britain of the early dark ages."[159]

Though he insisted that *The Anathemata* was "neither a history of the Britons nor a history of any sort," Jones grounded his stylistic principles in a declaration from the *Historia Brittonum: coacervavi omne quod inveni*, "I have made a heap of all that I could find."[160] As Nennius had

---

[153] Roberts (1964) 7.
[154] Jones (1937) x.
[155] Jones (1937) x.
[156] Dilworth (2017) 259.
[157] Collingwood (1993) 315; Jones (1937) x; Jones (1952) 106n2.
[158] Jones (1952) 11.
[159] David Jones, Letter to Rev. Desmond Chute (January 26, 1953) in Jones *IN* (1984) 34. Borrowing the Greek Christ used when consecrating bread and wine, Jones insisted that poetry could hallow, bless and curse, and was thus, by parallel, "a kind of *anamnesis* of, i.e. is an effective recalling of, something loved." Like the transubstantiation accomplished at Mass, the poet's task was to "uncover a valid sign," to re-embody ancient fragments, to re-present them and thereby "propagand" the presence of the past. See Jones (1952) 21, 27. On *anamnesis* and *The Anathemata*, see Miles (1990) 1–22, Heath-Stubbs (1998) 128–33, and Williams (2005) 58–63.
[160] Jones (1952) 9.

composed "partly from writings and monuments of the ancient inhabit-
ants of Britain, partly from the annals of the Romans and the chronicles
of the sacred fathers," Jones stitched his verse from "mixed data" whose
stylization might shed light on a period in British history where the
"cross-currents" of cultural evolution had thus far eluded rationalization
and clear narrative structure.[161] The poem's hybrid idiom thus reflected
the "halting, broken & complicated and Babel-like" character of Roman
Britain and, for that reason, Jones refused to nativize its "mixed data" by
translating foreign fragments into familiar English; instead he offered his
readers explanatory footnotes in the interest of "mere politeness."[162] To
get at "something of this historic situation" only "fractured & fused
forms," only "hyphenated words," he wrote, could best transmute the
ethos of upheaval and linguistic fluidity endemic to that era.[163] *The
Anathemata*, though "in no real sense concerned to experiment with
words, with forms," he wrote, could not sacrifice the "overtones & undertones evoked by the words used," not if the poem were to excavate more
deeply the hidden metamorphoses of Romanity.[164] In the poem's third
section "Angle-Land," Jones depicted these metamorphoses in bricolage,
writing of the waste moors and fens on Crowland, where the "ancra-
man," the Mercian hermit, Saint Guthlac, had settled in AD 699.

> Past where the ancra-man, deeping his holy rule
>   in the fiendish marsh
>   at the *Geisterstunde*

---

[161] Jones (1952) 9; Collingwood and Myres (1937) 456.

[162] Jones, Letter to Rev. Desmond Chute (January 26, 1953) in Jones *IN* (1984) 34; Jones (1952) 9;
Orr (1966) 100. Jones' footnotes were met with palpable disdain. "[P]eople have said," he told
Peter Orr in 1964, "that they think that notes are pedantic, *I* think they are the reverse, because it
is useless to pretend that there's a common culture existing, as there might perhaps still be in
different parts of the world where the poet would be understood because he was within a
confined and received and inherited tradition. I would give anything to have Dante's annotations
to 'Il Paradiso', for instance. After all, one might say even the word 'Aphrodite' might not be
understood now by lots of chaps, and as civilization gets more complicated I think that the place
for explanation may be in notes, it seems only mere politeness." Orr (1966) 100. See Conclusion,
pp. 250–52.

[163] Jones, Letter to Rev. Desmond Chute (January 26, 1953) in Jones *IN* (1984) 34.

[164] Jones described his method at length in a self-deprecating way to Desmond Chute: "My
'method' is merely to arse around with such words as are available to me until the passage takes
on something of the shape I think it requires & evokes the image I want. I find, or think I find,
the process almost identical to what one tries to do in paintin' or drawin'. Having tried to the
best of one's powers, to make the lines, smudges, colours, opacities, translucencies, tightnesses,
hardnesses, pencil marks, paint marks, chalk marks, spit-marks, thumb marks, etc. evoke the
image one requires as much as poss., one only hopes that some other chap someone looking at
the picture, may recognize the image intended." Jones, Letter to Rev. Desmond Chute
(December 29, 1952) in Jones *IN* (1984) 24.

> on *Calangaeaf* night
> heard the bogle-*baragouinage.*
> Crowland-*diawliaidd*
> *Wealisc*-man lingo speaking?
> or Britto-Romani gone *diaboli?*
> or Romanity gone *Wealis?*[165]

According to legend, Guthlac had struggled with demons on Crowland where torments were expressed in Old Brythonic murmuring, the primitive tongue once widely spoken across Roman Britain.[166] With the rise of Anglo-Saxon, that language had all but disappeared by the eighth century, but the hermit, however, heard its strange pitch, its *strimulentas loquelas* lingering out on the marshes, and he thought it, according to the poem, the babble and "bogle-*baragouinage*" of devils.[167] What Guthlac encountered was not, however, simply an execration of the demonic, the *diawliaidd* of Brittania come again, it was a remnant of the Britto-Romani, the once powerful people who had for more than four centuries reputedly absorbed *Romanitas.* Jones hoped, by setting Latin, Welsh, Anglo-Saxon, German and French against each other at this moment, that he could give voice to the synthetic agglutination of Anglo-Saxon England.[168] Driven out to the wastelands of Crowland, what remained of the Roman had "gone *Wealis,*" passed among outlaws on the fringe of civilization. With sweeping multilingual style, Jones reflected the "unintentional, unconscious hybridization" of "historical life and evolution of all languages" in this period following the collapse of Roman rule.[169] Elsewhere in "Angle-Land" his hybridization of the Roman is enacted as paradox – as both dispersal and a kind of transubstantiation – a metamorphosis of what once had been distinctively Latin into 'new' linguistic forms in Welsh, English, French and German.

> Is Marianus wild Meirion?
> is Sylvánus
>   Urbigéna's son?
> has toga'd Rhufon
>   (gone Actaéon)
> come away to the Wake

[165] Jones (1952) 112.
[166] As recounted in section 34 of the *Vita Sancti Guthlaci Auctore Felice.* See *Felix's Life of Saint Guthlac: Texts, Translation and Notes,* ed. Bertram Colgrave (Cambridge: Cambridge University Press, 1956) 108–11; see also Rhys (1901) 676–77; as well as Jackson (1953) 235–37.
[167] Colgrave (1956) 110.
[168] On this passage see Robichaud (2007) 157–62.
[169] Jones (1952) 112. Bakhtin (1981) 358.

> in the bittern's low aery?
> along with his towny
>   Patricius gone the *wilde Jäger?*
>
> From the *fora*
>   to the forests.
> Out from *gens Romulum*
>   into the *Weal*-kin
> *dinas*-man gone *aethwlad*
> *cives* gone wold-men
>   … from Lindum to London
> bridges broken down.[170]

The "toga'd Rhufon" – the urbane Roman once a "*dinas*-man" – has been driven from the center of imperial power, and like Actaeon, turned stag on Mount Cithaeron, he appears Romanized yet "forced," as René Hague (1905–81) argued, "back into a life of hunted and hunter."[171] Likewise, the "towny Patricius [has] gone the *wilde Jäger*," and Sylvánus too, his Latin toponymic, has been pushed from the city though he remains "Urbigéna's son," the offspring of a 'city-born' mother. The rise of Anglo-Saxon civilization had irrevocably altered the intricate synthesis of the Roman and the Brythonic, the classical and the Celtic; and in these lines Jones sought to scatter the Roman into uncharted forms of language and culture. The *gens Romulum* had become *aethwlad*, "outlawed" on an island country where their classical inheritance was now, bit by bit, being metamorphosed by the "*Weal*-kin" of medieval England.[172]

In layering this passage with foreign borrowings Jones stretched his idiom across the "densely wooded, inherited and entailed domains" of language and its histories in Britain.[173] In so doing he fashioned a macaronic form that functioned, as Christopher Dawson (1889–1970) suggested, like the Hisperic Latin of sub-Roman Britain. The Celts of that age, Dawson told Jones, had inventively deployed the Roman tongue, making up "'new words because they liked the sound of them, whereas with you," he wrote, "it is a question of increasing the density & meaning."[174] Though Jones pled ignorance to Dawson's claim of a parallel between Late Latin and his "'Davidic English'," he was flattered: "Dear

---

[170] Jones (1952) 112–13.

[171] Hague (1977) 138. See also Ovid, *Metamorphoses* (3.162–205). *Dinas* is typically taken as "city" in modern Welsh, but its roots are in related words for "fort" and "citadel." See Thomas (1967).

[172] On the contraction of *Romulorum* to the unusual and mistaken genitive form, *Romulum*, see David Jones, Letter to Rev. Desmond Chute (January 26, 1953) in Jones *IN* (1984) 31, 35n1.

[173] Jones (1952) 20.

[174] Jones, Letter to Rev. Desmond Chute (February 4, 1953) in Jones *IN* (1984) 46. "According to Nora Chadwick, in a passage marked by Jones, Hisperic Latin 'consists of a highly specialized

Xtopher, he always thinks that chaps are as learned as he is himself," he wrote, "I fear I don't know at all what the 6th Cent. Celts did to the Latin language."[175] Nonetheless Jones thought Dawson's analogy "pertinent & meaningful," for he had "*never* known him to make a wrong guess yet, not where historical comparisons were involved."[176] Nowhere was the suggested parallel more apparent than in the neologisms and his hyphenated forms. In the above-cited passage the word "*Weal*-kin" is a "germane example," for, as Jones noted, to keep the literal meaning, he might have written *Wealcyn*, the Anglo-Saxon word for 'Welsh race' or 'Welsh people'.[177] Yet to do this, he argued, would have marred the poem with "a dead word, a student's word"; "It would have been just a straight A. S. word," he explained,

> taken from any Anglo-Saxon document ... but by hyphenating *Weal* with 'kin', the word can be made to take on a certain life, because we still use the word 'kin' and can't see it without thinking of 'kith', whereas *cyn* is remote, & anyway I believe is pronounced 'kune' or something like it.[178]

Alternatively, Jones could have translated it "'Welshmen' or 'Welsh folk'," but this too, he thought, "would have given no historic undertone, or, in the case of 'Welsh folk' a rather bogus, or 'poetic' or dated feeling."[179] By joining an Anglo-Saxon root to a more familiar modern word Jones believed he could balance the native against the foreign, the more contemporary against the more ancient, compressing in a single compound the "Babel-like" character of Roman Britain. In doing so he syntactically scattered the *gens Romulum*, pushing the semblance of a 'pure' Latinity out into a neologism whose hybridity symbolized something of Britain's metamorphic history.[180]

---

and fantastic vocabulary containing a large foreign element and an extremely artificial figurative style combined with alliteration'. Certainly this suggests 'parallels' with 'Davidic English'." Miles (1990) 47.

[175] Jones *IN* (1984) 46.

[176] Jones *IN* (1984) 46.

[177] Jones, Letter to Rev. Desmond Chute (January 26, 1953) in Jones *IN* (1984) 34. For reference, see *wealh* and *cyn* in Toller (1898) 1173. See also -*cyn* in Toller (1921) 761; and Jackson (1953) 227–28.

[178] Jones *IN* (1984) 34.

[179] Jones *IN* (1984) 34.

[180] Jones *IN* (1984) 46. Saunders Lewis admired Jones' foreignizing of "nouns, especially the proper nouns." Their presence could make readers "more aware of life richly meshed in complexities ... 'Poetry is the song of deeds' he says, and he is the poet of proper names. He loves more particularly the names that travel and change, and by their changes tie up the centuries and are some clue to them." After hearing an excerpt of *The Anathemata* read on the BBC in 1958, Lewis told Jones "how very, very much I was moved by it. And you were well served; the production was

As noted – Jones was, on the surface, sympathetic to the cause of Welsh Wales, but more intimately he also expressed a deep wariness towards publicly engaging in political advocacy. British modernity did bear, he felt, "a resemblance to the beginnings of the Dark Ages," but no mere change in official policies towards Welsh alone would redeem the time.[181] On the contrary, for this "late and complex phase of a phenomenally complex civilization," Jones saw the art of writing his poetry itself as a more significant act of political resistance and remembrance, one wherein he could bear witness to the deep cultural memory of Britain's classical and Celtic traces.[182] In the preface to *The Anathemata* he wrote:

> When rulers seek to impose a new order upon any such group belonging to one or other of those more primitive culture-phases, it is necessary for those rulers to take into account the influence of the poets as recalling something loved and as embodying an ethos inimical to the imposition of that new order.[183]

Although Britain was "very far removed" from a time when "the poet was explicitly and by profession the custodian, rememberer, embodier, and voice of the mythus," Jones felt that he remained a "dangerous" figure for rulers of a "new order," dangerous on account of his ability and authority to evoke and recall the ethos, forms and civilizational fragments of earlier "culture-phases."[184] The residue of those fragments and forms, Jones argued, still remained part of the vast fabric which patterned the present age, and it was critical that the poet embody that fabric, to 'propagand' its fullness however inimical it might be to the "imposition" of a "new order."[185] In this sense Jones believed poetry to be "inevitably 'propaganda'," not political pamphleteering but an art that gave "real formal expression"

---

sensitive and human, Cockney voices and Welsh and plain chant all made an understanding unity of your poem, a reflection of all you were putting together in your lines. Yes, it was good." Saunders Lewis, Letter to David Jones (April 7, 1958) folio 18. David Jones Papers, CT 1/4, NLW. See Lewis (1967) 114–15.

181 Jones, "Art in Relation to War," in Jones (1978) 147.

182 Jones (1952) 21.

183 Jones (1952) 21.

184 Jones (1952) 21.

185 Jones (1952) 21. Saunders Lewis saw this aspect of Jones' literary work as radically anti-imperial. Writing later to Jones about his poem "The Tribune's Visitation," Lewis called the work both "moving and terrible. An indictment of all empires, of all that destroy the local thing, not merely military conquests but industrial and commercial expansions; and it's all put into the mouth of the representative of all that uniformity, – and it even kills willingly its own fountain-head, its own local thing. So that the poem is a cry to the England of today also, – for the English lares as well as the Welsh are being quite forgotten. It's a very contemporary poem." Saunders Lewis, Letter to David Jones (December 31, 1969) folio 58, David Jones Papers, CT 1/4, NLW.

to that which "propagands the reality which caused those forms and their content to be."[186] If *The Anathemata* could be said to document the time-worn hybridity of *Romanitas*, its legacy could not easily serve forms of ideological nativism. To cede the "very subtly meshed" past to either the notion of Welsh purity or an 'accessible' English would be tantamount to imposing "new order" on a 'primitive culture-phase' "inimical to the impo-sition of that new order."[187] *Romanitas* was too centripetal a force, not a static phenomenon but a catalytic agent through which the "survivals" from "an older condition of culture" could be successively translated into new hybrid shapes.[188] To represent it in poetry was thus not so much a nostalgic obsession for Jones – the seeking after a 'pure' past or 'lost' origin – as an obsession with its power to forge continual cultural and linguistic evolution in the future. For this reason, *The Anathemata* has been said to radiate "an incomparable imaginative reach over vast temporal spans."[189]

Jones' attempts to depict the synoptic transmission of many 'Romes' into British civilization were indebted, without doubt, to his immersion in Britto-Romanic sources and the study of its histories, but the complex influence of James Joyce proved pivotal to him as well. Joyce's preoccupa-tion with the so-called "Celtic hinterland" long dominated his thinking about the "formal problems" of literary art.[190] Saunders Lewis had likewise once expressed admiration for Joyce, confessing that a Dedalean impulse to "fly by the nets" of nationality, language, and religion drove him to enlist and fight in the First World War.[191] By the war's end, however, Lewis had eschewed Joyce entirely, for his experience, he felt, had taught him that Welsh identity was "not a net but a root."[192] Rejecting

---

[186] Jones (1952) 21.

[187] Jones (2016) [10]; Jones (1952) 21.

[188] The English anthropologist E. B. Tylor (1832–1917) defined "survivals" in *Primitive Culture: Researches into the Development of Mythology, Philosophy, Religion, Art, and Custom* (1871), as those "processes, customs, opinions, and so forth, which have been carried on by force of habit into a new state of society different from that in which they had their original home, and they thus remain as proofs and examples of an older condition of culture out of which a newer has been evolved." Tylor (1871) vol. 1: 15.

[189] Carne-Ross (1980) 42.

[190] Jones, "James Joyce's Dublin," in Jones (1959) 305. See also Jones (1952) 26. On Jones' debt to Joyce, see Staudt (1994) 129–38.

[191] In a 1955 interview broadcast on the BBC Home Service, Lewis recalled the notorious words of Stephen Dedalus: "When the soul of a man is born in this country there are nets flung at it to hold it back from flight. You talk to me of nationality, language, religion. I shall try to fly by those nets." Joyce *Portrait* (1993) 230, as in Lewis (1955) 12. On Lewis' military service, see Chapman (2006b) 20–38.

[192] Lewis (1955) 12.

the novelist as a "waste of ingenuity" crippled by "self-torment and self-analysis," Lewis embraced the far-right *l'enraciné* nationalism of the French novelist Maurice Barrès (1862–1923) instead.[193] It was not Joyce who had immersed himself in Ireland's 'rootedness', he argued, but rather the dramatic verse of Yeats, Synge, Lady Gregory and Pádraic Colum. Their work contained a "[p]oetic speech and regionalism and nationalism" that could be an example for Welsh writers, perhaps even the beginning of "an answer" to the central problem plaguing its national life, namely the "all-invading industrialism of the time."[194] By contrast with the Irish theatre, Joyce had rejected the notion that "[p]oetry and poetic drama needed roots in a community."[195] While he remained "of Irish race," he had refused, Lewis argued, to "write for Ireland."[196] For David Jones, however, Joyce's work not born of hate or disregard of country, "because of all artists ever," the novelist was "the most dependent on the particular, on place, site, locality."[197] Despite a "life-long exile" on the European continent, Joyce had no less feeling for "his natal place," his self-imposed banishment having served "only to sharpen, clarify and deepen his devotion to the *numina* of place, not of any place, but of this place, Eblana … '*Hircus Civis Eblanensis*'."[198] As Jones saw it, Joyce's loathing for the rigid ideological structures specific to his experience of Ireland – those 'nets' of race, language and crude persuasion so despised by Dedalus – had pushed many critics to regard him wrongly as an iconoclast. "The notion that Joyce was destructive is so ludicrous," he wrote, "because nobody could have been more concerned with informing every word and every jot and tittle with some sort of significance. It was rebellious, of course, rebellious against superficiality and preconceived notions."[199] It was in fact that very rebellion against the preconceived and conventional which had made Joyce's work "absolutely incomparable" in its devotion to 'local' character of particular places in language and in landscape – for Joyce could show, Jones explained, how "one word, even a comma," could "have more facets of

---

[193] Saunders Lewis, Letter to Margaret Gilcriest (October 20, 1920) in Lewis (1993) 425. See also Humphreys (1983) 217–19.

[194] Lewis (1955) 11.

[195] Lewis (1955) 11.

[196] Lewis (1939) 7.

[197] Jones (1959) 304. See also Jones (1952) 26.

[198] Jones (1959) 304, quoting the Latin of Joyce's *Finnegans Wake* (215.26–27): "Latin me that, my trinity scholard, out of eure sanscreed into oure eryan! *Hircus Civis Eblanensis*!"

[199] Orr (1966) 103.

[200] Orr (1966) 103.

meaning" and "recall more things than any writer that I know."²⁰⁰ He
understood the "amalgam" of "Celtic deposits," how these "incorporated
pre-Celtic ones and these together underlie the Germanic-Latin fusion"
and could therefore generate a sonic or linguistic hybridity "in as
compact a space as possible" matched to the stratigraphic sequence of a
specific place.²⁰¹ "All great things are like that," Jones insisted, "I mean,
you just strip off layers and you find more underneath, and you strip off
another and there is more underneath."²⁰² Joyce's "thick description" of
Dublin life had indeed satirized the Revival's forced marriage of ideological nationalism and contemporary literature, but it did so, Jones
thought, in "absolute fidelity to a specified site, and the complex historic
strata, special to that site."²⁰³ In this way Joyce had not broken faith with
Ireland but balanced the complexities of its chaotic history against
contemporary reality; the "immemorial thought-patterns of a genuine
'folk'" he enmeshed in a "modern industrial slum-culture" and "saloon-
bar folk-lore."²⁰⁴

Although the impulses that shaped *The Anathemata* were, as Jones once
told W. H. Auden, "indebted" to "stupendous old Joyce," the work was
seen by some critics as a form of "seedless fruit" when compared with
Joyce and the earlier writings of Eliot and Pound (as well as Jones' own *In
Parenthesis*).²⁰⁵ Hugh Kenner, in his 1954 review for *Poetry*, complained of
the poem's lack of "voice."²⁰⁶ "We get a word, and a word, and a word,"
he argued,

> we don't hear anyone speak. Mr. Jones is a scrupulous bard with a
> word-hoard, and the words are cleanly and lovingly juxtaposed. But the
> juxtapositions remain oddly antiseptic. They are always evocative, in a
> quickeningly un-sensual way; but one keeps looking at the footnotes to see
> what it is that they are supposed to evoke.²⁰⁷

Where in *In Parenthesis* Jones had inflected the Cockney "speech and
habit of mind" of Private John Ball and others as a "perpetual showing",
one that revealed both the past narrative in the present and the present

---

²⁰¹ Jones (1959) 305; Orr (1966) 103.
²⁰² Orr (1966) 103.
²⁰³ Geertz (1973) 3–30, esp. 5–6, 9–10; Jones, "Notes on the 1930s," in Jones (1978) 46.
²⁰⁴ Jones (1959) 304. See also David Jones, Letter XXIII to Aneirin Talfan Davies (November 27,
      1962) in Jones (1980) 88.
²⁰⁵ Jones, "To W. H. Auden, 24 February 1954," in Jones *DG* (1980) 161. Kenner (1954) 295–301. See
      Miles (1990) 74–76.
²⁰⁶ Kenner (1954) 298. See Conclusion, pp. 254–56.
²⁰⁷ Kenner (1954) 298.

narrative in the past, the allusions of *The Anathemata* seemed "less systematically ventilated," its deposits of "Welsh and Romanic provenance" insufficiently linked to "our contemporary, less intimate, larger unities."[208] Although Jones did think himself beholden to Joyce – "*Lux perpetua luceat ei*. But what person of my generation could not be?" – he grumbled at the suggestion that his work was derivative, perhaps no more than a "'direct imitation'."[209] As he saw it, he had not derived his style: he felt rather that he and Joyce shared a parallel "civilisational situation" with respect to their 'natal places', that they were motivated by "*absolute* necessity to find a 'form' that somehow or other 'fits' the contemporary situation."[210] "I see how perfectly natural it is for critics to suppose," he observed,

> that I based my 'style' on Joyce. Of course, I knew about him. And an Irishman read to me *Anna Livia Plurabelle* in the nineteen-twenties and I was deeply impressed. But I believe the truth is that a given civilisational situation will, necessarily, produce the same problems for people of certain sorts of perception, and that therefore, both in form and content, their work will show an affinity that looks like direct borrowing but which is, in reality, a similar response to an identical 'situation' on the part of persons of similar perception.[211]

Faced with pressure to advance Celtic 'purity' in language and literature, Joyce was skeptical: composing his work in exile, he too remained "elusive of social or religious orders," trying, like Dedalus, to "learn his own wisdom apart from others or to learn the wisdom of others himself wandering among the snares of the world."[212] Yet, as Jones noted sympathetically, the self-imposed exile Joyce endured did not drive him from Ireland but only deeper into a more intense examination of its "vast fabric," into the very "lore of semantics" that evoked the country's history and hybridity.[213] It was Joyce's development of this lore – "this language thing" – that most attracted the admiration of Jones.[214] Though the result often seemed like "verbal

---

[208] Jones (1937) xi; Kenner (1954) 298; Jones (1952) 11; Jones (1937) xi.

[209] Jones, "To W. H. Auden, 24 February 1954," in Jones *DG* (1980) 161, 160. In his review of February 1954, Auden defended the originality of *The Anathemata*, writing that "Joyce certainly, and Dante probably, have had a hand in Mr. Jones' development, but his style is in no sense an imitation. Nor is this verse as 'free' as at a superficial glance it looks." Auden (1954) 68.

[210] David Jones, Letter to William Hayward (July 12, 1961) in Jones (1979) 58. See also David Jones, Letter to John Johnston (May 2, 1962), as discussed in Johnston (1964) 321–22.

[211] Jones, Letter to William Hayward (July 12, 1961) in Jones (1979) 58.

[212] Joyce *Portrait* (1993) 188.

[213] Joyce *CWJJ* (1989) 165. Lewis (1967) 115.

[214] Jones, Letter to Harman Grisewood (March 19, 1940), as in Staudt (1994) 130.

chaos," his "linguistic virtuosity" was "not an 'emancipation' from the rules of language."[215] On the contrary, what "knowledge of language and its structure" Joyce did have informed a technical and thematic brilliance that exposed "affinities not previously caught, because it concertinas history."[216] Jones likewise composed his own polyglot *prosimetrum* from something of a parallel position with respect to Welsh history and the far-right politics of Saunders Lewis. Eager to distill a new experimental idiom, he forged a vernacular whose webs of multilingual connection seemed "endless ... the possibilities infinite."[217] Nonetheless, Jones still felt that a radical deprivation – stemming in part from inadequate exposure and lack of formal instruction in the "root languages" of Welsh, Latin, Greek and Anglo-Saxon – had hampered his abilities as a poet, especially as compared with Joyce. His ignorance, however, proved inventive, essential even in shedding light, both linguistically and historically, on the "shared and objective world to which each of us," he thought, "is attached by the same texture of living strands."[218] Yet Jones still worried that the complicated archaeological structure and style of *The Anathemata*, its sheer allusiveness and difficulty, would be too much for most readers in the contemporary world – a world that would at times regard his work as eccentric, obscure and prone to a kind of spiritual solipsism. "[I]t is a very, very painful process," he confessed,

> I found in writing *The Anathemata* that I went out so far on limbs, as it were, that I couldn't get back again to the main trend with any sort of intelligibility ... You see an enormous number of facets of the thing, and one thing suggests another, but if you aren't very careful it takes you too far from the concept and you can't get back to it again except at very great length, and that might be artistically bad.[219]

Nonetheless, with the "living strands" he did know, in the tongues he cherished, Jones shaped into *The Anathemata* a culturally hybrid vision of the classical, one which moved the contemporary reception of *Romanitas* beyond baser forms of ideology, beyond nativism and Welsh-Wales purism, to recall the "deep roots and the ancient springs" of Britain's "mixed mess-up" in history.[220]

---

[215] Raine (1974–75) 5.
[216] Raine (1974–75) 5; Lewis (1967) 115.
[217] Jones, Letter to Harman Grisewood (March 19, 1940), as in Staudt (1994) 130.
[218] As in Staudt (1994) 130; Raine (1982) 126.
[219] Orr (1966) 99.
[220] Raine (1982) 126; Raine (1974–75) 5; Jones, Letter to Rev. Desmond Chute (January 26, 1953) in Jones *IN* (1984) 34.

CHAPTER 5

"A Form of Doric Which Is No Dialect in Particular"
Scotland and the Planetary Classics of Hugh MacDiarmid

Emboldened by the success of his 1926 poem *A Drunk Man Looks at the Thistle*, the Scottish poet and critic Christopher Grieve – better known by his pseudonym, Hugh MacDiarmid – set sight on a new creative endeavor, a work that could "glimpse the underlying pattern of human history," what MacDiarmid called "Cencrastus, the Curly Snake."[1] For MacDiarmid, Cencrastus represented the "Gaelic (or Scottish) version of the idea common to Indian and other mythologies that underlying Creation there is great snake," a snake symbolic of "the principle of change and the main factor in the revolutionary development of human consciousness, 'man's incredible variation'."[2] If this new work, he thought, could engage "an intricate linguistic apparatus which involves Scottish and Irish Gaelic, German, French, Italian, Spanish, Latin, and Greek," he might "sing as never Scotsman sang afore," developing a synthetic style as a "Homage of Consciousness – a paean to creative thought."[3] Yet to write this new poem – the poem that became *To Circumjack Cencrastus* (1930) – proved difficult. Frustrated after nearly four years' work, MacDiarmid complained to a friend that *Cencrastus* had not achieved what he "intended – I deliberately deserted my big plan."[4] While the poem demonstrated "an astonishing knowledge of the whole range of modern European philosophy and religious speculation," it possessed an "intellectual arrogance," "pretentious pedantry" and a "super-abundance of needless personalities – scurrilous vilification of

---

[1] Christopher Grieve, Letter to Helen Cruickshank (February 1939) in MacDiarmid *LHM* (1984) 128.

[2] Grieve, Letter to Helen Cruickshank (February 1939) in MacDiarmid *LHM* (1984) 128.

[3] Hugh MacDiarmid (credited as "Pteleon"), "Blasphemy and Divine Philosophy Mixed: Hugh M'Diarmid's Extraordinary Poem," *The Scots Observer* (October 2, 1930) in MacDiarmid *RT2* (1997) 200; MacDiarmid *CP1* (1993) 241; Grieve, Letter to Helen Cruickshank (February 1939) in MacDiarmid *LHM* (1984) 128.

[4] Christopher Grieve, Letter to George Ogilvie (December 16, 1930) in MacDiarmid *LHM* (1984) 103.

great Scotsmen past and present."[5] Moreover, he argued, *Cencrastus* had not illuminated what Scottish literature then needed most, he thought, namely a "new classicism" – one that could extend the country's "national principle of freedom on the plane of world-affairs" while rebalancing "Europe in accordance with [Scotland's] distinctive genius."[6]

MacDiarmid's pursuit of a "new classicism" for Scotland was unique from the start: what he desired was not the institutionalized "puerilities, elementary, trifling, schoolboy drilling, and very bad drilling" of nineteenth-century Scottish classical instruction but a form of reception that went well beyond the patriotic vision of antiquity espoused by the Scottish radical John Stuart Blackie (1809–95), professor of Greek at the University of Edinburgh from 1852 to 1882.[7] Blackie, the author of the 1853 essay *On the Living Language of the Greeks*, had once argued that the Scottish people needed "not new editions of trite Greek plays already edited so often, and tortured so critically, that many a luckless word in them has been put into more antic attitudes" but instead "a scholarship with a large human soul, and a pregnant social significance, which shall not seek with a studious feebleness to avoid, but rather with a generous vigour to find contact with all the great intellectual and moral movements of the age."[8] As the outlines of MacDiarmid's vision of nationalism became clear, he built on Blackie's thought, believing that, if a 'new' Scottish classicism did arise, it would engage more intensely with the fraught politics and social movements of the present while also resolving a central problem plaguing Scottish scholars of the previous century. Though many of Scotland's prominent Victorians were eager to distinguish themselves from "the dry-as-dust, anti-life affair which English classicism was," the nineteenth-century Scottish reception of antiquity still seemed to have been effectively split.[9] Against a 'Northern' expression of idealism – motivated by cultural nationalism and a particularly Scottish stress on "democratic intellectualism" – there emerged an opposing 'Southern' principle that accentuated "'Blood and Culture', according to which, a system of racial exclusiveness was presented as preferable to the

---

[5] MacDiarmid *RT2* (1997) 200.
[6] See also C. M. Grieve ("Hugh McDiarmid"), "English Ascendancy in British Literature," *The Criterion* 10.41 (July 1931) 593–613, as in MacDiarmid *SP* (1992) 80. Hugh MacDiarmid, "The Caledonian Antisyzygy and the Gaelic Idea" (1931–32) in MacDiarmid *SEHM* (1970) 68, 67.
[7] Pillans (1848) 28, as cited in Davie (1961) 231. On Blackie's life and influence, see Davie (1961) 232–44, as well as Wallace (2006).
[8] Blackie (1855) 10.
[9] Davie (1961) 223.

anarchism of Scottish democracy."[10] While Southern scholars, Davie suggested, were keen to amass "out-of-the-way erudition, their Northern counterparts were animated with the purpose of elevating public taste and impressing on the nation at large a respect for classical restraint in the Arts."[11] MacDiarmid, in seeking a 'new classicism', aimed to merge something from both these impulses, not merely amassing erudition but articulating a democratic 'public voice' in his verse as well. Yet, as he sought this, MacDiarmid's vision of reception was transformed – not only by his auto-didacticism and incendiary politics but by the erosion of classics' critical position in British society. As classical learning became increasingly dis-embedded both from its central institutional role as a guardian of British imperial interests and increasingly even from its role as a key accelerant in the 'nation-building' movements of Celtic revival, MacDiarmid generated a new and more complex vision. Though he had become, by the early 1930s, irritated with the pragmatism of the National Party, MacDiarmid still believed a 'new classicism' might emerge as a catalytic force for Scottish interests, one that would fuse together the project of national reinvention with an anti-imperial, global ideology – principally, the communism of V. I. Lenin (1870–1924).[12] With this in mind, MacDiarmid turned from the heteroglossic Lallans developed for *A Drunk Man* to a polyglossic, synthetic English, "a vision of world language."[13] Born from his admiration of Joyce, this multilingual idiom proved artistically promising, but, as MacDiarmid adumbrated it throughout the 1930s, he was led into increasingly radical forms of stylistic eccentricity and ideological isolation. His new aesthetic engendered a deep solipsism for which his synthetic vernacular became emblematic: MacDiarmid's 'global' idiom was, as Matthew Hart notes, "the speech of no singular person, place, or nation-state."[14] Nonetheless these "private imaginings of a new public discourse" impacted both the range of his poetry and his reputation.[15] This eccentric vision of 'classicism' untethered MacDiarmid's work from clear substantive links to the literatures of Greece and Rome, and in so dominating his later work, his

---

[10] Davie (1961) 244.

[11] Davie (1961) 223.

[12] On MacDiarmid's political and 'spiritual' adoption of Marxism, see Lyall (2011) 68–81, and this chapter, pp. 221–24.

[13] MacDiarmid's *In Memoriam James Joyce, From a Vision of World Language* was first published in 1955 with William Maclellan of Glasgow.

[14] Hart (2010) 38.

[15] Haynes (2019b) 16.

penchant for both the idiosyncratic and the incendiary made his poetry a "form of Doric" that was indeed "no dialect in particular."[16]

Though frustrated with the failures of *Cencrastus*, MacDiarmid outlined his "big plan" in a polemical essay he proposed for the pages of T. S. Eliot's *The Criterion*.[17] Writing to Eliot he asked:

> Would you care to consider an article ... discussing the way in which, instead of pooling their resources, or at least acting and reacting freely upon each other (and a common bilingual or multi-lingual public) and giving British literature far more variety, Irish, Scottish Gaelic, Welsh, and, to a lesser extent, Scottish Vernacular, and even English dialect literature ... have been practically excluded from the knowledge of most British people – and consequently have had their potentialities inhibited – by the English ascendancy tendency.[18]

Eliot accepted the proposal, and MacDiarmid later dispatched the essay entitled "English Ascendancy in British Literature." The piece was published in July 1931, motivated by MacDiarmid's desire to discuss at some length a recent report on primary education by the London Board of Education. MacDiarmid praised some findings from the *Report of the Consultative Committee on the Primary School* (1931), especially the new stress laid on the "need to realize that there are many varieties of English; that it is not the function of schools to decry any special or local peculiarities of speech; and that a racy native turn of speech is better than any stilted phraseology, especially for literary purposes."[19] As he saw it, the suggestion that schools not discourage "varieties of English" was a welcome departure from long-established practice and policy in Britain, for from the time of Matthew Arnold only the "narrow ascendancy tradition" of English had been encouraged across public life.[20] The Elementary Education Acts 1870 to 1893 had notably "made no provision for the teaching of/in anything other than English" so that an entire generation, though "intelligent readers of English," were "content to ignore Scottish,

---

[16] Hugh MacDiarmid under the pseudonym, J. G. Outterstone Buglass, "Arne Garborg, Mr Joyce, and Mr M'Diarmid" (September 1924) in MacDiarmid *RT1* (1996) 237.

[17] Grieve, Letter to George Ogilvie (December 16, 1930) in MacDiarmid *LHM* (1984) 103.

[18] Christopher Grieve, Letter to T. S. Eliot (December 9, 1930) in MacDiarmid *LHM* (1984) 434.

[19] MacDiarmid *SP* (1992) 61.

[20] Grillo (1989) 101. MacDiarmid *SP* (1992) 61, 67. On language and educational policy in this period, see Grillo (1989) 84–106, and Heffer (2013) 412–68.

Irish, and Welsh Gaelic literatures, and Scots Vernacular literature."[21] Rather than "broad-basing" knowledge of literature through "all the diverse cultural elements and the splendid variety of languages and dialects, on the British Isles," the public had been systematically confined to the "English central stream" of British literature.[22] As a result, the British people had heard "but one side of a complicated case" and become victims of what MacDiarmid called "an extensive spiritual and psychological blindness."[23] Yet this new report suggested that distinctions were to be drawn between "local variations" of dialect and the clear incorrect use of standard English among children.[24]

> There can be no doubt that an attempt to correct local peculiarities too early has a depressing effect upon the child's power of speech. With young children, the capital aim must be to secure that they begin to use language freely and easily; a nearer approach to the standard speech may be dearly bought by an unnatural reticence on their part. The teacher must boldly face the fact that there are many varieties of the English language; it is not the duty of the school to decry any special or local variations. As the children grow older, more should be done to teach the habits of standard speech. The best dialect words have a picturesque value, especially for literary purposes ... Above all, the degenerate speaking of standard English should not be confused with the speaking of dialect.[25]

While the report's recommendations focused largely on dialect, the insistence that certain linguistic variations could develop "freely and easily" gave MacDiarmid hope that the languages of Scotland, Ireland and Wales might perhaps someday enjoy greater recognition.[26] Like English dialects these languages were "products of substantially the same environment, and concerned for the most part with the same political, psychological, and practical issues, the same traditions and tendencies, the same landscapes, as poets in English."[27] Yet they were often ignored or dismissed as "valuably complementary" to the central stream of English expression.[28] As MacDiarmid saw it, however, their "ancient technique" provided a "corrective" to contemporary English, for

---

[21] MacDiarmid *SP* (1992) 67.
[22] MacDiarmid *SP* (1992) 67, 68.
[23] MacDiarmid *SP* (1992) 68, 69.
[24] Board of Education (1931) 157.
[25] Board of Education (1931) 157.
[26] Board of Education (1931) 157.
[27] MacDiarmid *SP* (1992) 68.
[28] MacDiarmid *SP* (1992) 68.

> Few literatures offer within themselves so rich a range of alterative values,
> of material for comparative criticism, as does, not English, but British,
> meaning by the latter that common culture – in *posse*, rather than *in esse* –
> which includes not only English (and English dialect) literature, but the
> Gaelic and Scots Vernacular literatures as well.[29]

Though Britain still possessed these elements within the wider range of
its literary culture, the "narrow ascendancy tradition" had shut forms of
Welsh, Gaelic and Scots vernacular literature out, keeping the more salu-
brious cultural influences of the Celtic far from the collective imagination.[30]

The report did provide hope, but MacDiarmid felt that the Celtic
languages still faced threats on many sides, not least the various attempts
to standardize "'correct English'" as an International Auxiliary Language
(IAL), a movement that in the wake of the First World War had gained
greater favor among some prominent intellectuals, linguists and politicians.[31] Led by Cambridge University critics C. K. Ogden (1889–1957)
and I. A. Richards (1893–1979), advocates of "Basic English" felt that if
language could be simplified and stripped largely of its idiomatic characteristics, then English might be made a more effective mode of international communication.[32] Since the Armistice of 1918, Ogden and
Richards had pushed for the development of a condensed English,
believing that the continued prosperity of postwar Europe depended to
some extent on the deployment of a secondary tongue, or common interlanguage, which could more easily traverse national boundaries of
language and culture.[33] "The so-called national barriers of today are ultimately language barriers," Ogden declared in 1931,

> The absence of a common medium of communication is the chief obstacle
> to international understanding, and therefore the chief underlying cause of
> War. It is also the most formidable obstacle to the progress of international

---

[29] MacDiarmid *SP* (1992) 69, 68, 69.

[30] MacDiarmid *SP* (1992) 67.

[31] MacDiarmid *SP* (1992) 62. On twentieth-century efforts to form an international language, see
Eco (1995) 317–36, as well as Pei (1958) and Crystal (1997).

[32] On the beginning of Basic English in Britain, see Koeneke (2004) 22–52, Stern (2014) 86–97, as
well as Howatt and Widdowson (2004) 283–88.

[33] "During a discussion with I. A. Richards on 11 November 1918 Ogden outlined a work to correlate
his earlier linguistic studies with his wartime experience of 'the power of Word-Magic' and the
part played by language in contemporary thought. Ogden converted the *Cambridge Magazine*
into a quarterly in which he and Richards published a series of articles as a first draft of the book
which appeared in 1923 as *The Meaning of Meaning*. This empirical approach to theoretical confusion about language, setting forth principles for the understanding of the function of language,
rapidly became one of the important books of the decade." Scott (2004).

Science, and to the development of international Commerce. As to the desirability of a Universal Language, therefore, there can be little difference of opinion.[34]

In combatting the problem of 'Babel' in Europe, "'Basic English for all'" offered to do the work that Latin was thought to have once accomplished as the dominant tongue of political, academic and religious discourse – albeit without demanding "the faith of a fanatic" for Rome's dead language.[35] Though it comprised only 850 words, Ogden insisted that Basic could "meet the universal demand for a compact and efficient technological medium" of speech.[36] Complex problems of translation mitigated, 'Basic' linguistic exchange could steer nations clear of threats to the

> economic, moral, cultural, social, or political status or independence of any person or any people. It must carry no implications of intellectual, technological, or other domination. No one in learning the world language must have excuse for even the least shadow of a feeling that he is submitting to an alien influence or being brought under the power of other groups ... We can guard against this danger only by conceiving a world language in a truly planetary spirit – as a universal medium, not as an extension of the sphere of influence of some one pressure group.[37]

Moreover, as they envisioned it, the language would not be imposed upon any people but would rather come "into use freely, as a general convenience, under the urge of the everyday motives of mankind," for as Anglophone countries grew in power and global prestige, English too had become far more pervasive.[38] For Ogden and Richards, "Standard English" had been so "enriched and cosmopolitanized," especially "through the expansion of modern science," that the spread of its more Basic form might forge greater global understanding and combat claims of a new linguistic imperialism.[39]

---

[34] Ogden (1931) 13–14.
[35] Ogden (1931) 13. "Five hundred years ago Latin was the literary language of Western Europe. Its downfall was due to the awakening of the masses, to their revolt against the routines and dictates of a caste. Today the English schoolboy can acquire no more than a smattering of its complexities after ten years' intensive misery; the scholar still writes slowly and faultily after twenty years of practice. Outside of Italy, even in the universities, Latin is losing all along the line. As the language of Radio, the language of Africa, the language even of American business, its mere advocacy demands the faith of a fanatic." Ogden (1934) 11.
[36] Ogden (1932) 14.
[37] Richards (1943) 11.
[38] Richards (1943) 11.
[39] Ogden (1932) 13–14. On the charge that Basic English itself constituted a form of "linguistic imperialism," see Russo (1989) 397–404.

On a popular level, the desire to see idiomatic English debrided, to see its dialects condensed to the most basic and 'standard' of components, had already had a broad impact, especially in West End theatres of the postwar period.[40] The notion, espoused by Ogden and Richards, that English was an efficient "Universal medium" for the swift communication of ideas had been, in a crude way, advanced across the daily criticism of London drama throughout the 1920s.[41] A less literary and less artificial English – an English marked by lack of dialect, accent or artifice – was thought more appealing, better for the understanding of general audiences than anything too experimental. Driven by an aversion for "ornate literary stuff," St. John Ervine (1883–1971) – the Ulster-born playwright and Unionist – had thus discouraged dialect in theatre, dismissing as "contrived" and "withdrawn from reality" the recent drama of Ireland and England.[42] Such "'literary drama'" was, he asserted, "generally full of stiff sentences that have more resemblance to the language used in editorial articles and 'middles' printed in the weekly reviews than to the language used in conversation."[43] The especial "business" of the modern playwright was, he believed, "to write dialogue which shall have the look of literature and the sound of the street: it must have the similitude of ordinary conversation and, at the same time, be attractive and compact and shapely."[44] As such, dialect that was not "selected and shapely" could perhaps become an impediment to effective dramatic speech, an obstruction, Ervine thought, both to the clear communication of a playwright's "ideas and intentions" and to the commercial success of theatre itself.[45] His critique – elaborated across a series of reviews he wrote for *The Observer* in February 1931 – drew out MacDiarmid's scorn. Ervine had declared "[a]nything that makes oral communication difficult ...

---

[40] On theatre in this period, see Barker and Gale (2000).
[41] Ogden (1931) 14.
[42] Ervine (1928) 17. On the life and dramatic work of Ervine, see Cronin (1988) 7–16.
[43] Ervine (1928) 16.
[44] Ervine (1928) 22. Ervine himself had, in fact, first embraced and exploited his own dialect of Ulster English on stage. In the 1915 tragedy *John Ferguson*, he deliberately employed an Anglo-Irish idiom, hoping to build on the work begun by Yeats, Synge and Lady Gregory. However, he could not get his plays produced in the West End or recognized in London, and in light of the political drama unfolding in Ireland, he turned against the impulses that motivated the dialect-driven drama of the Abbey, telling George Bernard Shaw (1856–1950) that Ireland had become a land dominated by "bleating Celtic Twilighters, sex-starved Daughters of the Gael, gangsters and gombeen-men." See Ervine, Letter to George Bernard Shaw (February 16, 1932) British Library Add. MS 50533 folio 145, as in Vance (1990) 189. On Ervine's disdain for the Irish Literary Revival, see Vance (1990) 176–89. On the unionist impulses of his work, see McIntosh (1999) 144–79.
[45] Ervine (1931b).

essentially evil."[46] Citing the amateur linguist Richard Paget (1869–1955), he insisted that, though English was "a wild growth" with its "learned words ... a potpourri compounded of hedgerow flowers – Greek and Latin," its speech could be tamed and "made more useful by conscious effort on our part."[47] To develop a plainer idiom, Ervine encouraged actors and writers to read Paget's 1930 treatise *Babel, or The Past, Present, and Future of Human Speech*, specifically for its methods on making English a "flexible instrument for communication" across the globe.[48] English was to be standardized through "systematic and scientific study ... with a view to its future improvement" even if the "great majority of the literary world at present" still believed that "the fate of our language ought properly to be left to chance, or rather to herd instinct."[49] As Paget saw it, artists and writers fond of this "comfortable policy" – this *"laissez-faire"* approach to linguistic development – were wrong; it was not "practicable to-day, for the fate of English speech is in the balance."[50] "If we do nothing," he exclaimed, "one thing will be likely to happen, namely, that the English language will break up – America going one way, Australia another, and so on, till in the end these different communities will no longer be able to understand one another."[51] In this moment of apparent crisis, there were, however, unique opportunities as well, for already "[b]roadcasting, long-distance telephony, the talking film, and the gramophone" had conspired to make better forms of "standardization possible, and even comparatively easy to establish."[52] New technological media could indeed provide a "unifying influence," allowing language to overcome the more tribal and fractious impulses of human socialization.[53] The scientific precision of a more universal English was within grasp, he thought, but "only by systematic and conscious effort" would there be "unity and an approach to perfection in the future," an approach that would fulfill the "words of

---

[46] Ervine (1931b).
[47] Paget (1930) 8, 11.
[48] Ervine (1931a). Paget's contribution to the study of speech lay in his development of a "theory of pantomimic action of the tongue and lips," the principles of which became the foundation for the Paget Gorman Sign System. Designed for the deaf and deaf mute, this form of signing was not a language but rather a system of signs, providing a "one-to-one, sign-to-word match" between gestures and English words. On the structure of the Paget Gorman Sign System, see Sutton-Spence and Woll (1999) 14.
[49] Paget (1930) 83, 9.
[50] Paget (1930) 92.
[51] Paget (1930) 82–83.
[52] Paget (1930) 83.
[53] Paget (1930) 92.

Genesis," that there be "'one language – and now nothing will be restrained from them which they have imagined to do'."[54]

Eager to advance Paget's vision, Ervine promoted the notion that "[c]lear speech and strong speech and fine speech" was not merely an aesthetic preference but a political imperative of great importance.[55] English had already, he thought, fast become an "exact and simple" tongue, and indeed it was that very "simplicity" that had made it "peculiarly suitable to be a world-language."[56] On that account alone, he claimed, the continued existence (to say nothing of revivals) of other dialect forms and "obsolete languages" across the British Isles served no useful purpose.[57] The surviving traces of Goedelic and Brythonic tongues in Scotland, Ireland and Wales had done little, he felt, to further the "first principle of speech, that its use is to make us clearly understand each other."[58] Echoing to some extent the criticism of Irish that Mahaffy once leveled, Ervine mocked

> those reactionaries who are all for the revival of obsolete languages. It would not upset me if knowledge of Gaelic perished out of these islands, and if I had the power of dictating in these matters I should forbid the Highlander and the Irishman and the Welshman to continue in the use of his dying speech. When I hear reactionaries orating about the desirability of a diversity of tongues I feel inclined to remind them that what was wrought at the Tower of Babel was confusion. "Go to," said the Lord, according to Genesis, "let us go down, and there confound their language, that they may not understand one another's speech."[59]

For Ervine, the desire to preserve a diversity of languages was tantamount to warding off "the day when all men will be able to understand each other," a time when simply English alone would provide plain-spoken understanding between culturally different peoples.[60] No longer could language then be exploited for artificial, "sophisticated" aims – the putting on of so-called "literary airs" – but rather "for its purpose, the understanding of each other, and not the preservation of quaintness or the indulgence of literary idiosyncrasies."[61]

---

[54]   Paget (1930) 93. See also Genesis 11:6.
[55]   Ervine (1931c); Paget (1930) 92.
[56]   Ervine (1931a).
[57]   Ervine (1931c).
[58]   Ervine (1931c).
[59]   Ervine (1931c).
[60]   Ervine (1931c).
[61]   Ervine (1931a, 1931b).

Hugh MacDiarmid vilified the Anglophilia of Ervine's universal "world-language."[62] Denouncing his criticism, MacDiarmid insisted that Ervine had not simply abandoned advocacy for Gaelic languages in Britain but had willingly betrayed his homeland in Ulster as well. Rather than write an English idiom inflected by local dialects of the North, he had chosen to defend the commercial theatre of the bourgeoisie instead, supporting poor, digestible drawing-room comedies focused almost entirely on "winning the London success, and international vogue of a kind, denied to his earlier and better work."[63] Robbed of its Ulster English, Ervine's drama had fallen victim to the same "sorry imperialism which has thrust Gaelic and dialect literatures outwith the pale and concentrated on what has become to use Sir William Watson's phrase, 'scriptive English'."[64] Contrary to Ervine, MacDiarmid believed that as English slowly became "more and more of a world-language," the language was "progressively useless for higher literary purposes."[65] Without the corrective pressures brought by Scottish, Welsh and Irish literatures, English had become a "far less concentrated and expressive language."[66] British literature needed, he argued, not only strong infusions from a variety of local English dialects, but those Gaelic, Scots vernacular and Welsh literary traditions that had been "virtually proscribed by the 'English Ascendancy' policy."[67] If even Scots alone had been "concurrently maintained with the development of 'English Literature'," he speculated

---

[62] Ervine (1931b).

[63] MacDiarmid *SP* (1992) 62.

[64] MacDiarmid *SP* (1992) 63. MacDiarmid cites the popular Georgian poet William Watson. Watson received a knighthood in 1917 in part for composing the patriotic panegyric "The Man Who Saw" (a poem he dedicated to the prime minister, David Lloyd George). In a 1916 book entitled *Pencraft*, he argued that literature could be divided "into three kinds or orders, and to call them the cantative, the scriptive, and the loquitive." These designations formed a range upon which one could plot kinds of language and speech, the 'cantative' applying to those instances "capable of uttering themselves through but one medium, the medium of quite obviously and literally chanted words," the 'scriptive' being "the essentially *written*, as distinguished from that not necessarily greater but perhaps more elemental thing, the essentially *chanted* word," and the 'loquitive' which "in form and substance is little if at all distinguishable from conversational speech." According to Watson, "the immense middle region" that comprised the 'scriptive' was "absolutely literature; neither a sublimely abnormal, half preternatural phenomenon nor a transfiguration of everyday chit-chat, but absolutely literature." With its "deliberate and ordered language," the 'scriptive' represented language as the "preeminently efficient manner of speech." Watson (1916) 9, 10, 13, 16, 18, 21, 22. On Watson's life and work, see Wilson (1981).

[65] MacDiarmid *SP* (1992) 66.

[66] MacDiarmid *SP* (1992) 62.

[67] MacDiarmid *SP* (1992) 63.

> what the results today would have been ... Would such a synthesis or duality of creative output (each element of it so very different that they could have complemented and 'corrected' each other in a unique and invaluable fashion) not have been infinitely better ...?[68]

Nonetheless, in light of the suggestions by the Board of Education, there seemed to be a greater openness to the possibility of better synthesis between the "diverse cultural elements and the splendid variety of languages and dialects, in the British Isles."[69] The "children of tomorrow," MacDiarmid observed, might yet be relieved of that "subtle but far-reaching psychological outrage which has been inflicted on many generations of pupils and seriously affected the quality and direction of those of them who had literary inclinations."[70]

Relief had already begun to appear in Ireland where the Irish language and literature were experiencing something of an unexpected resurgence in popularity and prestige. During the late nineteenth century, MacDiarmid noted,

> highly-educated Irishmen were incapable of conceiving that in this whole corpus [of Gaelic literature] there was anything worth recovering, let alone an entire classical tradition, with its own elaborate technique, its own very different but (if only because incomparable) not inferior values which maintained itself intact – in active intercourse with all contemporary European developments, but unadulterated by them in the integrity of its own modes – for at least two thousand years.[71]

This revitalization of an Irish "classical tradition" had not come about, however, through imitating or adapting the literatures of Greek or Roman antiquity: there had been no need to replicate either its forms or its content, for Irish Gaelic, MacDiarmid insisted, possessed an "alternative value of prime consequence when set against the Greek and Roman literatures which are all that most of us mean when we speak of 'the Classics'."[72] As MacDiarmid saw it, the meaning of 'Classics' had been grossly misinterpreted by poets and artists throughout the European Renaissance. In mimicking the formal trappings of Greek and Roman art, that which was in fact unique and 'classical' in their own native literatures had been filtered through false international standards. The canons

---

[68] MacDiarmid SP (1992) 63.
[69] MacDiarmid SP (1992) 67.
[70] MacDiarmid SP (1992) 61.
[71] MacDiarmid SP (1992) 63.
[72] MacDiarmid SP (1992) 63.

of such neoclassicism, allegedly derived from Greece and Rome, were not classical in any sense but only imitative and productive of arid reformulations of antiquity. Citing Daniel Corkery's study, *The Hidden Ireland* (1924), MacDiarmid declared that "Renaissance standards" were clearly "not Greek standards. Greek standards in their own time and place were standards arrived at by the Greek nation; they were national standards."[73] "Caught up at second hand into the art-mind of Europe," Greek principles were acclaimed universal, and under their influence "the youthfully tender national cultures of Europe" slowly atrophied.[74] The "standards of a dead nation" thus overwhelmed and "killed" the native genius of many latent 'classical' traditions in Europe.[75] Those "aptitudes through which they themselves had become memorable" were, bit by bit, washed away in largely botched efforts to imitate and "re-discover the secret power that lay behind Greek art."[76] That power was never retrieved, MacDiarmid felt, and all attempts at doing so had produced only the "sham strength," "uneasy energy" and "death in life" of "mere neo-classical" formalism.[77]

Although imitations of the Greek and the Roman had helped snuff out forms of "national art" across Europe, MacDiarmid thought contemporary Scottish writers could challenge English dominance and break down its "limited channels" with a "new classicism today."[78] Scottish classicism, however, could not be born of neoclassical rigor nor of mere nostalgia for the Celtic past. On the contrary, the country had to "get down to *Ur-motives* – to get back behind the Renaissance" if it were to "undo that deplorable whitewashing whereby Greek and Latin culture has prevented other European nations realizing their national genius in the way Greece and Rome themselves did."[79] Rather than ape a foreign tradition, Scottish writers needed to do for their place, their time, what "Greece and Rome themselves" had achieved in their own.[80] In this endeavor MacDiarmid felt Ireland's recent Literary Revival was instructive. While the reputedly Gaelic "values" prized by Yeats and others were,

[73] Corkery (1925) xiv, as in MacDiarmid *SP* (1992) 79.
[74] Corkery (1925) xiv–xv, as in MacDiarmid *SP* (1992) 79.
[75] Corkery (1925) xv, as in MacDiarmid *SP* (1992) 79.
[76] Corkery (1925) xv, xvi, as in MacDiarmid *SP* (1992) 79, 80.
[77] Corkery (1925) xv, as in MacDiarmid *SP* (1992) 79, 80.
[78] Corkery (1925) xv; MacDiarmid *SP* (1992) 77, 80. On MacDiarmid's view of the Reformation and Renaissance, see Lyall (2006) 41–43.
[79] MacDiarmid *SP* (1992) 80; Hugh MacDiarmid, "Towards a Celtic Front" (1953) in MacDiarmid *SEHM* (1970) 173.
[80] MacDiarmid *SEHM* (1970) 173.

he confessed, "largely phoney and based on misunderstanding and falsification," the "Celtic Twilight" had provided "probably the only way at first to get even a modicum of Gaelic culture across in an overwhelmingly hostile environment. It succeeded in doing so and led on to the genuine article."[81] That genuine article was to be found not only in the apparent revival of the Irish language but also in new "re-translations" of Irish poetry that stressed not "the stars and shadows of Yeats" but the "hard realism and sharp satire" of Gaelic literature.[82] Yet, even with the gains made in Ireland, Scotland was

> still practically a *terra nullius*. We have no study of it a thousandth part as good as Corkery's or de Blacam's or Douglas Hyde's or Eleanor Hull's books on Irish Literature; and non-Gaelic readers can still only approach the best Scottish Gaelic poems through such inadequate and distorting translations as were those, in Ireland, of Sir Samuel Ferguson and the beginners of the Irish Literary Revival, which have only to be compared with the re-translations, far 'harder' and truer to the original Gaelic spirit and free of the 'Twilight' nonsense, of such recent translators as Professor Bergin, Mr Robin Flower, or Mr James Stephens, to show how much has still to be done.[83]

For too long Scottish poets had been focused on composing work in English and thus neglected an "all-in view of the literary production of our country."[84] A "mere subsidiary to English letters," Scottish literary culture had produced no seemingly "first-class work, indispensable or even relevant to the main line of English literary evolution."[85] To escape this "creatively inferior" position, poets had to cut through the "crust of imitation" to manifest Scotland's "potentialities of incalculable difference."[86]

Though recent Scottish writing had been too "'hit and miss' and unscientific" to advance a "renewed manifestation" of the classics in Scotland, MacDiarmid nonetheless set forth three conditions for a broad cultural renaissance.[87] First, the "rising tide of Scottish national consciousness"

---

[81] MacDiarmid *SEHM* (1970) 173.
[82] MacDiarmid *SP* (1992) 78, 70.
[83] MacDiarmid *SP* (1992) 77–78. Translations by Osborn Bergin (1873–1950), Robin Flower (1881–1946) and James Stephens (1882–1950) were said to have captured the essence of Irish better.
[84] MacDiarmid *SP* (1992) 69.
[85] MacDiarmid *SP* (1992) 70.
[86] MacDiarmid *SP* (1992) 70, 73.
[87] MacDiarmid *SP* (1992) 73. The term "Scottish Renaissance" was first coined in French by the Toulousian critic Denis Saurat (1890–1958). See Saurat (1924) 295–307. On the Renaissance and the rise of modernism in Scotland, see McCulloch (2009).

had to grow to greater heights: for too long, he argued, the central differences between the English and the Scottish imagination had been obscured by the "increasing Anglicization of the latter" even though Scotland's "assimilation to the English" had never been effective or complete.[88] Many "deep-seated and unalterable psychological differences remain," he argued, "Only the 'surface minds' (in the Bergsonian sense) of the Scots have been Englished."[89] For that reason, it seemed possible – as a second condition – that the formal education at Scottish institutions could be recentered on the study of native literature. "No other people in the world," he argued,

> have ever preferred an alien literature to their own, and practically excluded the latter from the curricula of their schools and universities, in this way; and it is not to be wondered at that English literature, which has never suffered from any such neglect, should have acquired an importance out of all proportion to Scottish. The disparity between the two today may yet be redressed to some extent if anything like the same attention is given to Scottish literature in Scottish schools and elsewhere in Scotland as is presently given to English.[90]

According to MacDiarmid, this "thorough-going reconcentration" would help spread an "all-in view of Scottish poetry," not a "hopelessly one-sided" view but one that would see Scotland foster and maintain its own "separate literary tradition."[91] To an extent, some of the groundwork for meeting these two conditions was already developing: the National Party was founded in June 1928, and as such the nationalist movement slowly began to gain better organization and wider public recognition. Its establishment brought together previously separated associations and political interest groups, and in so doing, forced these once "somewhat remote, residually cultural organization[s]" to generate a more concrete ideological

---

[88] MacDiarmid *SP* (1992) 73, 72.
[89] MacDiarmid *SP* (1992) 72–73. Drawn by the notion of a "surface mind," MacDiarmid interpreted Henri Bergson's *An Introduction to Metaphysics* (1912), applying his description of the "crust of imitation" to a distinctively Scottish linguistic context. "When I," Bergson wrote, "direct my attention inward to contemplate my own self (supposed for the moment to be inactive), I perceive at first, as a crust solidified on the surface, all the perceptions which come to it from the material world. These perceptions are clear, distinct, juxtaposed or juxtaposable one with another; they tend to group themselves into objects. Next, I notice the memories which more or less adhere to these perceptions and which serve to interpret them. These memories have been detached, as it were, from the depth of my personality, drawn to the surface by the perceptions which resemble them; they rest on the surface of my mind without being absolutely myself." Bergson (1912) 9–10.
[90] MacDiarmid *SP* (1992) 73.
[91] MacDiarmid *SP* (1992) 73.

platform with clear political objectives.[92] Despite these developments, however, no advent of a renaissance in Scotland could survive, MacDiarmid thought, without mending the radical division of Scottish languages. "The third point," he suggested therefore, was

> the necessity to bridge the gulf between Gaelic and Scots. Both have been tremendously handicapped by circumstances, and yet in their evolution, thus miserably attenuated and driven underground by external factors, they have continued to complement and correct each other in the most remarkable way. I am not going to make use of the terms 'Romantic' and 'Classical', although these dubious counters do roughly correspond to the Scots and Gaelic traditions in poetry respectively.[93]

As he saw it, if contemporary writers were to somehow fuse together Scotland's disseminated tongues, ranging from Highland Gaelic through varieties of Lallans, then they might "lead the way in the great new movement in poetry which is everywhere being sought for."[94] To "effectively bridge this Gaelic-Scots gulf," however, was a unique challenge, not least because the number of fluent speakers of Scottish Gaelic had been gradually diminishing for well over a century.[95] In 1891 more than 250,000 people spoke the language, but only forty years later that number had dropped precipitously: the British census of 1941 reported less than 130,000 speakers.[96] As Scottish Gaelic slowly became a cultural curiosity from a once Celtic past, its idiom also was said to have been "choked by an excessive formalism."[97] By contrast, most varieties of Lowland Scots faced no threat of extinction, yet their parochial reputation preceded discussion of Lallans serving the national interest. Lack of standardization and a "formlessness" reigned over its twentieth-century writing.[98] Unfit for literary use, Scots had "gradually lost all the qualities befitting them for major expressive purposes rather than for homely, local uses."[99] With

---

[92] Brand (1978) 195. The National Party largely grew out of the Scottish Home Rule Association (founded in 1886) led by Roland Eugene Muirhead, the Scots National League (founded in 1904), the Scottish National Movement (founded in 1926) and the Glasgow University Student Nationalist Association (founded in 1927). On the origins of these organizations and their particular contributions to the Party, see Brand (1978) 169–227; Tanner (2004) 63–65; Hanham (1969) 119–30; Finlay (1994) 71–125; as well as Harvie (2004) 28–31.

[93] MacDiarmid SP (1992) 73–74.

[94] MacDiarmid SP (1992) 74.

[95] MacDiarmid SP (1992) 74.

[96] On Scottish Gaelic in the twentieth century, see MacKinnon (1991) 121–49 and MacKinnon (2000) 44–55.

[97] MacDiarmid SP (1992) 74.

[98] MacDiarmid SP (1992) 74.

[99] MacDiarmid SP (1992) 74.

the dialects of one language disseminated so widely and the other stran-gled with a slavish stress on form, English made inroads in a Scotland "miserably attenuated and driven underground by external factors."[100]

Still MacDiarmid believed the "role of our race in history – the special qualities and functions of Scottish nationality" could be articulated in a unifying national language with "necessary dynamic force."[101] There would be no nostalgic return to Scottish Gaelic nor indeed a "puerile" retreat to the parochial – "prevalent conceptions" of Scottish language were "all out of date" and had to change, he thought; what was needed was the innovation of a new synthetic vernacular, a flexible idiom that could then merge various Scots dialects with Scottish Gaelic.[102] Only by bridging this gulf – by forging a new sense of Scottish hybridity – would a "new classicism" begin to take shape.[103] Advocates of Home Rule, notably Ruaraidh Erskine of Mar, had argued that Scots vernacular possessed no literary merit, that Highland Gaelic alone was fit for national purpose, but MacDiarmid insisted that a new vernacular could be forged if "all the *disjecta membra* of the Doric" were worked "back from the bits to the whole" through a "synthetic process."[104] This remaking of Scots was no ploy to animate further literary provincialism. Scottish letters had already had enough of "Doric infantilism" with its "instinctive suspicion of cleverness and culture."[105] What was needed was not further "mental inertia," he argued, but an idiom that embraced "all

---

[100] MacDiarmid *SP* (1992) 73.

[101] MacDiarmid *SP* (1992) 75.

[102] MacDiarmid *SP* (1992) 75.

[103] MacDiarmid *SP* (1992) 74. For discussions of cultural and linguistic hybridity in Scotland, see Crawford (1998) 238–44, Crawford (2000) 111–75, as well as Craig (2004) 229–53.

[104] Hugh MacDiarmid, "The New Movement in Vernacular Poetry: Lewis Spence, Marion Angus" (November 27, 1925) in MacDiarmid *CSS* (1995) 198. Hugh MacDiarmid, "Towards a Synthetic Scots" (August 13, 1926) in MacDiarmid *CSS* (1995) 368–69. Following the publication of Allan Ramsay's play, *The Gentle Shepherd* (1725), the epithet 'Doric' was often used to describe the rough speech of Northumbria and the Scottish Lowlands. The term was appropriated by the critic Alexander Fraser Tytler, Lord Woodhouselee (1747–1813), who, in praising Ramsay's work, stressed the rusticity and simplicity of his Scots vernacular when compared with the urbane English of London. "To us," he wrote, "their dialect is an antiquated tongue, and as such it carries with it a Doric simplicity." Woodhouselee (1852) xxxv, lviii. Gradually, Doric became identified with the dialects of northeast Scotland, and this insistence on a "Grecian Doric" character was common in subsequent criticism. Later, in an unsigned review of N. F. Moore's *Lectures on the Greek Language and Literature* (1835), an anonymous critic echoed this conceit, arguing that, in "English, the dialect of Allan Ramsay's Gentle Shepherd, and of many of the sweetest songs of Burns, corre-sponds in no slight degree with the Grecian Doric." Review of "Moore's Lectures on the Greek Language and Literature," *The North American Review* 42 (January 1836) 107. On the development of the 'Doric' in the modern era, see McClure (2000) 1–13; as well as McClure (2002).

[105] C. M. Grieve, Letter to the *Aberdeen Free Press* (January 30, 1922) in MacDiarmid *LHM* (1984) 756, 754.

progressive and creative tendencies" present in modern literature and forced Scottish poets from their "anti-cultural prejudices," the

> mental and spiritual agoraphobia which has driven them – and to all intents and purposes the rest of Scotland with them! – into a cul de sac, where they bury their minds (as ostriches bury their heads) in the shadow of the blind wall which blocks them out from literature and from life.[106]

MacDiarmid derived his experimental vision for Scots in large part from Joyce's *Ulysses* (1922), but it was also the *Landsmål* movement – perhaps Arne Garborg's *Odyssevskvædet*, a Nynorsk verse translation of *The Odyssey* (1918) – which first showed him a synthetic language of national scope.[107] With the publication of "The Watergaw" in 1922, MacDiarmid began his own unique renovation of the Doric, and its growing "evolutionary momentum" would see him, over the next four years, "think himself back" into its spirit across three collections of synthetic poetry: *Sangschaw* (1925), *Penny Wheep* (1926) and, finally, his landmark long poem *A Drunk Man Looks at the Thistle* (1926).[108] Composed in 2,685 lines, *A Drunk Man* was a "gallimaufry," a satirical *patois* steeped in polyglot intrusions from other European languages.[109] The work's linguistic heterogeneity, he claimed, "pit in a concrete abstraction / My country's contrair qualities," what the critic G. Gregory Smith (1865–1932) had called "the Caledonian antisyzygy," the "zigzag of contradictions" and "sudden jostling of contraries" at work in the modern Scot.[110] Its "polemical restlessness" set out with some belligerence the "latent potentialities" of "distinctive Scots psychology."[111] "(To prove my saul is Scots," MacDiarmid declared,

> I maun begin
> Wi' what's still deemed Scots and the folk expect,
> And spire up syne by visible degrees
> To heichts whereo' the fules ha'e never recked.

---

[106] Grieve, Letter to the *Aberdeen Free Press* (January 30, 1922) in MacDiarmid *LHM* (1984) 754, 755, 756.

[107] On MacDiarmid's decision to write in synthetic Scots, see Bold (1990) 121–30.

[108] C. M. Grieve, "Introducing 'Hugh M'Diarmid'," *The Scottish Chapbook* 1.41 (August 1922), as in MacDiarmid *SP* (1992) 10. On writing "The Watergaw," see Bold (1990) 137–40. On the development of *A Drunk Man* from manuscript to publication, see Herbert (1992) 42–67, as well as Bold (1990) 180–224. For a broader comparative, transnational account of 'synthetic' writing and twentieth-century modernism, see Hart (2010).

[109] M'Diarmid, "Author's Note," in M'Diarmid (1926) vii.

[110] Hugh MacDiarmid, *A Drunk Man Looks at the Thistle*, as in MacDiarmid *CP1* (1993) 145. Smith (1919) 4, 20.

[111] Smith (1919) 4. MacDiarmid *CSS* (1995) 198.

> But aince I get them there I'll whummle them
> And souse the craturs in the nether deeps,
> – For it's nae choice, and ony man s'ud wish
> To dree the goat's weird tae as weel's the sheep's!)[112]

Though he thought his work had drawn on Scotland's "common trough," MacDiarmid's 'synthesis' did not fare well commercially, and *A Drunk Man* was met with some vociferous, critical reviews.[113] Some considered it sloppy, confusing and peculiar – "It is idle to attempt a coherent account of a poem so deliberately and provocatively incoherent" – while others castigated MacDiarmid for the "constant plangent grieving over his inhibitions."[114] Nonetheless, the poem had many early admirers, among them the Irish writer and ancient Greek enthusiast Oliver St John Gogarty, (who lauded *A Drunk Man* for its "wonderfully flexible and containing form") and the poet Edwin Muir (who praised its "instinctive rightness").[115] "The form of the present poem," Muir observed,

> fixed by the psychological state of the principal character, permits him to express with their appropriate degree of conviction his various intuitions of the world, some of them realistic, some of them fantastic or grotesque. The scheme of the poem might be called indifferently psychological or philosophical; it is the picture of a mind; it is an image of the world as symbolized in the thistle. The world changes its shape, is lost, appears again as Mr M'Diarmid follows the transitions, daring and yet natural, in the mind of the monologist.[116]

Yet Muir also detected "frequent carelessness of style" in *A Drunk Man*, a "hasty, slipshod manner," which suggested, perhaps, that this artificial fusion of dialects could not be sustained as a shared language across Scottish literature.[117] "Hugh M'Diarmid," he later asserted,

> has recently tried to revive [Scots Vernacular] by impregnating it with all the contemporary influences of Europe one after another, and thus galvanize it into life by a series of violent shocks. In carrying out this experi-

---

[112] MacDiarmid *CP1* (1993) 83.

[113] MacDiarmid *CP1* (1993) 86. Of its initial print run of 500 copies, only 99 copies sold before the end of 1926. On the poem's lack of commercial success, see Bold (1990) 222–24.

[114] Unsigned review, *Times Literary Supplement* 1338 (September 22, 1927) 650–51, as in McCulloch (2009) 46. Unsigned review, *Aberdeen Press and Journal* (November 27, 1926) 5, as in Bold (1990) 223. On the poem's early reception, see McCulloch (2009) 29–52.

[115] Oliver St John Gogarty, under the pseudonym "Gog." "Literature and Life: A Drunk Man Looks at the Thistle," *Irish Statesman* (January 8, 1927) 432, as in Bold (1990) 223. Edwin Muir, "Verse," *Nation and Athenaeum* (January 22, 1927) 568, as in McCulloch (2004) 74.

[116] Edwin Muir, "Verse," *Nation and Athenaeum* (January 22, 1927) 568, as in McCulloch (2004) 73.

[117] Edwin Muir, "Verse," *Nation and Athenaeum* (January 22, 1927) 568, as in McCulloch (2004) 74.

ment he has written some remarkable poetry; but he has left Scottish verse
very much where it was before. For the major forms of poetry rise from
the collision between emotion and intellect on a plane where both meet
on equal terms; and it can never come into existence where the poet feels
in one language and thinks in another, even though he should translate his
thoughts into the language of his feelings. Scots poetry can only be
revived, that is to say, when Scotsmen begin to think *naturally* in Scots.
The curse of Scottish literature is the lack of a whole language, which
finally means the lack of a whole mind.[118]

According to Muir, MacDiarmid's experiments with synthetic language,
however intriguing, were "an isolated phenomenon" unsuited to creating
a "complete and homogeneous Scottish literature."[119] The "landscape" of
its literary world "is not noticeably diversified with poets chanting in
synthetic Scots"; he explained: "the village bards who have excruciated us
for so long still calmly proceed on their traditional way."[120] To have "a
complete and homogeneous" literature, writers had to choose "a
complete and homogeneous language," either Gaelic or English: "There
seems to me to be no choice except for these: no half-way house if
Scotland is ever to reach its complete expression in literature."[121]
Although the country once possessed a vernacular in which "everything
can be expressed that a people wishes to express ... we cannot return to
it," Muir insisted, "to think so is to misunderstand history."[122] By the
time Robert Burns (1759–96) began composing in Scots poetry, the
vernacular was said to have already "lost its richness and thinned to a
trickle. It could express feeling, but not sustained thought."[123] Dispersed
as a variety of provincial dialects, the vernacular had become "what the
babbling of children is to the speech of grown men and women; it is
blessedly ignorant of the wider spheres of thought and passion, and when
it touches upon them its response is as irresponsible as that of the irreme-
diably immature."[124] Doubtful that Scottish Gaelic provided a better
alternative, Muir saw English as the "only practicable" choice for the
country.[125] "This may be a regrettable fact, but it must be accepted," he

[118] Muir (1936) 21–22.
[119] Muir, "Scotland Once Had a Scots Literature," *The Bulletin* (January 27, 1938) 18, as in
       MacDiarmid and Muir (2005) 70. Muir (1936) 178.
[120] MacDiarmid and Muir (2005) 70.
[121] Muir (1936) 178.
[122] Muir (1936) 177–78.
[123] MacDiarmid and Muir (2005) 69.
[124] Muir (1936) 70–71.
[125] Muir (1936) 178.

explained, "for there is no Scots language to which we can pass over from the restricted and local province of dialect: there is only English."[126] There was no present impediment to a national literature, he maintained: the country had simply to "assert its identity" in English following after "the contemporary case of Ireland."[127] "Irish nationality cannot be said to be any less intense than ours," he explained, "but Ireland produced a national literature not by clinging to Irish dialect, but by adopting English and making it into a language fit for all its purposes. The poetry of Mr Yeats belongs to English literature, but no one would deny that it belongs to Irish literature pre-eminently and essentially."[128] Yeats' example had demonstrated clearly that, even with the strictures of English, new and appropriate forms of expression could be found to express a variety of 'Celtic identities' on the British Isles. The tragedy of contemporary Scottish writing lay, as Muir saw it, not in any failure to revive Gaelic or reimagine Scots but with those who clung mulishly to the "bits and patches" of fading dialects while ignoring the precedent of the Irish Revival.[129]

MacDiarmid abhorred the "absurd pro-English prejudice" of Muir's "sudden attack," his "stab-in-the-back" betrayal.[130] He proclaimed him an enemy of Scotland, viciously casting doubt on the Orcadian's national loyalty and critical skill:

> Scotland's worst enemies have always been Scotsmen themselves, and it is therefore not surprising to find a Scottish writer going far farther in his denigration of Scottish language and literature than even Sir John Squire ... Mr Muir is not exactly a Scotsman himself. He is an Orcadian, and in arguing as he does that a writer in Scots handicaps a critic because the critic must criticise in a different language to that in which the work is written he unwittingly destroys the supposed value of his own remarks on Scots literature, which, by his own criterion, he is incapable of judging save through the disabling medium of a different language. The argument is a nonsensical one.[131]

---

[126]   Muir (1936) 71.
[127]   Muir (1936) 182, 179.
[128]   Muir (1936) 179.
[129]   Muir (1936) 179.
[130]   C. M. Grieve, "Scots As a Literary Medium: Point of View for Burns Day," *The Bulletin* (January 24, 1938) 13, as in MacDiarmid and Muir (2005) 61. See also C. M. Grieve, Letter to P. H. Butter (December 22, 1966) in MacDiarmid *LHM* (1984) 868. On Muir's interest in nationalist causes, see Hanham (1969) 160–62, and Bold (1990) 340–43.
[131]   MacDiarmid and Muir (2005) 61–62; MacDiarmid never forgave "slithy Edwin" Muir for the opinions he espoused in *Scott and Scotland*, and he often attacked Muir's poetry and his character. "I cannot agree," he told Peter Herbert Butter (1921–99), Regius Professor of English

For MacDiarmid, Muir's insistence that remaking Scots was a "petty provincial fad" was tantamount to a "wholesale attack" on both his poetic idiom and the national aspirations of Scotland.[132] Muir's "contemptuous dismissal" simply reflected a characteristically "English inability to tolerate anything that does not 'do pujah' to themselves. It is this inordinate English ascendancy policy," MacDiarmid complained, "that has determined all their history, and accounts for their ruthless treatment of Irish and Scottish and Welsh Gaelic, the Scots vernacular, and their own dialects."[133] Yet such a "snobbish English Tendency," he argued, had certain key facts wrong, for

> the Normans at the time of the conquest were as inferior in literary culture and barbarous compared with the inhabitants of England as the Romans were inferior to the Greeks when they made themselves masters of Greece. In precisely the same way it is true that there is nothing inherently inadequate in Scots for the expression of the full range of modern literary purposes – the fact that Scots is not used for a fraction of these is due to other factors than its own inadequacy altogether.[134]

Furthermore, the examples Muir had offered of Yeats and the Irish Revival were equally mistaken, not least because Yeats himself "was an enthusiastic supporter of the Lallans movement and used to go about reciting certain Lallans lyrics which he greatly admired and had memorised."[135] Moreover, "the whole Celtic Twilight business" had at best, he claimed, "only tinkered with the fringes" of an authentic renaissance in

---

Language and Literature at the University of Glasgow, "that he is a good, let alone an important, poet. I do not believe at all from my knowledge of him in his professed Christianity or his near saint-hood of character. On the contrary I do not believe he had any intellectual integrity at all." C. M. Grieve, Letter to P. H. Butter (December 22, 1966) in MacDiarmid *LHM* (1984) 868. See also C. M. Grieve, Letter to F. G. Scott (July 13, 1940) in MacDiarmid *NSLHM* (2001) 184. Muir, for his part, later insisted that MacDiarmid's work with Lallans had helped to revive something of Scottish language. "Because of [MacDiarmid's] example," he wrote in 1951, "there has been a revival of the Scottish language, a language which has proved that it is full of vigour, colour, and potentiality. A new poetry without the mark of parochialism which used to cling to Scottish verse, has been written in it, along with poetry by Scotsmen in English, and the remarkable work of Somerled MacLean in Gaelic. There is no parallel to all this in Scottish literature since the days of Fergusson and Burns." Muir (1951) iii–iv. On Muir's unwillingness to engage with MacDiarmid's persistent attacks, see Butter (1966) 152–56.

[132] MacDiarmid and Muir (2005) 64, 62.
[133] MacDiarmid and Muir (2005) 62, 61.
[134] MacDiarmid and Muir (2005) 61.
[135] MacDiarmid enjoyed noting that he had once sent "Mr Yeats and 'A.E.' (the late Mr G. W. Russell) representative collections of contemporary poems in English by Scottish poets like Mr Edwin Muir, the late Messrs William Jeffrey, William Soutar, Frederick Branford and others. They found the entire collection quite devoid of merit and said that this confirmed them in their support of the Lallans movement." Hugh MacDiarmid, Letter to *The Scotsman* (December 5, 1950) in MacDiarmid *LHM* (1984) 795.

Celtic literature, perhaps even "dodging ... the issue."[136] No new reign of classicism in Irish literature had emerged from the behest of Yeats' literary politics, MacDiarmid argued, and the poet himself had admitted as much, having often confessed profound disappointment with Revival-era writing, writing that spoke in the

> sweet insinuating feminine voice of the dwellers in the country of shadows & hollow images. I have dwelt there too long not to dread all that comes out of it. We possess nothing but the will & we must never let the children of vague desires breathe upon it nor the waters of sentiment rust the terrible mirror of its blade.[137]

For MacDiarmid, Yeats had recognized too late the need for a "Gaelic classical tradition," a tradition forged not with "fine-spun, tenuous, shadowy stuff" – the "accepted products" of Revival – but with a "distinctive Irish-English," a hard, hybrid idiom whose "variety" and "virility" could "get back, through the twilight, to the Gaelic sunshine."[138]

By the time his fierce debate with Muir took place, however, MacDiarmid's incendiary approach to art, life and politics had already embroiled him in significant turmoil of both a political and a personal nature. By the early 1930s his thirteen-year marriage to Margaret Grieve, née Skinner, was disintegrating as broader support for his involvement in the nationalist movement was evaporating as well.[139] In spring 1933 John MacDonald MacCormick (1904–61), secretary for the Council of the National Party, notified him that the party had declined his renewal of membership.[140] MacDiarmid's desire to use "the National Party as a means of introducing Communism into Scotland," his penchant for preaching "from the Nationalist platform Scots Communism, Republicanism etc.," was, MacCormick explained, "completely at variance with the Policy of the National Party," and so

[136] Hugh MacDiarmid, Letter to Kenneth Buthlay (March 4, 1953) in MacDiarmid *LHM* (1984) 863.

[137] Yeats, "To George Russell (Æ)" (April 1904) in Yeats *CL3* (1994) 577, cited by Hugh MacDiarmid in "A Roland for an Oliver" (April 1955) in MacDiarmid *RT3* (1998) 343.

[138] Hugh MacDiarmid, "The Norman Conquest" (July 1955) in MacDiarmid *RT3* (1998) 347. Hugh MacDiarmid, "An Irish Poet: Oliver St John Gogarty" (September 1928) in MacDiarmid *RT2* (1997) 221. On the parallel positions that MacDiarmid and Yeats occupied within revival movements whose aims included "the wider cultural repudiation of English hegemony," see Crotty (2011) 20–38.

[139] Amid allegations of infidelity, the couple divorced on January 16, 1932. On their marriage, see Bold (1990) 242–46, 259–64, 267–68.

[140] MacDiarmid had allowed his membership in the National Party to lapse "some time after 10 May 1930." He was not, therefore, as has often been repeated, expelled from the party so much as prohibited from reinstatement. See Manson (2011) 76.

by a vote of fifty-five against thirty-eight, MacDiarmid was deemed a political isolate, ineligible for renewed membership.[141] His strong left-wing sympathies as well as his propensity to savage any opponent were considered too great a liability for the National Party's plan to merge with the more conservative, more unionist Scottish Party led by John Kevan MacDowall (1891–1958). As MacCormick put it, MacDiarmid was "politically one of the greatest handicaps with which any national movement could have been burdened."[142]

> Grieve had joined our platform and in characteristic manner had hurled contempt at everything English … His love of bitter controversy, his extravagant and self-assertive criticism of the English, and his woolly thinking, which could encompass within one mind the doctrines of both Major Douglas and Karl Marx, were taken by many of the more sober-minded of the Scots as sufficient excuse to condemn the whole case for Home Rule out of hand.[143]

MacDiarmid, in reaction, poured his venom into a series of Scots verses, mocking 'King John' MacCormick and his band of moderate Home Rule enthusiasts. That "troupe of gibbering lunatics" had convinced him that there was "nae ither country 'neath the sun / That's betrayed the human spirit as Scotland's done, / And still the betrayal proceeds to the complete / Dehumanisin' o' the Scottish breed."[144] Ostracized, he felt that "Nae man, nae spiritual force, can live / In Scotland lang," and so he encouraged his contemporaries to disavow the National Party:

> For God's sake leave it tae.
> Mak' a warld o' your ain like me, and if
> 'Idiot' or 'lunatic' the Scots folk say
> At least you'll ken – owre weel to argue back –
> You'd be better that than lackin' a' they lack.[145]

In remaking his own world – his political and aesthetic vision as well as his domestic world – MacDiarmid sought isolation and self-imposed exile, moving with his Cornish companion Valda Trevlyn (1906–89) to

---

[141] "37. From J. M. MacCormick, National Party of Scotland" (May 10, 1933) in Manson (2011) 73–74. The vote was not without controversy: some considered MacCormick decidedly "narrow-minded" in his view of MacDiarmid's contributions to the Party. See "39. From N. C. Jack, National Party of Scotland" (May 31, 1933) in Manson (2011) 74, 76.

[142] MacCormick (1955) 35, as in Bold (1990) 235.

[143] MacCormick (1955) 35, as in Bold (1990) 235.

[144] Hugh MacDiarmid, Letter to Neil Gunn (May 19, 1933) in MacDiarmid *LHM* (1984) 250; Hugh MacDiarmid, "Letter to R. M. B.," in MacDiarmid *CP2* (1994) 1273.

[145] MacDiarmid *CP2* (1994) 1273.

Whalsay in summer 1933. The "Outer Isles," exclaimed Ezra Pound, "How the hell *you* are ever to find out anything in Outer Isles with nothing but the shit of Fleet Street and the Pooping of McFarty and Co. governing 96% of British printing kzrrist alone xknoze."[146] Despite Pound's exasperation at this move – he risked becoming, like Basil Bunting (1900–85) off on the Canary Islands, "no more central" Pound warned – MacDiarmid remained on Whalsay for nearly nine years, his imagination kindled by the strange visual character of the Shetland and Faroes' 'stone' worlds.[147] Its "impression of barrenness and monotony" was deceptive, for in radiating a "very moderate aspect," its apparent "absence of variety of colour and form and the landscape, however different to that which one been accustomed, has its own completeness and complexity."[148] Its "Deictic, fiducial stones" engendered something of a creative renewal, and thus MacDiarmid began experimenting with a "synthetic English – not Scots," a new, more multilingual 'world' language that 'got' into

> this stone world now.
> Ratchel, striae, relationships of tesserae,
> > Innumerable shades of grey,
> > Innumerable shapes,
> And beneath them all a stupendous unity,
> Infinite movement visibly defending itself
> Against all the assaults of weather and water,
> Simultaneously mobilised at full strength
> At every point of the universal front,
> > Always at the pitch of its powers,
> > The foundation and end of all life.
> I try them with the old Norn words – hraun
> Duss, rønis, queedaruns, kollyarun;
> They hvarf from me in all directions
> Over the hurdifell – klett, millya hellya, hellyina bretta,
> Hellyina wheeda, hellyina grø, bakka, ayre, –
> > And lay my world in kolgref.[149]

---

[146] "84. From Ezra Pound" (December 28, 1934) in Manson (2011) 122–23.

[147] "84. From Ezra Pound" (December 28, 1934) in Manson (2011) 123.

[148] Hugh MacDiarmid, "Faeröerne" (January 12, 1934) in MacDiarmid *RT2* (1997) 357.

[149] Hugh MacDiarmid, "On A Raised Beach," in MacDiarmid *CP1* (1993) 423, 426–27. C. M. Grieve, Letter to William Soutar (July 5, 1933) in MacDiarmid *LHM* (1984) 148. MacDiarmid likely knew these Norn words from Jakob Jakobsen's 1897 book, *The Dialect and Place Names of Shetland: Two Popular Lectures*. The words in this passage can be roughly glossed as follows: hraun, meaning "rough, rocky place, wilderness"; duss, meaning "thrown-up heap"; rønis, meaning "cairn" or "stone-heap"; queedaruns, meaning "white rocky place"; kollyarun, meaning

Moving beyond the Doric of *A Drunk Man* and *Cencrastus*, he brought his "aesthesis in vain to bear" on Whalsay, retrieving many languages, living and extinct, to make a 'learnèd' poetry of "kindred form … Alpha and Omega, the Omnific Word. These stones have the silence of supreme creative power."[150] He became "an angle-titch to all" the stones' "corrugations and coigns," and as his interest in linguistic hybridization grew further, MacDiarmid began to insist that a new poetics of world language might, in fact, give voice to forms of genius present in all literatures and nationalities.[151] In juxtaposing "alternative value(s) of prime consequence," poetry – perhaps the mind itself, MacDiarmid suggested – could be unshackled from "our helpless submission to a fraction of our expressive possibilities."[152] "[D]espite minor differences," all restrictive forms of dialect and standardized language, he explained,

> employ only a very small fraction – and for the most part all the same
> fraction – of the expressive resources of the language in question … The
> reason why nineteen-twentieths of any language are never used is shrewdly
> related to the problem of the freedom of the consciousness. As Dostoevski
> said, all human organizations tend to stabilise and perpetuate themselves –
> to become a 'church' and to short-circuit human consciousness. This is
> most marked in our language-habit.[153]

The "particular habits of intellection" encouraged by industrial capitalism and the concomitant dominance of English had choked the public with "incrustations" masked with the names of thought and reason, for "what we call 'thought'," he explained, "is generally only 'rationalism' of our preconceived or inherent prejudices, or limitations, conscious or unconscious, of our powers of thought to suit our interests."[154] Drawing on the metaphysics of Bergson, MacDiarmid argued that the "misleading superficial 'crusts'" of prejudice had to be "broken through to release the

---

"high rocky place"; hvarf, meaning "turning, disappearance"; hurdifell, meaning "steep, rocky hill, full of downfallen boulders"; klett, meaning "shore rocks"; millya hellya, meaning "between the smooth rocks"; hellyina bretta, meaning "the steep or sloped rock"; hellyina wheeda, meaning "the white rock"; hellyina grø, meaning "the gray rock"; bakka, meaning "cliff, or steep rocky shore"; ayre, meaning "beach or piece of sandy shore"; kolgref, meaning "a pit for burning coals." See Jakobsen (1897), especially 79–80, 84–85, 88–89, 92.

[150] MacDiarmid *CP1* (1993) 423, 428, 429.
[151] MacDiarmid *CP1* (1993) 423.
[152] MacDiarmid *SP* (1992) 63; C. M. Grieve, Letter to *The Free Man* (December 9 1933) in MacDiarmid *LHM* (1984) 771.
[153] Grieve, Letter to *The Free Man* (December 9, 1933) in MacDiarmid *LHM* (1984) 771.
[154] Hugh MacDiarmid, "Constricting the Dynamic Spirit: We Want Life Abundant" (May 2, 1936), as in MacDiarmid *RT2* (1997) 548.

dynamic spirit which has no more to do with these incrustations than a running stream has to do with a layer of ice which forms on its surface."[155] To unleash this kind of dynamism, one had to seek *le mot libre*, a '"freedom of speech' in the real meaning of the term – something completely opposed to our language habits and freely utilising not only all the vast vocabulary these automatically exclude, but illimitable powers of word formation in keeping with the free genius of any language."[156] Thus, in contrast to the Basic English encouraged by Ogden and Richards, MacDiarmid felt that no adequate 'world' language could take the shape of rudimentary, seemingly straightforward intercultural communication. On the contrary, given the sheer diversity of language and literatures, only a difficult synthetic medium could resist the 'imperial' or broad 'ascendancy' model of international language, one which would see a single language feign translation of all human cultures, nationalities and knowledge through its idiom.

While MacDiarmid's vision for this collective medium was more literary, its politics more expressly aesthetic, he drew on parallel, practical models of 'Interlanguage', especially those advanced by contemporaneous communist thinkers in Britain. One was the suffragette and anti-fascist agitator E. Sylvia Pankhurst (1882–1960), whose 1926 book *Delphos: The Future of International Language* bemoaned that "language-barriers" still obstructed the "desire for world-friendship long latent amongst the kindlier and wiser people of all nations, and now quickened to an ardent flame by the agonies of the World-war."[157] Pankhurst believed, nonetheless, that the cause of "world-friendship" could be helped, in part, by developing an international "Interlanguage," if such a tongue could indeed *"provide the greatest possible intelligibility: therefore it must reach the widest possible internationality."*[158] In no way could it be characterized as global if other distinctively national modes of expression were eradicated through the official imposition of a more 'basic' form.

> The Interlanguage cannot be the creation of Governments. No Government attempts to dictate in regard to the grammar and syntax of the national tongue. Even in France such matters are left to the *Académie*. Government schools everywhere teach according to the generally accepted

---

[155] MacDiarmid *RT2* (1997) 548.
[156] Grieve, Letter to *The Free Man* (December 9, 1933) in MacDiarmid *LHM* (1984) 771.
[157] Pankhurst (1926) 6, 7. On Pankhurst's communism and its influence over her view of world language, see Romero (1987) 181–82.
[158] Pankhurst (1926) 7, 48 (emphasis in the original).

canons established by those who make a special study of the given subject. So with the Interlanguage: it will develop with the general consensus of world-opinion, led by the specialists. Its discovery and perfection must be mainly the work of philologists, working, not as propagandists and politicians, but as scientists and students. After the philologists will come the stylists; the poets, and thinkers.[159]

According to Pankhurst, no national tongue could be especially equitable serving as a "world auxiliary" language: to encourage global prosperity, the Interlanguage had to emerge from "definite scientific principles," the "general consensus of world philological opinion" and not forms of political and linguistic aggression.[160] To this end she promoted endowing "interlanguage research" and establishing "[c]hairs of synthetic philology ... in all universities."[161] Far from antagonizing existing national languages, the Interlanguage would operate "much like Latin," the "master-key to the most universally employed of the great speech-families" and would engender "a readier and deeper understanding" of many national tongues.[162] Employed in separate fields of human endeavor, national and international language could therefore work in harmony, she argued, their knowledge together doing much to "accelerate the spread of learning and the breaking down of social barriers."[163]

> Probably fifty (perhaps even thirty) years hence no one will be troubled by learning the Interlanguage. It will be acquired at the toddling age, side by side with the mother-tongue. The schools will be wholly bi-lingual. The Interlanguage and the native language will be used in teaching children, who will enter school with a familiar-speaking knowledge of both. For arithmetic, geometry, mathematics, astronomy, chemistry, the geography and history of foreign countries, the Interlanguage will be the vehicle of instruction, the national language being employed for the literature,

---

[159]   Pankhurst (1926) 86.
[160]   Pankhurst (1926) 44, 41, 87–88.
[161]   Pankhurst (1926) 87.
[162]   Pankhurst (1926) 50, 47. Pankhurst favored the adoption of Interlingua, a form of scientifically simplified, uninflected Latin (*Latino sine flexione* or IL) designed by the Italian mathematician and linguist Giuseppe Peano (1858–1932). According to Pankhurst, IL deserved the "palm for linguistic excellence, amongst the existing interlanguages ... because it is the first systematic attempt to build up an inter-European vocabulary on a consistent scientific basis; because it goes furthest in the elimination of grammar, under the guidance of observed tendencies in natural language; above all, because it is a logical etymological attempt to create the poor man's simplified Latin, which will open to him the nomenclature of the sciences, and will enable him to understand the prescription of his doctor and the legal phrases contained in the lawyer's presentment of his case." Pankhurst (1926) 84–85.
[163]   Pankhurst (1926) 50.

history, and geography of the native land. Elocution will be practised in both tongues.[164]

MacDiarmid felt likewise: a synthetic 'world' language would not threaten parochial idioms or diminish the importance of national literary expression. On the contrary, its essential quality would be its sheer complexity, its ability to house the exceptional character of all literatures while creating a "vivid sense" of their "very different historical, psychological and practical affiliations."[165] These polyglossic aspirations moved MacDiarmid beyond heteroglossia, synthesizing not dialects of the same tongue but the very 'classical' essences drawn from "the whole range of *welt-literatur*" and its forms of "many-sided knowledge."[166]

For MacDiarmid, no conflict existed between this vision and the nationalist ambitions of his early verse, for "the Communist Party of Great Britain," he noted, was "the only party which has the restoration to Scotland of a Parliament of its own as a plank in its platform."[167] More than any other progressive party, Communist Britain understood that Scotland "with its splendid old Radical and Left Wing tendency" had an essential role to play in a "United Front against Fascism and War," for if the country were to "pull its full weight on the side of Peace and the Commonwealth of Mankind at this great turning-point in human history," then the "possibility of the development of the Scottish culture" might be more fully ensured.[168] While a certain "fascisising pseudo-satisfaction" – that of Oswald Mosley (1896–1980) and the British Union of Fascists – was on the rise, even among some Scottish nationalists, MacDiarmid considered his "adequate synthetic medium" an essential

---

[164] Pankhurst (1926) 93–94.
[165] MacDiarmid (1943) 7.
[166] MacDiarmid *LP* (1994) 354.
[167] Hugh MacDiarmid, "Burns Today and Tomorrow" (1959) in MacDiarmid (1996a) 276. On MacDiarmid's "Nationalist Internationalism," see Hart (2010) 51–78.
[168] Hugh MacDiarmid, "Scottish Culture and Imperialist War" (1937) in MacDiarmid *RT3* (1998) 8. MacDiarmid believed a "Celtic USSR" – a socialist union of Ireland, Scotland and Wales – could diminish English ascendancy. See Hugh MacDiarmid, "Celtic Front" (1939) in MacDiarmid *RT3* (1998) 21–26. His interest in a "Celtic USSR" originated, in part, from his formative experiences during the First World War: "I was associated with soldiers," he later explained, "who were English, Welsh, Irish and so on. And I found that wherever these elements were brigaded together, we got on very well – Irish, the Welsh, the Scots but not the English. That caused me to think. And when I came back to Scotland, after serving several years for a war that was ostensibly fought for the determination of small nations – poor little Belgium and all that – I was suddenly confronted by the fact that I didn't know anything about my own country of Scotland, and I didn't see why on earth so many friends of mine had been slain fighting a war that we didn't know anything about." Hugh MacDiarmid, as interviewed in *Hugh MacDiarmid: No Fellow Travelers*, a film for the 1972 Edinburgh Festival, directed by Oscar Marzaroli (Ogam Films, 1972).

way by which human consciousness might be freed from the bonds that had long "cribbed, cabbined, confined" expression among the disenfranchised and impoverished.[169] Its idiom could help throw off "the bias given to human mentality by economic, political, religious, and other factors (including above all the *vis inertia*)," thus fulfilling Lenin's dictum that communism "must not abandon the old."[170] "Communism," he had declared – in remarks MacDiarmid fondly repeated –

> becomes an empty phrase, a mere façade, and the Communist a mere bluffer, if he has not worked over in his consciousness the whole inheritance of human knowledge ... made his own, and worked over anew, all that was of value in the more than two thousand years of development of human thought.[171]

However marginal a country's wealth, military power or global prestige might be, each "nation, once fully realised on its own terms" could articulate its political genius and aesthetic potential free from imperial forms of interference, whether such forms were officially imposed or culturally inherited.[172]

Given such influence, it is of little surprise that MacDiarmid hoped to wean 'classicism' and the 'classical' off abstract principles drawn from Greek and Roman civilization. Imitating or conforming to a kind of marmoreal, or neoclassical, reception of antiquity would inevitably limit vital expressions of contemporary national culture. "I have," he explained,

> no more use for 'consistency' of this kind than I have for any other shibboleth which tries to confine the infinite vitality and potentiality of humanity to any particular 'rut', and my objection to any such process is precisely the root of my nationalism. I do not believe in – or in the desirability of – any 'likemindness', any 'common purpose', any 'ultimate

[169] MacDiarmid *RT3* (1998) 8. Grieve, Letter to *The Free Man* (December 9, 1933) in MacDiarmid *LHM* (1984) 771. MacDiarmid *RT2* (1997) 548. See also Linehan (2000) 124–49, and Pugh (2006).

[170] MacDiarmid *RT2* (1997) 548. Lenin (1973) 439.

[171] Often incorrectly cited (as by MacDiarmid himself in *Lucky Poet*) as originating in Lenin's final speech from 1922, "Speech at a Plenary Session of the Moscow Soviet," these remarks are from a speech to the Russian Young Communist League given in October 1920. MacDiarmid knew this English translation from the 1933 book *Lenin*, written by the journalist Rajani Palme Dutt (1896–1974). Dutt argued of Lenin that he saw communism not as a "special body of doctrines or dogmas ... 'ready-made conclusions' to be learnt from textbooks," but rather as "the outcome of the whole of human science and culture, on the basis of an exact study of all that previous ages, including especially capitalist society, had achieved." Dutt (1933) 64–65. See the text of Lenin's speech in a later translation in Lenin (1974) 286. See also Hugh MacDiarmid, under the pseudonym "Arthur Leslie," "The Poetry and Politics of Hugh MacDiarmid" (1952) in MacDiarmid *SEHM* (1970) 29–30, as well as MacDiarmid *LP* (1994) xxxi–xxxii, 153, 355.

[172] Lyall (2006) 19.

objective', but simply in 'life and all that more abundantly', in the lifting of all suppressions and thwarting and warping agencies. My communism in this sense is purely Platonic.[173]

Despite these aspirations, however, Hugh MacDiarmid was no trained linguist. Christopher Grieve had come into the world with few social or educational advantages, having been raised by working-class parents in the mill town of Langholm. He had little exposure to the classics or even to contemporary European languages in his schooling at Langholm Academy. When he did move to Edinburgh in 1908 to train as a teacher at Broughton Junior Student Center – an institution whose curriculum was said to include the "Liberal Arts subjects – English, Languages, Maths, Science, History, Classics, Geography and Art" – the instruction he received was little more than basic.[174] Nonetheless, MacDiarmid continued to associate a certain creative magnetism (as well as his own frustration, sexual and otherwise) with the presence of classics, Greek in particular. He wrote later how

> ... greatly I love to hear a girl
> Back from three years at school
> Say to her father in fluent Greek
> 'Morning, old lad: like your eggs fried or boiled?
> Going to be cursed hot to-day
> But thank Heaven I've nothing to do
> But grill ἡλιάζω on the lawn
> And smoke καπνίζω a handful
> Of cigarettes σκιρτεῖν or χειροπηδᾶν'
> – All in Plato's or Xenophon's style and vocabulary,
> Only borrowing from the modern language
> The few words necessary
> For purely 20th century things,
> And wish I might be found so speaking too
> fhios dom fhéin some fine day
> Tho' I appreciate Euripides' use
> Of archaic diction too,
> But alas I can speak no Greek,
> And am now too old to learn.
> And nil leiyeas ogam air.[175]

---

[173] MacDiarmid *RT2* (1997) 549.

[174] Kerrigan (1988) xv. On his early education, see MacDiarmid *LP* (1994) 218–32, Lyall (2006) 56–65 and Gish (1984) 8–19.

[175] MacDiarmid *CP2* (1994) 797. ἡλιάζω, meaning "to bask in the sun"; καπνίζω, meaning "to smoke"; σκιρτεῖν, meaning to "leap, dance, frisk, buck" (commonly of calves); and χειροπηδᾶν,

MacDiarmid left Broughton without receiving a certificate to qualify him as a teacher. He was glad of it, though, it seems, for he did not want to become institutionalized by the "Scottish teaching profession," by those "hopeless Safety-Firsters ... conscienceless agents of the Powers-that-Be" who continually bend "the knee to Baal in this connexion or that, or grovelling together, obliged, in order to secure their jobs, to tout and belly-crawl."[176] Grieve's failures with formal schooling, however, only emboldened his belief that Scotland's guardian institutions remained irrepressibly Anglicized and British; they were therefore not suited to the educational needs of the more 'authentic' Scottish student, a student he considered not unlike himself. From a young age he had "an unusual readiness of speech," "a fluency in the use of a very extensive vocabulary," which later helped him become an ardent autodidact.[177] MacDiarmid's profound self-regard often saw him preen:

> I have never met anyone who has read anything like as much as I have, though I have known most of our great bookmen; and it is a common experience of mine to have professors and other specialists in this or that language or literature, or in subjects ranging from geology to cerebral localization or the physiological conditions of originality of thought, admit that I am far better read even in their own particular subject than they are themselves. The range of reference in all my books bears this out.[178]

MacDiarmid's "pugnacious pride" about his learnedness masked, as Scott Lyall suggests, an "insecurity as to the absence of an institutional basis for such learning," but, however much he fretted about his own lack of formal instruction, MacDiarmid took a decidedly dim view of the "Scottish Educational System as a whole," believing it had "been utterly de-Scoticized and adapted in the most shocking fashion to suit the exigencies of English Imperialism and the Capitalist system."[179] For that

---

meaning "to be bound, handcuffed." Some of the Greek used by MacDiarmid in this passage alludes obliquely to the capture of Dionysus in Euripides' *Bacchae* (434–60). On the source of the Irish Gaelic in the passage, see Introduction, p. 11n57.

[176] MacDiarmid *LP* (1994) 229.
[177] MacDiarmid *LP* (1994) 229.
[178] MacDiarmid *LP* (1994) 13.
[179] Lyall (2006) 57. MacDiarmid *LP* (1994) 229. MacDiarmid's pugnaciousness often found impressive expression in insults against the political and literary establishment. For example: "My aim all along has been (in Ezra Pound's terms) the most drastic *desuetization* of Scottish life and letters, and, in particular, the de-Tibetanization of the Highlands and Islands, and getting rid of the whole gang of high mucky-mucks, famous fatheads, old wives of both sexes, stuffed shirts, hollow men with headpieces stuffed with straw, bird-wits, lookers-under-beds, trained seals, creeping Jesuses, Scots Wha Ha'evers, village idiots, policemen, leaders of white-mouse factions

reason, in part, he felt that his "interest in *welt-literatur*," his own half-read exposure to many languages and literatures, was more than enough to carry synthetic verse "much further than it has yet been carried by anyone else known to me."[180]

As MacDiarmid pushed ahead with his synthetic experiments, he began composing in 1937 a sprawling poem, *Cornish Heroic Song for Valda Trevlyn*, dedicated to his second wife.[181] Drawing on "corrective" 'classical' values from literatures past and present, MacDiarmid no longer sought, as he had done for Scots, simply "a form of Doric which is no dialect in particular" but a "new literary language" drawn from many expressions of human speech.[182] In so doing, however, he felt himself at odds with, if not a rival of, the prior examples of Celtic revival and nationalist renaissance, especially the example of Yeats and the Irish Literary Revival.[183] As Hart has noted, MacDiarmid's earliest attempts to remake Scots came at something of cross purposes, marked with an ambivalence as to whether he wanted revival and preservation – a "project of linguistic recovery" – or something aimed more purely at experimentation and invention, what Hart calls the "avant-garde hypostatization of linguistic scholarship."[184] As the writing of *Cornish Song* progressed, MacDiarmid pushed the impulse towards revival and preservation aside emphatically, and instead embraced a transnational cosmopolitanism modeled on Arne Garborg (1851–1924) and Joyce whose "European range in technique and ideas" had "striking affinities" with his own practice.[185] "Theoretically – and to some extent practically," he told *The Free Man*,

and noted connoisseurs of bread and butter, glorified gangsters, and what 'Billy' Phelps calls Medlar Novelists (the medlar being a fruit that becomes rotten before it is ripe), Commercial Calvinists, makers of 'noises like a turnip', and all the touts and toadies and lickspittles of the English Ascendancy, and their infernal women-folk, and all their skunkoil skulduggery." MacDiarmid *LP* (1994) 149.

[180] MacDiarmid *LP* (1994) 13; C. M. Grieve, Letter to William Soutar (January 14, 1938) in MacDiarmid *LHM* (1984) 168.

[181] On the composition and publication history of *Cornish Heroic Song for Valda Trevlyn*, see Herbert (1992) 157–225. See also Bold (1990) 346–80.

[182] MacDiarmid *SP* (1992) 68; MacDiarmid *RT1* (1996) 237.

[183] On MacDiarmid's competitive relationship with Yeats, see Crotty (2011) 32–36. For his view of the Irish Revival, see also Bold (1985) 4–5.

[184] Hart (2010) 67.

[185] MacDiarmid *RT1* (1996) 237, 233. Alan Bold suggests that MacDiarmid's "opinion of Yeats was qualified by his disapproval of Yeats's 'pro-Fascist' politics. Yeats's Celtic Twilight period did not appeal to MacDiarmid though he felt that Yeats would be acknowledged as 'the greatest poet of his period in the English language ... mainly by virtue of his later work.'" Bold (1985) 8.

> I go further and agree with Joyce in regard to the utilisation of a multi-
> linguistic medium – a synthetic use, not of any particular language, but of
> all languages. Personally, I write in English, or in dialect Scots, or in
> synthetic Scots – or in synthetic English – with bits of other languages. I
> recognise the values of any language or any dialect for certain purposes,
> but where I am concerned with the free consciousness I cannot employ
> these – I must then find an adequate synthetic medium.[186]

Likening himself to Joyce, MacDiarmid insisted (often in pseudonymous
reviews praising his own work) that "in cerebral and psychological interpretation" he was doing for Scotland something "like what Mr Joyce has
done for Ireland," for "Mr M'Diarmid thus resembles Mr Joyce in his
attitude to the religion of his countrymen, to sexual problems, to political and cultural nationalism, to humbug, hypocrisy, and sentimentalism,
[and] in his preoccupation with 'interior revelation.'"[187] Whether or not
MacDiarmid's work reflected an authentically Joycean character, he did
go far, by sheer number, with his synthetic idiom, producing between the
years of 1937 and 1939 more than 20,000 lines of verse, an amount that
showed, he claimed, how he had left "Joyce at the starting-post so far as
the use of multi-linguistics is concerned."[188]

Yet, as critics of *Cornish Heroic Song* have suggested, MacDiarmid's
attempts at 'world' poetry still remained clearly marked with "the ineradi-
cability of English."[189] His idiom was not so much a global language
inflected with a wide range of syntactic patterns and complex code-
switching but instead an "English coloured with exotic quotations."[190]
When faced with the poem's synthesis, English readers can with relative
ease, as Hart observes,

> recognize textual representations of nonstandard language precisely
> because of the homogeneity of modern spellings and the parallel homoge-
> neity of phonemic representations of the nonstandard. Likewise, the devi-
> ations from English that are such a marked feature of MacDiarmid's
> poetry are largely sketched against more familiar syntactic and phonolog-
> ical canvasses, so that his "World Language" requires that we own a good
> dictionary (or have access to Google) but not, in Kamau Brathwaite's
> words, that we reprogram the very "software of the language."[191]

[186] Grieve, Letter to *The Free Man* (December 9, 1933) in MacDiarmid *LHM* (1984) 771.
[187] MacDiarmid *RT1* (1996) 238, 237.
[188] Grieve, Letter to William Soutar (January 14, 1938) in MacDiarmid *LHM* (1984) 168.
[189] Hart (2010) 68.
[190] Bold (1990) 360.
[191] Hart (2010) 68.

MacDiarmid's idiom – suffused in foreign intrusions – did ensure that his verse would appear "lexically deterritorialized" for English readers, especially when compared with other conventional or seemingly 'accessible' forms of poetry, yet it is important to note that this 'deterritorialization' was not absolute.[192] His idiom does not require to any substantive degree the parallel activation of multiple languages, semantically or phonologically, nor does it effectively generate meaning across multiple tongues – not as Joyce had tried perhaps to do more effectively through the "strange slithery slipping, dreamy nightmarish prose" of *Anna Livia Plurabelle*.[193] Its idioglossic fusion radiated what Æ called "wild meanings arising out of arcane affinities with other words, the whole gurgling and slipping like water."[194] Nevertheless, though many have thought the poem's apparent "erudition … sometimes bogus," MacDiarmid still believed his "huge" *Cornish Heroic Song* had "worked out all the interconnexions," the "mutual inter-activity" needed, to exorcise the "linguistic imperialism" of English ascendancy.[195] That tendency with its "magnificent insularity / Which is the pride of the Anglo-Saxon mind," he wrote, had been seen squarely in calls that Basic English be adopted "as the supra-national language," a reality which

> Would imply the acknowledgment of Anglo-Saxon supremacy.
> The proof of this is that all arguments adduced
> By Professor Richards and his colleagues
> Are all based on our manifold superiorities:
> We are richer, more numerous,
> More civilised, more virtuous than the rest!
> – All dreams of 'imperialism' must be exorcised,
> Including linguistic imperialism, which sums up all the rest.[196]

Criticism of Basic English notwithstanding, the synthetic poetry MacDiarmid was producing with a "vast international vocabulary" reflected parallel schemes for summing "up all the rest."[197] The self-taught insularity and crippling isolation MacDiarmid experienced on the

---

[192] Hart (2010) 68.
[193] Æ, "*Anna Livia Plurabelle*," *Irish Statesman* xi (December 29, 1928) 339, in Deming (1970) vol. 2: 396.
[194] Æ, "*Anna Livia Plurabelle*," *Irish Statesman* xi (December 29, 1928) 339, in Deming (1970) vol. 2: 396. For a comparative account of *Finnegans Wake* and *In Memoriam James Joyce*, see Freedman (1992) 253–73.
[195] Freedman (1992) 269; MacDiarmid *LP* (1994) 26; MacDiarmid *CP2* (1994) 790.
[196] MacDiarmid *CP2* (1994) 789–90.
[197] MacDiarmid *CP2* (1994) 790.

Shetlands made him more vulnerable, it seems, to delusions of apocalyptic clairvoyance: the "multitudinous waves of speech" his verse possessed had "language elements," he fantasized, which "effectively combined" could "utterly change the nature of man."[198]

> Even as the recently-discovered plant growth hormone,
> Idole-acetic acid, makes holly-cuttings in two months
> Develop roots that would normally take two years to grow,
> So perchance can we outgrow time
> And suddenly fulfil all history
> Established and to come.[199]

Addressing not just the Scottish but Anglophobic nationalists drawn from across "Cornwall, Scotland, Ireland, Wales," he exhorted "young Celts arise with quick tongues intact" to do what their "elders" lying "tongueless under the ocean of history" had reputedly not done: claim alternative 'classical' values and rive away "the heavy oily blood-rich tongue" of the "white whale," England's "hideous khaki Empire."[200] By effectively depleting any clear connection to Greek and Roman literature from the 'classical' and 'classicism', MacDiarmid dislodged classics from the once seminal role it played in enfranchising the English ruling class; the culturally enforced guardianship of the Celtic and other minority literatures was to be deposed. As the "identity-forming power" of classics shifted elsewhere, its authority was employed to serve 'new' postcolonial constituencies, where "Anglocentric" hegemony was not reinforced or seen as a given condition of British imperial inheritance.[201] "Red blasts of the fire come quivering – yes, we dare," MacDiarmid declared,

> To shoot out our tongues under the very noses of the English.
> The fate of our forefathers has not made us afraid
> To open our mouths and show our red glory of health;
> Nay, we sail again, laughing, on the crown of the sea,
> "Not so much bound to any haven ahead
> As rushing from all havens astern,"
> The deepest blood-being of the white race crying to England
> "Consummatum Est! Your Imperial *Pequod* is sunk."[202]

---

[198] MacDiarmid *CP2* (1994) 787, 781.
[199] MacDiarmid *CP2* (1994) 781.
[200] MacDiarmid (1977) 10.
[201] Haynes (2019b) 12; Crawford (2000) 30.
[202] MacDiarmid (1977) 10.

That his global synthesis possessed an eschatological vision, heralding new international unity, that this vision moreover did not subject particular forms of national expression to a forced assimilation imposed by "supra-national language," was never in doubt for MacDiarmid.[203] Yet the difficulty of his synthetic English – to say little of the fact that his work was forged in radical isolation – made finding a venue for publication troublesome, even among those considered more sympathetic to the avant-garde. Writing to Eliot in February 1938, MacDiarmid proposed a large, 4,000 to 5,000 line section of *Cornish Heroic Song* for publication in *The Criterion*, a portion he had re-entitled *Mature Art*. The work was

> a "hapax legomenon of a poem – an exercise in schlabone, bordatini, and prolonged scordatura" and it is, I am very safe in saying, a very advanced example of 'learned poetry', much of it written in a multi-linguistic diction embracing not only many European but also Asiatic languages, and prolific in allusions and 'synthetic poetry', demanding for their complete comprehension an extremely detailed knowledge of numerous fields of world-literature. At the same time the logic of the whole is quite clear, and most of the poem should be understood by almost anyone who reads while he runs – if he runs fast enough.[204]

Eliot responded politely, noting that, while his poem appeared to be an "extremely interesting, individual, and indeed very remarkable piece of work," *The Criterion* could not afford to print it in its entirety: "There can be no doubt that it is something that ought to be published, but the question is how, and by whom … I cannot get my colleagues to consider undertaking a work in verse of this size. I cannot afford to lose much money for them on poetry."[205] Instead, for *The Criterion*'s final issue of January 1939, Eliot chose to publish only a small, nine-page excerpt – the "First Appendix (Cornwall)" – of MacDiarmid's "extremely long unpublished poem."[206] Later, larger portions of *Mature Art* would appear in 1955 when MacDiarmid pledged himself to the "forward-straining vision" of Joyce, refashioning parts of his long poetic sequence as *In Memoriam James Joyce, From A Vision of World Language*.[207]

[203] MacDiarmid *CP2* (1994) 789.
[204] C. M. Grieve, Letter to T. S. Eliot (February 4, 1938) in MacDiarmid *LHM* (1984) 446.
[205] T. S. Eliot, Letter to C. M. Grieve (June 8, 1938) in MacDiarmid *LHM* (1984) 447.
[206] The poem was published under the title "Cornish Heroic Song for Valda Trevlyn." See MacDiarmid (1939a) 195–203. On Eliot's exchanges with MacDiarmid in this period, see Harding (2002) 101–2.
[207] Eugène Jolas, "Style and the Limitations of Speech," *Irish Statesman* (January 26, 1929) in Deming (1970) vol. 2: 399. On the composition of *In Memoriam James Joyce*, see Benstead (2019).

The initial difficulty, however, of finding a publisher – or indeed of appealing to a wide audience – did not faze MacDiarmid. Years earlier he had scoffed at the suggestion that *A Drunk Man Looks at the Thistle* ought to be divided into sections for the common reader. Such divisions would simply be "'hand-rails'" to "raise false hopes in the ingenuous minds of readers whose rational intelligences are all too insusceptible of realising the enormities of which 'highbrows' of my type are capable – even in Scotland."[208] In similar fashion he once demanded that the nationalist periodical *The Voice of Scotland* (of which he was then editor) maintain its "highly specialised appeal to the ablest minds," impacting opinion solely among the social, political and artistic elite, not among commoners.[209] A "continuity of culture" could be maintained not by popular acclamation but "by a very small number of people indeed – and these not necessarily the best equipped with worldly advantages."[210] Far from shirking the ambition of *Cornish Heroic Song*, MacDiarmid plunged himself further into work. Beginning a memoir, *Lucky Poet* (1943), to recount his "desperate" struggles, he cast himself as a 'learned' poet then embarking "on a course … in the teeth of all the opposition of those who hate versatility," and versatility, MacDiarmid boasted, was at the heart of *Cornish Heroic Song*: its virtuosic synthesis of languages deployed nothing less than what Coleridge called the mind's "prime & loftiest Faculty," the "esemplastic power" of human imagination.[211] "Is this not what we require?" he declared,

> Coleridge's esemplasy and coadunation
> Multeity in unity – not the Unity resulting
> But the mode of the conspiration
> (Schelling's *In-Eins-Bildung Kraft*)
> Of the manifold to the one,
> For, as Rilke says, the poet must know everything,
> Be μυριόνους (a phrase I have borrowed

---

[208] M'Diarmid (1926) viii.

[209] MacDiarmid (1939b) 19. On MacDiarmid's approach, see Baker (2016) 315–17.

[210] MacDiarmid (1939b) 19. Eliot (1939) 274.

[211] MacDiarmid *LP* (1994) xxxi, xvi, as first introduced by Coleridge in chapter 10 of *Biographia Literaria* (1817). Coleridge (1983) vol. 1: 168–71. On "esemplastic power," see also Samuel Taylor Coleridge, chapter 13 of *Biographia Literaria* in Coleridge (1983) vol. 1: 295–306 as well as Coleridge, *Notebook* 24.72 (February–June 1813), where esemplasy is contrasted with the "Imagunculation": "His Imagination, if it must be so called, is at all events of the pettiest kind–it is an Imagunculation–How excellently the German Einbildungskraft expresses this prime & loftiest Faculty, the power of co-adunation, the faculty that forms the many into one, *in eins Bildung*." Coleridge (1973) note 4176. See also Kathleen Coburn's explanatory notes on this passage in Coleridge (1973) note 4176.

From a Greek monk, who applies it
To a Patriarch of Constantinople),
Or, as the *Bhagavad-Gita* puts it, *visvato-mukha.*[212]

While Coleridge had coined "esemplastic" from the Greek, εἰς ἕν πλάττειν – an anglicization of Friedrich Schelling's notion, *Ineinsbildung* (the so-called interweaving of opposites) – MacDiarmid saw in the neologism further evidence that his synthetic techniques – those he had worked out with the "sudden jostling of contraries" of the "Caledonian antisyzygy" – had broader reach across history.[213] According to Coleridge it was Shakespeare, above all, who possessed not merely "poetic genius" but the "power of reducing multitude into unity of effect … modifying a series of thoughts by some one predominant thought or feeling."[214] That fact made Shakespeare "our myriad-minded" poet – an ἀνὴρ μυριόνους – whose mastery of "combination" and "intertexture" authenticated the aphorism (sometimes attributed to the Roman grammarian Pseudo-Acro): "Poeta nascitur non fit."[215]

Yet the 'myriad-mindedness' that Christopher Grieve was eager to arrogate to his own pseudonymous mask, Hugh MacDiarmid, was not as inborn as the grammarian imagined but one which MacDiarmid had acquired on the Shetlands, where by January 1942 he had spent nearly nine years "rowing about on lonely waters; lying brooding in uninhabited islands; seeing no newspapers and in other ways cutting myself completely away from civilised life."[216] As a student at Langholm Academy, Grieve had been considered "utterly unamenable to discipline of any kind," so much so that his headmaster spoke of a "terrible vein of recklessness" that ran through him.[217] It was the development of Grieve's irreverence, though, that drove him to invent Hugh MacDiarmid and his 'myriad-minded' global classicism. That classicism prized, he thought,

---

[212] In *Lucky Poet* (1943) MacDiarmid did not write μυριόνους but instead "mindedness" in Greek lettering, with no accentuation: "μινδεδνεος." See MacDiarmid *LP* (1994) 122, as well as MacDiarmid *CP2* (1994) 1016.

[213] On "esemplastic," see Coleridge (1983) vol. 1: 168–171. Smith (1919) 20, 4.

[214] Coleridge (1983) vol. 2: 20.

[215] From the Latin: "a poet is born, not made." From the Greek μυριόνους, Coleridge translated "myriad-minded." This can be roughly rendered as "complex and multiform in the variously versatile wisdom," as by House (1953) 33. Coleridge encountered the term μυριόνους in 1801 in Naucratius' eulogy of *Theodorus Studites* (759–826), published in William Cave's *Scriptorum Ecclesiasticorum Historia Literaria* (1688–99) vol. 1: 509–13; and in the 1743 edition, vol. 2: 8–11. Parts of the passages from Cave are reproduced in Coleridge's notebook 21.195 (December 1801). See Coleridge (1957) note 1070. On "Poeta nascitur non fit," see Ringler (1941) 497–504.

[216] C. M. Grieve, Letter to Neil M. Gunn (May 19, 1933) in MacDiarmid *LHM* (1984) 250.

[217] MacDiarmid *LP* (1994) 227.

not neoclassical forgeries of the Greek and Roman but a broad openness to the possibility that all nations could realize their genius "to classic effect as the Greeks themselves did."[218] However, even as MacDiarmid desired "something far more radical than a return to any 'classical' formalism," he himself possessed little fluency with those modern and ancient languages on which he purported to draw to classic effect.[219] Yet still he bullishly called on these, convinced that his being "an omnivorous reader" would help him bring together "vital contemporary poetry no matter in what European country or language it was being produced."[220] Thus while a sense of being cut off from an operative "continuity of culture" always haunted MacDiarmid, that "remoteness" proved to be a "stimulating rather than obstructive" force for his work.[221] Opposing "intellectual apathy" he claimed to work with

> ... material founded, like Gray's, on difficult knowledge
> And its metres those of a poet
> Who has studied Pindar and Welsh poetry,
> But, more than that, its words coming from a mind
> Which has experienced the sifted layers on layers
> Of human lives – aware of the innumerable dead
> And the innumerable to-be-born,
> The voice of the centuries, of Shakespeare's history plays
> Concentrated and deepened,
> 'The breath and finer spirit of all knowledge,
> The impassioned expression
> Which is in the countenance of all science.'[222]

Although MacDiarmid's forms of linguistic appropriation were compromised by his aggression, they still nonetheless fertilized powerful synthetic experiments in Scots and in English, experiments predicated not on nostalgia for the purity of classics but on a vision of greater global integration. This future MacDiarmid marked with spectacular fantasies of multilingual fusion on which the "whole life" of all traditions and cultures would depend.[223] To enact again what "Greece itself had done,"

---

[218] Hugh MacDiarmid, "Wider Aspects of Scottish Nationalism" (November 1927) in MacDiarmid *RT2* (1997) 61.
[219] MacDiarmid *RT2* (1997) 60.
[220] Hugh MacDiarmid, "The Future of Scottish Poetry" (June 24, 1933) in MacDiarmid *RT2* (1997) 209.
[221] Eliot (1939) 274. Carne-Ross (1979) 9.
[222] MacDiarmid *CP2* (1994) 1013, 1014.
[223] Carne-Ross (1979) 5.

to understand the "Ur-motives" that had shaped the fundamental form of all literatures, one had to turn the 'classical' impulse away from a fatal drift towards imitation.[224] The 'classical' was, for him, a predominantly local phenomenon, something that could be weaponized in forms of invention and resistance against English ascendancy. By deploying something akin to what the historian C. L. R. James (1901–89) defined as the "postcolonial prerogative," MacDiarmid believed the "native potentialities" of so-called minor languages and peripheral literatures could reconfigure themselves and upset the dominant linguistic, economic and social conditions of the present.[225] Mere revival, mere renaissance, could aspire to something beyond, a reality bent closer to the synthetic manifestation of a "world-soul," a "cosmical unity still more perfect."[226]

---

[224] MacDiarmid *LP* (1994) 375. See also MacDiarmid, "The Caledonian Antisyzygy and the Gaelic Idea" (1931–32) in MacDiarmid *SEHM* (1970) 74.

[225] MacDiarmid *RT2* (1997) 61. See also Gikandi (1996) 18–20, Bhabha (2004) 248–52, as well as Greenwood (2019) 576–607.

[226] MacDiarmid, "A Russo-Scottish Parallelism," in MacDiarmid *SEHM* (1970) 41.

Conclusion

Literary modernism developed on the 'Celtic fringe' in the early twentieth century at the same time as revivals of self-declared Celtic civilizations were underway and as the character of British and Irish classical education was also evolving in drastic fashion.[1] As such, classical reception was transformed in this period, in conjunction with – and in reaction to – nationalist narratives of rebirth. As classical learning slowly became dislodged from a central role in marking a sense of civic entitlement for the British Empire's elite, formal knowledge of Greek and Roman antiquity saw its wider cultural prestige diminish, leaving receptions of antiquity open to new forms of social, political and aesthetic reconfiguration. Hannah Arendt once observed that the "end of a tradition does not necessarily mean that traditional concepts have lost their power over the minds of men": the "full coercive force" of such "concepts" might be unleashed, she wrote, "only after its end has come" when the "well-worn notions and categories" of a tradition could become perhaps "more tyrannical as the tradition loses its living force and as the memory of its beginning recedes."[2] As classics and the institutions that governed its transmission gradually lost something of their living authority, the "well-worn notions and categories" of classical knowledge did indeed become more coercive: the range of possible receptions was widened, and the notion of the 'classical' became a far more pliable but volatile phenomenon. In this context of dislocation and recovery – a moment of "particularly intense hybridization" to borrow from Peter Burke's analysis in *Cultural Hybridity* – a variety of new, eccentric stylizations of classics also emerged.[3] Poets, artists, political extremists and

---

[1] On the 'Celtic fringe,' see Gikandi (1996) 29 and O'Connor (2006). See Introduction, pp. 3–5, especially n23.
[2] Arendt (2006) 25–26.
[3] Burke (2009) 66.

social controversialists offered radical attempts to revive or reinvent the cultural credibility of antiquity. Greek and Roman antiquity thus remained a vital and compelling force in both Anglophone politics and in the literature of the period, its "more tyrannical" appeal driving fresh, unconventional ways of engaging the ancients to new, experimental heights.

In 1925, in a piece she composed for *The Common Reader*, Virginia Woolf (1882–1941) observed this tyranny at work, noting in her essay "On Not Knowing Greek" how powerful yet enigmatic the place of ancient Greek had become. Although Woolf had spent some of her youth, as Quentin Bell (1910–96) noted, "fairly active learning both Greek and Latin," it then seemed "vain and foolish" to still "talk of knowing Greek, since in our ignorance we should be at the bottom of any class of schoolboys."[4] Greek had been "taught her by Miss Clara Pater, the sister of Walter Pater" and then by the Cambridge-educated suffragette Janet Elizabeth Case (1863–1937), but by 1925 Woolf felt her 'schoolboy' drills had done little to teach the true nature of the language.[5] However lamentable that was, she thought, too few scholars had addressed the deeper reality of classics' present position in European culture – namely, the "tremendous breach of tradition" – the "very real and very great" difficulties at play in struggling to 'know' the ancients.[6] "To our thinking the difficulty of Greek is not sufficiently dwelt upon," she observed, "chiefly perhaps because the sirens who lure us to these perilous waters are generally scholars of European reputation."[7] Haunted perhaps by her tutor's work in translating *Prometheus Bound* – Janet Case's efforts to "grope after Aeschylus' meaning in the uncertain light of what is left of the Trilogy" – Woolf insisted that forms of error and ignorance held all claims to knowing Greek under their sway.[8] No scholarly approach could lift the veil from the ancients, for the "few hundred years" that separated

---

[4] Bell (1972) 68. Virginia Woolf, "On Not Knowing Greek," in Woolf *EVW4* (1994) 38.

[5] Bell (1972) 68.

[6] Woolf *EVW4* (1994) 38. Virginia Woolf, "The Perfect Language," in Woolf *EVW2* (1987) 115.

[7] Woolf *EVW2* (1987) 115. On Woolf's sometimes dismissive attitude towards classical scholarship, and its effects on her knowledge of Greek, see Prins (2017) 38–45.

[8] Case (1905) 7. In the introduction to her translation, Case argued that the "attitude of Aeschylus" in *Prometheus* could not be deciphered. The "loss of the *Prometheus Unbound* leaves us sadly in the dark." Particularly difficult to discern were the "conflicting and often degrading conceptions" of Zeus. Against the "old crude Zeus" which Aeschylus had inherited from the "early myths" was set a "more spiritual conception of deity ... much in common with the monotheism of the Hebrew prophets" found in his other dramatic work. In composing *Prometheus*, however, "Aeschylus," she surmised, "had here such savage old tales to deal with that not even his genius could wholly purge them of their grosser elements, and he was confronted by the stubborn task of

"John Paston from Plato, Norwich from Athens," had made "a chasm which the vast tide of European chatter can never succeed in crossing."[9] Greek literature thus appeared written "in the shadow," "just on the far side of language" where ambiguity clouded "exactly what it means."[10]

> But again (the question comes back and back), Are we reading Greek as it was written when we say this? When we read these few words cut on a tombstone, a stanza in a chorus, the end or the opening of a dialogue of Plato's, a fragment of Sappho, when we bruise our minds upon some tremendous metaphor in the *Agamemnon* instead of stripping the branch of its flowers instantly as we do in reading *Lear* – are we not reading wrongly? losing our sharp sight in the haze of associations? reading into Greek poetry not what they have but what we lack?[11]

As Woolf saw it, the "whole of Greece" still lay heaped behind every line, every word of Greek literature, yet claims to understand that heap required a "dangerous leap through the air."[12] "When we read Chaucer," she explained, "we are floated up to him insensibly on the current of our ancestors' lives, and later, as records increase and memories lengthen, there is scarcely a figure which has not its nimbus of association, its life and letters, its wife and family, its house, its character, its happy or dismal catastrophe."[13] By contrast, few such associations could be easily drawn out for Greek literature. Yet it was because the Greeks had left only "their poetry, and that is all" that the imagination was nonetheless compelled to "fashion itself surroundings," to import new details with which to stamp the more impersonal nature of Greek.[14] "[S]ome background, even of the most provisional sort" had to be drawn from elsewhere even when such backgrounds could result in further "sources of misunderstanding, of distorted and romantic, of servile and snobbish passion."[15]

---

grafting his own more spiritual conception on the rugged stock of early myth." Shelley understood that stubborn task and took note of Aeschylus' failure to fully moralize Zeus in *Prometheus* "making good spring from the seeming cruelty." Recognizing the "impossibility of reconciliation between Prometheus and the malevolent Zeus of the *Prometheus Bound*," the English poet "abandoned Aeschylus in his own *Prometheus Unbound*" and gave "his own solution of the difficulty by recasting the *dénoüement*," overwriting an absent original with "certain arbitrary discretion." See Case (1905) 8, 13, 8, 11–12, 11, 8 as well as Percy Bysshe Shelley, "Author's Preface," in Shelley (2002). On Woolf's efforts to translate *Agamemnon*, see Prins (2017) 35–56.

[9] Woolf *EVW4* (1994) 39.
[10] Woolf *EVW4* (1994) 39, 50, 45.
[11] Woolf *EVW4* (1994) 48.
[12] Woolf *EVW4* (1994) 48, 44.
[13] Woolf *EVW4* (1994) 39.
[14] Woolf *EVW4* (1994) 39.
[15] Woolf *EVW4* (1994) 39, 49–50.

With the best will in the world the translators are bound to stamp their individuality or that of their age upon the text. Our minds are so full of echoes that a single word such as 'aweary' will flood a whole page for an English reader with the wrong associations. And such is the power of the Greek language that to know even a little of it is to know that there is nothing more beautiful in the world.[16]

These difficulties, though, were not unique to the 'amateur' experience of Greek, she thought, but evidence rather of an all too human compulsion to 'fill in' the apparent emptiness of ambiguity, of 'not knowing'. Seduced by the classical, one might invent from variously "incongruous odds and ends" an "all the more strange" vision of the ancients, which, though forged in ignorance or in partial knowledge, could be passed off as bearing "slight resemblance to the real meaning of Greek."[17] "Back and back," she declared, "we are drawn to steep ourselves in what, perhaps, is only an image of the reality, not the reality itself, a summer's day imagined in the heart of a northern winter."[18]

By questioning the possibility of an authentic translation 'matching the original', Woolf presented Greek as a volatile linguistic enigma whose sheer difficulty invited one to stamp the classical with the contemporary, to re-embed or reorganize the ancient along a wide spectrum of current knowledge and ignorance. Thus to translate, allude, adapt or appropriate aspects of antiquity was not to transfer something stable into the present but rather to work openly in an "ethically charged and politically engaged act of interpretation," one in which a profound sense of "linguistic estrangement" provoked a fusion, a fluid hybridization of the past and present.[19] Woolf's remarks – what Nancy Worman has called a "feminist critique of imperial adventuring" and "triumphalist Hellenism" – glimpse suggestively at a growing pattern at work in the receptions then given to classical learning.[20] As classics' authority diminished among elite institutional communities, it remained subject to "continual processes of recontextualization, of recombination in the widest variety of forms of politics, religion, and social life."[21] With respect to literature, these processes often hybridized or set classics more expressly in a comparative relation to modern vernacular literatures, sometimes in ways that advanced the

[16] Woolf *EVW2* (1987) 118.
[17] Woolf *EVW4* (1994) 38, 39.
[18] Woolf *EVW4* (1994) 48.
[19] Venuti (2019) 40. Prins (2017) 37.
[20] Worman (2019) 5.
[21] Haynes (2019b) 6.

political, social, economic and aesthetic interests of some 'Englishness',
and at other times in ways that resisted the dominance then being ceded
to or encoded in English as a language, literature and institutional power.
Thus growing avant-garde interest in antiquity during this period was
bred in oscillation, caught between forces or "traditions of appropriation"
and those of "resistance" as well.[22] For nearly a century prior, a reputedly
authentic knowledge of Latin and Greek (or at least instruction in them)
had played a relatively secure role in Victorian society. The growth and
professionalization of university instruction in classics had been linked to
the "expanding bourgeois demand for an education which would make
gentlemen of their sons" and thus help legitimize the emerging commercial classes.[23] Classical education thus became, for a time, a critical mechanism in settling the broader cultural processes of "distinction and social
exclusion," learning Greek and Latin being essential to anchoring a sense
of "self-recognition and social closure" among an "assimilated noble-
bourgeois élite."[24] However, as the century drew to a close, the "linguistic
hierarchy of Greek, Latin, and English" that had been a marked feature
of British social stratification began to break down, leaving classics'
ability to resolve questions of "social incorporation and enfranchisement"
in a more volatile state.[25] "The contest," Stray observes, "between an aristocratic ideology of indeterminacy (grace and mysterious style) and bourgeois ideology of determinacy (the following of explicit rules)" had long
been enacted in Victorian society through "the differential status and
definition of Greek and Latin."[26]

> The bourgeois groups who completed the social ascent to gentlemanly
> status may have seen Greek learning as something above them; Latin,
> however, formed the material for their maintenance of barriers against
> their aspirant inferiors ... the centre of gravity of such exclusionary prac-
> tices moved down the social scale, paralleled by a gradual shift from the
> predominance of Greek to that of Latin.[27]

Yet as educational practices and university curricula evolved, the "centre
of gravity" moved further still, shifting the social ladder and resetting the
significance of antiquity primarily in terms of its relationship with the

---

[22] Burke (2009) 67.
[23] Stray (1998) 21.
[24] Stray (1998) 29.
[25] Stray (1998) 32.
[26] Stray (1998) 32.
[27] Stray (1998) 32.

dominant national vernacular: English.[28] In this context calls for formalized ways of studying of English letters first became louder at British and Irish universities, there being something "national and classical in the genius of English literature."[29]

By the mid-1880s, as universities took on a central role in determining what the critic John Churton Collins (1848–1908) called "the organization and control of a system of advanced popular education," it was thought that the "genius of the Schools" had to be brought into "harmony with the genius of national life."[30] No longer would mere adherence to "the local interests of specialism and Philology" suffice: institutions of higher education had to cultivate what Robert Bulwer-Lytton (1831–91) called "the preservation of what is national and classical in the genius of English literature."[31] Yet, even as the push to 'classicize' the vernacular grew stronger, fear abounded too. Would this "specious but perilous gift" only "disturb or weaken the existing classical system"?[32] "The study of the classics," wrote Henry Howard Molyneux Herbert (Earl of Carnarvon),

> – the most useless if inaccurate – is, if exact, the best instrument for forming the mind; it has stood the test of "infinite time," and it has been immemorially honoured in the University. Further, it is not too much to say that a real understanding of English literature is impossible without a knowledge of at least Latin. For these reasons it seems to me that a further reduction of classical instruction in the supposed interests of English literature would be only a melancholy delusion, and a fresh and mischievous tribute to the "smattering" tendencies of modern education.[33]

Calls for the study of English were often predicated explicitly on connecting modern literature with the Greek and the Roman. Matthew Arnold notably insisted that "the great works of English literature" could be "taken in conjunction with those of Greek and Latin literature in the

---

[28] Stray (1998) 32.

[29] Collins (1891) 115.

[30] Collins (1891) 149. George Goschen (1831–1907), president of the London Society for the Extension of University Teaching, noted in 1887 that there was "no subject in which there is greater demand for courses of Lectures than English Literature," even though many universities across the United Kingdom had yet to take serious steps to meet this need. Goschen (1887) 381. On the "extramural" nature of early study in English literature, see Lawrie (2014). For a series of primary source materials on English studies in Victorian Britain, see Bacon (1998).

[31] As quoted in "Petition Addressed to Hebdomadal Council for the Foundation of a School of Modern Literature," *Quarterly Review* 164.327 (January 1887) 256, as cited in Collins (1891) 115.

[32] "English at the Universities – III, Letters from Mr. Bright, Mr. Gladstone, and the Earl of Carnarvon," *Pall Mall Budget* 34.949 (December 2, 1886) 8.

[33] "English at the Universities – III, Letters from Mr. Bright, Mr. Gladstone, and the Earl of Carnarvon," *Pall Mall Budget* 34.949 (December 2, 1886) 8.

final examination for *Literae Humaniores*."[34] However, anything less than teaching English with the ancients in clear sight would be, as William Gladstone also suggested, "injurious to the interests of education."[35] Conversely, for others, formalizing English literary studies was seen as a means to wholly renew the classical system, to give "more life and reality to the method of studying Greek and Latin authors."[36] "[T]here can be no doubt," observed Collins, "that they would greatly gain in interest and educational value if their relations to Modern Literature were made more generally intelligible."[37] Nevertheless, Oxford and Cambridge both remained slow to bring the study of modern English literature into their curricula, for, as D. J. Palmer noted, it was "one matter to illustrate the debt of English literature to the Classics, and therefore to expect a student of English to know something of Greek and Latin literature, but quite another matter to design a school on the basis of such a relationship."[38] However, the reluctance of these prestigious institutions did not deter other provincial colleges and universities from sanctioning English as a form of "broad cultural education" in "the spirit of Classics."[39] Used

---

[34] Matthew Arnold, as in Collins (1891) 107–8. See also Arnold (1910) and Arnold (1977) 500–1.

[35] English at the Universities – III, Letters from Mr. Bright, Mr. Gladstone, and the Earl of Carnarvon," *Pall Mall Budget* 34.949 (December 2, 1886) 8. It was to be taken for granted, William Walter Merry (1835–1918), rector of Lincoln College, wrote in 1886, that the subject "be taught in connection with the Greek and Latin classics. It seems to me the only scholarly method of such a study. A knowledge of the classics may not indeed be necessary to the ordinary reader for the appreciation and enjoyment of English literature, but it is quite indispensable to the student of English literary history. Without such a knowledge much of the matter and form of our literature can have no intelligible meaning." As quoted in Collins (1891) 104.

[36] Merry, as in Collins (1891) 104.

[37] Collins (1891) 104–5.

[38] Palmer (1965) 85. Since the University Commission of 1877, Oxford and Cambridge had in fact been slowly adapting their curricula to meet growing interest in English studies. At first, though, it was the scientific study of English Philology that was stressed, not the humanist examination of literature. Oxford conferred some legitimacy on the academic study of English in 1885, naming a specialist in Germanic languages, Arthur Sampson Napier (1853–1916), as the first Merton Professor of English Language and Literature. Napier's approach, however, remained mostly philological (notably to John Churton Collins' displeasure – he vowed to free English literature "from its present degrading vassalage to Philology"). It would not be until 1904 when Sir Walter Raleigh (1861–1922) took up the newly established Chair of English Literature at Oxford that its study moved beyond largely philological considerations to include the study of literature in its "wide acquaintance with human life and human passion." At Cambridge, English with a heavy philological emphasis was likewise admitted for study in 1878 under the umbrella of the medieval and modern languages tripos. However, it was not until 1917 that a Cambridge University report recommended that the modern languages tripos be separated and an independent English literature tripos be created. Arthur Quiller-Couch (1863–1944), then holder of the King Edward VII Chair of English Literature, warmly supported it. See Collins (1891) 4; Walter Raleigh, *Shakespeare* (1907) 3, as in Palmer (1965) 124.

[39] Palmer (1965) 79.

to forge greater "agreement on fundamental social goals" – perhaps even to impose a "sense of spiritual continuity" on the nation – English studies made especially significant inroads in the more geographically 'peripheral' areas of the United Kingdom and, eventually, across the empire itself.[40] As such, it became an "ideal carrier for the propagation of the humanist cultural myth of a well-educated, culturally harmonious nation."[41] Prominent professors of literature and history in Ireland, Scotland and Wales were some of the first academics to take up its cause. It has been suggested that because their relationship to the core of Englishness was more "ephemeral," those on the "periphery – the Celtic fringe, and even the emerging lower classes – came to have greater emotional investment in an invented British nationalism than the old aristocratic classes did."[42] English literature, with its images of an "old thatched and timbered romantic England," possessed an appeal that promised not only greater national cohesion but the extension of broad civic privileges beyond the British Isles as well.[43] Across the empire devotion to the 'civilizing' spirit of its literature motivated many fledgling academics, for just as it was thought that "English cultural history and the internal history of the race" might advance "the privilege of citizenship" on the British Isles, so too was knowledge of England's literary inheritance increasingly regarded elsewhere as "an intrinsic measure of the progress of 'civilization'."[44] In this way the study of English literature became an imperially minded *via media*, a "class-conscious alternative" between both the reputed rigor and elitism of classics on one hand and the "utilitarianism and the vulgarities of a *declassé* society" on the other.[45]

Advocates of Celtic languages and their revival, however, were often incensed that English literature had been proclaimed an "instrument of great moral and spiritual influence," and accorded a "special rôle at the centre of the humanities, supplanting the declining Classics."[46] Both Matthew Arnold and Henry Morley (1822–94), professor of English

---

[40] Court (1992) 14.
[41] Court (1992) 14. See also Eagleton (1996) 23–24, and Palmer (1965) 78.
[42] Gikandi (1996) 29. See Introduction, pp. 3–5, especially n23. As the Newbolt Report noted, it could be said that "the teaching of academic English began in Scotland and Ireland." Newbolt Report (1921) 243.
[43] Court (1992) 155.
[44] Court (1992) 132. See, for example, the account of Mungo William MacCallum's experiences and influence in Wales and Australia, in Dale (2012) 65–77, as well as the analyses of John Nichol's and David Masson's careers in Scotland, in Court (1992) 123–41.
[45] Court (1992) 155.
[46] Palmer (1965) 169.

Literature at University College London, had tried, throughout the 1860s, to insist on a "union of native races" across Britain and Ireland, on the essential "brotherhood" between "Celts, Gael and Cymry" and the "Teutonic races, or the Anglo-Saxons" – but both nonetheless largely presented Celtic influence as significant so far as it had contributed to the flowering of English literature.[47] Morley put it squarely in 1867 when he asserted that "without help of the Celts the Anglo-Saxons could not have produced a Shakespeare."[48] "[T]he honest, earnest, practical, God-fearing Anglo-Saxon mass," he argued, "was leavened with the artistic feeling of the Celt," and "there it was, and only there, that the best energy of a true literature appeared in England, before the establishment of a dominating centre of thought among men gathered from all districts to the capital."[49] The presentation of the Celt as indispensable to the apotheosis of the "solid Saxon mind" did not mitigate the Anglophobia that pervaded Irish writing in the 1890s.[50] As noted, while advocates of the Literary Revival sought to generate new 'classical' forms for the country's vernacular literature(s), the value of English itself and its relationship to Irish literary work was hotly debated. At Trinity College, Dublin, professors Edward Dowden (1843–1913) and J. P. Mahaffy were perhaps the most vociferous agitators for English literary studies, seeing its growth as an extension of the legacy left by Greek and Roman antiquity. Though Mahaffy did bemoan the diminishment of Latin – "the purest, the most grammatical, the most logical idiom which a man could learn" – he nonetheless accepted the "growth of English influence and English speech" as "a matter of certainty" that would ensure the "commercial and political progress of the world."[51] Bolstering this new "imperial language" across the university would not only help secure greater political consensus on the British Isles but ward off "modern confusion" as well.[52] "The test point is this," he declared, "which is made compulsory, the imperial or the local tongue? If the former, we are advancing, if the latter, we are receding, in civilisation."[53] The legacy of Greece and Rome would be best advanced when English attained the position once occupied by Latin – a language to be acquired by all educated classes across Europe.

---

[47] Morley (1871) 279, 283. On Morley's contributions to English studies in the United Kingdom, see Palmer (1965) 50–54 as well as Court (1992) 141–48.
[48] Morley (1871) 283.
[49] Morley (1871) 283.
[50] Solly (1898) 305.
[51] Mahaffy (1896) 782, 791, 784.
[52] Mahaffy (1896) 784, 788.
[53] Mahaffy (1896) 784–85.

It is obvious that the use of one common language in addition to the mother tongue of each people would produce an enormous saving of time, and tend to the nearer and better knowledge of the world's progress among them all. This position of the common language was once attained by Greek, then in a wider sense by Latin, both of which commanded not only the business transactions, but even the literature of the world for some centuries.[54]

Provided that English remained the primary "means of easy and wide communication" in matters "of the courts, of Parliament, of science," Mahaffy was content to have some "indulgence and consideration" given to some tongues whose existence was thought to reflect "purely national sentiment."[55] "[L]et us have poetry and prose in every tongue," he declared:

> let the Scotch heart beat faster to the jargon of Burns, or the Dorsetshire to that of Barnes; let us have the flavour of each nationality, and the perfume of its finest bloom, expressed in myriad tongues; but when we come to international questions, imperial policy, discoveries in science, history, economic and social problems, we should surely insist upon some limitation in the vehicle employed.[56]

Dowden, a staunch Unionist and prominent scholar of Shakespeare, likewise saw English as an essential tool for maintaining national unity and advancing global progress. Eager to see its study elevate the "democratising of literature" above the "merely utilitarian" and "merely commercial," Dowden stressed the humane value of English's "higher spirit," a spirit whose careful examination could help keep democracy from drifting towards indecency and vulgarity.[57] Though present forms of democracy were sometimes derided as "devoted to mediocrity" and "intellectual sterility," "literary research" he thought provided a wide-ranging means to "save the democracy, if possible, from what is unfruitful in its own way of thinking and feeling."[58] With an "exact and thorough" approach, its careful study would cultivate a

> temper of mind ... fitted to hold in check the rash ardours of the democratic spirit, a temper of mind at once courageous and cautious, strong in serious hopes and free from illusions, faithful to the best traditions of our

---

[54] Mahaffy (1896) 795.
[55] Mahaffy (1896) 784, 785.
[56] Mahaffy (1896) 785.
[57] Dowden (1895) 7, 6, 31.
[58] Dowden (1895) 6, 30, 9.

forefathers and not bound in subjection to them, but rather pressing forward to those high ends towards which they and we together work.[59]

In this way Dowden felt that a "people educated and intellectually alive" might have their past illuminated, their sympathies widened; rather than remain in a "state of half-culture," a "multitude of readers" could learn how to "meet this half-culture with a culture less incomplete, trained to exact methods of thought and observant of the details of fact."[60] Like Mahaffy, he too remained highly skeptical of forming any "separate channels" in British letters, treating those who sought to "cut for the flow" of "several streams of sentiment in literature" with studied distance.[61] Though Dowden had heard of "plaintive demands for an Irish literature with a special character of its own," of the "enthusiasm with which Welsh bards are listened to at the national Eisteddfods" and even of the "spirit of Scottish patriotism," he was convinced that political and aesthetic unity could be best maintained in English.[62] The variety, the "distinctive genius characterising each of the peoples of Scotland, Wales and Ireland," would be better explored within "the unity of our literature," a unity that "if twisted together should make up a cord which is both strong and delightfully coloured."[63]

Although these other traditions had claims of being "rooted in the soil," Dowden saw the study of English as essentially "Imperial or cosmopolitan" like classics, and thus he dismissed the "conscious effort to promote a provincial spirit" across literature.[64] No clamor, no "flapping a green banner in the eyes of the beholders," he warned, could persuade those "who 'speak the tongue that Shakespeare spake'" to "nurse the dream of four separate streams of literature."[65] In this way Dowden saw the nationalism of the fledgling Literary Revival as provincial.[66] Its kneejerk impulse to court "dear delusions" – to "view all things through an emerald mist" – was a "huge absurdity," as, for example, when on reading "a popular life of Lord Edward Fitzgerald [*sic*],

[59] Dowden (1895) 30, 13.
[60] Dowden (1895) 6, 9, 8, 10.
[61] Dowden (1895) 16.
[62] Dowden (1895) 15.
[63] Dowden (1895) 17.
[64] Dowden, as quoted in Boyd (1918) 156. See Kiberd (1996) 159–60.
[65] Dowden (1895) 18, 15.
[66] The notion, as Kiberd writes, that the Revival itself comprised a variety of attempts to "revolt *against* imitative provincialism completely escaped Dowden." On Dowden's struggle with cultural politics of Irish revivalism, see Kiberd (1996) 160, 159–65, and Murphy (2017) 105–10.

published in Dublin," Dowden found himself outraged with the following poetical exordium.[67]

> "Not Greece of old in her palmiest days, the Greece of Homer and Demosthenes, of Aeschylus, Euripides, and Sophocles, of Pericles, Leonidas, and Alcibiades, of Socrates, Plato, and Aristotle, of Solon and Lycurgus, of Apelles and Praxiteles, not even this Greece, prolific as she was in sages and heroes, can boast such a lengthy bead-roll as Ireland can of names worthy of the immortality of history." How partial, then, have been the awards of history! How true the saying that the world knows nothing of its greatest men! And how modest the writer of this life of Lord Edward Fitzgerald, to set forth the bead-roll of Greece in such ample detail and to throw the veil of a general statement over the glories of his native land! If in the Irish literary movement we are to step to such a tune as this, I think on the whole I should rather fall out of the ranks, or even step to music as rhetorical as that of "Rule Britannia."[68]

For Dowden, "art & literature as a whole" would "move with the general movement of society ... & reflect its ideals" but "the poet & artist," he argued, still "ought seldom to meddle with the details of practical politics."[69] Therefore no matter how loud "literary claims of contending nationalities" might grow, artists and students of history had to remain "patient, disinterested, and exact," in a word "to hold in check, chiefly in ways that are indirect, the superficial views, the partisan representations, the crude generalisations of the amateur sociologist and political manipulator of half knowledge."[70] "Let an Irish poet teach his countrymen to write a song free from rhetoric," he declared,

> free from false imagery, free from green tinsel, and with thoroughly sound workmanship in the matter of verse, and he will have done a good and a needful thing. Let an Irish prose writer show that he can be patient, exact, just, enlightened, and he will have done better service for Ireland, whether he treats of Irish themes or not, than if he wore shamrocks in all his buttonholes and had his mouth for ever filled with the glories of Brian the Brave.[71]

---

[67] Dowden (1884) 164–65. See also Dowden (1895) 18.

[68] Dowden (1895) 18.

[69] MS No. 3124/4, Manuscripts Room, Trinity College Library, as in Court (1992) 151.

[70] Dowden (1895) 15, 13.

[71] Dowden (1895) 20. Yeats publicly criticized Dowden's condescension, writing that, though the professor had been "for years our representative critic" in Ireland, he had given the "new creative impulse" of Irish literature "too little attention." Yeats, "To the Editor of the *Daily Express*, 26 January 1895," in Yeats *CL1* (1986) 431.

The views that Dowden found clumsy in various Revival-era manipulations of the literary and the political, had done little to arrest what he saw as an inexorable reality, namely that modernity's "larger movement" had made English letters a new "head-quarters of literature," a place which nonetheless still had to be conceived "aright" using "a broad outline map of the whole course of history, a map not crowded with petty names, but clearly setting forth the facts of prime importance."[72]

The convergence of English studies with classical learning proved consequential. Though it would take at least another fifty years, the expansion of liberal arts education swept across the Anglo-American world, and the study of England's 'national' literature slowly stepped out from classics' shadow, overtaking it as a seemingly more democratic, more accessible "status marker" among those "seeking distinction in relation to ... perceived superiors and inferiors."[73] More immediately, however, the commingling of English and classics stoked fierce resistance in what might be called the linguistically 'peripheral' parts of the British Empire. As Jason Harding and John Nash have observed, "the near-global spread of English by the dawn of the twentieth century, and in particular its dominant status in colonies and former colonies, encouraged dissonant voices of artistic and linguistic experimentation, of resistance and of co-optation."[74] Across Ireland, Scotland and Wales, a widespread – though politically and aesthetically diverse – backlash openly disputed the coming of English as an all-pervasive language for commerce, journalism, literature, the academy and government. Armed with nationalized claims regarding the classical character of ancient Gaelic and Brythonic languages, these reactive, revival movements aimed to resuscitate the Celtic and to resist the encroachment of English on a national scale.[75] In such anti-colonial or postcolonial contexts of the early twentieth century, receptions of classical antiquity often emerged as important sites in the struggle between metropolitan and provincial interests, providing what Emily Greenwood has called "a rich source of literature and myth" to circumvent (or perhaps even to advance) the notion of "'English literature' as a national institution."[76] What is especially notable about these 'Celtic' contestations is that they first arose as the very claims of England's

---

[72] Dowden (1895) 421, 420.
[73] Stray (1998) 29.
[74] Harding and Nash (2019) 13.
[75] Kiberd (1996) 136–54.
[76] Greenwood (2019) 577.

own national 'tradition' were still openly under dispute in the curricula of many British and Irish institutions of higher education. Though attempts to enshrine English literature as canonical were pervasive, the literature then possessed only the promise of becoming a so-called "single 'great' or 'classical' tradition."[77] That threat alone, however, emboldened a number of writers towards revival and resistance. In an effort to displace, or at the very least obstruct, English dominance, many agitators fused a rabid Anglophobia with broader efforts to distinguish alternative channels of national culture on the British Isles.[78] Though the resulting movements of 'Celtic' resistance would inflame popular rancor and cruder expressions of nationalist sentiment, their impact was also felt in more unexpected ways. Principally, they nurtured a complex, multiform "aesthetic of renovation" across various 'Celtic' engagements in English literature – one whose renewed openness to linguistic hybridization and creative invention helped articulate their formative, 'peripheral' experiences of modernity on "new grounds of recognition and understanding."[79]

This aesthetic permeated the eccentric receptions that Yeats, Joyce, Jones and MacDiarmid gave to classical literature, receptions which complicated the widespread ideological animus against the growth and dominance of English. On the whole their work oscillates between two poles – first, a belief that preserving and fusing the classical and Celtic together could somehow be effective for immediate political and social ends and then, also, an avant-garde impulse to disrupt, to twist Celtic and classical *residua* in more experimental forms of self-critical exploration and critique. At one end classical learning was sought after because its prestige, it was thought, could be recentered or recontextualized as a key accelerant in the heroic romance of national rebirth. As a catalyst in these coming-of-age stories, the classics were enlisted to contest the dominance of conventional English, giving voice to what Yeats called "the spontaneous expression of an impulse which has been gathering power for decades."[80] At the other end, however, nationalized mergers of the classical and Celtic fell victim to deepening skepticism, one which nonetheless generated, in its wake, further exploits of stylistic divergence. Often these exploits rearticulated the collective appetite for a national vernacular made classical, but they did so also while radically undercutting the very

---

[77] Greenwood (2019) 577.
[78] Gikandi (1996) 27–29.
[79] Castle and Bixby (2019) 14.
[80] Yeats, "To the Editor of the *Daily Express*, 26 January 1895," in Yeats *CL1* (1986) 431.

same phenomenon simultaneously. The broad arc of Yeats' engagement with Greek antiquity encompasses the tension, from his neo-Romantic desire to forge for the Irish "plays and poems like those of Greece" to the *saeva indignatio* of his later poetry and drama.[81] There claims of Hellenic beauty no longer advanced the prospect of a new classical age in Ireland but stood only in stern counterpoint to modernity, "like a tightened bow, a kind / That is not natural in an age like this."[82] Joyce, by contrast, believed that ancient Greece, like Ireland and ancient Egypt, was dead and beyond revival or resurrection. In *Ulysses*, however, he set forth elements of the *Odyssey* as a "cracked lookingglass" through which pivotal events from Dublin, June 16, 1904, could at once be skewed and illuminated.[83] The collage of narrative experiments that resulted – experiments Joyce developed around notions of error, satire and misinterpretation – willfully mistranslated the 'original' classical world, throwing light on the folly of using a Homeric pattern as a master key to unleash Irish nationality. In this way Joyce's reconfigurations of antiquity in *Ulysses* did not order, or tame, the ragged forces of quotidian Dublin: they extorted instead, by comic misalignment, the revivalist obsession with Homer, with his power to make Ireland a 'nation once again'.

While David Jones regarded Joyce as "super-sensitive" to "the formal problems of art" and the "artistic dilemmas" of modernity, he did not see a "radical incompatibility," a satirical pastiche in *The Anathemata*'s alignments of mythologies and languages.[84] The poem was rather a "series of fragments, fragmented bits, chance scraps really, of records of things, vestiges of sorts and kinds of *disciplinae*" whose irregularity nonetheless accorded with Jones' own eccentric sense of a whole.[85] Its heaping-up of ancient languages, myths and cultural deposits had adumbrated an "ancestral mound," but Jones' synoptic vision of cultural translation did not smooth out this heap – acculturating its complexity with the "loppings off of meanings or emptyings out" of linguistic particularity – Jones instead hoped to integrate its difference and diversity across wide chasms of linguistic and cultural variety.[86] The "modernist drive toward effects of simultaneity through juxtaposition" drew him to the reception of

---

[81] Yeats, "The Galway Plains" (1903) in Yeats *CW4* (2007) 158.
[82] Yeats *VE* (1987) 256–57. See Introduction, pp. 33–34, Chapter 2, pp. 88–91, and Chapter 3, pp. 135–38.
[83] Joyce *Ulysses* (1986) 6 (1.154). See Introduction, pp. 34–36.
[84] Jones, "Preface to *The Anathemata*," in Jones (1952) 26, 17.
[85] Jones (1952) 34.
[86] Jones (1952) 26, 24.

Romanitas espoused by Collingwood, Myres and Cochrane.[87] While discussions of Welsh history, and this phenomenon in particular, were popularly peddled across nationalist circles, it was not sympathy for crude Welsh-Wales claims on cultural purity that attracted Jones. It was rather the reputed hybridity of *Romanitas* that drew his interest; historically understood, he thought, its enduring historical pattern demonstrated the possibility of authentically integrating many literatures and cultures within a tradition and across time – one wherein the foreign was not sacrificed to the native, nor the local to the universal, nor even the national to the imperial. As Jones saw it, *The Anathemata*'s "mixed data," its many languages, did not unnaturally warp the poem's greater unity, a unity informed by Jones' sacramental vision of art and making in human history.[88] Marked with devotion to the rhythmic structures of Catholic ritual – in "'time of the Mass'" – the poem's "trains of distraction and inadvertence" and "sprawl of the pattern – if pattern there is" were "initially set in motion, shunted or buffered into near sidings or off to far destinations, by some action or word, something seen or heard, during the liturgy."[89] Thus the "'ambivalences'" of culture and history registered in the poem's hybridized "meanderings to and fro" across language and myth were linked analogically – indeed ordered, as Jones saw it – by one central event, the original act of sign-making given in Christ's anamenetic command to "'Do this for a recalling of me'."[90] That moment, Jones believed, promised a "totality of connotation" for the poet, a moment that could authenticate "this whole business of sign and what is signified," with all its "loves and validities of many sorts and kinds."[91] "It would seem," he explained,

> that the forms which strategy shows forth can be typic only of that archetypal form-making and ordering implicit in the credal clause *per quem omnia facta sunt.* That is to say they partake in some sense, however difficult to posit, of that juxtaposing by which what was *inanis et vacua* became radiant with form and abhorrent of vacua by the action of the Artifex, the Logos, who is known to our tradition as the Pontifex who formed a bridge 'from nothing' and who then, like Brân in the *Mabinogion,* himself became the bridge by the Incarnation and Passion and subsequent Apotheoses.[92]

---

[87] Wray (2019) 428.
[88] Jones (1952) 9. See also Collingwood (1924) 14.
[89] Jones (1952) 31–32.
[90] Jones (1952) 31.
[91] Jones (1952) 24, 25.
[92] Jones, "Art and Sacrament," in Jones (1959) 159–60.

Despite such bold statements of faith – 'in some sense' affirming the divine significance of art and 'making' – Jones had his own doubts about the very making of *The Anathemata*. He frequently complained of being badly read in the many languages the poem employed, and that he had failed, too, formally in the very arrangement of the first published edition.[93] Because of the difficulties inherent in his polyglot idiom, Jones provided footnotes to the poem, insisting that these might help *"incant* something for the English reader" of "the undertones and overtones" of foreign fragments he drew on.[94] The footnotes may have lessened some caustic accusations – especially those that rejected the poem for intellectualism and spiritual obscurantism – but the crudity and brevity of the 'translations' Jones offered in the footnotes also betrayed the poem's *"main fundamental* difficulty": both reader and poet remained at arm's length from the "raw stuff" of "the past," stuff whose contexts were "virtually forgotten and available perhaps (as in the Welsh case), in another linguistic tradition and moreover a tradition separated fm [*sic*] us by centuries of a contrary tradition."[95] Though Jones laid some claim to the catalytic power of *Romanitas*, seeing it as a living and ideal, integrative model of cultural translation, the reception he gave it was troubled too by the forces of entropy and widespread ignorance – forces that would indeed mar Jones' practice of composition and influence contemporaneous criticism of his work.

By contrast Hugh MacDiarmid, despite his relative lack of formal schooling, betrayed no fundamental misgivings about the adequacy of his own knowledge of other languages, or their place within his poetic idiom. He would have little use for footnotes. His own eccentric liaisons with ancient and modern literatures – those that became characteristic of his 'synthetic English' – were made possible, he felt, by his exceptional imagination, which was "accustomed to contemplating the unity of the human spirit."[96] For MacDiarmid, "differences between languages and cultures" appeared seemingly "less marked," so much so that *In Memoriam James Joyce* commonly apposed "Graeco-Roman references with elements of other cultural origin, usually including Asian material as an instantiation of the 'East–West synthesis."[97] This "great range of allusions and references" was, to MacDiarmid at least, "rarely obscure and often exciting,"

---

[93] Jones (1959) 171. See Chapter 4, pp. 182–84.
[94] David Jones, Letter to Vernon Watkins (April 11, 1962) in Jones (1976) 57.
[95] Jones (1976) 58. On Jones' footnotes, see Chapter 4, p. 185n162.
[96] Hugh MacDiarmid, "Author's Note," in MacDiarmid (1955) 14.
[97] MacDiarmid (1955) 14. Wray (2019) 423.

no less because it allowed him to bring together the 'classical' from many languages and civilizations.[98] The multilinguistic hybridity that resulted documented the "cerebral pattern" of an autodidact whose "magpie-like appropriation of ideas," polyglot intromissions and incongruous juxtapositions MacDiarmid proudly hailed as "jujitsu for the 'educated'."[99] The poem's focus, however, remained anchored in a 'spiritual' Marxism, in MacDiarmid's belief that a growing "planetary consciousness" across art and literature would soon give better expression to the "consciousness of the millions of the dead, of the multiplicity of souls, of the profounds of Times."[100] *In Memoriam*'s internationalized idiom had suggested a world seemingly beyond tribal affiliations and "our Western chaos," a 'new classicism' global in scope and thus more resistant to "British Imperialism, English Ascendancy and centralization in London."[101] Despite MacDiarmid's ambition, however, his kaleidoscopic celebration of the classical-in-the-global carried profound risk. In manipulating antiquity in this way MacDiarmid tried to disrupt the predominant "nimbus of association" that had surrounded Victorian forms of classical reception, the very reality which kept the growing strength of English literature tethered closely to the legacy and 'leftover' prestige of Greek and Latin learning.[102] No claim of equality with classical languages ought to serve, he thought, the imperial ambitions of Englishness. Yet his efforts to untether English from such exclusive claims became increasingly idiosyncratic, MacDiarmid's "hectic pursuit of new forms of radicalism" leading him, by the mid-1930s, to a "career as a political heretic" and poetic eccentric.[103] His notion, moreover, of revolutionizing 'classics' – of casting its presence as the organizing principle by which all 'minor' traditions could authenticate their value – slowly emptied classical literature of clear substantive links to Greece and Rome; and many in MacDiarmid's audience, it seems, wondered whether his very interest in 'exotic' languages, to say nothing of his incendiary and ferocious Anglophobia, reflected simply a predilection for "the cachet and shibboleth" of the foreign or, worse, what William Aitken (1913–98) called an "objective admiration for anything which claims to oppose the existing order."[104]

[98] MacDiarmid (1955) 11, 12.
[99] MacDiarmid (1955) 11, 18. Hart (2010) 71.
[100] MacDiarmid (1955) 14, 15. See also Lyall (2011) 68–81. See Chapter 5 pp. 196–98, 221–24.
[101] MacDiarmid (1955) 18. MacDiarmid *LP* (1994) 376.
[102] Woolf *EVW4* (1994) 39.
[103] Hart (2010) 74.
[104] Collins (1891) 149. William Aitken, as in Hart (2010) 74. See also W. Aitken "The Puzzle of Mr. Grieve," *Free Man* (August 13, 1932), as in McCulloch (2004) 342.

By the early 1950s the eccentricity at work in the receptions of Celtic modernism had become apparent; moreover, by that time the volatility of classical learning had been roughly restabilized within the Anglo-American academy. This process of institutional restabilization had itself, in fact, helped curricularize some of the achievements of literary modernism, but the work of Yeats, Joyce, Jones and MacDiarmid were treated in different ways. By the time Jones published *The Anathemata* in 1952 and MacDiarmid *In Memoriam James Joyce* in 1955, there existed a desire to 'sweep the stage', to rediscover "rational structure and comprehensible language" and be "empirical in its attitude to all that comes."[105] Enough already had been written by the so-called "Lallans-mongers" and the other "Residual nuisances like the Social-realists ... the church-furnishers and the neo-Georgians."[106] Moreover, the "tendency to over-intellectualise" poetry and poetics had become a mark of critical opprobrium, driving some writers from polyglot solutions to the problems of cross-cultural encounter to writing new work that was "deliberately and self-confessedly *provincial*," fixed in the "central tradition of all English poetry, classical or romantic."[107] "[N]obody wants any more poems on the grander themes for a few years," declared Kingsley Amis (1922–95), "but at the same time nobody wants any more poems about philosophers or paintings or novelists or art galleries or mythology or foreign cities or other poems. At least I hope nobody wants them."[108] The difficulty of such poetry, Hugh Kenner suggested, lay in the fact that certain poets, and their poetry with all its erudition, lacked a "conception of an active culture" to which they "might contribute."[109] Despite his "devotion and learning," Kenner argued, David Jones appeared in *The Anathemata* without a distinctive voice, as though his interests had been "channelled into mere book-making, on the assumption that someone else will be able to think up a use for the results."[110] The mid-life work of both Jones and MacDiarmid suffered from this reception, lying down fatefully, it seems, in the idiosyncratic semantic codes that both writers had traced to preserve, or revive, the dying, minority languages and cultures they cherished. Whatever 'active cultures' they might have thought to defend, these too had become – as the Scottish classicist Douglas Young (1913–73)

---

[105] Conquest (1956) xviii, xv.
[106] Conquest (1956) xii.
[107] Conquest (1956) xvi, xv. Davie (1977) 47.
[108] Kingsley Amis, as in Enright (1955) 17.
[109] Kenner (1954) 301. See Chapter 4, pp. 192–94.
[110] Kenner (1954) 301.

once noted of Scots – "more and more diluted, through education and the mass media, with standard English or American."[111]

Yet, even as Jones' work and MacDiarmid's work failed to gain wide public acclaim, the popular canonization of Yeats and Joyce as exemplars of so-called high modernism was well underway by this time; and ironically, it was largely British and American educational establishments – with their wholesale 'Englishing' of the liberal arts (and of modernism at large) following the end of the Second World War – that provided the 'active culture' in which Irish modernist receptions of antiquity were embraced. It should be noted, too, that both Yeats and Joyce were seen not just as key contributors to the modern canon of English literature but as the most recent inheritors of a reputedly European 'classical tradition'. As reimagined by Gilbert Murray and other prominent American and English academics, nothing in the matrices of reception seemed excessively fraught: all that was classical had served a common, elevated purpose across history, namely the "common worship" of the Muses. Between Europe's many linguistic, religious, national and ethnic differences there was no "competition," Murray wrote, "in which each individual writer is expected to produce something new, to assert his personal claims, to outstrip his neighbor, and to put the old poets into the shade";[112] and yet, despite Murray's insistence, the concentric force of institutionalizing this 'classical tradition' at Anglo-American universities stripped, in part, some modernist engagements with the ancients of their deeper cultural and linguistic contexts. Academic interest in links between the classical and the contemporary increased, but the ambiguities modernist works enacted through their adaptations and allusions were often misjudged by the early proponents of 'tradition'.[113] The classics, though read primarily in

---

[111] Young (1966) 395.

[112] Murray (1927) 260. Following the "long strain" of the First World War, Murray saw Hellenism and the classical tradition as "the basis of a reforming and educative mission" for European civilization, one which could help mend the then "widespread degradation of political conduct." Molded by his involvement with Liberal politics and commitment to the League of Nations, Murray argued that classics' ongoing influence in Europe betokened a "central and permanent" civilizational unity. He himself had been shaped by an "intense immersion in ancient Greek philosophy and history," and Murray hoped his own teaching could likewise lead "some undergraduates to a commitment to change the world, or at least to become enlightened administrators of the British Empire." Invited by Harvard University in 1925 to take the inaugural Charles Eliot Norton Chair of Poetry, Murray lectured on the tradition at length, aiming to forge a "proper instrument for detecting" those aspects of style "which are the direct though unconscious fruit of ancient influence and have been in poetry from the beginning." See Murray (1921) vii; Stray (2007b) 3; as well as Murray (1927) xvii, 26, 27. See also Griffith (2007) 51–80.

[113] On the scholarly turn from the classical tradition to an emphasis on reception, see Hardwick and Stray (2008) 4–5; Budelmann and Haubold (2008) 13–25, as well as Martindale (1993) 23–29 and Haynes (2019b) 7–15.

translation at university, were then often said to exude a "strong, noble, statuesque" presence in modern literature.[114] On the whole, their reception and contemporary literary purpose was said to document "how sordid the men and women of to-day have made themselves." "[B]y contrast with the heroism or beauty of classical legend," modernity was, Gilbert Highet (1906–78) once claimed of *Ulysses*, an "explosion in a cesspool."[115] The works of Yeats and of Joyce, like those of MacDiarmid and Jones, however, had simmered in a far more complex and capricious world, a world where the hydra-headed forces of classical reception could be used to bolster competing aesthetic claims and a variety of aggressive nationalisms – not only those that would 'outstrip neighbors' and rival nations of civic authenticity but also those of artists and scholars all too eager to put other poets, other nations and other languages "into the shade."[116] Thus the early codification of some forms of Celtic modernism as the "latest stage" of 'classical' growth at times divested their experimentalism of more controversial accretions.[117] References to antiquity were often glossed as though they passed on a largely unwavering or invariant sense of cultural stability – conceived, Lawrence Venuti suggests, as though "contained in or caused by the source text, an invariant form, meaning, or effect."[118] With the further democratic expansion of the university, the volatility of modernist receptions could thus be steadied and rebranded for broad institutional consumption. Echoes of the struggles to define the classical grew fainter, and the stylistically eccentric forms of Celtic modernism were domesticated or sometimes ignored, leaving allusions and adaptations of the Greek and the Roman fraught with misreading. Their presence then evoked not the labyrinth of ways in which the classics were mediated to Yeats, Joyce, Jones and MacDiarmid but a more contemporary need to claim comfort from the ancient 'Western' world, to engender some "aesthetic consolation against the stresses, dangers and vulgarities of life."[119]

---

[114] Highet (2015) 512.
[115] Highet (2015) 512. Having studied with Gilbert Murray at Balliol College, Oxford, Highet became professor of Latin and Greek at Columbia College in 1938. He first published *The Classical Tradition: Greek and Roman Influences on Western Literature* in 1949.
[116] Murray (1927) 260.
[117] Highet (2015) 546.
[118] Venuti (2019) 1.
[119] Highet (2015) 518.

References

Æ. 1899. "Nationality and Cosmopolitanism." *Literary Ideals in Ireland*. Ed. John Eglinton. London: T. Fisher Unwin, 79–88.

Acoe. 1889. "The Wanderings of Oisin." *Clonmel Chronicle*, February 23.

Adams, Matthew. 2015. *Teaching Classics in English Schools, 1500–1840*. Newcastle upon Tyne: Cambridge Scholars.

Adams, Michael. 1968. *Censorship: The Irish Experience*. Dublin: Scepter Publishers.

Adamson, Sylvia. 1998. "Literary Language." *The Cambridge History of the English Language, Volume 4: 1776–1997*. Ed. Suzanne Romaine. Cambridge: Cambridge University Press, 589–692.

Aldington, Richard. 1921. "The Influence of Mr. James Joyce." *The English Review* 32.149 (April): 333–41.

Allen, Nicholas. 2010. "'out of eure sanscreed into oure eryan': Ireland, the Classics and Independence." *Classics and National Culture*. Ed. Susan A. Stephens and Phiroze Vasunia. Oxford: Oxford University Press, 16–33.

Alspach, Russell K. 1943. "Some Sources of Yeats's *The Wanderings of Oisin*." *PMLA* 58.3 (September): 849–66.

Ames, Keri Elizabeth. 2005. "Joyce's Aesthetic of the Double Negative and His Encounters with Homer's *Odyssey*." *Beckett, Joyce and the Art of the Negative*. Vol. 16. Ed. Colleen Jaurretche. European Joyce Studies. Amsterdam: Rodopi Press, 15–48.

d'Arbois de Jubainville, H. 1903. *The Irish Mythological Cycle and Celtic Mythology*. Trans. Richard Irvine Best. Dublin: Hodges, Figgis & Co.

Arendt, Hannah. 2006. *Between Past and Future*. New York: Penguin.

Arkins, Brian. 1990. *Builders of My Soul: Greek and Roman Themes in Yeats*. Savage, MD: Barnes and Noble Books.

Arkins, Brian. 1994. "Passionate Syntax: Style in the Poetry of Yeats." *Yeats: An Annual of Critical and Textual Studies*. Vol. 12. Ed. Richard J. Finneran. Ann Arbor: University of Michigan Press, 3–26.

Arkins, Brian. 1999. *Greek and Roman Themes in Joyce*. Lewiston, NY: Edwin Mellen Press.

Arkins, Brian. 2005. *Hellenizing Ireland: Greek and Roman Themes in Irish Literature*. Newbridge: The Goldsmith Press.

Arkins, Brian. 2009. "Greek and Roman themes." *James Joyce In Context*. Ed. John McCourt. Cambridge: Cambridge University Press, 239–49.

Armstrong, Richard Hamilton. 2005. "Translating Ancient Epic." *A Companion to Ancient Epic*. Ed. John Miles Foley. Malden, MA: Blackwell Publishing, 174–95.

Arnold, Matthew. 1910. *Letters from Matthew Arnold to John Churton Collins*. n.p.

Arnold, Matthew. 1960. *The Complete Prose Works of Matthew Arnold, Volume 1: On the Classical Tradition*. Ed. R. H. Super. Ann Arbor: University of Michigan Press.

Arnold, Matthew. 1962. *The Complete Prose Works of Matthew Arnold, Volume 3: Lectures and Essays in Criticism*. Ed. R. H. Super. Ann Arbor: University of Michigan Press.

Arnold, Matthew. 1965. *The Poems of Matthew Arnold*. Ed. Kenneth Allott. London: Longmans, Green and Co.

Arnold, Matthew. 1977. *The Complete Prose Works of Matthew Arnold, Volume 11: The Last Word*. Ed. R. H. Super. Ann Arbor: University of Michigan Press.

Arnold, Matthew. 1993. *Selected Letters of Matthew Arnold*. Ed. Clinton Machann and Forrest D. Burt. Houndmills: Macmillan.

Arts Council of Ireland. 2014. *Review of the Abbey Theatre, Report*. June.

Atkinson, Robert. 1896. *The Yellow Book of Lecan: A Collection of Pieces (Prose and Verse) in the Irish Language*. Dublin: Royal Irish Academy House.

Auden, W. H. 1954. "A Contemporary Epic." *Encounter* (February): 67–71.

Bacon, Alan, ed. 1998. *The Nineteenth-Century History of English Studies*. Abingdon: Ashgate Publishing.

Baker, Gregory. 2016. "'Attic Salt into an Undiluted Scots': Aristophanes and the Modernism of Douglas Young." *Brill's Companion to the Reception of Aristophanes*. Ed. Philip Walsh. Leiden and Boston: Brill, 307–30.

Baker, William E. 1967. "The Strange and the Familiar." *Syntax in English Poetry, 1870–1930*. Berkeley: University of California Press, 84–106.

Bakhtin, M. M. 1981. *The Dialogic Imagination, Four Essays*. Austin: University of Texas Press.

Ballantyne, Archibald. 1888. "Wardour-Street English." *Longman's Magazine* 72 (October): 585–94.

Barcus, James E., ed. 1975. *Shelley: The Critical Heritage*. London: Routledge and Kegan Paul.

Barker, Clive, and Maggie B. Gale, eds. 2000. *British Theatre Between the Wars, 1918–1939*. Cambridge: Cambridge University Press.

Barnes, Ben. 2008. *Plays and Controversies: Abbey Theatre Diaries 2000–2005*. Dublin: Carysfort Press.

Barrett, S. J., ed. 1899. *The Proceedings of the Third Oireachtas, Held in Dublin on Wednesday, 7th June, 1899*. Dublin: Sealy, Bryers and Walker.

Barry, William. 1902. "The Gael and the Greek." *New Ireland Review* 17.6 (August): 321–35.

Bell, Quentin. 1972. *Virginia Woolf: A Biography*. New York: Harcourt Brace Jovanovich.

Benstead, James. 2019. "A Study of Hugh MacDiarmid's *In Memoriam James Joyce*." Ph.D. Diss., University of Edinburgh.

Bérard, Victor. 1902. *Les Phéniciens et l'Odyssée*. Vol. 1. Paris: Librairie Armand Colin.

Berenato, Thomas. 2018. "David Jones, Essay on Gerard Manley Hopkins, c. 1968." *David Jones on Religion, Politics, and Culture: Unpublished Prose*. Ed. Thomas Berenato, Anne Price-Owen and Kathleen Henderson Staudt. London: Bloomsbury Academic, 101–267.

Bergson, Henri. 1912. *An Introduction to Metaphysics*. Trans. T. E. Hulme. London: G. P. Putnam's Sons.

Berlin, Isaiah. 1976. *Vico and Herder: Two Studies in the History of Ideas*. New York: Viking Press.

Bhabha, Homi K. 2004. *The Location of Culture*. New York: Routledge.

Birmingham, Kevin. 2017. "'Truman Capote Award Acceptance Speech', Iowa City, 19 October 2016." *The Chronicle of Higher Education*, February 12.

Blackie, John Stuart. 1855. *On the Advancement of Scottish Learning: A Letter to the Right Honourable Lord Provost and Town Council of Edinburgh, Patrons of the University*. Edinburgh: Sutherland and Knox.

Blackmur, R. P. 1935. "Statements and Idyls." *Poetry* 46.2 (May): 108–12.

Blair, Hugh. 1763. *A Critical Dissertation on the Poems of Ossian, The Son of Fingal*. London: T. Beckett and P. A. De Hondt at Tully's Head.

Blair, Hugh. 1765. *The Works of Ossian, the Son of Fingal in Two Volumes*. Vol. 2. 3rd ed. London: T. Beckett and P. A. De Hondt at Tully's Head, 445–60.

Blair, Peter Hunter. 2003. *An Introduction to Anglo-Saxon England*. 3rd ed. Cambridge: Cambridge University Press.

Blank, Paula. 1996. *Broken English: Dialects and the Politics of Language in Renaissance Writings*. London: Routledge.

Blanshard, Alastair, Shane Butler and Emily Greenwood. 2015. "Series editors' Preface." Leah Culligan Flack. *Modernism and Homer: The Odysseys of H. D., James Joyce, Osip Mandelstam, and Ezra Pound*. Cambridge: Cambridge University Press, ix–xii.

Bloom, Harold. 1970. *Yeats*. New York: Oxford University Press.

Board of Education. 1931. *Report of the Consultative Committee on the Primary School*. London: H. M. Stationery Office.

Bold, Alan. 1985. *Scots Steel Tempered wi' Irish Fire: Hugh MacDiarmid and Ireland*. Edinburgh: Edinburgh College of Art.

Bold, Alan. 1990. *MacDiarmid: Christopher Murray Grieve, a Critical Biography*. Amherst: University of Massachusetts Press.

Bolgar, R. R. 1954. *The Classical Heritage and Its Beneficiaries*. Cambridge: Cambridge University Press.

Borach, Georges. 1954. "Conversations with James Joyce." Trans. Joseph Prescott. *College English* 15.6 (March): 325–27.

Borges, Jorge Luis. 1932. "Las versiones homéricas." *La Prensa* (May 8).

Borges, Jorge Luis. 2001. *The Total Library: Non-Fiction 1922–1986*. Ed. Eliot Weinberger. Trans. Esther Allen, Suzanne Jill Levin and Eliot Weinberger. London: Penguin Books.

Bornstein, George. 1970. *Yeats and Shelley*. Chicago, IL: University of Chicago Press.

Boyd, Ernest A. 1918. *Appreciations and Depreciations: Irish Literary Studies*. New York: Lane.

Bradley, Bruce. 1982. *James Joyce's Schooldays*. New York: St. Martin's Press.

Bradley, Mark, ed. 2010. *Classics and Imperialism in the British Empire*. Oxford and New York: Oxford University Press.

Brand, Jack. 1978. *The National Movement in Scotland*. London: Routledge and Kegan Paul.

Brooker, Peter, Andrzej Gasiorek, Deborah Longworth and Andrew Thacker. 2010. "Introduction." *The Oxford Handbook of Modernisms*. Ed. Peter Brooker, Andrzej Gasiorek, Deborah Longworth and Andrew Thacker. Oxford: Oxford University Press, 1–16.

Brooks, Alaisdair. 2003. "Crossing Offa's Dyke: British ideologies and late eighteenth- and nineteenth-century ceramics in Wales." *Archaeologies of the British: Explorations of Identity in the United Kingdom and Its Colonies 1600–1945*. Ed. Susan Lawrence. New York: Routledge, 119–37.

Brown, Terence. 1985. *Ireland: A Social and Cultural History, 1922 to the Present*. Ithaca, NY: Cornell University Press.

Browne, Henry. 1917. *Our Renaissance: Essays on the Reform and Revival of Classical Studies*. London: Longmans, Green and Co.

Browning, Gary K. 2004. *Rethinking R. G. Collingwood: Philosophy, Politics and the Unity of Theory*. Basingstoke: Palgrave Macmillan.

Budelmann, Felix, and Johannes Haubold. 2008. "Tradition and Reception." *A Companion to Classical Receptions*. Ed. Lorna Hardwick and Christopher Stray. Malden, MA: Wiley-Blackwell, 13–25.

Budgen, Frank. 1972. *James Joyce and the Making of Ulysses, and Other Writings*. London: Oxford University Press.

Bullough, Geoffrey. 1934. *The Trend of Modern Poetry*. London: Oliver and Boyd.

Burke, Peter. 2009. *Cultural Hybridity*. Cambridge: Polity Press.

Bush, Ronald. 1976. *The Genesis of Ezra Pound's Cantos*. Princeton, NJ: Princeton University Press.

Bush, Ronald. 1983. "Gathering the Limbs of Osiris: The Subject of Pound's *Homage to Sextus Propertius*." *Ezra Pound and William Carlos Williams*. Ed. Daniel Hoffman. Philadelphia: University of Pennsylvania Press, 61–79.

Bush, Ronald. 1996. "The Modernist under Siege." *Yeats's Political Identities: Selected Essays*. Ed. Jonathan Allison. Ann Arbor: University of Michigan Press, 325–33.

Bush, Ronald. 2019. "*Ulysses* and Joyce's Museum of Homers." *The Oxford History of Classical Reception in English Literature, Volume 5: After 1880*. Ed. Kenneth Haynes. Oxford: Oxford University Press, 322–57.

Butcher, S. H. 1884. "Sophocles." *The Fortnightly Review* 41 (June 1): 794–811.

Butcher, S. H., and A. Lang, trans. 1879. *The Odyssey, Done into English Prose*. London: Macmillan and Co.

Butler, Samuel. 1893. *On the Trapanese Origin of the Odyssey*. Cambridge: Metcalfe and Co.

Butler, Samuel. 1898. *The Iliad of Homer: Rendered into English Prose for Those of Us Who Cannot Read the Original.* London, New York and Bombay: Longmans, Green and Co.

Butter, P. H. 1966. *Edwin Muir: Man and Poet.* Edinburgh: Oliver and Boyd.

Buxton, John. 1978. *The Grecian Taste: Literature in the Age of Neo-Classicism, 1740–1820.* New York: Barnes and Noble.

Byrne, J. F. 1953. *Silent Years: An Autobiography with Memoirs of James Joyce and Our Ireland.* New York: Farrar, Straus and Giroux.

C. M. P. 1908. "The Bagpipe and the Gael." *Guth Na Bliadhna* 5.4 (Autumn): 361–80.

Carne-Ross, D. S. 1979. *Instaurations.* Berkeley: University of California Press.

Carne-Ross, D. S. 1980. "The Last of the Modernists." *The New York Review of Books* 27.15 (October 9): 41–43.

Carne-Ross, D. S. 2010. *Classics and Translation.* Ed. Kenneth Haynes. Lewisburg, PA: Bucknell University Press.

Carpentier, Martha C. 2016. *Ritual, Myth and the Modernist Text: The Influence of Jane Ellen Harrison on Joyce, Eliot and Woolf.* London and New York: Routledge.

Case, Janet. 1905. *The Prometheus Bound of Aeschylus, Edited with Introduction, Translation and Notes by Janet Case.* London: J. M. Dent and Co.

Castle, Gregory. 2001. *Modernism and the Celtic Revival.* Cambridge: Cambridge University Press.

Castle, Gregory, and Patrick Bixby. 2019. "Introduction: Irish Modernism from Emergence to Emergency." *A History of Irish Modernism.* Ed. Gregory Castle and Patrick Bixby. Cambridge: Cambridge University Press, 1–24.

Chapman, T. Robin. 2006a. "Theism's Last Hurrah: Saunders Lewis's Caernarfon Court Speech of 1936." *Idiom of Dissent.* Ed. T. Robin Chapman. Llandysul: Gomer Press, 24–42.

Chapman, T. Robin. 2006b. *Un Bywyd o Blith Nifer: Cofiant Saunders Lewis.* Llandysul: Wasg Gomer.

Char, René. 2007. *Feuillets d'Hypnos.* Paris: Éditions Gallimard.

Chrisafis, Angelique. 2004. "Dublin's Abbey in Centenary Crisis." *The Guardian,* September 8.

Chrisafis, Angelique. 2005. "How a Backstage Farce Nearly Ruined the Abbey Theatre." *The Guardian,* July 22.

Clark, Frank L. 1923. "On Certain Imitations or Reminiscences of Homer in Matthew Arnold's *Sohrab and Rustum.*" *Classical Weekly* 17.1 (October 1): 3–7.

Cochrane, C. N. 1940. *Christianity and Classical Culture.* Oxford: Clarendon Press.

Coffey, Diarmid. 1938. *Douglas Hyde, President of Ireland.* Dublin and Cork: Talbot Press.

Cohen, Edward. 2009. *The Athenian Nation.* Princeton, NJ: Princeton University Press.

Coleridge, Samuel Taylor. 1957. *The Notebooks of Samuel Taylor Coleridge, Volume 1: 1794–1804.* Ed. Kathleen Coburn. New York: Pantheon Books.

Coleridge, Samuel Taylor. 1973. *The Notebooks of Samuel Taylor Coleridge, Volume 3: 1808–1819*. Ed. Kathleen Coburn. Princeton, NJ: Princeton University Press.

Coleridge, Samuel Taylor. 1983. *Biographia Literaria, The Collected Works of Samuel Taylor Coleridge, Volume 7*. Ed. James Engell and Walter Jackson Bate. 2 vols. Princeton, NJ: Princeton University Press.

Collingwood, R. G. 1924. *Roman Britain*. London: Oxford University Press.

Collingwood, R. G. 1993. *The Idea of History*. Rev ed. Oxford: Oxford University Press.

Collingwood R. G. and J. N. L. Myres. 1937. *Roman Britain and the English Settlements*. 2nd ed. Oxford: Clarendon Press.

Collins, John Churton. 1891. *The Study of English Literature: A Plea for Its Recognition and Organization*. London: Macmillan and Co.

Committee of Council on Education. 1848. *Reports of the Commissioners of Inquiry into the State of Education in Wales*. London: Committee of Council on Education.

Committee on Evil Literature. 1927. *Report of the Committee on Evil Literature*. Dublin: Stationery Office.

Committee to Inquire into the Position of Classics in the Educational System of the United Kingdom. 1921. *Report of the Committee Appointed by the Prime Minister to Inquire into the Position of Classics in the Educational System of the United Kingdom*. London: H. M. Stationery Office.

Comyn, David, ed. and trans. 1880. *Laoid Oisín air Tír na n-Óg*. Dublin: A. E. Chamney.

Comyn, David, ed. and trans. 1881. *Mac-Ghníomhartha Fhinn. The Youthful Exploits of Fionn*. Dublin: M. H. Gill and Son.

Conquest, Robert. 1956. *New Lines: An Anthology*. London: Macmillan and Co.

Coolahan, John. 1981. *Irish Education: Its History and Structure*. Dublin: Institute of Public Administration.

Corcoran, Neil. 1982. *The Song of Deeds: A Study of The Anathemata of David Jones*. Cardiff: University of Wales Press.

Corkery, Daniel. 1925. *The Hidden Ireland: A Study of Gaelic Munster in the Eighteenth Century*. Dublin: M. H. Gill and Son.

Court, Franklin. 1992. *Institutionalizing English Literature: The Culture and Politics of Literary Study, 1750–1900*. Stanford, CA: Stanford University Press.

Craig, Cairns. 2004. "Scotland and Hybridity." *Beyond Scotland: New Contexts for Twentieth-century Scottish Literature*. Ed. Gerard Carruthers, David Goldie and Alastair Renfrew. Amsterdam: Rodopi, 229–53.

Crawford, Robert. 1998. "The Scottish Invention of English Literature." *The Scottish Invention of English Literature*. Ed. Robert Crawford. Cambridge: Cambridge University Press, 225–46.

Crawford, Robert. 2000. *Devolving English Literature*. 2nd ed. Edinburgh: Edinburgh University Press.

Crawford, Robert. 2011. "The Classics in Modern Scottish and Irish Poetry." *Modern Irish and Scottish Poetry*. Ed. Peter Mackay, Edna Longley and Fran Brearton. Cambridge: Cambridge University Press, 131–46.

Cronin, John. 1988. "Introduction." *Selected Plays of St. John Ervine*. Ed. John Cronin. Gerrards Cross: Colin Smythe, 7–16.

Cronin, Michael. 1996. *Translating Ireland: Translation, Languages, Culture*. Cork: Cork University Press.

Crotty, Patrick. 2011. "Swordsmen: W. B. Yeats and Hugh MacDiarmid." *Modern Irish and Scottish Poetry*. Ed. Peter Mackay, Edna Longley and Fran Brearton. Cambridge: Cambridge University Press, 20–38.

Crowley, Tony. 2000. *The Politics of Language in Ireland, 1366–1922*. London and New York: Routledge.

Crowley, Tony. 2005. *Wars of Words, The Politics of Language in Ireland 1537–2004*. Oxford: Oxford University Press.

Crystal, David. 1997. *English As a Global Language*. Cambridge: Cambridge University Press.

Cullingford, Elizabeth. 1981. *Yeats, Ireland and Fascism*. New York: New York University Press.

Curley, Thomas M. 2009. *Samuel Johnson, the Ossian Fraud, and the Celtic Revival in Great Britain and Ireland*. Cambridge: Cambridge University Press.

Dale, Leigh. 2012. *The Enchantment of English: Professing English Literatures in Australian Universities*. Sydney: Sydney University Press.

Dalzel, Andrew. 1821. "Lecture XXVIII, Pastoral Poetry." *Substance of Lectures on the Ancient Greeks, and on the Revival of Greek Learning in Europe*. Vol. 2. Edinburgh: Archibald Constable and Company, 233–52.

Davenport, Guy. 1987. "Ariadne's Dancing Floor." *Every Force Evolves a Form*. San Francisco, CA: North Point Press, 53–63.

Davenport, Guy. 1997. "Another Odyssey." *The Geography of the Imagination*. Boston, MA: David R. Godine, Publisher, 29–44.

Davie, Donald. 1977. *The Poet in the Imaginary Museum: Essays of Two Decades*. New York: Persea Books.

Davie, George Elder. 1961. *The Democratic Intellect: Scotland and Her Universities in the Nineteenth Century*. Edinburgh: Edinburgh University Press.

Davies, Aneirin Talfan. 1961. "Dylanwadau: Saunders Lewis." *Taliesin* 2: 5–18.

Davies, Ceri. 1995. *Welsh Literature and the Classical Tradition*. Cardiff: University of Wales Press.

Davies, Ceri. 2009. "Classics and Welsh Cultural Identity in the Nineteenth Century." *British Classics Outside England: The Academy and Beyond*. Ed. Judith P. Hallett and Christopher Stray. Waco, TX: Baylor University Press, 35–47.

Davies, D. Hywel. 1983. *The Welsh Nationalist Party, 1925–1945: A Call to Nationhood*. New York: St. Martin's Press.

Davies, Janet. 2000. "Welsh." *Languages in Britain and Ireland*. Ed. Glanville Price. Oxford: Blackwell Publishers, 78–108.

Davies, John. 2007. *A History of Wales*. Rev. ed. London: Penguin Books.

De Quincey, Thomas. 1845. "Suspiria de Profundis: Being A Sequel to the Confessions of An Opium-Eater. Part I. Concluded. The Palimpsest." *Blackwood's Edinburgh Magazine* 57.356 (June): 739–51.

Dean, Joan Fitzgerald. 2004. *Riot and Great Anger: Stage Censorship in Twentieth-century Ireland.* Madison, WI: University of Wisconsin Press.

Deming, Robert H., ed. 1970. *James Joyce: The Critical Heritage.* 2 vols. London: Routledge and Kegan Paul.

Dentinger, Hannah. 2004. "'Cydgyfarfyddiad' Cymreig: Gohebiaeth David Jones a Saunders Lewis." *Y Traethodydd* 159: 222–34.

Devane, R. S. 1925. "Indecent Literature: Some Legal Remedies." *Irish Ecclesiastical Record* 5th ser. 25 (February): 182–204.

Devine, T. M. 1999. *The Scottish Nation: A History, 1700–2000.* New York: Viking.

Dillon, John. 1991. "The Classics in Trinity." *Trinity College Dublin and the Idea of a University.* Ed. C. H. Holland. Dublin: Trinity College Dublin Press, 239–54.

Dilworth, Thomas. 1988. *The Shape of Meaning in the Poetry of David Jones.* Toronto: University of Toronto Press.

Dilworth, Thomas. 2000. "Antithesis of Place in the Poetry and Life of David Jones." *Locations of Literary Modernism, Region and Nation in British and American Modernist Poetry.* Ed. Alex Davis and Lee M. Jenkins. Cambridge: Cambridge University Press, 66–88.

Dilworth, Thomas. 2012. *David Jones in the Great War.* London: Enitharmon Press.

Dilworth, Thomas. 2017. *David Jones: Engraver, Soldier, Painter, Poet.* Berkeley, CA: Counterpoint.

Dickson, David. 2014. *Dublin: The Making of a Capital City.* Cambridge, MA: The Belknap Press of Harvard University Press.

Donoghue, Denis. 1997. "Yeats, Eliot, and the Mythical Method." *The Sewanee Review* 105.2 (Spring): 206–26.

Donovan, Robert. 1902. "Lady Gregory's New Book." *The Freeman's Journal* (May 2): 5.

Dowden, Edward. 1884. "Dublin City." *The Century Magazine* 29.2 (December): 163–79.

Dowden, Edward. 1895. *New Studies in Literature.* London: Kegan Paul, Trench, Trübner & Co.

Doyle, Aidan. 2015. *A History of the Irish Language.* Oxford: Oxford University Press.

Dunleavy, Janet Egleson, and Gareth W. Dunleavy. 1991. *Douglas Hyde: A Maker of Modern Ireland.* Berkeley, CA: University of California Press.

Dutt, R. Palme. 1933. *Lenin.* London: Hamish Hamilton Publisher.

Eagleton, Terry. 1996. *Literary Theory: An Introduction.* 2nd ed. Minneapolis: University of Minnesota Press.

Earle, Ralph Harding. 1988. "Questions of Syntax, Syntax of Questions: Yeats and the Topology of Passion." *Yeats: An Annual of Critical and Textual Studies*, Vol. 6. Ed. Richard J. Finneran. Ann Arbor: University of Michigan Press, 19–48.

Earp, F. R. 1944. *The Style of Sophocles.* Cambridge: Cambridge University Press.

Earp, F. R. 1948. *The Style of Aeschylus.* Cambridge: Cambridge University Press.

Easterling, Pat. 2005. "'The Speaking Page': Reading Sophocles with Jebb." *The Owl of Minerva: the Cambridge Praelections of 1906 – Proceedings of the Cambridge Philological Society*. Ed. Christopher Stray. Cambridge: Cambridge Philological Society, 25–46.

Eco, Umberto. 1995. *The Search for the Perfect Language*. Trans. James Fentress. Oxford: Blackwell Publishers.

Edwards, Owen M. 1901. *Wales*. London: T. Fisher Unwin.

Eliot, T. S. 1920. "Euripides and Professor Murray." *The Sacred Wood*. London: Methuen and Co., 64–70.

Eliot, T. S. 1923. "*Ulysses*, Order, and Myth." *The Dial* 75.5 (November): 480–83.

Eliot, T. S. 1939. "Last Words." *The Criterion* 18.71: 269–75.

Eliot, T. S. 2009a. *The Letters of T. S. Eliot, Volume 1: 1898–1922*. Rev. ed. Ed. Valerie Eliot and Hugh Haughton. London: Faber and Faber.

Eliot, T. S. 2009b. *The Letters of T. S. Eliot, Volume 2: 1923–1925*. Ed. Valerie Eliot and Hugh Haughton. London: Faber and Faber

Ellis, E. L. 1972. *The University College of Wales, Aberystwyth, 1872–1972*. Cardiff: University of Wales.

Ellis, Peter Berresford. 1972. *A History of the Irish Working Class*. London: Victor Gollancz.

Ellmann, Richard. 1950. "Joyce and Yeats." *The Kenyon Review* 12.4 (Autumn): 618–38.

Ellmann, Richard. 1982. *James Joyce*. Rev. ed. Oxford: Oxford University Press.

Enright, D. J., ed. 1955. *Poets of the 1950's: An Anthology of New English Verse*. Tokyo: Kenkyusha.

Erskine, Ruaraidh. 1904a. "Ireland and Scotland." *Guth Na Bliadhna* 1.2 (Spring): 197–206.

Erskine, Ruaraidh. 1904b. "The Church and the Highlands." *Guth Na Bliadhna* 1.1 (Winter): 1–11.

Erskine, Ruaraidh. 1905a. "St. Columba." *Guth Na Bliadhna* 2.2 (Spring): 105–110.

Erskine, Ruaraidh. 1905b. "Cas no Bas." *Guth Na Bliadhna* 2.4 (Autumn): 300–308.

Erskine, Ruaraidh. 1906. "Gaelic Confederation." *Guth Na Bliadhna* 3.1 (Winter): 11–25.

Erskine, Ruaraidh. 1908. "The Recent Crisis in the Gaelic Movement." *Guth Na Bliadhna* 5.3 (Summer): 233–50.

Ervine, St. John. 1928. *How to Write a Play*. New York: The Macmillan Company.

Ervine, St. John. 1931a. "At the Play. Speech and the Actor's Craft – I." *The Observer*, January 25: 13.

Ervine, St. John. 1931b. "At the Play. Speech and the Actor's Craft – II." *The Observer*, February 1: 13.

Ervine, St. John. 1931c. "At the Play. Speech and the Actor's Craft – III." *The Observer*, February 8: 13.

Ervine, St. John. 1956. *Bernard Shaw: Life, Work and Friends*. New York: Morrow.

Evans, D. Emrys. 1953. *The University of Wales, A Historical Sketch*. Cardiff: University of Wales Press.

Evans, Geraint. 1987. "The Correspondence of Saunders Lewis and David Jones." MA Thesis, University College of Swansea.

Evans, Geraint. 2019. "Welsh Modernist Writing in Wales and London." *The Cambridge History of Welsh Literature*. Ed. Geraint Evans and Helen Fulton. Cambridge: Cambridge University Press, 446–67.

Fanning, Ronan, Michael Kennedy, Dermot Keogh and Eunan O'Halpin, eds. 1998. "The Anglo-Irish Treaty (December 1920–December 1921)." *Documents on Irish Foreign Policy, Volume 1: 1919–1922*. Dublin: Royal Irish Academy, 204–370.

Farrell, Joseph. 2012. "Joyce and Modernist Latinity." *Reception and the Classics, An Interdisciplinary Approach to the Classical Tradition*. Ed. William Brockliss, Pramit Chaudhuri, Ayelet Haimson Lushkov and Katherine Wasdin. Cambridge: Cambridge University Press, 57–71.

Fathers of the Society of Jesus, comp. 1930. *A Page of Irish History: Story of University College, Dublin, 1883–1909*. Dublin and Cork: The Talbot Press.

Ferguson, Samuel. 1888. *Lays of the Western Gael, And Other Poems*. Dublin: Sealy, Bryers and Walker.

Finlay, Richard J. 1994. *Independent and Free, Scottish Politics and the Origins of the Scottish National Party 1918–1945*. Edinburgh: John Donald Publishers.

Fishlock, Trevor. 1976. "The Men Who Lit the Torch That Set the Whole of Wales Alight." *The Times*, September 4: 12.

Flack, Leah Culligan. 2015. *Modernism and Homer: The Odysseys of H. D., James Joyce, Osip Mandelstam, and Ezra Pound*. Cambridge: Cambridge University Press.

Flack, Leah Culligan. 2020. *James Joyce and Classical Modernism*. London: Bloomsbury Academic.

Flannery, James. 1976. *W. B. Yeats and the Idea of a Theatre: The Early Abbey Theatre in Theory and Practice*. New Haven, CT: Yale University Press.

Foster, John Wilson. 1987. *Fictions of the Irish Literary Revival: A Changeling Art*. Syracuse, NY: Syracuse University Press.

Foster, R. F. 1997. *W. B. Yeats, A Life, Volume 1: The Apprentice Mage, 1865–1914*. Oxford: Oxford University Press.

Foster, R. F. 2003. *W. B. Yeats, A Life, Volume 2: The Arch-Poet, 1915–1939*. Oxford: Oxford University Press.

Fowell, Frank, and Frank Palmer. 1913. *Censorship in England*. London: Frank Palmer.

Freedman, Carl. 1992. "Beyond the Dialect of the Tribe: James Joyce, Hugh MacDiarmid, and World Language." *Hugh MacDiarmid: Man and Poet*. Ed. Nancy Gish. Edinburgh: Edinburgh University, 253–73.

Freeman, Edward Augustus. 1867–1876. *The History of the Norman Conquest of England*. 6 vols. Oxford: Clarendon Press.

Garland, Hamlin, ed. 1926. *Nature's Alchemy, Special Bulletin of the Turck Foundation for Biological Research*. New York: The Turck Foundation for Biological Research.

Geertz, Clifford. 1973. *The Interpretation of Cultures*. New York: Basic Books.

Gere, Cathy. 2009. *Knossos and the Prophets of Modernism*. Chicago, IL: University of Chicago Press.

Gere, Cathy. 2019. "Myth and Ritual." *The Oxford History of Classical Reception in English Literature, Volume 5: After 1880*. Ed. Kenneth Haynes. Oxford: Oxford University Press, 200–25.

Gikandi, Simon. 1996. *Maps of Englishness: Writing Identity in the Culture of Colonialism*. New York: Columbia University Press.

Gilbert, Stuart. 1950. *James Joyce's Ulysses: A Study*. London: Faber and Faber.

Gillespie, Michael Patrick and Erik Bradford Stocker. 1986. *James Joyce's Trieste Library: A Catalogue of Materials at the Harry Ransom Humanities Research Center, Texas*. Austin, TX: Humanities Research Center.

Gish, Nancy K. 1984. *Hugh MacDiarmid, The Man and His Work*. London: Macmillan.

Godley, A. D. 1914. "The Present Position of Classical Studies in England." *Louis Clark Vanuxem Foundation, Lectures Delivered in Connection with the Dedication of the Graduate College of Princeton University in October, 1913*. Princeton, NJ: Princeton University Press, 67–94.

Goff, Barbara, ed. 2005. *Classics and Colonialism*. London: Duckworth.

Gogarty, Oliver St John. 1971. *Many Lines to Thee – Letters to G. K. A. Bell*. Ed. James F. Carens. Dublin: Dolmen Press.

Gogarty, Oliver St John. 2001. *The Poems and Plays of Oliver St John Gogarty*. Ed. A. Norman Jeffares. Gerrard's Cross: Colin Smythe.

Goldhill, Simon. 2002. *Who Needs Greek? Contests in the Cultural History of Hellenism*. Cambridge: Cambridge University Press.

Gomes, Daniel. 2014. "Reviving Oisin: Yeats and the Conflicted Appeal of Irish Mythology." *Texas Studies in Literature and Language* 56.4 (Winter): 376–99.

Gordon, Gregory S. 2017. *Atrocity Speech Law: Foundation, Fragmentation, Fruition*. Oxford: Oxford University Press.

Gorman, Herbert. 1939. *James Joyce*. New York: Farrar and Rinehart.

Goschen, George J. 1887. "To the Vice-Chancellor of the University of Oxford." *University Gazette* 17.582 (April): 381–82.

Graver, Bruce. 2007. "Romanticism." *A Companion to the Classical Tradition*. Ed. Craig W. Kallendorf. Malden, MA: Blackwell Publishing, 72–86.

Green, John Richard. 1878–1880. *History of the English People*. 4 vols. Oxford: Clarendon Press.

Green, Jonathon, and Nicholas J. Karolides. 2005. "Theatre Regulation Act (U. K.) (1843)." *The Encyclopedia of Censorship*, New ed. New York: Facts on File Press, 568.

Greenwood, Emily. 2019. "Subaltern Classics in Anti- and Post-Colonial Literatures in English." *The Oxford History of Classical Reception in English Literature, Volume 5: After 1880*. Ed. Kenneth Haynes. Oxford: Oxford University Press, 576–607.

Gregory, Augusta. 1913. *Our Irish Theatre: A Chapter of Autobiography*. New York and London: G. P. Putnam's and Sons and The Knickerbocker Press.

Gregory, Augusta. 1970. *Cuchulain of Muirthemne*. Coole Edition. Gerrards Cross: Colin Smythe.

Gregory, Augusta. 1976. *Seventy Years: Being the Autobiography of Lady Gregory*. New York: Macmillan.

Gregory, Augusta. 1996. *Lady Gregory's Diaries, 1892–1902*. Ed. James Pethica. New York: Oxford University Press.

Grene, David. 1942. *Three Greek Tragedies in Translation*. Chicago, IL: University of Chicago Press.

Grene, Nicholas. 2008. *Yeats's Poetic Codes*. Oxford: Oxford University Press.

Grieve, Dorian. 2011. "MacDiarmid's Language." *The Edinburgh Companion to Hugh MacDiarmid*. Ed. Scott Lyall and Margery Palmer McCulloch. Edinburgh: Edinburgh University Press, 23–35.

Griffin, Gerald. 1938. *The Wild Geese: Pen Portraits of Famous Irish Exiles*. London: Jarrolds.

Griffith, Arthur. 1903. "All Ireland." *The United Irishman*, October 17: 1.

Griffith, Mark. 2007. "Gilbert Murray on Greek Literature: The Great/Greek Man's Burden." *Gilbert Murray Reassessed*. Ed. Christopher Stray. Oxford: Oxford University Press, 51–80.

Griffiths, Bruce. 1979. *Saunders Lewis*. Writers in Wales Series. Cardiff: University of Wales Press.

Grillo, R. D. 1989. *Dominant Languages: Language and Hierarchy in Britain and France*. Cambridge: Cambridge University Press.

Groden, Michael. 1977. *Ulysses in Progress*. Princeton, NJ: Princeton University Press.

Groom, Bernard. 1937. *The Formation and Use of Compound Epithets in English Poetry from 1579*. Oxford: Clarendon Press.

Hacking, Ian. 1989–1990. "Two Kinds of 'New Historicism' for Philosophers." *New Literary History* 21: 343–64.

Hague, René. 1977. *A Commentary on The Anathemata of David Jones*. Toronto: University of Toronto Press.

Hall, Edith, and Fiona Macintosh. 2005. *Greek Tragedy and the British Theatre 1660–1914*. Oxford: Oxford University Press.

Hall, Granville Stanley. 1911. *Educational Problems*. 2 vols. New York: D. Appleton and Co.

Hall, Jonathan. 1997. *Ethnic Identity in Greek Antiquity*. Cambridge: Cambridge University Press.

Hallam, Tudur. 2019. "The Legacy of Saunders Lewis." *The Cambridge History of Welsh Literature*. Ed. Geraint Evans and Helen Fulton. Cambridge: Cambridge University Press, 507–28.

Hanham, H. J. 1969. *Scottish Nationalism*. Cambridge, MA: Harvard University Press.

Hanink, Johanna. 2017. "It's Time to Embrace Critical Classical Reception." *Eidolon*, May 1.

Harding, Jason. 2002. *The Criterion: Cultural Politics and Periodical Networks in Inter-War Britain*. Oxford: Oxford University Press.

Harding, Jason, and John Nash, eds. 2019. *Modernism and Non-Translation.*
Oxford: Oxford University Press.

Hardwick, Lorna. 2000. *Translating Words, Translating Cultures.* London:
Duckworth.

Hardwick, Lorna, and Christopher Stray. 2008. "Introduction: Making
Connections." *A Companion to Classical Receptions.* Ed. Lorna Hardwick
and Christopher Stray. Malden, MA: Wiley-Blackwell, 1–9.

Hardwick, Lorna, and Carol Gillespie, eds. 2007. *Classics in Post-colonial Worlds.*
Oxford: Oxford University Press.

Harrison, Jane Ellen. 1903. *Prolegomena to the Study of Greek Religion.*
Cambridge: Cambridge University Press.

Harrison, Stephen. 2009. "Introduction: The Return of Classics." *Living Classics:
Greece and Rome in Contemporary Poetry in English.* Ed. S. J. Harrison.
Oxford: Oxford University Press, 1–16.

Harrison, Stephen. 2019. "Heaney As Translator, Horace and Virgil." *Seamus
Heaney and the Classics: Bann Valley Muses.* Ed. Stephen Harrison, Fiona
Macintosh and Helen Eastman. Oxford: Oxford University Press, 244–62.

Hart, Matthew. 2010. *Nations of Nothing but Poetry: Modernism,
Transnationalism, and Synthetic Vernacular Writing.* Oxford: Oxford
University Press.

Harvie, Christopher. 2004. *Scotland and Nationalism: Scottish Society and Politics,
1707 to the Present.* 4th ed. New York: Routledge.

Haverfield, Francis. 1905. *The Romanization of Roman Britain.* Oxford:
Clarendon Press.

Haynes, Kenneth. 2003. *English Literature and Ancient Languages.* Oxford:
Oxford University Press.

Haynes, Kenneth. 2007. "Modernism." *A Companion to the Classical Tradition.*
Ed. Craig W. Kallendorf. Malden, MA: Blackwell Publishing, 101–14.

Haynes, Kenneth. 2013. "Gentleman's Latin, Lady's Greek." *The Oxford
Companion to the Victorian Novel.* Ed. Lisa Rodensky. Oxford: Oxford
University Press, 413–37.

Haynes, Kenneth. 2019a. "Preface." *The Oxford History of Classical Reception
in English Literature, Volume 5: After 1880.* Ed. Kenneth Haynes. Oxford:
Oxford University Press, xi–xv.

Haynes, Kenneth. 2019b. "An Introduction to Classical Reception in English
Literature after 1880: The Modern Spiritual Practice of Antiquity." *The
Oxford History of Classical Reception in English Literature, Volume 5: After
1880.* Ed. Kenneth Haynes. Oxford: Oxford University Press, 1–22.

Haywood, Christina. 2003. *The Making of the Classical Museum: Antiquarians,
Collectors and Archaeologists: An Exhibition of the Classical Museum, University
College Dublin.* Dublin: Classical Museum, University College Dublin.

Heaney, Seamus. 1990. *The Cure at Troy: A Version of Sophocles' Philoctetes.*
London: Faber and Faber.

Heaney, Seamus. 2004. *The Burial at Thebes: A Version of Sophocles' Antigone.*
New York: Farrar, Straus and Giroux.

Heath-Stubbs, John. 1998. "Daughters of Memory: *The Anathemata* of David Jones." *The Literary Essays of John Heath-Stubbs*. Manchester: Carcanet Press, 128–33.

Heffer, Simon. 2013. *High Minds: Victorians and the Birth of Modern Britain*. London: Random House Books.

Heil, Günter, and Adolf Martin Ritter, eds. 1991. *Corpus Dionysiacum II*. Berlin: Walter de Gruyter.

Heller, Erich. 1988. "Yeats and Nietzsche: Reflections on Aestheticism and a Poet's Marginal Notes." *The Importance of Nietzsche*. Chicago, IL: University of Chicago Press, 127–40.

Henderson, Jeffrey, ed. and trans. 2002. *Aristophanes: Frogs, Assemblywomen, Wealth*. Cambridge, MA: Harvard University Press.

Henebry, Richard. 1902. "Best Method of Learning Irish." *An Claidheamh Soluis* 4.17 (July): 295.

Henebry, Richard. 1903. "Literary and Old Irish." *An Claidheamh Soluis* 4.51 (February): 857.

Henebry, Richard. 1909. "Revival Irish." *The Leader: A Review of Current Affairs, Politics, Literature, Art and Industry* 17.22 (January): 522–24.

Herbert, W. N. 1992. *To Circumjack MacDiarmid: The Poetry and Prose of Hugh MacDiarmid*. Clarendon: Oxford University Press.

Herder, Johann Gottfried. 1985. *Über die neuere deutsche Literatur, Fragmente. Erste Sammlung* (1768). *Werke in zehn Bänden. Band. 1. Frühe Schriften, 1764–1772*. Ed. Ulrich Gaier. Frankfurt: Verlag.

Herder, Johann Gottfried. 1993. *Werke in zehn Bänden. Band. 2. Schriften zur Ästhetik und Literatur 1767–1781*. Frankfurt: Verlag.

Herring, Phillip F. 1977. "*Ulysses* Item V.A.8, Early Draft of 'Cyclops'." *Joyce's Notes and Early Drafts for Ulysses: Selections from the Buffalo Collection*. Charlottesville: University of Virginia Press, 152–77.

Higgins, Geraldine. 2012. *Heroic Revivals from Carlyle to Yeats*. New York: Palgrave Macmillan.

Highet, Gilbert. 2015. *The Classical Tradition: Greek and Roman Influences on Western Literature*. Oxford: Oxford University Press.

Hill, Geoffrey. 1998. *The Triumph of Love*. Boston and New York: Houghton Mifflin.

Hingley, Richard. 2005. *Globalizing Roman Culture: Unity, Diversity and Empire*. London: Routledge.

Hodgkins, R. H. 1935. *A History of the Anglo-Saxons*. 2 vols. Oxford: Clarendon Press.

Hölderlin, Fredrich, trans. 1804. *Die Trauerspiele des Sophokles*. Erster Band. Frankfurt: Friedrich Wilmans.

Holloway, John. 1967. *Widening Horizons in English Verse*. Evanston, IL: Northwestern University Press.

Holloway, Joseph. 1968. *Joseph Holloway's Irish Theatre, Volume 1: 1926–1931*. Ed. Robert Hogan and Michael J. O'Neill. Dixon, CA: Proscenium Press.

Homer. 1905. *L'Odissea: Testo, costruzione, versione letterale e argomenti. Libro I*. Milano: Societá Editrice Dante Alighieri di Albrighi.

Homer. 1915. *Il libro XIV dell'Odissea*. With notes by Salvatore Rossi. Livorno: Raffaello Giusti.

Homer. 1998. *The Odyssey*. 2nd ed. Trans. A. T. Murray and Rev. George E. Dimock. Cambridge, MA: Harvard University Press.

Hooley, Daniel. 1988. *The Classics in Paraphrase: Ezra Pound and Modern Translations of Latin Poetry*. Selinsgrove, PA: Susquehanna University Press.

Hopkins, Gerard Manley. 2013a. *The Collected Works of Gerard Manley Hopkins: Correspondence, Volume 1: 1852–1881*. Ed. R. K. R. Thornton and Catherine Phillips. Oxford: Oxford University Press.

Hopkins, Gerard Manley. 2013b. *The Collected Works of Gerard Manley Hopkins: Correspondence, Volume 2: 1882–1889*. Ed. R. K. R. Thornton and Catherine Phillips. Oxford: Oxford University Press.

Hopkins, Gerard Manley. 2015. *The Collected Works of Gerard Manley Hopkins, Volume 3: Diaries, Journals, and Notebooks*. Ed. Lesley Higgins. Oxford: Oxford University Press.

House, Humphry. 1953. *Coleridge*. London: Rupert Hart-Davis.

Howatt, A. P. R. and H. G. Widdowson. 2004. "Choosing the Right Words." *A History of English Language Teaching*. 2nd ed. Oxford: Oxford University Press, 278–93.

Hulme, T. E. 1924. *Speculations: Essays on Humanism and the Philosophy of Art*. London: Routledge and Kegan Paul.

Humphreys, Emyr. 1958. *A Toy Epic*. London: Eyre and Spottiswoode.

Humphreys, Emyr. 1983. *The Taliesin Tradition: A Quest for the Welsh Identity*. London: Black Raven Press.

Hunter-Evans, Jasmine. 2014. "You're Awfully Unorthodox, David." *New Welsh Review* 104 (Summer): 24–31.

Hyde, Douglas. 1890. *Beside the Fire*. London: David Nutt.

Hyde, Douglas. 1894. "The Necessity for De-Anglicising Ireland." Charles Gavan Duffy, George Sigerson and Douglas Hyde. *The Revival of Irish Literature, Addresses by Sir Charles Gavan Duffy, K.C.M.G., Dr. George Sigerson, and Dr. Douglas Hyde*. London: T. Fisher Unwin, 116–61.

Hyde, Douglas. 1899. "Dr. Atkinson on Gaelic Literature – To the Editor of the 'Daily Express.'" *The Daily Express*, February 25: 3.

Hyde, Douglas. 1986. *Language, Lore, and Lyrics: Essays and Lectures*. Ed. Breandán Ó Conaire. Dublin: Irish Academic Press.

Impens, Florence. 2018. *Classical Presences in Irish Poetry after 1960: The Answering Voice*. New York: Palgrave Macmillan.

Impens, Florence. 2019. "Classics and Irish Poetry After 1960." *The Oxford History of Classical Reception in English Literature, Volume 5: After 1880*. Ed. Kenneth Haynes. Oxford: Oxford University Press, 525–48.

Intermediate Education (Ireland) Commission. 1899. *Final Report of the Commissioners Intermediate Education (Ireland) Commission [with Evidence]*. Dublin, H. M. Stationery Office.

Jackson, Kenneth. 1953. *Language and History in Early Britain*. Edinburgh: University Press.

Jakobsen, Jakob. 1897. *The Dialect and Place Names of Shetland: Two Popular Lectures*. Lerwick: T. and J. Manson.

Jakobson, Roman. 1959. "On Linguistic Aspects of Translation." *On Translation*. Cambridge, MA: Harvard University Press, 232–39.

Jansen, Laura. 2018. *Borges' Classics: Global Encounters with the Graeco-Roman Past*. Cambridge: Cambridge University Press.

Jebb, Richard. 1877. *Greek Literature*. London: Macmillan and Co.

Jebb, Richard, ed. and trans. 1883. *Sophocles, The Plays and Fragments, Part I, With Critical Notes, Commentary and Translation in English Prose. Volume 1: The Oedipus Tyrannus*. 1st ed. Cambridge: Cambridge University Press.

Jebb, Richard, ed. 1885. *The Oedipus Tyrannus*. Cambridge: Cambridge University Press.

Jebb, Richard. 1893. *The Growth and Influence of Classical Greek Poetry*. Boston and New York: Houghton Mifflin.

Jebb, Richard. 1907. "The Influence of the Greek Mind on Modern Life." *Essays and Addresses*. Cambridge: Cambridge University Press, 560–80.

Jebb, Richard, and A. W. Verrall, trans. 1887. *The Oedipus Tyrannus of Sophocles: As Arranged for Performance at Cambridge, November 1887*. Cambridge: Macmillan and Bowes.

Jeffares, A. Norman, ed. 1977. *W. B. Yeats: The Critical Heritage*. London: Routledge and Kegan Paul.

Jenkins, Dafydd. 1998. *A Nation on Trial, Penyberth 1936*. Trans. Ann Corkett. Cardiff: Welsh Academic Press.

Jenkyns, Richard. 1980. *The Victorians and Ancient Greece*. Cambridge, MA: Harvard University Press.

Johnson, Anna. 2010. "'Wounded Men and Wounded Trees': David Jones and the Anglo-Saxon Culture Tangle." *Anglo-Saxon Culture and the Modern Imagination*. Ed. David Clark and Nicholas Perkins. Cambridge: D. S. Brewer, 89–109.

Johnston, John H. 1964. *English Poetry of the First World War: A Study in the Evolution of Lyric and Narrative Form*. Princeton, NJ: Princeton University Press.

Jones, C. P. 1996. "ἔθνος and γένος in Herodotus." *Classical Quarterly* 46: 315–20.

Jones, Darryl. 1996. "'I Failed Utterly': Saunders Lewis and the Cultural Politics of Welsh Modernism." *The Irish Review* 19 (Spring–Summer): 22–43.

Jones, David. 1937. *In Parenthesis*. London: Faber and Faber.

Jones, David. 1952. *The Anathemata*. London: Faber and Faber.

Jones, David. 1959. *Epoch and Artist*. London: Faber and Faber.

Jones, David. 1972. "A Letter." *Poetry Wales* 8.3 (Winter): 5–9.

Jones, David. 1974. "Yr Iaith." *Planet* 21 (January): 3–5.

Jones, David. 1976. *Letters to Vernon Watkins*. Ed. Ruth Pryor. Cardiff: University of Wales Press.

Jones, David. 1978. *The Dying Gaul and Other Writings*. London: Faber and Faber.

Jones, David. 1979. *Letters to William Hayward*. Ed. Colin Wilcockson. London: Agenda Editions.

Jones, David. 1980. *Dai Greatcoat, A Self-Portrait of David Jones in His Letters.* Ed. René Hague. London: Faber and Faber.

Jones, David. 1980. *David Jones, Letters to a Friend.* Ed. Aneirin Talfan Davies. Swansea: Christopher Davies.

Jones, David. 1984. *Inner Necessities, The Letters of David Jones to Desmond Chute.* Ed. Thomas Dilworth. Toronto: Anson Cartwright Editions.

Jones, David. 1996. *Ten Letters to Two Young Artists Working in Italy.* Ed. Derek Shiel. London: Agenda Editions.

Jones, David. 2016. "An Edition of Jones's Address to the University of Wales, on Receiving the Honorary Degree of Litterarum Doctor, 15 July 1960." Ed. Gregory Baker. *David Jones, Culture and Artifice. Flashpoint* 18 (Summer): 1–12.

Jones, David. 2018. *David Jones on Religion, Politics, and Culture: Unpublished Prose.* Ed. Thomas Berenato, Anne Price-Owen and Kathleen Henderson Staudt. London: Bloomsbury Academic.

Jones, R. Brinley. 1970. *The Old British Tongue: The Vernacular in Wales, 1540–1640.* Cardiff: Avalon Press.

Jones, Richard Wyn. 2014. *The Fascist Party in Wales? Plaid Cymru, Welsh Nationalism and the Accusation of Fascism.* Cardiff: University of Wales Press.

Jones, Siân. 1997. *The Archaeology of Ethnicity.* London: Routledge.

Jordan, Eamonn, and Eric Weitz. 2018. "Introductions/Orientations." *The Palgrave Handbook of Contemporary Irish Theatre and Performance.* Ed. Eamonn Jordan and Eric Weitz. London: Palgrave Macmillan, 1–28.

Joyce, James. 1957. *Letters of James Joyce.* Ed. Stuart Gilbert. New York: Viking Press.

Joyce, James. 1965. "Section 5, The Pola Notebook." *The Workshop of Daedalus: James Joyce and the Raw Materials for A Portrait of the Artist as a Young Man.* Ed. Robert Scholes and Richard M. Kain. Evanston, IL: Northwestern University Press, 80–91.

Joyce, James. 1966. *Letters of James Joyce, Volumes II and III.* Ed. Richard Ellmann. New York: Viking Press.

Joyce, James. 1975. *Selected Letters of James Joyce.* Ed. Richard Ellmann. New York: Viking Press.

Joyce, James. 1979. *Notes, Criticism, Translations & Miscellaneous Writings. A Facsimile of Manuscripts and Typescripts,* Vol. 2. Ed. Hans Walter Gabler. New York: Garland Publishing.

Joyce, James. 1986. *Ulysses.* Ed. Hans Walter Gabler. New York: Random House.

Joyce, James. 1989. *The Critical Writings of James Joyce.* Ed. Ellsworth Mason and Richard Ellmann. Ithaca, NY: Cornell University Press.

Joyce, James. 1993. *A Portrait of the Artist As a Young Man.* Ed. Hans Walter Gabler, with Walter Hettche. New York and London: Garland Publishing.

Joyce, James. 1993. *Dubliners.* Ed. Hans Walter Gabler, with Walter Hettche. New York: Garland Publishing.

Joyce, James. 2012. *Finnegans Wake.* Ed. Robbert-Jan Henkes, Erik Bindervoet and Finn Fordham. Oxford: Oxford University Press.

Joyce, Stanislaus. 2003. *My Brother's Keeper: James Joyce's Early Years*. Cambridge, MA: Da Capo Press.

Kavanagh, Peter. 1950. *The Story of the Abbey Theatre: From Its Origins in 1899 to the Present Day*. New York: Devin-Adair Company.

Keats, John. 1958. *The Letters of John Keats 1814–1821, Volumes 1 and 2*. Ed. Hyder Edward Rollins. Cambridge, MA: Harvard University Press.

Kelleher, John V. 1950. "Matthew Arnold and the Celtic Revival." *Perspectives of Criticism*. Ed. Harry Levin. Cambridge, MA: Harvard University Press, 197–221.

Kenefick, William. 2007. *Red Scotland! The Rise and Fall of the Radical Left, c. 1872 to 1932*. Edinburgh: Edinburgh University Press.

Kennedy, Christopher M. 2010. *Genesis of the Rising, 1912–1916: A Transformation of Nationalist Opinion*. Irish Studies, Vol. 10. Ed. Christopher Berchild. New York: Peter Lang Publishing.

Kenner, Hugh. 1954. "Seedless Fruit." *Poetry* 83.5 (February): 295–301.

Kenner, Hugh. 1969. "Homer's Sticks and Stones." *James Joyce Quarterly* 6.4 (Summer): 285–98.

Kenner, Hugh. 1978. *Joyce's Voices*. Berkeley: University of California Press.

Kenner, Hugh. 1987. *Dublin's Joyce*. Morningside Edition. New York: Columbia University Press.

Kerrigan, Catherine. 1988. "Introduction." *The Hugh MacDiarmid-George Ogilvie Letters*. Ed. Catherine Kerrigan. Aberdeen: Aberdeen University Press, xiii–xxxiii.

Keynes, Simon. 2003. "Introduction: Changing Perceptions of Anglo-Saxon History." Peter Hunter Blair, *An Introduction to Anglo-Saxon England*. 3rd ed. Cambridge: Cambridge University Press, xvii–xxxv.

Kiberd, Declan. 1996. *Inventing Ireland*. Cambridge, MA: Harvard University Press.

Kiberd, Declan. 2001. "Augusta Gregory's Cuchulain: The Rebirth of the Hero." *Irish Classics*. Cambridge, MA: Harvard University Press, 399–419.

Kilroy, James. 1971. *The 'Playboy' Riots*. Dublin: Dolmen Press.

Knirck, Jason K. 2006. *Imagining Ireland's Independence: The Debates over the Anglo-Irish Treaty of 1921*. Lanham, MD: Rowman and Littlefield.

Koeneke, Rodney. 2004. *Empires of the Mind: I. A. Richards and Basic English in China, 1929–1979*. Stanford, CA: Stanford University Press.

Krause, David. 1982. *The Profane Book of Irish Comedy*. Ithaca, NY: Cornell University Press.

Kutzinski, Vera M. 2012. *The Worlds of Langston Hughes: Modernism and Translation in the Americas*. Ithaca, NY: Cornell University Press.

Lauriola, Rosanna. 2017. "Oedipus the King." *Brill's Companion to the Reception of Sophocles*. Ed. Rosanna Lauriola and Kyriakos N. Demetriou. Leiden and Boston, MA: Brill, 149–325.

Lavan, Rosie. 2019. "'Mycenae Lookout' and the Example of Aeschylus." *Seamus Heaney and the Classics: Bann Valley Muses*. Ed. Stephen Harrison, Fiona Macintosh and Helen Eastman. Oxford: Oxford University Press, 50–68.

Lawrie, Alexandra. 2014. *The Beginnings of University English: Extramural Study, 1885–1910*. Basingstoke: Palgrave Macmillan.

Lenin, V. I. 1973. "Speech at a Plenary Session of the Moscow Soviet" [November 20, 1922]. *Collected Works*. Vol. 33. 2nd ed. Trans. David Skvirsky and George Hanna. Moscow: Progress Publishers, 435–43.

Lenin, V. I. 1974. "'The Tasks of the Youth Leagues.' Speech Delivered at the Third All-Russia Congress of the Russian Young Communist League" [October 5, 1920]. *Collected Works*. Vol. 31. 2nd ed. Trans. Julius Katzer. Moscow: Progress Publishers, 283–99.

Lewis, J. Saunders. 1919. "Anglo-Welsh Theatre, The Problem of Language." *The Cambria Daily Leader*, September 10: 4.

Lewis, J. Saunders. 1921. *The Eve of Saint John*. Newtown: The "Welsh Outlook" Press.

Lewis, Saunders. 1930. *The Banned Wireless Talk on Welsh Nationalism*. Caernarvon: Swyddfa'r Blaid Genedlaethol.

Lewis, Saunders. 1936. "The Case for Welsh Nationalism." *The Listener*, May 13: 915–16.

Lewis, Saunders. 1939. *"Is there an Anglo-Welsh Literature?" Being the Annual Lecture Delivered to the Branch on December 10th, 1938*. Caerdydd: Swyddfa Gofrestri, Parc Cathays.

Lewis, Saunders. 1941–1942. *Wales after the War*. Caernarfon: J. E. Jones, Publisher, Nationalist Office.

Lewis, Saunders. 1955. "By Way of Apology." *Dock Leaves* 6.18 (Winter): 10–13.

Lewis, Saunders. 1967. "Epoch and Artist." *Agenda, David Jones Special Issue* 5.1–3 (Spring–Summer): 112–15.

Lewis, Saunders. 1973. *Presenting Saunders Lewis*. Ed. Alun R. Jones and Gwyn Thomas. Cardiff: University of Wales Press.

Lewis, Saunders. 1975. *Egwyddorion Cenedlaetholdeb – Principles of Nationalism*. Trans. Bruce Griffiths. Cardiff: Plaid Cymru. [Welsh edition first published in 1926.]

Lewis, Saunders. 1993. *Saunders Lewis, Letters to Margaret Gilcriest*. Ed. Mair Saunders Jones, Ned Thomas and Harri Pritchard Jones. Cardiff: University of Wales Press.

Liebregts, P. Th. M. G. 1993. *Centaurs in the Twilight: W. B. Yeats's Use of the Classical Tradition*. Amsterdam: Rodopi Press.

Lilly, Gweneth. 1943. "The Welsh Influence in the Poetry of Gerard Manley Hopkins." *The Modern Language Review* 38.3 (July): 192–205.

Linehan, Thomas. 2000. *British Fascism, 1918–1939: Parties, Ideology and Culture*. Manchester: Manchester University Press.

Livingstone, R. W. 1912. *The Greek Genius and Its Meaning to Us*. Oxford: Clarendon Press.

Lloyd, D. Tecwyn. 1988. *John Saunders Lewis, Y Gyfrol Gyntaf*. Dinbych: Gwasg Gee.

Long, A. A. 1968. *Language and Thought in Sophocles: A Study of Abstract Nouns and Poetic Technique*. London: University of London and The Athlone Press.

Longenbach, James. 1988. *Stone Cottage: Pound, Yeats and Modernism.* Oxford: Oxford University Press.

Longenbach, James. 2010. "Modern Poetry." *Yeats In Context.* Ed. David Holdeman and Ben Levitas. Cambridge: Cambridge University Press, 320–29.

Lowe, Elizabeth. 2014. "Revisiting Re-translation: Re-creation and Historical Re-vision." *A Companion to Translation Studies.* Ed. Sandra Bermann and Catherine Porter. West Sussex: John Wiley & Sons, 413–24.

Luce, John Victor. 1992. *Trinity College Dublin: The First Four Hundred Years.* Dublin: Trinity College Press.

Lyall, Scott. 2006. *Hugh MacDiarmid's Poetry and Politics of Place: Imagining a Scottish Republic.* Edinburgh: Edinburgh University Press.

Lyall, Scott. 2011. "MacDiarmid, Communism and the Poetry of Commitment." *The Edinburgh Companion to Hugh MacDiarmid.* Ed. Scott Lyall and Margery Palmer McCulloch. Edinburgh: Edinburgh University Press, 68–81.

Lyons, F. S. L. 1979. *Culture and Anarchy in Ireland, 1890–1939.* Oxford: Oxford University Press.

Lysaght, Meadhbh. 1996. "Trinity College Schools' Competition Junior Gold Medal Winner: Dublin's Wholesale Fruit and Vegetable Market." *History Ireland* 4.3 (Autumn): 42–45.

M'Diarmid, Hugh. 1926. *A Drunk Man Looks at the Thistle.* Edinburgh and London: William Blackwood & Sons.

MacCormick, J. M. 1955. *The Flag in the Wind.* London: Victor Gollancz.

MacDiarmid, Hugh. 1939a. "Cornish Heroic Song for Valda Trevlyn." *The Criterion* 18.71 (January): 195–203.

MacDiarmid, Hugh. 1939b. "A Letter to the Editor." *The Voice of Scotland* 1.4 (March–May): 17–20.

MacDiarmid, Hugh. 1943. "Foreword" in Douglas Young, *Auntran Blads: An Outwale o Verses.* Glasgow: William MacLellan and Co., 5–9.

MacDiarmid, Hugh. 1955. *In Memoriam James Joyce, From A Vision of World Language.* Glasgow: William Maclellan.

MacDiarmid, Hugh. 1967–1968. "Credo for a Celtic Poet." *Agenda, Double Issue: Hugh MacDiarmid and Scottish Poetry* 5.4–6.1 (Autumn–Winter): 12–15.

MacDiarmid, Hugh. 1968. "Scotland." *Celtic Nationalism.* London: Routledge and Kegan Paul, 299–358.

MacDiarmid, Hugh. 1970. *Selected Essays of Hugh MacDiarmid.* Ed. Duncan Glen. Berkeley: University of California Press.

MacDiarmid, Hugh. 1977. *Cornish Heroic Song for Valda Trevlyn and Once in a Cornish Garden.* Padstow: Lodenek Press.

MacDiarmid, Hugh. 1984. *The Letters of Hugh MacDiarmid.* Ed. Alan Bold. Athens: University of Georgia Press.

MacDiarmid, Hugh. 1988. *The Hugh MacDiarmid-George Ogilvie Letters.* Ed. Catherine Kerrigan. Aberdeen: Aberdeen University Press.

MacDiarmid, Hugh. 1992. *Selected Prose.* Ed. Alan Riach. Manchester: Carcanet Press.

MacDiarmid, Hugh. 1993. *Complete Poems, Volume 1*. Ed. Michael Grieve and W. R. Aitken. Manchester: Carcanet Press.

MacDiarmid, Hugh. 1994a. *Complete Poems, Volume 2*. Ed. Michael Grieve and W. R. Aitken. Manchester: Carcanet Press.

MacDiarmid, Hugh. 1994b. *Lucky Poet*. Ed. Alan Riach. Manchester: Carcanet Press.

MacDiarmid, Hugh. 1995. *Contemporary Scottish Studies*. Ed. Alan Riach. Manchester: Carcanet Press.

MacDiarmid, Hugh. 1996a. *Albyn: Shorter Books and Monographs*. Ed. Alan Riach. Manchester: Carcanet Press.

MacDiarmid, Hugh. 1996b. *The Raucle Tongue, Hitherto Uncollected Prose, Volume 1*. Ed. Angus Calder, Glen Murray and Alan Riach. Manchester: Carcanet Press.

MacDiarmid, Hugh. 1997. *The Raucle Tongue, Hitherto Uncollected Prose, Volume 2*. Ed. Angus Calder, Glen Murray and Alan Riach. Manchester: Carcanet Press.

MacDiarmid, Hugh. 1998. *The Raucle Tongue, Hitherto Uncollected Prose, Volume 3*. Ed. Angus Calder, Glen Murray and Alan Riach. Manchester: Carcanet Press.

MacDiarmid, Hugh. 2001. *New Selected Letters of Hugh MacDiarmid*. Ed. Dorian Grieve, O. D. Edwards and Alan Riach. Manchester: Carcanet Press.

MacDiarmid, Hugh, and Edwin Muir. 2005. "For the Vernacular Circle." *Scottish Studies Review* 6.1 (May): 59–73.

Macintosh, Fiona. 1994. *Dying Acts: Death in Ancient Greek and Modern Irish Tragic Drama*. Cork: Cork University Press.

Macintosh, Fiona. 1997. "Tragedy in Performance: Nineteenth- and Twentieth-Century Productions." *The Cambridge Companion to Greek Tragedy*. Ed. P. E. Easterling. Cambridge: Cambridge University Press, 284–323.

Macintosh, Fiona. 2008. "An Oedipus for Our Times? Yeats's Version of Sophocles' *Oedipus Tyrannus*." *Performance, Iconography, Reception: Studies in Honour of Oliver Taplin*. Ed. Martin Revermann and Peter Wilson. Oxford: Oxford University Press, 524–47.

Macintosh, Fiona. 2011. "Irish Antigone and Burying the Dead." *Antigone on the Contemporary World Stage*. Ed. Erin B. Mee and Helene Foley. Oxford and New York: Oxford University Press, 90–103.

Macintosh, Fiona. 2016. "Conquering England: Ireland and Greek Tragedy." *A Handbook to the Reception of Greek Drama*. Ed. Betine van Zyl Smit. Chichester: John Wiley and Sons, 323–36.

MacIntyre, Alasdair. 2007. *After Virtue*. 3rd ed. Notre Dame, IN: University of Notre Dame Press.

Mackail, J. W. 1895. *Latin Literature*. New York: Charles Scribner's Sons.

MacKenna, Stephen. 1936. *Journal and Letters of Stephen MacKenna*. Ed. E. R. Dodds. London: Constable and Co.

MacKinnon, Kenneth. 1991. "Language-Retreat and Regeneration in the Present-Day Scottish Gàidhealtachd." *Linguistic Minorities, Society and Territory*. Ed. Colin H. Williams. Clevedon, Avon: Multilingual Matters, 121–49.

MacKinnon, Kenneth. 2000. "Scottish Gaelic." *Languages in Britain & Ireland*. Ed. Glanville Price. Oxford: Blackwell Publishers, 44–55.

Macpherson, James. 1765. *The Works of Ossian, The Son of Fingal. In Two Volumes*. London: T. Beckett and P. A. De Hondt at Tully's Head.

Macpherson, James. 1805. *The Poems of Ossian &c. Containing the Poetical Works of James Macpherson, Esq., in Prose and Rhyme: With Notes and Illustrations by Malcolm Laing, Esq.* 2 vols. Edinburgh: Archibald Constable and Company.

Macpherson, James. 1996. *The Poems of Ossian and Related Works*. Ed. Howard Gaskill. Edinburgh: Edinburgh University Press.

Mahaffy, J. P. 1882. "Education in Hungary." *The Athenaeum*, October 7: 464–65.

Mahaffy, J. P. 1896. "The Modern Babel." *The Nineteenth Century* 40 (November): 782–96.

Mahaffy, J. P. 1899. "The Recent Fuss Over the Irish Language." *The Nineteenth Century* 46 (August): 213–22.

Mahaffy, J. P. 1909. *What Have the Greeks Done for Modern Civilization?* New York and London: The Knickerbocker Press.

Mahony, Christina Hunt. 2016. "Reinscribing the Classics, Ancient and Modern: The Sharp Diagonal of Adaptation." *The Oxford Handbook of Modern Irish Theatre*. Ed. Nicholas Grene and Chris Morash. Oxford: Oxford University Press, 654–70.

Mandle, W. F. 1987. *The Gaelic Athletic Association and Irish Nationalist Politics 1884–1924*. Dublin: Gill and Macmillan.

Mangan, James Clarence. 1846. "Prince Aldfrid's Itinerary Through Ireland." *Specimens of the Early Native Poetry of Ireland in English Metrical Translations*. Ed. Henry R. Montgomery. Dublin: James McGlashan, 60–65.

Mannix, Patrick. 2012. *The Belligerent Prelate: An Alliance between Archbishop Daniel Mannix and Eamon de Valera*. Newcastle upon Tyne: Cambridge Scholars Publishing.

Manson, John, ed. 2011. *Dear Grieve, Letters to Hugh MacDiarmid*. Glasgow: Kennedy and Boyd.

Marks, Emerson R. 1998. *Taming the Chaos: English Poetic Diction Theory since the Renaissance*. Detroit, MI: Wayne State University Press.

Martin, Richard. 2007. "Homer Among the Irish: Yeats, Synge, Thomson and Parry." *Homer in the Twentieth Century*. Ed. Barbara Graziosi and Emily Greenwood. Oxford: Oxford University Press, 75–91.

Martindale, Charles. 1993. *Redeeming the Text: Latin Poetry and the Hermeneutics of Reception*. Cambridge: Cambridge University Press.

Masqueray, Paul, trans. 1922. *Sophocle: Ajax, Antigone, Oedipe-Roi, Electre*. Vol. 1. Paris: Société d'Édition "Les Belles Lettres."

Mathews, P. J. 2003. *Revival: The Abbey Theatre, Sinn Féin, the Gaelic League, and the Co-operative Movement*. Notre Dame, IN: University of Notre Dame.

Mattar, Sinéad Garrigan. 2004. *Primitivism, Science, and the Irish Revival*. Oxford: Oxford University Press.

Mattingly, David. 2006. *An Imperial Possession: Britain in the Roman Empire, 54 BC – AD 409*. London: Allen Lane.

McCleery, Alistair. 1990. "The One Lost Lamb." *James Joyce Quarterly* 27.3 (Spring): 635–39.

McCleery, Alistair. 1994. "The Gathered Lambs." *James Joyce Quarterly* 31.4 (Summer): 557–63.

McClure, J. Derrick. 2000. *Language, Poetry, and Nationhood: Scots As a Poetic Language from 1878 to the Present*. East Linton: Tuckwell Press.

McClure, J. Derrick. 2002. *Doric: The Dialect of North-East Scotland*. Amsterdam: John Benjamins Publishing.

McCormack, W. J. 1985. *Ascendancy and Tradition in Anglo-Irish Literary History*. Oxford: Clarendon Press.

McCormack, W. J. 2005. *Blood Kindred: W. B. Yeats, The Life, The Death, The Politics*. London: Pimlico Press.

McCourt, John. 2000. *The Years of Bloom, James Joyce in Trieste 1904–1920*. Madison: University of Wisconsin.

McCrea, Barry. 2015. *Languages of the Night*. New Haven, CT and London: Yale University Press.

McCulloch, Margery Palmer, ed. 2004. *Modernism and Nationalism: Literature and Society in Scotland 1918–1939*. Glasgow: Association for Scottish Literary Studies.

McCulloch, Margery Palmer. 2009. *Scottish Modernism and Its Contexts 1918–1959: Literature, National Identity and Cultural Exchange*. Edinburgh: Edinburgh University Press.

McDonald, Marianne. 2000. "Classics As Celtic Firebrand: Greek Tragedy, Irish Playwrights and Colonialism." *Theatre Stuff: Critical Essays on Contemporary Irish Theatre*. Ed. Eamonn Jordan. Dublin: Carysfort Press, 16–26.

McDonald, Marianne. 2002. "The Irish and Greek Tragedy." *Amid Our Troubles: Irish Versions of Greek Tragedy*. Ed. Marianne McDonald and J. Michael Walton. London: Methuen, 37–86.

McDonald, Peter. 1995. "The Greeks in Ireland: Irish Poets and Greek Tragedy." *Translation and Literature* 4.2: 183–203.

McGarrity, Maria. 2009. "Primitive Emancipation: Religion, Sexuality and Freedom in Joyce's *A Portrait of the Artist as a Young Man* and *Ulysses*." *Irish Modernism and the Global Primitive*. Ed. Maria McGarrity and Claire A. Culleton. New York: Palgrave Macmillan, 133–52.

McIntosh, Gillian. 1999. *The Force of Culture: Unionist Identities in Twentieth-Century Ireland*. Cork: Cork University Press.

McKinsey, Martin. 2001. "Counter-Homericism in Yeats's 'The Wanderings of Oisin'." *W. B. Yeats and Postcolonialism*. Ed. Deborah Fleming. West Cornwall, CT: Locust Hill Press, 235–51.

McLane, Maureen. 2001. "Ballads and Bards: British Romantic Orality." *Modern Philology* 98.3: 423–43.

Melchiori, Giorgio. 1981. "The Politics of Language and the Language of Politics." *James Joyce Broadsheet* 1.4 (February): 1.

Michelet, Jules. 1835. *Histoire de France*. 17 vols. Paris: Librarie Classique de L. Hachette.

Miles, Jonathan. 1990. *Backgrounds to David Jones: A Study in Sources and Drafts*. Cardiff: University of Wales Press.

Millet, Martin. 1990. *The Romanization of Britain*. Cambridge: Cambridge University Press.

Mitchell, Arthur. 1995. *Revolutionary Government in Ireland: Dáil Éireann 1919–22*. Dublin: Gill & Macmillan.

Moore, George. 1911. *Hail and Farewell! Ave*. London: Heinemann.

Moore, George. 1914a. "Yeats, Lady Gregory, and Synge." *The English Review* 16 (January): 167–70.

Moore, George. 1914b. *Hail and Farewell! Vale*. London: Heinemann.

Moore, N. F. 1835. *Lectures on the Greek Language and Literature*. New York: Windt and Conrad.

Moorhouse, A. C. 1959. *Studies in the Greek Negatives*. Cardiff: University of Wales Press.

Moran, D. P. 2006. *The Philosophy of Irish Ireland*. Dublin: University College Dublin Press.

Morash, Chris. 2020. "Yeats and Oedipus: The Dark Road." *Classics and Irish Politics, 1916–2016*. Ed. Isabelle Torrance and Donncha O'Rourke. Oxford: Oxford University Press, 218–34.

Morgan, Kenneth O. 1971. "Welsh Nationalism: The Historical Background." *Journal of Contemporary History* 6.1: 153–59, 161–72.

Morgan, Kenneth O. 1981. *Rebirth of a Nation: Wales, 1880–1980*. New York: Oxford University Press.

Morley, Henry. 1871. "Influence of the Celt on English Literature." *Clement Marot and Other Studies, Volume 2*. London: Chapman and Hall, 248–84.

Morris, Mowbray. 1888. [Review of Matthew Arnold]. *The Quarterly Review* 167.334 (October): 398–426.

Muir, Edwin. 1936. *Scott and Scotland*. London: George Routledge and Sons.

Muir, Edwin. 1951. "Preface." *Catalogue of an Exhibition of 20th-century Scottish Books at the Mitchell Library, Glasgow*. Glasgow: Robert MacLehose and Co., iii–iv.

Murphy, Andrew. 2017. *Ireland, Reading and Cultural Nationalism, 1790–1930*. Cambridge: Cambridge University Press.

Murphy, William M. 1978. *Prodigal Father: The Life of John Butler Yeats (1839–1922)*. Ithaca, NY: Cornell University Press.

Murray, Christopher. 1997. *Twentieth-Century Irish Drama: Mirror Up to Nation*. Manchester: Manchester University Press.

Murray, Gilbert. 1897. *A History of Ancient Greek Literature*. New York: D. Appleton and Company.

Murray, Gilbert, trans. 1911. *Oedipus, King of Thebes*. New York: Oxford University Press.

Murray, Gilbert. 1921. *The Problem of Foreign Policy*. Boston, MA: Houghton Mifflin.

Murray, Gilbert. 1927. *The Classical Tradition in Poetry.* Cambridge, MA: Harvard University Press.

Murray, Gilbert. 1954. *Hellenism and the Modern World.* Boston, MA: The Beacon Press.

Murray, Gilbert. 1977. "Letter to W. B. Yeats. 27 January 1905." *Letters to W. B. Yeats.* Vol. 1. Ed. Richard Finneran, George Mills Harper and William M. Murphy. New York: Columbia University Press, 145–46.

Nash, John. 2006. *James Joyce and the Act of Reception: Reading, Ireland, Modernism.* Cambridge: Cambridge University Press.

Newbolt Report. 1921. *The Teaching of English in England.* London: Board of Education, His Majesty's Stationery Office.

Newman, F. W., trans. 1856. *The Iliad of Homer, Faithfully Translated into Unrhymed English Metre.* London: Walton and Maberly.

Nietzsche, Friedrich. 1878. *Menschliches, Allzumenschliches: Ein Buch für freie Geister.* Chemnitz: Ernst Schmeitzner.

Nietzsche, Friedrich. 1901. *Nietzsche as Critic, Philosopher, Poet and Prophet.* Trans. Thomas Common. London: Grant Richards.

Nietzsche, Friedrich. 1986. *Human, All Too Human: A Book for Free Spirits.* Trans. R. J. Hollingdale. Cambridge: Cambridge University Press.

Nikopoulos, James. 2017. "The Wisdom of Myth: '*Ulysses*, Order, and Myth'." *Brill's Companion to the Reception of Classics in International Modernism and the Avant-Garde.* Ed. Adam J. Goldwyn and James Nikopoulos. Leiden and Boston: Brill, 292–311.

Novillo-Corvalán, Patricia. 2011. *Borges and Joyce: An Infinite Conversation.* New York: Taylor and Francis.

Ó Conchubhair, Brian. 2009. *Fin de Siècle na Gaeilge: Darwin, an Athbheochan agus Smaointeoireacht na hEorpa.* Gaillimh: An Clóchomhar.

O'Connor, Laura. 2006. *Haunted English: The Celtic Fringe, the British Empire, and De-Anglicization.* Baltimore, MD: Johns Hopkins University Press.

O'Connor, Ulick. 1964. *Oliver St John Gogarty: A Poet and His Times.* London: Jonathan Cape.

Ó Dochartaigh, Cathair. 2000. "Irish in Ireland." *Languages in Britain and Ireland.* Ed. Glanville Price. Oxford: Blackwell Publishers, 6–36.

O'Driscoll, Robert. 1971. "Two Lectures on the Irish Theatre by W. B. Yeats." *Theatre and Nationalism in Twentieth-Century Ireland.* Ed. Robert O'Driscoll. Toronto: University of Toronto Press, 66–88.

O'Grady, Standish, ed. and trans. 1857. *Tóraíocht Dhiarmada agus Gráinne: The Pursuit of Diarmuid and Gráinne.* Dublin: The Ossianic Society. [Printed in *Transactions of the Ossianic Society for the Year 1855* 3 (1857).]

O'Grady, Standish. 1881. *History of Ireland: Critical and Philosophical.* 2 vols. London and Dublin.

O'Higgins, Laurie. 2017. *The Irish Classical Self: Poets and Poor Scholars in the Eighteenth and Nineteenth Centuries.* Oxford: Oxford University Press.

O'Leary, Philip. 1994. *The Prose Literature of the Gaelic Revival, 1881–1921: Ideology and Innovation.* University Park, PA: The Pennsylvania State University Press.

O'Looney, Bryan, ed. and trans. 1859. *Lay of Oisin on the Land of Youths*. Dublin: The Ossianic Society. [Printed in *Transactions of the Ossianic Society for the Year 1856* 4 (1859): 227–80.]

O'Shea, Edward. 1985. *A Descriptive Catalog of W. B. Yeats's Library*. New York and London: Garland Publishing.

Ogden, C. K. 1931. *Debabelization, With a Survey of Contemporary Opinion on the Problem of a Universal Language*. London: Kegan Paul, Trench, Trübner and Co.

Ogden, C. K. 1932. *Basic English, A General Introduction with Rules and Grammar*. London: Kegan Paul, Trench, Trübner and Co.

Ogden, C. K. 1934. *The System of Basic English*. New York: Harcourt, Brace and Company.

Oppel, Frances Nesbitt. 1987. *Mask and Tragedy, Yeats and Nietzsche, 1902–10*. Charlottesville: University of Virginia Press.

Orr, Peter. 1966. "David Jones." *The Poet Speaks*. London: Routledge and Kegan Paul, 97–104.

Owen, Rodney Wilson. 1983. *James Joyce and the Beginnings of Ulysses*. Ann Arbor: University of Michigan Research Press.

P. G. W. 1903. "Daily Chronicle Office, Wednesday Morning." *Daily Chronicle*, May 13: 7.

Paget, Richard. 1930. *Babel, or The Past, Present, and Future of Human Speech*. London: Kegan Paul, Trench, Trübner and Co.

Palmer, D. J. 1965. *The Rise of English Studies*. London: Oxford University Press.

Pankhurst, E. Sylvia. 1926. *Delphos: The Future of International Language*. London: Kegan Paul, Trench, Trübner and Co.

Parkinson, Thomas. 1964. *W. B. Yeats, The Later Poetry*. Berkeley: University of California Press.

Parkinson, Thomas. 1971. *W. B. Yeats, Self-Critic*. Berkeley: University of California Press.

Pašeta, Senia. 1998–99. "Trinity College, Dublin, and the Education of Irish Catholic, 1873–1908." *Studia Hibernica* 30: 7–20.

Pater, Walter H. 1876a. "The Myth of Demeter and Persephone." *The Fortnightly Review* 19.109 (January): 82–95.

Pater, Walter H. 1876b. "The Myth of Demeter and Persephone." *The Fortnightly Review* 19.110 (February): 260–76.

Pater, Walter. 1910. *Greek Studies: A Series of Essays*. New Library ed. London: Macmillan.

Patmore, Coventry. 1854. Rev. of *Poems* by Matthew Arnold. *North British Review* 21 (August): 493–504.

Paulin, Tom. 1985. *The Riot Act: A Version of Sophocles' Antigone*. London: Faber and Faber.

Pearse, P. H. 1898. *Three Lectures on Gaelic Topics*. Dublin: M. H. Gill.

Pearse, Pádraic H. 1924. *Collected Works of Padraic H. Pearse – Songs of the Irish Rebels and Specimens from an Irish Anthology, Some Aspects of Irish Literature, Three Lectures on Gaelic Topics*. Dublin: Phoenix Park.

Pei, Mario. 1958. *One Language for the World*. New York: Devin-Adair.

Pillans, James. 1848. *A Word for the Universities of Scotland; and a Plea for the Humanity Classes in the College of Edinburgh*. Edinburgh: Maclachlan, Stewart and Co.

Platt, L. H. 1992. "Joyce and the Anglo-Irish Revival: The Triestine Lectures." *James Joyce Quarterly* 29.2 (Winter): 259–66.

Platt, Len. 1998. *Joyce and the Anglo-Irish: A Study of Joyce and the Literary Revival*. Amsterdam: Rodopi Press.

Plumptre, E. H. 1867. *The Tragedies of Sophocles*. London: Alexander Strahan.

Porter, James I. 2004. "Homer: The History of an Idea." *The Cambridge Companion to Homer*. Ed. Robert Fowler. Cambridge: Cambridge University Press, 324–43.

Pound, Ezra. 1913. "Xenia." *Poetry* 3.2 (November): 58–60.

Pound, Ezra. 1914. "The Later Yeats." *Poetry* 4.2 (May): 64–69.

Pound, Ezra. 1918. "A Retrospect." *Pavannes and Divisions*. New York: Alfred A. Knopf.

Pound, Ezra. 1970. *Pound/Joyce: The Letters of Ezra Pound to James Joyce, with Pound's Essays on Joyce*. Ed. Forrest Read. New York: New Directions.

Pound, Ezra. 1971. *The Selected Letters of Ezra Pound, 1907–1941*. Ed. D. D. Paige. New York: New Directions.

Pound, Ezra. 1988. *Ezra Pound and Margaret Cravens: A Tragic Friendship, 1910–1912*. Ed. Omar Pound and Robert Spoo. Durham, NC: Duke University Press,

Power, Arthur. 1974. *Conversations with James Joyce*. New York: Harper and Row.

Prins, Yopie. 2017. *Ladies' Greek: Victorian Translations of Tragedy*. Princeton, NJ: Princeton University Press.

Pseudo-Dionysius. 1899. "On the Heavenly Hierarchy." *The Works of Dionysius the Areopagite, Part II – The Heavenly Hierarchy and The Ecclesiastical Hierarchy*. Trans. Rev. John Parker. London and Oxford, 1–66.

Pugh, Martin. 2006. *Hurrah for The Blackshirts! Fascists and Fascism in Britain Between the Wars*. London: Pimlico.

Purdom, C. B. 1955. *Harley Granville Barker, Man of the Theatre, Dramatist, and Scholar*. London: Rockliff Press.

Puttenham, George. 2007. *The Arte of English Poesy: A Critical Edition*. Ed. Frank Whigham and Wayne A. Rebhorn. Ithaca, NY: Cornell University Press.

R. M. 1904. "The National Theatre Society, Its Work and Ambitions, A Chat with Mr. W. B. Yeats." *Evening Mail*, December 31: 4.

R. M. 1905. "The National Theatre Society, A Chat with Mr. W. B. Yeats." *Daily Express*, January 2: 6.

Raby, Peter. 1991. *Samuel Butler: A Biography*. Iowa City: University of Iowa Press.

Raine, Kathleen. 1974–75. *David Jones, Solitary Perfectionist*. Ipswich: Golgonooza Press.

Raine, Kathleen. 1982. "David Jones and the Actually Loved and Known." *The Inner Journey of the Poet*. New York: George Brazilier, 118–36.

Ramsay, A. A. W. 1933. *Challenge to the Highlander*. London: John Murray.

Read, Herbert Edward. 1937. "War and the Spirit." *Times Literary Supplement* 1846 (June 19): 457.

Rees, William, ed. 1938. *The Transactions of the Honourable Society of Cymmrodorion, Session 1937*. London, 27–100.

Reynolds, Matthew. 2006. "Principles and Norms of Translation." *The Oxford History of Literary Translation in English, Volume 4: 1790–1900*. Ed. Peter France and Kenneth Haynes. Oxford: Oxford University Press, 59–82.

Rhys, John. 1901. "Race in Folklore and Myth." *Celtic Folklore, Welsh and Manx*. Vol. 2. Oxford: Clarendon Press, 639–88.

Riach, Alan. 1991. *Hugh MacDiarmid's Epic Poetry*. Edinburgh: Edinburgh University Press.

Richards, I. A. 1943. *Basic English and Its Uses*. New York: W. W. Norton and Company.

Richardson, Edmund. 2013. *Classical Victorians: Scholars, Scoundrels and Generals in Pursuit of Antiquity*. Cambridge: Cambridge University Press.

Ringler, William. 1941. "Poeta Nascitur Non Fit: Some Notes on the History of an Aphorism." *Journal of the History of Ideas* 2.4 (October): 497–504.

Roberts, Nesta. 1964. "Sign of the Bear." *The Guardian*, February 17: 7.

Robichaud, Paul. 2007. *Making the Past Present: David Jones, the Middle Ages and Modernism*. Washington, DC: The Catholic University of America Press.

Roche, Anthony. 1988. "Ireland's *Antigones*: Tragedy North and South." *Cultural Contexts and Literary Idioms in Contemporary Irish Literature*. Ed. Michael Kenneally. Gerrards Cross: Colin Smythe, 221–50.

Rodgers, W. R., ed. 1973. "J. M. Synge." *Irish Literary Portraits*. New York: Taplinger Publishing Co., 94–115.

Romero, Patricia W. 1987. *E. Sylvia Pankhurst: Portrait of a Radical*. New Haven, CT: Yale University Press.

Ross, Iain. 2013. *Oscar Wilde and Ancient Greece*. Cambridge: Cambridge University Press.

Royal Commission on University Education in Ireland, 1901. *Second Report of the Commissioners*. Dublin.

Rudd, Niall. 1994. "Pound and Propertius: Two Former Moderns" with "Appendix: Professor Hale and *Homage* as a Document of Cultural Transition." *The Classical Tradition in Operation*. Toronto: University of Toronto Press, 117–58.

Russo, John Paul. 1989. *I. A. Richards: His Life and Work*. Baltimore, MD: Johns Hopkins University Press.

Ruthven, K. K. 1979. "Criteria of Complexity and Simplicity." *Critical Assumptions*. Cambridge: Cambridge University Press, 33–50.

Ryan, William P. 1902. "Kiltartan, Mr. Yeats, and Cuchulain." *The Leader: A Review of Current Affairs, Politics, Literature, Art and Industry*, July 5: 297–99.

Saint-Girons, Baldine. 2014. "Sublime." *Dictionary of Untranslatables: A Philosophical Lexicon*. Ed. Barbara Cassin. Princeton, NJ: Princeton University Press, 1091–1096.

Saurat, Denis. 1924. "Le Groupe de la Renaissance écossaise." *Revue Anglo-américaine* 1.4 (April): 295–307.

Schork, R. J. 1991. "Buck Mulligan As *Grammaticus Gloriosus* in Joyce's *Ulysses*." *Arion* 3rd series. 1.3 (Fall): 76–92.

Schork, R. J. 1997. *Latin and Roman Culture in Joyce*. Gainesville: University of Florida Press.

Schork, R. J. 1998. *Greek and Hellenic Culture in Joyce*. Gainesville: University of Florida Press.

Schuchard, Ronald. 2008. *The Last Minstrels: Yeats and the Revival of the Bardic Arts*. Oxford: Oxford University Press.

Schwartzman, Myron. 1974–1975. "The V.A.8 Copybook: An Early Draft of the 'Cyclops' Chapter of *Ulysses* with Notes on its Development." *James Joyce Quarterly* 12.1/2: 64–122.

Scott, J. W. 2004. "Ogden, Charles Kay (1889–1957)," revised by W. Terrence Gordon. *Oxford Dictionary of National Biography*. Oxford: Oxford University Press.

Seidel, Michael. 1976. *Epic Geography: James Joyce's Ulysses*. Princeton, NJ: Princeton University Press.

Senn, Fritz. 1984. "Book of Many Turns." *Joyce's Dislocutions: Essays on Reading As Translation*. Ed. John Paul Riquelme. Baltimore, MD: Johns Hopkins University Press, 121–37.

Senn, Fritz. 1987. "In Classical Idiom: Anthologia Intertextualis." *James Joyce Quarterly* 25.1 (Fall): 31–48.

Senn, Fritz. 1992. "'In the Original': Buck Mulligan and Stephen Dedalus." *Arion* 3rd series. 2.1 (Winter): 215–17.

Shelley, Percy Bysshe. 2002. *Shelley's Poetry and Prose*. 2nd ed. Ed. Donald H. Reiman and Neil Freistat. New York: W. W. Norton and Company.

Sidnell, Michael. 1996. "The Allegory of *The Wanderings of Oisin*." *Yeats's Poetry and Poetics*. New York: St. Martin's Press, 160–75.

Sidney, Philip. 1983. "The Defence of Poesy." *Sir Philip Sidney: Selected Prose and Poetry*. 2nd ed. Ed. Robert Kimbrough. Madison: University of Wisconsin Press, 99–158.

Simonsuuri, Kirsti. 1979. *Homer's Original Genius: Eighteenth-century Notions of the Early Greek Epic (1688–1798)*. Cambridge: Cambridge University Press.

Smith, Alexander. 1857. "Keats, John." *Encyclopedia Brittanica, Or Dictionary of Arts, Sciences, and General Literature. Eighth Edition. Volume 13*. Boston, MA: Little, Brown, and Co., 55–57.

Smith, G. Gregory. 1919. *Scottish Literature, Character and Influence*. London: Macmillan and Co.

Solly, Henry Shaen. 1898. *The Life of Henry Morley, LL.D.* London: Edward Arnold.

Sophocles. 1899. *The Oedipus Tyrannus of Sophocles, Translated and Presented by the Students of Notre Dame University*. Notre Dame, IN: University Press.

Stanford, W. B. 1976. *Ireland and the Classical Tradition*. Dublin: Allen Figgis and Co.

Stanford, W. B. and R. B. McDowell. 1971. *Mahaffy, A Biography of an Anglo-Irishman*. London: Routledge and Kegan Paul.

Staudt, Kathleen. 1994. *At the Turn of a Civilization: David Jones and Modern Poetics*. Ann Arbor: University of Michigan Press.

Staudt, Kathleen Henderson. 2018. "David Jones: An Unpublished Appreciation of Gerard Manley Hopkins." *David Jones on Religion, Politics, and Culture: Unpublished Prose*. Ed. Thomas Berenato, Anne Price-Owen and Kathleen Henderson Staudt. London: Bloomsbury Academic, 321–25.

Stead, Henry, and Edith Hall, eds. 2015. *Greek and Roman Classics in the British Struggle for Social Reform*. London: Bloomsbury Academic.

Stenton, F. M. 1943. *Anglo-Saxon England*. Oxford: Clarendon Press.

Stephens, Edward. 1974. *My Uncle John, Edward Stephens's Life of J. M. Synge*. Ed. Andrew Carpenter. London: Oxford University Press.

Stephens, Susan A., and Phiroze Vasunia, eds. 2010. *Classics and National Culture*. Oxford and New York: Oxford University Press.

Stern, Bert. 2014. *Winter in China: An American Life*. Xlibris.

Storr, Francis. 1912. "Introduction." *Sophocles: With an English Translation by F. Storr, B.A. Volume 1*. London: Heinemann, vii–xiv.

Strand, Karin. 1978. "W. B. Yeats's American Lecture Tours." Ph.D. Diss., Northwestern University.

Stray, Christopher. 1998. *Classics Transformed: Schools, Universities, and Society in England, 1830–1960*. Oxford: Clarendon Press.

Stray, Christopher. 2007a. "Jebb's Sophocles: An Edition and Its Maker." *Classical Books, Scholarship and Publishing in Britain Since 1800*. London: Institute of Classical Studies, University of London, 75–96.

Stray, Christopher. 2007b. "Introduction." *Gilbert Murray Reassessed: Hellenism, Theatre and International Politics*. Oxford: Oxford University Press, 1–15.

Stray, Christopher, ed. 2013. *Sophocles' Jebb: A Life in Letters. Cambridge Classical Journal*, Supplement 38. Cambridge: Cambridge Philological Society.

Stubbs, J. W. 1892. "During the Nineteenth Century." *The Book of Trinity College, Dublin, 1591–1891*. Belfast: Marcus Ward and Co., 91–130.

Sullivan, J. P. 1964. *Ezra Pound and Sextus Propertius: A Study in Creative Translation*. Austin: University of Texas Press.

Sullivan, Kevin. 1957. *Joyce Among the Jesuits*. New York: Columbia University Press.

Sutton-Spence, Rachel, and Bencie Woll. 1999. *The Linguistics of British Sign Language*. Cambridge: Cambridge University Press.

Swinburne, Algernon Charles. 1904. "The Triumph of Time." *The Poems of Algernon Charles Swinburne in Six Volumes, Volume 1: Poems and Ballads*. London: Chatto and Windus, 34–47.

Synge, J. M. 1966. *Collected Works, Volume 2: Prose*. Ed. Alan Price. London: Oxford University Press.

Tanner, Marcus. 2004. *The Last of the Celts*. New Haven, CT: Yale University Press.

Taylor, J. M. 1899. "Should the State Teach Morals in its Schools?" [December 10, 1898]. *The Schoolmasters' Association of New York and Vicinity 1898–99*. Newark: Baker Printing Co., 39–42.

Thackeray, W. M. 1845. "Punch in the East, from our Fat Contributor. III. Athens." *Punch, or The London Charivari* 8: 45.

Thomas, R. J., ed. 1967. *Geiriadur Prifysgol Cymru, A Dictionary of the Welsh Language, Volume 1: A-Ffysur*. Caerddydd: Gwasg Prifysgol Cymru.

Thomas, Ronald Edward. 1983. *The Latin Masks of Ezra Pound*. Ann Arbor: University of Michigan Research Press.

Thürlemann, Silvia. 1974. "Ceterum censeo Carthaginem esse delendam." *Gymnasium* 81: 465–75.

Toller, Thomas Northcote, ed. 1898. *An Anglo-Saxon Dictionary: Based on the Manuscript Collections of the Late Joseph Bosworth*. Oxford: Clarendon Press.

Toller, Thomas Northcote, ed. 1921. *An Anglo-Saxon Dictionary: Based on the Manuscript Collections of the Late Joseph Bosworth: Supplement*. Oxford: Clarendon Press.

Townshend, Charles. 2014. *The Republic: The Fight for Irish Independence, 1918–1923*. London: Penguin Books.

Trench, Dermot Chenevix. 1912. *What Is the Use of Reviving Irish?* Dublin: Maunsel and Co.

Tucker, Herbert. 2008. *Epic: Britain's Heroic Muse 1790–1910*. Oxford: Oxford University Press.

Turner, Frank M. 1981. *The Greek Heritage in Victorian Britain*. New Haven, CT: Yale University Press.

Tylor, Edward B. 1871. *Primitive Culture: Researches into the Development of Mythology, Philosophy, Religion, Art, and Custom*. 2 vols. London: John Murray.

Uí Chollatáin, Regina. 2004. *An Claidheamh Soluis agus Fáinne an Lae 1899–1932*. Baile Átha Cliath: Cois Life Teoranta.

Valente, Joseph. 2011. *The Myth of Manliness in Irish National Culture, 1880–1922*. Urbana, IL: University of Illinois Press.

Van Hamel, A. G. 1977. *On Anglo-Irish Syntax*. Chicago, IL: University of Chicago Press.

Vance, Norman. 1990. *Irish Literature: A Social History*. Oxford: Basil Blackwell.

Vance, Norman. 2015. "Myth and Religion." *Oxford History of Classical Reception in English Literature, Volume 4: 1790–1880*. Ed. Norman Vance. Oxford: Oxford University Press, 185–202.

Venuti, Lawrence. 2008. *The Translator's Invisibility: A History of Translation*. 2nd edition. New York: Routledge.

Venuti, Lawrence. 2013. *Translation Changes Everything: Theory and Practice*. New York: Routledge.

Venuti, Lawrence. 2019. *Contra Instrumentalism: A Translation Polemic*. Lincoln: University of Nebraska Press.

Villis, Tom. 2018. "David Jones, Essay on Adolf Hitler, 11 May 1939." *David Jones on Religion, Politics, and Culture: Unpublished Prose*. Ed. Thomas Berenato, Anne Price-Owen and Kathleen Henderson Staudt. London: Bloomsbury Academic, 45–99.

Wade-Evans, A. W., trans. 1938. *Nennius's History of the Britons*. London: Society for Promoting Christian Knowledge.

Wade-Evans, A. W. 1950. "Prolegomena to a Study of Early Welsh History." *The Historical Basis of Welsh Nationalism – A Series of Lectures*. Cardiff: Plaid Cymru, 1–41.

Waisman, Sergio. 2005. *Borges and Translation: The Irreverence of the Periphery*. Lewisburg, PA: Bucknell University Press.

Wallace, Stuart. 2006. *John Stuart Blackie: Scottish Scholar and Patriot*. Edinburgh: Edinburgh University Press.

Walton, J. Michael. 2002. "Hit or Myth: The Greeks and Irish Drama." *Amid Our Troubles: Irish Versions of Greek Tragedy*. Ed. Marianne McDonald and J. Michael Walton. London: Methuen, 3–36.

Washbourne, Kelly. 2016. "Revised Translations: Strategic Rationales and the Intricacies of Authorship." *Translation and Literature* 25.2: 151–70.

Watson, G. J. 1998. "Yeats, Macpherson and the Cult of Defeat." *From Gaelic to Romantic: Ossianic Translations*. Ed. Fiona Stafford and Howard Gaskill. Amsterdam: Rodopi, 216–25.

Watson, George. 2006. "Yeats, Victorianism and the 1890s." *The Cambridge Companion to W. B. Yeats*. Ed. Marjorie Howes and John Kelly. Cambridge: Cambridge University Press, 36–58.

Watson, William. 1916. *Pencraft, A Plea for the Older Ways*. London: John Lane and The Bodley Head.

Webb, Andrew. 2019. "R. S. Thomas, Emyr Humphreys, and the Possibility of a Bilingual Culture." *The Cambridge History of Welsh Literature*. Ed. Geraint Evans and Helen Fulton. Cambridge: Cambridge University Press, 529–56.

Webb, Timothy. 1983. "The Unascended Heaven: Negatives in *Prometheus Unbound*." *Shelley Revalued: Essays from the Gregynog Conference*. Ed. Kelvin Everest. Leicester: Leicester University Press, 37–62.

Wilde, Oscar. 1909. *The Complete Works of Oscar Wilde: Reviews, Volume 4*. New York: National Library Company.

Wilde, Oscar. 2000. *The Complete Letters of Oscar Wilde*. Ed. Merlin Holland and Rupert Hart-Davis. New York: Henry Holt.

Willett, Steven J. 2005. "Reassessing Ezra Pound's *Homage to Sextus Propertius*." *Syllecta Classica* 16: 173–220.

Williams, Glanmor. 1993. *Renewal and Reformation: Wales c.1415–1642*. Oxford: Oxford University Press.

Williams, Gwyn A. 1985. *When Was Wales? A History of the Welsh*. London: Black Raven Press.

Williams, J. Gwynn. 1985. *The University College of North Wales: Foundations 1884–1927*. Cardiff: University of Wales Press.

Williams, Raymond, 2003. *Who Speaks for Wales? Nation, Culture, Identity*. Cardiff: University of Wales Press.

Williams, Rowan. 2005. *Grace and Necessity: Reflections on Art and Love*. London: Continuum Books.

Wilson, J. M. 1981. *I Was an English Poet: A Critical Biography of Sir William Watson 1858–1936*. London: Cecil Woolf.

Wolf, F. A. 1797. *Briefe An Herrn Hofrath Heyne Von Professor Wolf*. Berlin: G. C. Nauk.

Wolf, F. A. 1985. *Prolegomena To Homer, 1795*. Trans. Anthony Grafton, Glenn W. Most and James E. G. Zetzel. Princeton, NJ: Princeton University Press.

Wolf, Nicholas M. 2014. *An Irish-Speaking Island: State, Religion, Community, and the Linguistic Landscape in Ireland, 1770–1870*. Madison: University of Wisconsin Press.

Wolfius, Frid. Aug. 1795. *Prolegomena Ad Homerum*. Halis Saxonum: E Libraria Orphanotrophei.

Woodhouselee, Lord [Alexander Tytler]. 1852. "Essay on Ramsay's Gentle Shepherd." *The Gentle Shepherd. A Pastoral Comedy by Allan Ramsay*. New York: William Gowans.

Woolf, Virginia. 1987. "The Perfect Language." *The Essays of Virginia Woolf, Volume 2: 1912–1918*. Ed. Andrew McNellie. London: Hogarth Press, 114–19.

Woolf, Virginia. 1994. "On Not Knowing Greek." *The Essays of Virginia Woolf, Volume 4: 1925–1928*. Ed. Andrew McNellie. London: Hogarth Press, 38–52.

Worman, Nancy. 2019. *Virginia Woolf's Greek Tragedy*. London: Bloomsbury Academic.

Wray, David. 2019. "'Learned Poetry' and the Classics: Three Case Studies." *Oxford History of Classical Reception in English Literature, Volume 5*. Ed. Kenneth Haynes. Oxford: Oxford University Press, 419–43.

Yao, Steven G. 2002. *Translation and the Languages of Modernism: Gender, Politics, Language*. New York: Palgrave Macmillan.

Yeats, W. B. 1895. Preface. *Poems*. London: T. Fisher Unwin, v–vi.

Yeats, W. B. 1955. *The Letters of W. B. Yeats*. Ed. Allan Wade. New York, Macmillan.

Yeats, W. B. 1966. "Sophocles' *King Oedipus*, A Version for the Modern Stage." *The Variorum Edition of the Plays of W. B. Yeats*. Ed. Russell K. Alspach. New York: The Macmillan Company, 809–51.

Yeats, W. B. 1970. *Uncollected Prose by W. B. Yeats, Vol. 1: First Reviews and Articles, 1886–1896*. Ed. John P. Frayne. New York: Columbia University Press.

Yeats, W. B. 1972. *Memoirs*. Ed. Denis Donoghue. New York: Macmillan.

Yeats, W. B. 1976. *Uncollected Prose by W. B. Yeats, Vol. 2: Reviews, Articles and Other Miscellaneous Prose, 1897–1939*. Ed. John P. Frayne and Colton Johnson. New York: Columbia University Press.

Yeats, W. B. 1986. *The Collected Letters of W. B. Yeats. Volume 1: 1865–1895*. Ed. John Kelly and Eric Domville. Oxford: Clarendon Press.

Yeats, W. B. 1987. *The Variorum Edition of the Poems of W. B. Yeats*. Ed. Peter Allt and Russell K. Alspach. New York: Macmillan Publishing Company.

Yeats, W. B. 1989a. *The Collected Works of W. B. Yeats. Volume 6: Prefaces and Introductions*. Ed. William H. O'Donnell. New York: Macmillan.

Yeats, W. B. 1989b. *The Writing of Sophocles' King Oedipus*. Ed. David R. Clark and James B. McGuire. Philadelphia: The American Philosophical Society.

Yeats, W. B. 1994a. *The Early Poetry: Manuscript Materials*. 2 vols. Ed. George Bornstein. Ithaca, NY: Cornell University Press.

Yeats, W. B. 1994b. *The Collected Letters of W. B. Yeats. Volume 3: 1901–1904*. Ed. John Kelly and Ronald Schuchard. Oxford: Oxford University Press.

Yeats, W. B. 1994c. *The Collected Works of W. B. Yeats. Volume 5: Later Essays*. Ed. William H. O'Donnell. New York: Charles Scribner and Sons.

Yeats, W. B. 1997. *The Collected Letters of W. B. Yeats. Volume 2: 1896–1900*. Ed. Warwick Gould, John Kelly and Deirdre Toomey. Oxford: Clarendon Press.

Yeats, W. B. 1999. *The Collected Works of W. B. Yeats. Volume 3: Autobiographies*. Ed. William H. O'Donnell and Douglas N. Archibald. New York: Scribner Press.

Yeats, W. B. 2000. *The Collected Works of W. B. Yeats. Volume 10: Later Articles and Reviews*. Ed. Colton Johnson. New York: Scribner Press.

Yeats, W. B. 2003. *The Collected Works of W. B. Yeats. Volume 8: The Irish Dramatic Movement*. Ed. Mary Fitzgerald and Richard J. Finneran. New York: Scribner Press.

Yeats, W. B. 2004. *The Collected Works of W. B. Yeats. Volume 9: Early Articles and Reviews*. Ed. John P. Frayne and Madeleine Marchaterre. New York: Scribner Press.

Yeats, W. B. 2005. *The Collected Letters of W. B. Yeats. Volume 4: 1905–1907*. Ed. John Kelly and Ronald Schuchard. Oxford: Oxford University Press.

Yeats, W. B. 2007. *The Collected Works of W. B. Yeats. Volume 4: Early Essays*. Ed. Richard J. Finneran and George Bornstein. New York: Scribner Press.

Yeats, W. B. 2018. *The Collected Letters of W. B. Yeats. Volume 5: 1908–1910*. Ed. John Kelly and Ronald Schuchard. Oxford: Oxford University Press.

Young, Douglas. 1966. "Whither the 'Scottish Renaissance'?" *Forum for Modern Language Studies* 2.4: 386–95.

Index